EMPLOYEE BENEFITS PROGRAMS
MANAGEMENT, PLANNING, AND CONTROL

Author and Editor
Ernest J. E. Griffes
Vice President
Watkins Ross & Co., Grand Rapids, Michigan
Employee Benefit Management Consultants
Former Director of Compensation and Benefits
Levi Strauss and Co., Georgia-Pacific Corporation
and Candle Corporation

Contributing Authors
John Barton
David M. Gladstone, FSA, JD.
Robert Griffith
William Kuehne
Joel Levy
William O. Shearer

Dow Jones-Irwin
Homewood, Illinois 60430

Dow Jones-Irwin is a trademark of Dow Jones & Company, Inc.

This publication is designed to provide accurate and
authoritative information in regard to the subject matter
covered. It is sold with the understanding that the
publisher is not engaged in rendering legal, accounting, or
other professional service. If legal advice or other expert
assistance is required, the services of a competent
professional person should be sought.

*From a Declaration of Principles jointly adopted by a Committee
of the American Bar Association and a Committee of Publishers.*

Project editor: Karen J. Murphy
Production manager: Diane Palmer
Cover Designer: Michael S. Finkelman
Compositor: TCSystems, Inc.
Typeface: 11/13 Times Roman
Printer: R. R. Donnelley & Sons Company

Library of Congress Cataloging-in-Publication Data

Griffes, Ernest J. E.
  Employee benefits programs:management, planning, and control/
author and editor, Ernest J. E. Griffes:contributing authors, John
Barton . . . [et al.].—2nd ed.
    p. cm.
  ISBN 1-55623-285-3
  1. Employee fringe benefits—United States. 2. Compensation
management—United States. I. Barton, John (John W.) II. Title.
HD4928.N62U63524   1990
658.3'25—dc20   89–39645
                                                        CIP

FOREWORD

A corporation's investment in employee benefits, including time off with pay, can constitute a profit or cost center: in effect a business within a business.

The way benefits are managed can quickly affect earnings per share. Benefits management for larger corporations has advanced from simple administration to a complex operation requiring the same degree of attention that is given to the management of any multimillion dollar operational unit with profit and loss responsibility.

While it is of critical importance to control the cost of employee benefits, it is equally essential to assure that those benefits contribute positively to the employment environment. Often it is the vehicle of benefits management that provides the means of effecting sensitive human resource policies and conveying to employees management's philosophy toward them.

The management of employee benefits, like so many institutions founded on social realities of the 1940s and 50s, today finds itself struggling with new social realities. New lifestyles and attitudes arise, develop and mature quickly, accompanied by a degree of openness and vocal expression from employees about their expectations that is unparalleled in America's social history.

Benefit programs designed decades ago around the nuclear family unit, with a working father and a homebound mother caring for the children, now contain anachronistic elements in a society where only 15 percent of the workforce comes from such a unit.

The challenge for benefits management in the 90s is to revitalize the positive role employee benefits can play in the work environment and as a spur to improved productivity. Upward spiraling costs must be brought under control at the same time plans are being restructured to answer the needs and expectations of the contemporary workforce.

This challenge places a premium on developing a higher degree of professionalism among employee benefits executives. It also demands top management involvement more than ever before.

Ernie Griffes and the others who contributed to this book offer significant insight into the challenges and issues of their field, but more important, they present many practical ideas for the planning, management, and control of employee benefit plans. This book is certain to contribute importantly to meeting the benefit challenges of the 90s.

Robert T. Grohman
President and Chief Executive Officer (retired)
Levi Strauss & Co.
San Francisco, California

"One always has to balance moral certainty
against insufficient knowledge. At a time when
the scope for action is greatest, knowledge is
usually at a minimum. When knowledge is greatest
the scope for action has disappeared. If one
wants absolute moral certainty, one must pay a
horrendous price."

—*Henry Kissinger*

"Straight Talk from Kissinger." Newsweek, *December 11, 1978,
reprinted with permission.*

PREFACE

Why is it that almost no one is entirely satisfied with either the amount and quality of the benefits in most employee benefit plans, or with the administration and operation of those plans?

Employee benefits managers and their staffs spend a great amount of time defending the benefit plans of their companies as being as good or better than competitors—or as being of great value to employees because the company invests so much money in those benefits.

Despite the huge expenditures on benefits, employees as a whole are generally not satisfied with their benefit coverages. At retirement the pension income is not large enough to live on, and it doesn't keep up with inflation. Various groups of employees are unhappy because the benefit plans provide benefits they see as being of little value to them while other benefits they need are not provided.

Top executives receive letters from disappointed retirees and employees and wonder why it is that with all the money being spent for benefits the needs of employees still aren't satisfied and why employees don't appreciate the benefits they have.

Government bureaucrats get complaints and fill their days finding new ways to push and pull employers to satisfy those complaints. Politicians get an earful from constituents and smell a hot political issue in the wind.

Is it simply human nature to always be dissatisfied with what we have and to want something more?

Have we passed the point where affluence assures the security needs that benefits are aimed at, thus placing benefits in the category of an expected part of compensation to be taken for granted and relegated to a low level of interest, noticeable only when deficient in some way?

Or have we done such a poor job of designing benefits and telling employees about them that our programs really don't meet their needs anymore and they don't want to understand them?

No doubt some measure of the institutionalized disaffection with benefits is attributable to all of these factors.

But there is more to it than that.

The world around us is changing dramatically every day. The underlying concepts and ideology that formed the basis of benefit plan formulation and operation are being subjected to enormous wrenching and tearing forces from these changes.

Somehow it has all held together, largely by gerrymandering and patch-and-paste techniques.

But this cannot continue.

Benefit plans in their role in the employment relationship, and also as an important factor in the social and economic fabric of our society, have become a force of their own. Benefits executives bear the burden of getting this force under control. It may take a generation in time to accomplish this formidable task.

The intention of this book is to make a contribution to the discussion about how we can and should approach the accomplishment of this task.

After first examining the changes in our long-standing assumptions about benefit design and management, we will undertake to consider the traditional and customary practices we now follow in the management and administration of benefits and how they are also changing. Finally, we will take a cautious glance ahead a few years to consider where benefit management is headed and what that means to us now—and in the future.

Mr. Kissinger's quote provides us a critical insight into managing uncertainty as we make decisions of great significance to our employees and employers. Often we will be faced with making those decisions without complete and certain knowledge that it is the correct decision. And yet, should we wait until all knowledge is certain, we may well have delayed beyond the point where we have genuine alternatives to influence changes in a way that is most meaningful and useful to those we serve.

To our friends and associates in all aspects of the benefits profession we entrust these thoughts and ideas, hoping they will consider and debate them for the betterment of the profession as well as for the employers and employees who depend on us.

Note on second edition:
Statistical data has been revised wherever possible. Many of the studies referenced in the first edition have not been repeated so updates were not possible. Since the trends reflected in those studies continue to evolve over decades, references to such studies continue to be valid into the decade of the 1990s.

Ernest J. E. Griffes

ACKNOWLEDGMENTS

A special expression of appreciation is due to Levi Strauss & Co. for permission to use in this book some materials developed for the company in the early 1980s.

Appreciation is also due to Bank of America NT & SA for permission to reprint their Personal Compensation Statement in the chapter on "Communications."

A debt of gratitude exists to the contributing authors, John Barton, David Gladstone, Bill Griffith, Joel Levy, and William Shearer, whose contributions have provided readers with a complete textbook.

E. G.

Ernest Griffes is Vice President and Senior Consultant for Watkins Ross and Co., Grand Rapids, Michigan. Mr. Griffes, former Director of Compensation and Benefits for Levi Strauss & Co, Georgia-Pacific Corporation, and Candle Corporation, is acknowledged as an authority on compensation and benefits management and older worker issues. For over 25 years he has conducted programs on these subjects for personnel, gerontological, legal, and financial organizations, including over 100 workshops for the American Society for Personnel Administration. He has also presented testimony before congressional committees and presidential commissions on these subjects.

Mr. Griffes is the creator of FIND-PRO©, a software program that communicates the role of benefits in financial planning and educates employees on their own responsibility for personal financial planning. During 1983 he was Executive Director of the International Society for Pre-Retirement Planning (ISPP). In 1980 he was selected Benefits Administrator of the Year by Pension World Magazine.

Author of *A Complete Guide to Organizing and Managing the Role of Plan Administrator* (Panel Publishers, 1978), Mr. Griffes has also published articles in *Personnel Administrator, Employee Benefits Journal, Pension World Magazine*, and many other publications. Since first published in 1983, *Employee Benefits Programs: Planning, Management and Control* has become a standard resource for practical ideas and approaches to solving the daily issues of benefits management.

John W. Barton is Vice President of Martin E. Segal Company in San Francisco. He is a cum laude graduate of Occidental College and was elected Phi Beta Kappa. He earned a Masters in Business Administration from Stanford University's Graduate School of Business. For many years he has advised all types of benefit plans in the corporate, multiemployer, and public fields and is a frequent speaker on benefits issues. He is an acknowledged authority on the measurement and control of benefits plan costs.

David M. Gladstone is a principle and director of Hazlehurst & Associates, an actuarial and consulting firm in Atlanta, GA. He is a Fellow of the Society of Actuaries, a Fellow of the Canadian Institute of Actuaries, a Fellow of the Conference of Actuaries in Public Practice, an enrolled actuary, and a member of the Bar of the State of Washington. He has been practicing as an actuary for over 20 years and has provided consulting services in all areas of employee benefits to corporations, municipal groups, and jointly managed trust funds. He has spoken nationally on many occasions on subjects related to employee benefits.

Robert Griffith is a managing consultant in the Los Angeles office of Foster Higgins. He consults corporate clients nationally in health plan administration, utilization, and design. He has worked with employers of all sizes from coast to coast, evaluating claim administrator performance and assessing administration options. Bob has over 17 years experience in the employee benefits field beginning as benefits manager for a manufacturer in Connecticut and then as regional claims director for a major commercial carrier. Bob graduated from Boston College and holds an MBA from the University of Connecticut.

William C. Kuehne is president of Kuehne, Rock and Mazour, a San Francisco investment advisory firm specializing in pension investments. He is past president of the Western Pension Conference, a graduate of UCLA, and a director of several companies. Prior to founding Kuehne, Rock and Mazour, he spent 29 years with Merrill Lynch, where he specialized in pension and benefit plan investments.

Joel F. Levy is a partner in the New York Actuarial, Benefits and Compensation Group of Coopers & Lybrand. His areas of responsibility include plan administration, benefits communications and human resources, system consulting, and operational reviews. Before joining Coopers & Lybrand, Mr. Levy's consulting experience included six years at George B. Buck Consulting Actuaries, Inc. He also was the president of his own benefit and compensation consulting firm. His experience in private industry spanned 13 years as Director of Personnel, Benefits and Labor Relations for several large employers.

William O. Shearer is a private business communications consultant, formerly with the San Francisco office of William M. Mercer, Incorporated. Mr. Shearer has a masters degree in Journalism from Northwestern University and over 10 years of experience in all phases of corporate business communications, including employee benefit communication programs.

Victor M. (Vic) Zink was General Director, Worldwide Employee Benefits, for General Motors Corporation at the time of his retirement on September 1, 1981. During his 35-year career with General Motors, he was responsible at one time or another for almost all areas of industrial relations and was a principal member of General Motors' bargaining team. He was also actively involved outside General Motors, particularly in the employee benefits area. These outside activities include membership on national boards and committees, service on federal advisory councils, and hundreds of talks and articles to regional and national audiences.

CONTENTS

1   THE CHANGING ROLE OF BENEFITS: A NEW PARADIGM
    by Ernest J. E. Griffes   1
    From the Fringe to the Center   1
    The Anachronistic Benefits Ideology   2
    The New Benefits Assumptions   6
    Changing Work/Life Attitudes   7
    Government, Stockholder, and Public Interests in Benefits   10
    The Economic Effects of Benefits   17
    Inflation, Depression, Economic Uncertainty   20
    The Demographics: An Older Society   22
    A New Benefits Paradigm   24
    General Assumptions of the New Paradigm   28
    Specific Assumptions of the New Paradigm   29

2   THE BENEFITS MANAGEMENT FUNCTION
    by Ernest J. E. Griffes   34
    Traditional Benefits Management   35
    Benefits Management in the New Role   35
    The Benefit Department in the Organizational Structure   38
    Benefit Department Organizational Structure   41
    Decision Making   44
    Positive Benefits Management: The Concept   47
    Applied Positive Management   49
    A Benefit Policy and Planning System (or Philosophy)   50
    A Planning Guide for Benefit Design and Management   53
    Summary   59

3   BENEFIT PLANNING SYSTEMS
    by Ernest J. E. Griffes   61
    The Components of a Benefits Planning System   63
    Assessment of Existing Benefits   65
    External and Internal Influences and Constraints   69
    The Function of the Benefits Executive   81
    Job Description versus Functional Role   81
    Long-Range Planning   86
    Components of Long-Range Planning   86
    Plan Sponsor Long-Range Plans   87
    Information about Developing Trends   89
    Introducing Long-Range Plans into the Organization   92
    Using Long-Range Plans Effectively for Short-Term Action   95
    Controlling Benefit Changes   96
    Conclusion   99

4   THE HUMAN ASPECT OF BENEFITS
    by Ernest J. E. Griffes   100
    Why Do Employers Provide Benefit Plans?   101
    People Perceptions of Benefits: Employee Expectations   101
    Employee Appreciation and Motivation   104
    Individualization of Attitudes toward Benefits   105
    Organized Employee Perceptions of Benefits   107
    Employer Perception of Benefits   108
    Why Do Benefits Cost So Much?   113
    The Influence of Benefits on Productivity and Work Behavior   117
    Theory of the Benefit Plan Life Cycle   121
    The Social Role of Employee Benefits   123
    Present Social Purposes of Benefits   124
    Benefits in Social Policy   125

5   ADMINISTRATION SYSTEMS AND SERVICES
    by Joel F. Levy   137
    Introduction   138
    Effective Administration   139
    Uses of Administration Manuals   143
    Preparing Step-by-Step Procedures   148

The Importance of Records   151
Keeping Participants Informed   153
Keeping Government Informed   154
Keeping Calculation Methods Up to Date   154
Checklists Can Help   154
Reviewing the Administrative Process   155
Looking Ahead   156

6   COMMUNICATIONS
     by William O. Shearer   157
     Effective Benefit Communication   158
     Planning   159
     Production   164
     Implementation   168
     Evaluation   169
     Future Trends in Benefit Communications   170
     Benefit Statements   172
     Social Security Benefits Statement   185
     Financial Education   193

7   CLAIMS ADMINISTRATION
     by Robert Griffith   207
     Introduction   207
     Importance of Effective Claims Administration   208
     Plan Costs   208
     Employee Satisfaction   211
     Elements of Effective Claims Administrators   212
     Types of Claims Administrators   216
     Selecting Claims Administrators   221
     Assessing the Claims Office   222
     Evaluating Claim Systems   225
     Negotiating Performance Agreements   227
     Future Trends in Claims Administration   229

8   COST MANAGEMENT AND CONTROL
     by John W. Barton   231
     Introduction   231
     Managing Benefit Costs   238

What Is Cost Control?   239
Hospital-Medical Benefits   242
Group Life Insurance Benefits   253
Use of the 501(c)(9) Trust in Managing Plan Costs   255
Long-Term Disability Benefits   257
Defined Benefit Pension Plans   259
Cost Control and Plan Administration   271
Cost Containment   273
Conclusion   281

9   MANAGING PLAN ASSETS
     by William C. Kuehne   282
     Introduction   282
     The Size of Employee Benefit Plan Assets   284
     Historical Answers   285
     New Services for Trustees   286
     ERISA Section 404—Fiduciary Responsibilities   287
     Customary Management Techniques   289
     Selecting Investment Advisers and Dealing with Them   294
     Other Investment Functions   296
     Performance and Risk Management   297
     Future Investment Trends   300

10   EVALUATING BENEFIT PLAN EFFECTIVENESS
     by Ernest J. E. Griffes   304
     Are Evaluations of Benefit Effectiveness Worth the Trouble and
     Expense?   305
     What Is the Objective of Evaluation Techniques?   306
     Effectiveness of Evaluation Techniques   307
     Selecting the Techniques to Be Used   309
     Employee Sensing Techniques   309
     Competitive Benefit Structure and Cost Analysis   312
     Benefit Indexing and Value Comparison   313
     Cost versus Impact Analysis   315
     Specific Plan Cost versus Benefit Analysis   320
     Practical Applications of Effectiveness Evaluation   320
     Correlation of Indexing Study and Employee Survey Data   324

APPENDIXES

1 Sample Benefits Department Annual Report 327

2 Sample Discussion Paper 333

3 Sample Employee Perception Survey 342

4 Lexicon of Benefit Terms and Acronyms 350

5 "The Winds of Change"
  by Victor Zink 364

6 "How to Use Your Consultants Effectively"
  by Ernest Griffes 370

Reference Sources 382

Index 389

CHAPTER 1

THE CHANGING ROLE OF BENEFITS: A NEW PARADIGM

By Ernest J. E. Griffes

FROM THE FRINGE TO THE CENTER
THE ANACHRONISTIC BENEFITS IDEOLOGY
THE NEW BENEFITS ASSUMPTIONS
CHANGING WORK/LIFE ATTITUDES
GOVERNMENT, STOCKHOLDER, AND PUBLIC
INTEREST IN BENEFITS
THE ECONOMIC EFFECTS OF BENEFITS
INFLATION, DEPRESSION, ECONOMIC
UNCERTAINTY
THE DEMOGRAPHICS: AN OLDER SOCIETY
A NEW BENEFITS PARADIGM
GENERAL ASSUMPTIONS OF THE NEW PARADIGM
SPECIFIC ASSUMPTIONS OF THE NEW PARADIGM
CHART: A BENEFIT SYSTEM MODEL

FROM THE FRINGE TO THE CENTER

Fringe benefits. The phrase is still in common use despite the fact that conditions of employment beneficial to employees (employee benefits) now include hundreds of different kinds of plans, programs, and policies.

Knowledgeable executives still use the phrase despite the fact that such employee benefits often cost employers 50 percent of payroll or more, significantly affect the earnings per share results every year, and sometimes accumulate assets greater in value than the book value of the entire corporation's outstanding stock.

Employees still use the term. When considering a prospective employer, the second question they ask after "How much does the job pay?" is "What are the fringe benefits?" And not infrequently the employee benefits available decide the matter.

It is apparent that employee benefits have gone through the fringe stage and are now moving toward center stage of management attention.

Top level executives, human resource and financial executives, union leaders, bankers and insurance company managers, insurance agents, consultants, actuaries, lawyers, brokers, politicians, and bureaucrats are all important participants in this unfolding drama of human resource management.

The lead role will be played by the employee benefit executives and managers. The present generation of such benefit specialists will lay the foundation for a new structure of benefit management. The next generation will build the new structure.

Throughout this book we will take a journey together to examine, probe, evaluate, and speculate on what employee benefits have meant, now mean, and will mean to the employers who provide them, the employees who use them, and the socioeconomic structure that houses them. Along the way, we will explore both old and new ideas about how to provide and manage employee benefits in the most effective manner.

THE ANACHRONISTIC BENEFITS IDEOLOGY

"The term *fringe benefits* can be traced back to about 1943, when a regional chairperson of the National War Labor Board referred to 'fringe issues,' a catchall phrase for all forms of employee compensation other than straight-time wages or salaries."[1]

Unfortunately, the term became fixed in the lexicon and for almost 50 years has characterized the ideology of employee benefits. The entire body of knowledge encompassing employee benefits (the benefits ideology), within which benefits have been developed and managed for five decades, has been created to deal with fringe issues.

A *fringe* is a decoration, it is a little extra something to make something else attractive, it is at the outside edge of whatever is considered really important, it is something that is nice to have but isn't really necessary. That is the connotation that has carried over as employee benefits have been characterized as fringe benefits—nice to have but not really necessary.

Employee benefits are now essential and basic features of the employment relationship—so basic that union members will strike over pension, vacation, or health benefits. They will actually give up income during a strike to gain some improvement in their benefits!

It is time to remove the phrase fringe benefits from the language and, with its removal, to clear away the ideological cobwebs associated with something that is on the "fringe".

Another feature of the benefits ideology has been the concept of paternalism. Employee benefits in the United States, at least until the New Deal days of Franklin D. Roosevelt and the advent of social security in 1935, were literally a gift from a generous employer.

The "gold watch" syndrome, with its images of a rotund and obviously very wealthy employer bestowing a wrinkled and wretched employee with a gold watch for 50 years of faithful service, is the personification of paternalism in the benefits ideology. Among corporate executives who were starting careers in the 1930s and 40s, and vividly remember the working conditions of the time, the residue of paternalism may still permeate ideas associated with employee benefits.

Paternalism is no longer an acceptable management concept and in fact is resented by most employees. While the basic thrust in employment may now be toward lifetime job security, that security derives from employee participation in employment decisions, mutual respect (between employee, union, and employer) and the consent of the governed (the employee), not from paternalistic impulses of an employer or union—at least as far as the employee is concerned.

Encouragement through tax relief, and negotiating benefits as a trade off against direct wages, are two more characteristics of the benefits ideology, and they are related, as so well described by Geraldine Leshin.

> What is considered on the "fringe" of wages is bargained for just as vigorously as union wage demands and, during inflationary periods, sometimes with greater vigor because benefits, while a form of compensation, are not taxable income.[2]

Thus both employers and unions, though for different reasons, may find themselves reaching agreement through trading off direct wages for fringes. Another way of putting it: the escalation over the years of the fringe benefit package has been a constructive means of reaching settlement since neither the union nor management is forced to put all its respective eggs in one wage basket—but rather can scramble the proposals and counter proposals so that hard-boiled direct wage intransigence on both sides can be softened by fringe benefit bargaining.[3]

During World War II, as wages skyrocketed because of a tight labor market and prices soared because of shortages of goods, the government granted special tax advantages to employee benefit plans in order to encourage developing benefits as a substitute for increasing direct wages and salaries. In general the special tax advantages permitted employers to deduct the expense. But for the most part, the employer expenditure was not taxable to the employee at the time the employer made the contribution, although it might be taxable to the employee at some future time. Encouraging benefits as an alternative to wages satisfied compensation problems in the tight labor market but kept money out of circulation in the economy, and also created a huge pool of savings for investment in capital goods for production. These tax advantages have been a cornerstone of the benefits ideology for four decades and have encouraged the growth of benefit plans. As we enter the 1990s many of these special tax advantages to employees are being challenged, and it is likely that some of them will be diminished or removed.

While employee benefits have been a convenient mechanism for resolving issues at the bargaining table, the tense and murky atmosphere that often exists in that setting has not been conducive to developing and coordinating benefit coverages in an orderly way to meet the needs of the covered employees in a cost-efficient manner.

It is unfortunate, but true, that it has sometimes been possible to almost magically negotiate flashy looking benefits for a low cost, thus making both sides of the table appear successful in the negotiation. When the smoke has cleared, occasionally the employees have been the losers as expected benefits sometimes failed to materialize.

The trade-off of wages for benefits has been an integral part of the benefits ideology for a long time, however. Union members know this game now very well and are demanding that benefits negotiated for them be those that they need and be properly secured financially. They no longer accept charades at the bargaining table that they do not understand.

Another major feature of the old benefits ideology has been the fundamental assumption that private employers could do pretty much as they pleased with respect to employee benefits with minimal interference from the government. In general, this was a reliable truism—until 1974 and the enactment of the Employee Retirement Income Security Act (ERISA).

Except for Internal Revenue Service regulations that placed some restraints on pension plan funding and design, government regulation of benefit plans was virtually nonexistent.

The only major governmental legislation until 1974 was the Welfare and Pension Plans Disclosure Act of 1958, which was aimed at gathering information and statistics on benefit plans through reporting requirements. The WPPDA was never adequately funded by Congress and thus was totally ineffective.

This demonstration of unconcern by Congress only encouraged the belief that government had little interest in employee benefit plans.

All of these features of the old benefits ideology combined to offer a set of assumptions that served well for almost 40 years. Those assumptions have been summarized by David Weeks of the Conference Board as follows:

1. Employee benefit plans will be improved indefinitely just as employee pay will be increased.
2. Government will not intervene directly in "private sector" benefit plans.
3. Employee contributions as a way of financing benefit plans have been dying.
4. Employee benefits and their planning affect only the company, the union, the employee, and his dependents—not the community, the poor, the aged, the unemployed, or state and federal governments.
5. Increases in benefit costs result primarily from attempts to enhance worker security, not from increases in paid time off or from the escalation of costs for benefits already in effect.
6. Increases in the costs of legally required benefits would continue in the same proportion to total benefit costs that they had over the last 20 years.
7. Employees would continue to make manifest new "needs" to be filled by private benefit planning.
8. Accountants and investors would continue to undervalue the long-range costs of today's employee benefit promises.

9. Companies which lead the pack in benefit "liberality" would be given credit for their progressiveness and farsightedness by their employees and by government.
10. Even-handed administration of benefits, such as the insistence upon compulsory retirement for all employees at age 65, was the same thing as justice.[4]

To these could be added even broader assumptions, such as:

a. Workers will continue to be motivated by the same employment factors in the future as the past.
b. Social values will be essentially the same in the future as in the past.
c. Employees and society will continue to accept without serious question whatever they are told.
d. The national economy will remain essentially stable over long periods of time.
e. Good benefits motivate employees to increased productivity through security and better morale.

It is now apparent that some of these assumptions (and thus some of the body of theory and even some of the knowledge) that have constituted the traditional benefits ideology have been declared anachronistic by the realities of social and economic change.

THE NEW BENEFITS ASSUMPTIONS

What are the changes that have occurred in the last four decades, and how have those changes affected the traditional benefits ideology?

There are at least six fundamental changes that can be considered more than transitory and can be expected to remain major factors in human resource management for at least the 1990s. Although there certainly will be shorter periods during this time when their individual influence will wax and wane, these factors are woven tightly enough into the socioeconomic fabric that their impact on benefits management can be expected to be significant and should be planned for in benefit management.

How these and other changes can be factored into benefit management and planning will be explored throughout this entire book. For the moment we are only going to examine how they have changed our assumptions about benefit management and what an appropriate set of new assumptions might be.

In summary these six major changes are:

1. Fundamentally different attitudes toward work and life and thus different expectations among employees about what the employer/employee relationship should be.
2. Steadily increasing real costs of providing benefits that are greater than the increase in wages.
3. Intense government, stockholder, and public interest in benefits plans, especially the weaknesses and perceived failures of such benefits.
4. The effect on the economies of the nation and the states of the huge expenditures on benefits and the accumulation of enormous assets and liabilities in pension plans.
5. Economic uncertainty and insecurity generated by institutionalized inflation, threats and forecasts of worldwide economic depression, and shortages of resources.
6. Demographic shifts to an older society and thus an older workforce.

CHANGING WORK/LIFE ATTITUDES

Are people's outlooks and attitudes toward life and work really different now than in the past? Equally as important, if attitudes are different, are they likely to remain fundamentally different than in the past?

The answer to both these questions is probably yes.

There is evidence everywhere that the work ethic has diminished in strength, that while people are still willing to give an honest days work, the perception of the quantity of productivity encompassed in that concept is different than in the past. Employees are less willing to give their all or dedicate themselves to work over other values. Enjoyment of other aspects of life is equally as important as work, and balance between the two is deemed necessary.

Demands for recognition, acknowledgement, and treatment as individuals, irrespective of sterotypes concerning sex, age, race, and so on, are more frequent and more vocal than in the past. Individualism, in the sense of individual recognition and treatment, is being demanded by employees as well as other segments of society not in the labor force.

This is not the antisocial rugged individualism of the John Wayne—Opening of the West Era but is a revolt against the computerized, numbered, DO NOT FOLD, SPINDLE, OR MUTILATE anonymity that technology has thrust upon society. It is individual acknowledgement within a social grouping that is sought.

Futurist Frank Ogden tells his college student audiences of 1989 that "at least 80 percent of what you were taught in school will be proved wrong. Knowledge is doubling at the rate of 100 percent every 20 months. What you know now will be obsolete by Christmas."[5] He also delights in the prediction "that robots will become increasingly human-like, and that by the turn of the century, men and women will be marrying humanoids." What type of benefits does an employer provide for "humanoid" dependents or workers? Certainly at the minimum, "maintenance insurance" for trips to the humanoid repair shop!

While it is comforting to discount such unnerving fanatasies of futurists, a Rand Corporation study in the 1980s concluded that futurists have the best record of predicting actual events that unfold, being correct about 30 percent of the time.

Activism, demands for equality of treatment, and assertiveness by everyone regarding whatever they deem important is encouraged and acceptable. Individuals and groups who in the past would have been considered accepting and docile are demanding satisfaction of their perceived rights, rectification of perceived maltreatment, and fulfillment of their expectations.

A higher level of both formal education and generalized awareness of what is occurring around us and in the world is creating more sophisticated and knowledgeable individuals who are less willing to believe on face value what they are told, who are ready to and capable of challenging the dictums handed down by any authority figure or unit.

There is some evidence of a trend back toward conservatism, a natural result of "baby boomers" growing older, having families, buying homes, and thinking more deeply about the long-term future. They are being replaced by the "yuppies," the young, urban, mobile, single-minded, ambitious, and upwardly striving professionals, who also demonstrate conservatism in the sense of protecting their personal and financial interests.

Workers are more independent in their thinking and behavior. The remarkable growth of the individual "consultant" businesses, small one- and two-person entreprenurial ventures, "remote" employees (working with computers from home) and family businesses run from the home, are indications of this drive for independence. But as a result, they are also more at risk in their employment experiences.

"What has happened is that the idea of a long-term job connection—of being a permanent employee of a company—has been reduced if not severed entirely. The phenomenon has been criticized as exploitation by employers, but it's more complex than that. Social change has been responsible," reports Columnist James Flanigan of the *Los Angeles Times*.[6]

"As laws and regulations (regarding employment and benefits) have proliferated, companies have increasingly contracted out for services—transferring to other firms or the individual workers the responsibility for health insurance, tax payments and liability insurance" as well as pensions, disability income, life insurance, and so on. "What will happen in the 1990s? Will an aging workforce put more emphasis on job security? Maybe, but it will be hard to deliver. Neither companies nor unions have power over employees lives anymore. What has been gained is today's individual opportunity and responsibility—which can sometimes be read as 'you're on your own.' "

Society's acceptance of nontraditional lifestyles is encouraging experimentaton with unusual relationships that are being legally sanctioned by the courts. Dual-career marriages, serial marriages, same-sex marriages, single and unwed parents, cohabitation, increasing divorce rates, group living, and so on are challenging the traditional family structure upon which many legal, social, and benefits practices have long been based. While some of this experimentation may be transitory, a complete return to the traditional nuclear family norm is unlikely, and some new legally sanctioned relationships are certain to develop. In any case a sudden reversal in a few years is unlikely, and adaptation of policies and practices to accommodate new lifestyles will be necessary during the next two decades.

The demand for participation in the making of decisions that affect the individuals life—either at work or away from work—is becoming louder and louder. Recognition of individual rights is being demanded through legal recourse.

Participation in job structuring, working hours, and all other conditions of employment is being sought and demanded, by both represented groups, and by individuals or groups of unrepresented individuals with common interests.

The memories of economic depression and legitimate war, and their associated hardships, are fading from the memories of the middle-aged

and older members of our workforce. Three decades of growing affluence are shifting attention to concerns about society's responsibility to
disadvantaged groups and global concerns about the quality of life. This
influences employee expectations of the role that business operations
and employers should play in utilizing economic power and profits.

The younger members of society and the workforce have no mem-
ory of the hardships of economic depression and have grown up in a
social environment that has encouraged them to expect equality of treatment and economic security. They look to their employers to fulfill their
expectations and loudly voice displeasure if their expectations are not
satisfied.

In short, the long-held assumption that people exist to serve the
productive processes of society is being turned upside down.

The belief is firmly entrenched in the new attitude that the productive processes of maintaining society exist to serve the needs of people.
This attitude alters traditional assumptions about conditions of employment. It foreshadows employment relationships that allow high levels of
employee participation in decisions about their work and conditions of
employment as well as flexibility that provides room for recognition of
individual needs and lifestyles.

The ramifications for benefits management are immense.

GOVERNMENT, STOCKHOLDER, AND PUBLIC INTEREST IN BENEFITS

The Government Interest

Federal, state, and local governments are responsible for protecting the
public interest. The public interest is defined by the elected politicians
and the bureaucrats who run government from day to day. Just as any
other human beings, politicians and bureaucrats are also motivated by
self-interest—for the politicians that means reelection; for the bureaucrats it means job security.

On the subjects of retirement income and public health, the public
interest and their self-interest coincide. For sponsors of employee benefit plans, this means intense government interest in the operation of
private pension and medical plans especially, but also, as a spillover,
considerable interest in all types of employee benefit plans.

It has also meant a costly and bewildering array of federal and state laws and literally thousands of regulatory decrees from federal and state agencies that define legitimate actions an employer may take in the operation of private benefit plans.

In 1974, ERISA became the first real indication of the deepening government interest in regulating benefits. Since then, there has been a plethora of federal legislation with acronyms like ADEA, TEFRA, COBRA, ERTA, REA, TAMRA, and several TRAs. As the 1990s dawn, the TRA of 1986, which spawned Section 89 of the Internal Revenue Code, is the most recent source of benefit executive nightmares. The Appendix Section includes a listing of definitions and abbreviations describing the significance of these acronyms.

The Tax Reform Act of 1986 enacted Section 89 of the Internal Revenue Code, effective in 1989, which created a furor with its labyrinth of tests for medical benefit plans. These tests attempted to determine the extent of discrimination in favor of highly compensated employees and the degree of value which should be included in the taxable income of such employees.

In the intensity of the furor over attempts to repeal Section 89, Fred Hunt, 1989 president of the Society of Professional Benefit Administrators, was prompted to offer this informed and thoughtful insight into the future of government involvement in benefits: "Like most things in Congress, this will probably fade into oblivion. Why? First, Congress believes that newly issued regulations give some relief to allow plans to adapt. Second, in the next few years there will probably be some minimum set of 'mandated or voluntary' benefits. Third, under pressure of the deficit, there is an increasing chance of taxation of benefits for the 'highly compensated.' Thus, I personally predict that Section 89 will stay, but its impact and possible necessity will dwindle."[7]*

At the time of ERISA in 1974 proposals arose to support minimum mandated pension plans for all employers. Every time social security issues come up in Congress, these proposals surface again as a means of taking financial pressure off the social security system. Such proposals are so persistent that the American Society of Pension Actuaries was prompted in 1989 to put forth a formal paper and proposal titled "A National Policy on Retirement Income." This proposal states: "The goal of the National Retirement Income Policy should be: Income from all

---

*Note: At press time section 89 was about to be repealed or greatly simplified by Congress. Either outcome increases the likelihood of mandated benefits and taxation of benefits for the "highly compensated."

sources throughout retirement that provides the same standard of living as that enjoyed in the later years of full-time employment. This requires a four-legged retirement structure:

1. Social Security.
2. Voluntary employer sponsored retirement plans that are virtually universal, with incentives for small employers.
3. Personal savings (including use of home equity as a form of savings).
4. Availability of gradual retirement."[8]

This courageous effort on a very controversial issue demonstrates a kind of wearing down effect in the private sector, a tiring of the endless stream of expensive legislation and regulation that is already virtually impossible to keep track of or understand, not to mention to comply with if you are a plan sponsor.

While few people in the private sector are ready to concede to federally mandated levels of pension and health benefits, many are becoming exhausted by the incremental incursion of government into plan design and management. The cumulative effect over the last 20 years has brought the nation close to the brink of mandated benefits anyway—or so it seems.

As frustrating, distasteful, and costly as it may be, the interest of government in the operation of employee benefit plans is legitimate, although a strong case can be made that, as practiced, it is excessive and unnecessarily punitive on plan sponsors. Forcing expanded benefits on employers is a politically popular "no lose" game for politicians and bureaucrats.

Government interest is legitimate for five basic reasons:

1. Promises by employers and unions made regarding benefits as a condition of employment should be kept, and legal protection seems to be necessary to assure fulfillment of those promises in some cases.
2. The government's viewpoint is necessarily broad and encompasses national perspectives and priorities, and it therefore must act to assure that benefit plans of employers support the social and economic objectives of the nation as a whole.
3. The incomprehensible size of asset accumulations and expenditures on benefit plans means that they are a major factor influencing the national and local economies and thus must be controlled (from a political perspective) simply because of their enormity.

4. The U.S. government is the plan sponsor of what is probably the largest benefit plan in the world—the social security system— and it therefore must act to protect that system and assure coordination between that system and private benefits.
5. Federal, state, and local governments are also employers and plan sponsors of benefits for their own employees and must be concerned with the adequacy and funding of those programs as well as the relationship between their own plans and private employer plans.

It would be comforting to believe that there is some sort of outer limit on government involvement in private benefits, that somehow this government interest and frustrating barrage of legislation will ease off during the next two decades.

To quote former HEW Secretary Joseph Califano, Jr.:

> Advances in health and life expectancy signal a dramatic change: The American Nation is about to become a four-generation society. The aging of the American population is an issue on the horizon: not yet clearly in political focus, but moving inexorably our way, freighted with opportunity and danger.
>
> The opportunity is the opportunity to plan: to study in advance how we shall cope with profound demographic change; to shape our ideas and programs for a new era.
>
> The danger is the danger of doing nothing, or too little, too late: the danger of ignoring approaching change until it sweeps over us; the danger of making drastic changes all at once, instead of careful, rational changes over time.[9]*

There should be no doubt in the mind of any reader of this book in the early 1990s that during his or her career in the benefits field, government interest and involvement in private benefit plans will be a major factor to cope with in benefit plan management.

And perhaps the biggest sleeper of all, from Nelson McClung:

> Essentially, I contend that it has been federal government policies which have created the present pension scheme and that *federal policy should be re-oriented toward the absorption of pension plans into a flexible and voluntary Old Age, Survivors and Disability Insurance program (OASDI*

---

*Note: At press time this statement was reinforced by repeal of the Catastrophic Health Care Program that had been in operation only one year. The program, intended to assist the elderly, was repealed because of outrage among this group over the income surtax they were required to pay to finance the program.

or social security) because employer arrangements for assuring income adequacy in retirement, disability and survivorship are (1) uneconomic and (2) incapable of achieving the objective.[10]

This idea was renewed by Secretary Califano in his remarks before the American Academy of Political and Social Science.

Benefits' executives of the 1990s will need to be prepared to defend the private benefits system against unwarranted government intrusion from every level of government. While government interest is legitimate in some respects and there is no apparent limitation to government interest in benefits, governmental meddling and tampering for political purposes is totally unjustified and unwarranted. Those associated with the benefits system are obligated to educate politicians and bureaucrats about where the line falls between legitimate interest and destructive meddlesomeness.

Stockholder Interest in Employee Benefits

Stockholders are interested primarily in a reasonable dividend return on their investment and in the financial strength and growth of companies as reflected in increasing stock value on the market. Anything that significantly affects the stock values or earnings per share or appears to reveal questionable financial management is certain to attract their attention.

Employee benefit costs and management, in particular pension plan management, has done exactly that in the last 10 years. Max Shapiro, a distinguished financial journalist, opened the eyes of stockholders concerning pension costs and liabilities in 1974.[11] Mr. Shapiro pointed out that for nonfinancial companies between 1955 and 1974:

   a. Pension contributions increased from $3.3 billion a year to $25.0 billion.
   b. Pension contributions as a percentage of cash increased from 6 percent to 41 percent.
   c. Pension contributions as a percentage of profits increased from 14 percent to 38 percent.[12]

In November of 1977, A. F. Ehrbar, following up on Mr. Shapiro's lead, took off the gloves and unleashed a controversy that is still vibrating through the financial world. In an article in *Fortune* entitled "Those Pension Funds Are Weaker Than You Think" he set forth the premise that pension liabilities are woefully understated and "when companies finally have to pay the bills, there may not be much left over for stock-holders."[13]

Coming out just ahead of hundreds of annual reports and annual stockholder meetings, his accusations sent company financial and benefit executives into overtime to examine anew the state of pension obligations and prepare defenses if necessary for inquisitions from stockholders and boards of directors.

With statements like: "Now it is the shareholders who had better watch out. From their point of view, the disquieting question is whether the companies whose pension funds are deeply in arrears will be able to pay off their obligations and still have much of anything left over for profits," and "The accounting and actuarial treatment of pension liabilities is a masterpiece of obfuscation," Mr. Ehrbar sensationalized for stockholders the sleepy processes of actuarial science by which pension liabilities are determined and funded.

Mr. Ehrbar's contentions were refuted profusely by the accounting and actuarial professions, but the damage had been done, and the only people listening to the complex refutations were financial executives in need of reassurance that it couldn't happen in their pension fund.

Since that period, every month sees business and financial publication articles expressing continuing concern over the impact of pension costs and liabilities on earnings, stock values, and corporate financial strength.

In 1976 the estimate of private pension plans' unfunded liabilities was $200 billion. At that time it was reported that 10 of the largest industrial corporations had unfunded liabilities in excess of 33 percent of their net worth and seven of those had unfunded pension liabilities exceeding the aggregate market value of their common stock.[14]

A long-smoldering question was fanned into flame by Mr. Ehrbar's article, and that is "Which generation of shareholders should bear the expense of paying for pension promises?" Actuarial assumptions and techniques may shift the cost of current pension promises far into the future, permitting current management to gain the credit for their generosity to employees but letting future generations of managers and stockholders bear the brunt of picking up the tab for those promises. The controversy continues in boardrooms and will be a stark spectre for benefits executives to contend with for the remainder of this century and well into the next.

In the last few years the accounting profession, through the Accounting Principles Board and its successor the Financial Accounting

Standards Board, has established standards for reporting pension liabilities as well as standards for what the accountants believe to be appropriate ways of determining funding, cost, and liabilities of pension plans. The actuarial profession has taken issue with the accounting profession over these standards, and the disagreements may well go on for many years.

The Securities and Exchange Commission has also set minimum disclosure requirements concerning pension costs and liabilities to be included in the annual reports of publicly traded companies.

Another aspect of benefits that has caught stockholder attention is the special perquisite benefits granted to top-level executives. The SEC has also established disclosure requirements concerning such benefits to be reported in proxy statements.

Stockholders express their concerns in two basic ways: by challenges to management at stockholder meetings and by selling off their holdings in the company and/or not investing in a company.

The first means can be easily observed, although it is not often publicly reported when stockholders raise such challenges at annual meetings. Some challenges concerning perquisites have been reported. However, the private decision to invest or sell is not usually discussed publicly—but it shows up in the stock market and stock price levels.

In the early 1980s, stock prices generally reflected a seven times multiple of the companies' earnings per share—at least that was the accepted rule of thumb for estimating the market value of a stock. A stock with earnings of $5 a year could be estimated at a $35 market price. On March 31, 1989 the average multiple of the Dow Jones Industrial Averages was 11 times earnings.

Of course many factors affect stock prices, and it would be inappropriate to imply that pension costs and liabilities alone have influenced stock prices negatively. Financial analysts, upon whom investors rely heavily in investment decisions, have not failed to note the financial impact of pension plans, however. Their reports reflect a sophisticated awareness of the effect on earnings and stock book values of pension plan costs and funding techniques.

If the simple rule of thumb concerning market values is applied, using a multiple of 11 times earnings, a pension funding decision or an increase in pension costs that reduces earnings 10 cents a share translates into $1.10 cents a share less in the market value. Applied to the millions of shares of stock outstanding for a given company, the increased pension costs have cost investors 11 times what they cost the company.

Consider further that annual pension costs may constitute only a fraction of total benefit costs. The Chamber of Commerce 1988 survey reported pension costs at 2.5 percent of payroll, only 6.4 percent of total benefit payments.[15] Stockholders and financial analysts are certain to have an increasing interest in what goes into benefits beyond the pension plan as the realization dawns about the effect on earnings per share (and thus on market value) of the enormous expenditures on employee benefits. How stockholders will reflect this interest is uncertain, of course.

It is certain, however, that benefit executives, in the decisions and recommendations they make and the directions they take their companies concerning benefits, will influence the earnings per share and the assets of stockholders to the tune of billions of dollars.

Sooner or later, benefits' executives will be held accountable by stockholders for their stewardship.

THE ECONOMIC EFFECTS OF BENEFITS

Expenditures for Benefits

In the mid-1970s New York City came to the brink of bankruptcy. Many observers attributed the near financial disaster to huge pension commitments made to city employees that drained off tax income needed for other services.[16] Ultimately, chaos was temporarily averted by using the assets of public employee pension plans to purchase New York City bonds and provide needed cash to meet payroll and other expenses.

In 1978, under great pressure to save the social security system from bankruptcy, Congress voted an increase in social security taxes that will cost workers $227 billion dollars in the decade of the 1980s alone. At the same time, benefits were actually reduced for those persons retiring near the end of the century. In 1978 social security benefit payments exceeded $115 billion. By 1988 they were forecast to reach $296 billion a year, almost a tripling in 10 years.

Based on the benefit structure in existence in 1979, combined employer-employee tax in the year 2051 would have to be 23.8 percent of payroll to meet this commitment, almost double the 1979 tax rate.[17] Based on 1979 tax rates, the social security system would be $3.4 trillion short over the next 75 years.[18]

The unfunded liabilities for public employee pension plans were estimated at $700 billion as of the late 1970s.

Employer costs to cover legally mandated workers' compensation benefits were $10.8 billion in 1978. Unemployment compensation benefits were $47 billion during the period 1974–77.[19]

Total benefit payments by private industry in 1987 were $813 billion, up from $245 billion in 1975.[20] The October 1989 stock market decline reduced private pension assets by $170 billion in three months.

Various proposals for a program of national health insurance contain costs ranging from $10 billion to $100 billion a year.

Benefits are big business. The numbers are so large that they become unreal and beyond our capacity to comprehend in a meaningful way.

Like the speed of light and the distance to the stars, the expenditures on benefits convey a sense of unreality. It may help to consider that based on a population of 244 million in 1987, employee benefit expenditures of $813 billion amounted to about $3,332 for every man, woman, and child in the United States. In 1977 based on a population of 217 million and benefit expenditures of $310 billion, the comparable number was $1,428.

Asset Accumulations

The Employee Benefits Reasearch Institute (EBRI) reported in early 1989 that the assets of private trusteed pension plans grew from $655 billion in 1982 to $1,274 billion in 1988, approximately a 12 percent annual growth rate.[21] The EBRI study revealed that this pool of investment funds reached a high point of $1,300 billion on September 30, 1987. In October 1987 the stock market took a shock equivalent to Black Friday of almost 60 years earlier. By the end of 1987 the value of these assets had dropped to $1,130 billion, down $170 billion in three months.

EBRI reported that at the end of 1988 private and public pension funds held nearly 25 percent of all corporate equity, up from 1 percent in 1950. Bond investments of this enormous pool of funds had declined from 20.1 percent in 1982 to 15.3 percent in 1988. Holdings in bank pooled funds during the same period had increased from 13.1 percent in 1982 to 21.8 percent in 1988, at which time 68 percent of these bank pooled funds were invested in cash funds.

During the period 1951–55 pension funds "accounted for new purchases amounting to 24 percent of the issues of corporate business, exclusive of the investment companies."[22] In the last 40 years pension funds have become virtually the primary source of new capital for financing the private sector economy of the United States.

What Does All This Mean?

From Mr. Drucker:

> Take-home pay in American mass production industries, it is often pointed out, did not increase faster than productivity until the late 60s, so that it had no inflationary impact until then. But in the early 60s total wage costs began to increase very much faster than productivity. One reason for this was the spiraling of health care costs; just as important was the steady increase in Social Security costs and especially private pension costs, which began around 1960.[23]

Benefits, in their cost expansion faster than wage increases, are a significant factor in the inflation of our national economy. Controlling benefit cost expansion is therefore an important factor in getting inflation under control.

"The major force that could initiate an upward trend in market investments is an increase in the level of equities to debt and short-term instruments held by institutional investors, especially pension funds,"[24] states Robert B. Ritter, technical market analyst of L. F. Rothschild.

Benefit plan assets (pension assets in particular) are a major force in the strength of the national and local economies. The manner in which these funds are managed, the strategies and philosophies of benefit asset managers, can and does influence the economy for better or for worse.

From Rifkin and Barber, authors of *The North Will Rise Again:*

> The battle over control of pension capital, and with it control over parts of the American economy, will be one of the central economic battles of the next decade. The private sector will continue its attempt at institutionalizing control over this new form of wealth in their hands. The unions and the northern states will begin a counter campaign to socialize pension fund capital under some rudimentary form of worker/community control.[25]*

It appears that there will be movement to apply the power of pension assets to serve many purposes other than the provision of retirement income to beneficiaries. Benefit executives will need to be very aware of this thrust and decide whether they want it for the assets under their guidance and, if so, how, where, and when. And if they don't want it, how are they going to resist and fight it?

---

*Note: At press time legislation was under consideration that would require employee trustees to be involved in managing pension plan assets.

From Professor Merton C. Bernstein:

> Both private plans and the social security system shift income. From where and to whom is quite important. Are the shifts fair and do they serve acknowledged public policies? The income shifting function of private plans has not received much attention—but should.[26]

And it certainly will during the 1990s. Benefit executives, wending their way daily through the frustrations and rewards of benefit management, need to have the perspective that the field in which they are working meshes with important economic and social activities in the nation. The strategies and actions developed and implemented by these benefit executives in their own companies have ramifications extending far beyond their own group of employees.

This is a new feature of benefit management that invalidates some of the long-standing assumptions and traditional practices.

INFLATION, DEPRESSION, ECONOMIC UNCERTAINTY

Employee benefits can be influenced by dramatic economic circumstances of a short-term nature because employees attitudes and lifestyles are affected in some drastic way. Some employee benefit plans may have a certain fluidity characteristic as they come into effect in response to a sudden dramatic change in economic conditions and phase out of importance as those conditions change or disappear.

The following excerpts from news articles illustrate such a phenomenon during the energy shortage of the late 1970s. Employers responded with some unusual short-term benefit policies to meet employee needs during this period.

Benefit executives increasingly will need to maintain an awareness of the ebb and flow of economic conditions and how the needs and attitudes of employees are influenced by these changes in the environment. Such fluctuations in the economic environment may present some opportunities to gain employee interest and morale value by low-cost, short-term benefits that respond to these needs and attitudes.

They may also present some traps, as employers are pressured to install programs (such as cost-of-living adjustments that are installed under great emotional pressure arising from current dramatic economic conditions) that cannot be withdrawn even though economic conditions change to diminish the value or need for that benefit.

Petrol Hunting: Many Employers Help Workers Surmount the Gasoline Crunch[27]

The story describes companies adopting lenient policies for tardiness in arriving at work, adoption of four-day weeks, increasing van fleets for commuting employees—all designed to help adjust to fuel shortages.

Heating Up: Outcry Begins on Plan to Curb Thermostats of Public Buildings—Will Office Workers Take It?[28]

The story describes the possible effects on productivity of federally mandated temperature controls, lower in winter and higher in summer, in order to conserve fuel.

A manager of a restaurant chain believes employees may get restless, slow down, and spend lots of time drinking water and going to the bathroom.

More time off from work, longer break periods, flexible work weeks, and help in commuting. The shortage of low-cost energy translates in the workplace to benefit programs.

Inflation, from Ray Kann:

Let's conclude with a couple of thoughts for the era ahead that might be worthwhile calling "keynotes" for what's coming up.

One of them we believe that the benefit field must learn better to cope with is inflation. First, we've got to recognize the problem. Inflation reduces the value of all fixed assets—personal and corporate. It increases the need for security benefits, it reduces the ability to provide them. Inflation is a problem that is exceedingly difficult to cope with in the benefit field. How are we going to get at it?[29]

Productivity:

Cars, Costs and Jobs: Rising Inflation Has a Silent Partner, Declining Productivity.[30]

The editorial considers General Motors frustrating phenomena: giving more time off with pay in order to combat absenteeism has no effect, and absenteeism continues to rise. Why? "The incentive to work declines when the cost of not working declines." Two incomes in the family, higher tax rates, double social security taxes reduce the net income lost by taking time off without pay. Employees may come out ahead if they use the time to work on homes and cars and thus save expensive repair bills that likely cost more than the lost wages. Expensive benefit programs not only do not help solve a serious problem but may even contribute to aggravation of the problem.

Recession, Depression:

> Recession, Oil and Tax Policy
> OPEC has done it again. The U.S. Recession is here.[31]

The article describes the intricate relationships between energy prices, recession, and tax policy to cope with these problems.

"Consumer prices in May spurted an adjusted 1.1 percent."[32] That's a 13.4 percent annual rate during a period when voluntary wage controls placed a 7 percent limit on wage increases.

In 1990 and 1995 the headlines will be different of course. They may have to do with an international monetary crisis, clashes over natural resource utilization between nations, or whatever. In the mid-1970s it was recession and unemployment; in the early 80s, inflation, in the late 80s a stock market crash.

Traditional benefit assumptions have been predicated on economic stability. Where specific consideration has been given to the effects on benefit plans of economic factors, such as inflation, wage growth, or investment return, the assumptions have factored in a degree of economic stability that events are proving does not exist, in either the short or long term. More often, the effect of economic fluctuations has not been considered in benefit design at all, for it has been assumed they would be moderate and of little impact.

It is becoming apparent that broad economic factors increasingly impact quickly on the attitudes and work environment of individual employees. If benefit programs are to fulfill a valid and useful function in the employment relationship, they must factor in somehow the economic factors that also impact the employment relationship, both in the short and long term.

THE DEMOGRAPHICS: AN OLDER SOCIETY

"Retirement age in the future may not come at a particular age, but at a time when the needs of all concerned are most adequately met."[33]

In the period following the raising of the permissible mandatory retirement age from 65 to 70 by federal law on January 1, 1979, this perception was entirely appropriate.

Interestingly, this statement was made in 1970 and arose from consideration of a developing trend to enhance early retirement in order to make room for younger workers entering the workforce. In fact during the 1970s that trend became very strong with innovations like 30 *and out* (unreduced pension after 30 years at any age), subsidized early retirement benefits (partial instead of full actuarial reductions), social security *fillers* (pension income to fill in for social security until it became payable at age 62), and retirement bonuses during *window* periods (supplemented pension income to employees who retired during specified periods of time). The thrust was clearly to move employees out of the workforce at earlier ages.

In the late 1980s, the realization dawned that the baby boom after World War II was working its way into middle age and ultimately, near the end of the century, to older age.

On top of this, genuine concerns about the funding of social security and the activism of older American groups combined to generate an irresistible political force powerful enough to shatter the arbitrary traditional retirement-at-65 practice.

It is very possible that during the 1990s the concept of mandatory retirement will pass into history altogether.

Despite all the sensationalism attached to the subject of an aging society, Tom Paine has correctly pointed out that during the 1980s and early 1990s we will have a "middle aging" society, not an "old aging" society. "It isn't until the later part of the 1980s that the population begins to age at all. Then the largest group is the 45 to 54 year-olds. But notice the year 1990. There is no change whatsoever in the number of people over 55. Thus, the 1980s will be a decade with many people in their 30s and 40s—not a time when the workforce is getting old."[34]

Nevertheless, there is complete evidence that the age makeup of the American population will continually shift toward the later ages.

The meaning of these demographics cannot be overestimated for they will influence the social structure, economics, politics, and employment relationships significantly for the next 50 years.

The management of benefit plans will share deeply in this shift to older ages. Fundamental assumptions and theories about benefit plan design will be challenged, found to be anachronistic, and replaced by new assumptions. Long-standing benefit plan practices will have to be adapted to the new realities and fresh concepts initiated to accommodate needs never perceived in the past.

"Inflation has convinced more than half of today's employees that they will have to work beyond age 65. Business will face much greater problems than it had expected."[35]

Consider what may arise when a middle-aging workforce, just hitting its stride for the period of greatest drive and productivity during a career, crashes into the generation ahead who decide not to move aside to make way, but to hold on to the positions, income, and security they have built over a lifetime. Benefit plans will play a role, perhaps a major role, in resolving this confrontation.

A NEW BENEFITS PARADIGM

"A *paradigm* is an explicitly structured set of assumptions, definitions, typologies, conjectures, analyses, and questions giving both a framework and a pattern of relationships: It is halfway between an analogy and a model, more rigorous than an analogy, not a model, relevant to the subject, but not a theory. It is a set of interrelated questions, typologies, conjectures, speculations, tentative themes, intuitions, insights, lists, and so on, which cover a subject about as far as you can go. It offers you a framework, at least, for thinking about the subject."[36]

Recall at the beginning of this chapter we listed a series of assumptions that have guided benefits management for three decades. David Weeks has pointed out:

> Basically, the unstated assumption that underlies all of these is that a trend of 25 or 30 years duration would continue forever. This, of course, can no longer be considered true. But to imply that none of these assumptions will hold as we move into the 1980s—or worse that a benefit catastrophe is at hand—is patent nonsense. To deduce that managements and the unions will eschew further changes in benefit packages is singularly naive, and to postulate government usurpation of the employee benefit field is totally unsupportable.
>
> However, a failure to reexamine the basic assumptions underlying this multibillion-dollar cultural and social enterprise that we call employee benefits is both poor stewardship and a missed opportunity.[37]

Using the concept of a paradigm is convenient as one way of reexamining the field of employee benefits. It is convenient because it permits expansive conceptualization of ideas and theories as well as consideration of specific narrow assumptions in the examination process.

In establishing a new benefits paradigm in the following pages, we will first set forth a series of ideas and theories that emanate from the changes which have occurred in the last three decades. Next we will postulate some general assumptions and then some specific principles about benefits management that the author views as appropriate to the current and anticipated future environment.

Throughout this book we will examine in detail existing and customary benefit management practices and how those may be altered by this new benefits paradigm.

A Benefit Paradigm for the 1990s

The role of employee benefits in the American socioeconomic system extends beyond fulfilling the economic security needs of employees in the employment relationship, *but satisfying those needs is the foremost primary function of any employee benefit program.*

The economic security needs of employees are influenced by factors generated from their personal circumstances, the employment relationship, and socioeconomic conditions during any given period of history. The range of economic needs to be met is fluid, fluctuating with changes in geographical, national, and worldwide economic and social conditions. The structure of benefit programs must therefore have some fluidity as well to permit them to expand and contract as conditions change.

Employees, both in their employment relationships and as members of the public community, are very interested in employee benefits. Employees and the public are encouraged by government actions and a generalized societal trend toward activism and assertive behavior to challenge authority, question employer policies, and seek redress of adverse circumstances through government agencies, the legal system, and publicity.

Increasingly, society through government expects employers to find ways to solve social problems of all kinds. The solution to many social problems lies in economic security, and employers are expected to provide such financial security so as to reduce the burden otherwise placed on public-income transfer systems. Some form of benefit plan is one method for transforming the pressure for meeting such social objectives into reality.

Tax advantages for employer-paid benefit programs generate a lower cost to the employer to provide the benefit than the cost if employees have to provide the benefit for themselves. Such tax advantages will probably be reduced for extra benefits provided to highly paid employees. Some additional tax advantage will be given employees in the private accumulation of personal assets toward pension income.

Benefit costs will continue to escalate because of (1) government-mandated changes aimed at transferring to employers social costs for economic security, (2) an expanding array of economic needs that derive from changing social values and economic conditions, and (3) expanding expectations of employees with regard to the nature of the employment relationship.

Total control over benefit costs is not possible under the traditional concepts of production cost control. In benefits, cost control derives from controlled utilization of the benefits (which may mean reduced or limited benefits), control of the costs of the systems for delivering benefits, and elimination of waste in the cost for benefits not needed (or not used) or inefficiently distributed between different groups of employees with different needs.

Cost control means managing the costs of benefits not necessarily lowering the costs. Shifting the cost to employees while reducing employer costs does not control the cost of benefits overall and is inefficient and more costly in total because tax advantages and group purchasing power enable employers to provide benefits for employees at a lower net cost. Further, the ultimate result is the need to pay higher levels of taxable direct compensation so employees can pay for their share of benefit costs.

Nonetheless, wherever tax advantages occur, employees must share in the cost to the maximum advantage point. Employees must also share in the cost of additional benefits that are in excess of basic survival levels because if they desire greater protection than necessary for survival, that is a choice which has an economic value they should recognize. Employees should also bear the major cost of noneconomic risk benefits—those benefits that enhance quality of life or standard of living but are not essential to survival or maintenance of health.

Employees and the public are capable of understanding information about benefit programs and benefit costs. Given sufficient information, they will respond by using their benefits efficiently and will cooperate in efforts toward cost control, especially if they gain other advantages by success in cost control.

Employees, the public, and managers of government, business, and unions need more information and concepts that can help them to better understand the purposes, values, limits, and operation of this benefits system so that expectations of what benefits can accomplish will become more realistic and consistent with capacities and limits of the system. The benefits profession in its entirety and those who serve it must undertake responsibility for leading the effort to strengthen the system as a whole, for correcting weaknesses, and in particular for enabling small employers to efficiently and economically extend survival-level benefits to every employed person and his or her dependents.

The basic benefit model consists of employer-paid benefits that meet economic risks up to comfortable survival levels (fully integrated with all government benefits), overlaid by a layer of supplements to these benefits with the cost shared by employees, and overlaid further by a layer of noneconomic risk benefits paid for by employer, employee, or both. (See Chart 1-1.)

CHART 1-1
Benefit System Model

Benefits Not Essential to Economic Survival

Educational expense payments
Product purchase discounts
Legal expense payment
Subsidized transportation
Flexible working hours
Stock ownership plans
Subsidized recreation programs
Physical fitness facilities
Assistance with personal problems
Payment of orthodontia expense
Many kinds of noneconomic survival benefits

Supplemental Economic Survival Benefits

Payment of expenses for dental care, vision care, preventive treatment Mental disorders Alcohol and drug abuse	Accidental death More life insurance or survivor income Family death benefits	Higher levels of disability income Mental and partial disability Additional sick days Unused sick pay buy back	Profit sharing Thrift savings Employee stock ownership plans Cost of living adjustments to pensions	More vacation and holidays Leave time, higher levels of income, and longer periods of payment during involuntary unemployment

Basic "Core" Economic Survival Benefits

Medical, hospital, doctor, maternity, accident, surgical expense payment	Survivor income life insurance death benefits	Income payments during illness or disability	Income in retirement	Income during time off, vacation, holidays, involuntary unemployment

---

GENERAL ASSUMPTIONS OF THE NEW PARADIGM

The assumptions that follow are part of the benefits paradigm appropriate to benefits management in the 1990s.

1. The primary purpose of benefit programs is to enable employees and their dependents to survive economic adversity that arises from involuntary illness or loss of earning capacity through illness, disability, retirement, or death, or other temporary loss of employment. Benefits designed for these objectives are "core benefits" in the total benefit system model.

2. Benefit programs should be designed and funded to maximize tax advantage to the employer and employee. Maximizing tax advantages represents a measure of efficiency and total cost minimization in the provision of benefits.

3. Benefit programs should be coordinated to the maximum extent with state and federal benefit programs. Coordination of all available benefits represents a measure of efficiency and cost minimization in the provision of benefits.

4. In no circumstance should a benefit plan or plans in combination pay in excess of 100 percent of expenses incurred for illness or 100 percent of basic compensation (not including bonuses) for income replacement. Income replacement plans will be reviewed every two years for ad hoc cost-of-living adjustments. Benefit payments that exceed such levels represent inefficiency and waste in the benefits system and waste in the utilization of productive resources.

5. Employees must expect to bear some portion of the economic risk of core benefits. The portion of risk borne by employees should bear a relationship to their capacity to survive; that is, the risk borne by employees should be less at low income levels and greater at higher income levels.

   The risk borne by employees should be limited under catastrophic circumstances to avoid complete destruction of basic economic survival. If the employee's economic survival is destroyed, the cost of maintaining the person becomes a cost borne by all of society through welfare.

6. Income replacement payments from benefit plans should fluctuate up or down with inflation so that the standard of living may be maintained relatively stable. The cost of maintaining in-

flation-related benefits should be shared by government, plan sponsors, and the employee.

7. Beyond the core group of benefits (survival level) there should be opportunities for individuals to augment these benefits or participate in other benefits that are appropriate to their personal circumstances. This feature of options is consistent with the developing social trends as well as with the basic principle that benefits should meet the needs of employees.

8. A third layer of benefits should be made available that is designed to accommodate social objectives, satisfy noneconomic purposes, and enable the employer to adapt to changes in the nature and desires of the workforce.

9. In overall design and availability, benefits should extend proportionately to all segments of the workforce, part-time as well as full-time employees, and in a relative manner to all classifications of employment. Every person employed should be covered to some degree by the core group of benefits.

10. Large employers and unions and all who serve the benefits industry must take some responsibility and action to enable small employers to extend core benefit protection to their employees. Government must ease the regulatory burden on small employers so they can more easily provide these benefits. Assuring extension of economic risk benefit protection to every employed person is a goal that must be acknowledged and preserved.

SPECIFIC ASSUMPTIONS OF THE NEW PARADIGM

1. Inflation will continue at an average of 5 percent per year or more for 20 years and present a major problem in benefit-plan management into the foreseeable future. This must be acknowledged by building a partial cost-of-living adjustment into all benefits that are income replacement in nature. Partial cost-of-living adjustments share the economic risk with employees and keep the pressure on government to act to lower inflation.

2. Benefit plans will continue to expand both in levels of coverage for basic survival benefits and in new plans. The nature of new plans will reflect attempts to ameliorate the increasing cost of

basic needs and services, such as housing, food, clothing, and energy by utilizing the group-purchasing-power concept and the bargaining power of the employer on behalf of employees.

3. Low wage earners are in the greatest need of expanded benefit programs. Unions and employers, in response to social and government pressure, must cooperate to accept the burden of providing both adequate wage levels and survival-level economic benefits for low-wage employees.

4. Government control over benefit plans will continue to expand, both in the regulation of plans and in the mandate for expanded coverage. The basic thrust will be to shift the burden of cost from the public sector to the private sector for benefit plans of all kinds. Such government control will severely limit the flexibility available to employers in providing benefits as the cost of government-mandated programs expand.

5. Benefit plan management increasingly will become legalized in every detail to avoid litigation. Still, litigation over benefits will increase dramatically, encouraged by government and aggressive social purpose-oriented groups. Plan sponsors will become more defensive in benefit management, more resistant to threats of litigation, and tougher in litigation.

6. Benefit management will entail more careful planning and closer control in order to manage costs as carefully as possible. Planning will be directed more carefully toward support of employer planning and objectives.

7. Benefits will increasingly become a right of employment as perceived by employees. Improvements in benefits will become expected just as salary increases are expected on a routine basis. The ability to gain productivity and morale values from benefit programs will diminish as they become a right of employment.

8. Communication of benefits will become more extensive, more open and direct, more individualized, more frequent, and more detailed, despite government efforts to simplify such communication, because generalized and simplified communications are too easily misunderstood and misinterpreted and thus subject to legal contest. Communications will reflect more cost data, even individualized cost data, as data processing systems improve.

9. Benefits will increasingly be presented as part of compensation

in communications as indirect benefit costs approach direct compensation costs.

10. Providers of services, such as insurers and consultants, will develop lower-cost packages of benefit programs including basic illness, disability, death, and pension benefits, along with all administration and communication so that small employers can provide for a single reasonable cost as a percent of payroll—a total package of survival-level benefits.

11. Within 15 years, basic levels of core benefits will be mandated by law for all employers and will cover all employees, including temporary and part-time employees.

12. The social thrust toward greater participation by employees in decisions affecting employment will lead to benefit systems permitting choices by employees among a variety of benefit programs and levels of coverage so that they may tailor benefit coverages to their individual circumstances and needs.

13. Data processing systems will dominate the administration of benefit programs eventually with virtually all administration— from eligibility through claims payment—being primarily a matter of data entering into a system.

14. As benefit costs increase and programs become more complex with greater legal exposure, benefit management will rise in responsibility within the organization structure. A new profession, replete with formal education and professional certification, will develop to supply the needed knowledge and talent to manage benefit programs.

Where do we begin in the process of accommodating the new benefits paradigm? Let's begin with benefits management.

REFERENCES

1. Geraldine Leshin, "EEO Law: Impact on Fringe Benefits," Institute of Industrial Relations, University of California, Los Angeles, January 1979, p. 1. Reprinted with permission.
2. Ibid., p. 5.
3. Ibid., p. 6.
4. David Weeks, *Rethinking Employee Benefit Assumptions* (New York: The Conference Board, 1978). Reprinted with permission.
5. Connie Koenenn, "Future Shocker," *Los Angeles Times*, January 31, 1989.
6. James Flanigan, "Workers Today More Independent, At Risk," Los Angeles Times Syndicate, Grand Rapids Press, March 10, 1989.
7. Letter to SPBA Membership, March 20, 1989, Society of Professional Benefit Administrators, Washington D.C., Frederick D. Hunt, Jr., President.
8. "A National Policy on Retirement Income, Part I: Overview," the American Society of Pension Actuaries, February 1989, Washington D.C.
9. "The Aging of America: Questions for the Four-Generation Society," Joseph A. Califano, Jr., Secretary of Health, Education and Welfare, speech before the American Academy of Political and Social Science, Philadelphia, 1978.
10. Nelson McClung, "Policy for Pension Plans," *Pension and Welfare News*, April 1971. Reprinted with permission. Italics and parenthetical expression are the authors.
11. Max Shapiro, "Can Companies Afford Pensions?" *Duns Review*, June 1974.
12. Ibid., p. 74.
13. A. F. Ehrbar, "Those Pension Funds Are Weaker Than You Think," *Fortune*, November 1977, p. 104. Copyright 1977 Time Inc. all rights reserved. Reprinted with permission.
14. Joseph A. Califano, Jr., "Critical Pension Policy Issues," speech before the American Academy of Political and Social Science, 1978.
15. "Employee Benefits 1988," (Washington, D.C.: U.S. Chamber of Commerce), p. 23.
16. Peter F. Drucker, *The Unseen Revolution: How Pension Fund Socialism Came to America* (New York: Harper & Row, 1976), p. 57.
17. *"Social Security,"* Congressional Action Special Report, U.S. Chamber of Commerce, February 9, 1979.
18. "A Compensation and Benefits Overview," remarks by Richard Schulz, October 2, 1978, p. 46.
19. Ibid., pp. 41–42.
20. "Employee Benefits 1988," U.S. Chamber of Commerce, p. 33.
21. "Employee Benefits Research Institute Quarterly Pension Investment Report," March 1989, EBRI, Washington, D.C.

22. Paul P. Harbrecht, S. J., "Pension Funds and Economic Power," The Twentieth Century Fund, 1959, p. 25.
23. Drucker, *The Unseen Revolution,* p. 57.
24. "Pension Funds Could Spur Market Rally," *Pension World,* May 1979, p. 29.
25. Jeremy Rifkin and Randy Barber, *The North Shall Rise Again: Pension, Politics and Power in the 1980s* (Boston: Beacon Press, 1978), p. 229.
26. "Private Pensions and the Public Interest," American Enterprise Institute for Public Policy Research, Washington, D.C., 1970, p. 184. Reprinted with permission.
27. *The Wall Street Journal,* June 26, 1979, p. 1.
28. *The Wall Street Journal,* June 26, 1979, p. 1.
29. "The Decade Ahead," Remarks by Ray Kann at UCLA Conference on Forecasting Employee Benefits, Los Angeles, December 7, 1978.
30. *The Wall Street Journal,* June 27, 1979, Editorial, p. 14.
31. *The Wall Street Journal,* June 27, 1979, Editorial, p. 14.
32. *The Wall Street Journal,* June 27, 1979, Editorial, p. 3.
33. Robert S. Butler, "Employee Benefits in the Environment of the 70s," *Bests Review,* September 1970, p. 38. Reprinted with permission.
34. Thomas Paine, *The Changing Role of Private Plans,* (New York: Hewitt and Associates, 1978).
35. "Retirement Revolution Brewing," *Duns Review,* May 1979, p. 96. Reprinted with special permission of *Duns Review,* copyright 1979, Dun & Bradstreet Publications Corporation.
36. Herman Kahn and B. Bruce Briggs, "Things To Come: Thinking about the 70s & 80s," copyright The Hudson Institute, Inc., 1972, p. 89. Reprinted with permission.
37. *Rethinking Employee Benefit Assumptions* (New York: The Conference Board, 1978), p. 2. Reprinted with permission.

CHAPTER 2

THE BENEFITS MANAGEMENT FUNCTION

Ernest J. E. Griffes

TRADITIONAL BENEFITS MANAGEMENT

BENEFITS MANAGEMENT IN THE NEW ROLE

THE BENEFIT DEPARTMENT IN THE
ORGANIZATIONAL STRUCTURE

BENEFIT DEPARTMENT ORGANIZATIONAL
STRUCTURES

DECISION MAKING

POSITIVE BENEFITS MANAGEMENT: THE CONCEPT

APPLIED POSITIVE MANAGEMENT

A BENEFIT POLICY AND PLANNING SYSTEM
(OR PHILOSOPHY)

A PLANNING GUIDE FOR BENEFIT DESIGN
AND MANAGEMENT

SUMMARY

TABLES/FIGURES

BENEFIT MANAGEMENT IN THE
ORGANIZATION STRUCTURE

BENEFIT DEPARTMENT ORGANIZATION
STRUCTURE

POSITIVE BENEFITS MANAGEMENT SYSTEM

TRADITIONAL BENEFITS MANAGEMENT

The "management" of benefits for most companies has traditionally meant "administration" of benefits.

The customary attributes of management—planning, objective setting, decision making—have traditionally not been entrusted to benefit managers who have generally been viewed as administrators. To some extent this traditional view derives from the perception of benefits as *giveaways* without a measurable return on investment.

It has also derived from the subordination of benefits to compensation, buried deep within a personnel function that itself has been discredited. Mr. Bere has described the weakness in personnel management:

> It is a paradox that you who are charged with the highest human responsibility—evoking the potentials of other human beings—have so often found your own work given "the character of uselessness." After enjoying rather fashionable status during and just after World War II, the personnel function, in the early 50s, began to lose some of its status. In many companies it became a stepchild of management, assigned to people not likely to go higher. I am glad to note this seems to be changing.[1]

Neither has there been a clear or attractive career path into benefits management that could excite talented managers. Virtually none of those persons now bearing the mantle of benefits management commenced their careers with the goal defined as benefits management.

Consequently, benefits management has traditionally been characterized by a crisis atmosphere, paste and patch tactics to deal with each crisis, and extraneous pressures from promoters and strong power centers in the organization. That structure is crumbling under the weight of social change, government actions, and the critical need for control and order in the conduct of business enterprise.

BENEFITS MANAGEMENT IN THE NEW ROLE

As we examined in Chapter 1, employee benefits are in transition to a new role. This role is being created by the changes occurring in the heightened expectations of employees, by the needs of all types of employers to plan for and control all operations more carefully, and by the intense interest of government in the totality of the employment relationship, including benefits.

All features of the human resource function are being dramatically affected by these forces, with the result that top management is concerned with personnel functions to a degree unparalleled in business history.

Benefits operations are dramatically affected because they are being thrust forward by the force of government actions and increasing costs. The realization that benefits are no longer simple and easy to manage is forcing benefit operations to a higher level of importance in organization structures. *Total compensation,* the phrase that has described compensation and benefits management, is still applicable, of course, and the need to integrate and coordinate these functions will always be appropriate.

The first apparent feature of benefits management in the new role, therefore, is that it is becoming a distinctive functional unit in its own right, on a par with the traditional personnel functions of compensation, employment, equal opportunity, training/development, and industrial relations. This new role for benefits changes the traditional nature of the benefits manager. The benefits manager of the past can be characterized essentially as a technician or mechanic. It was expected of them that their primary responsibility would be technical administration of benefit plans. Specific technical knowledge and ability are and always will be essential features of the benefit manager's skills. Maintaining technical competence is increasingly difficult for benefit managers confronted with rapid-fire technical changes in a multitude of complex benefit plans.

The benefits managers of the next decade will increasingly be thrust into genuine executive roles, with the concomitant responsibility for broad-gauge thinking, planning, and judgment that distinguish managers from administrators. They will carry heavy loads of decision influence and responsibility because they will have the specialized expertise to grasp the total impact of intricate and complex relationships between a vast array of programs that are beneficial to employees.

Evidence of this trend is already appearing. A survey of benefit managers published by the National Employee Benefits Institute revealed that "an overwhelming majority said that the employee benefit manager continues to assume a more significant role for the corporation, with increased direct responsibility and reporting to a higher management level."[2]

In the late 80s vice presidential titles for benefits executives began appearing in large corporations, sometimes associated with some other responsibility but sometimes specifically a Vice President, Employee

Benefits. Most significantly evidencing this trend is the professional Certified Employee Benefit Specialist educational program, first launched in 1976 by the International Foundation of Employee Benefit Plans and the Wharton School at the University of Pennsylvania. For the first time, in 1980, the program graduated students who had completed the equivalent of a college major in benefits management. This elevates benefits management to a professional level equal with Personnel, Industrial Relations, or Finance and separates benefits from the usual peer functions (compensation, employment, etc.) in that at the present time a specific college major in those fields is not available.

The next major organizational step for benefits management begins to take shape from this background. That is the identification of benefits as an organizational entity on a par with Personnel and Finance, incorporating within it the various aspects of personnel and finance that have hindered benefits management with conflicting objectives.

The second apparent effect then of benefits in the new role will be the appearance of highly trained benefits professionals, specifically prepared not only for the technical complexities of benefits administration but equally prepared to function as executives, confident of their professionalism and their ability to contribute in significant ways to the goals of the organization. These new professional benefits executives are bringing to bear a concentrated effort to achieve positive control over the management of benefit programs, the cost of those programs, and the support role of benefits in achieving organizational objectives.

The benefits management process is becoming more scientific, more controlled, and more stable. There will exist more thorough planning efforts coordinated with the organization planning activities. The basis for making decisions on benefit program changes will be a framework of criteria that provide solid, factual, and quantitative data on which judgments can be made.

Because of organizations' long-ingrained habits and outmoded assumptions concerning benefits' traditional role, the acceptance of this changing role for benefits management is evolving with reluctance by other organizational units. Political insecurities and territorial protectiveness will inhibit the development of this role as other units who have long cherished a benefits influence are forced to transfer those responsibilities to the benefits function. Success in realizing this new benefits management role will depend on the political aptitude and sensitivity of individual benefit executives, a character trait for which there is no formal training program. It will also depend on the perceptiveness of top corporate management in recognizing the advantage to the company of positive centralized benefits management.

THE BENEFIT DEPARTMENT IN THE ORGANIZATIONAL STRUCTURE

A survey of 337 of Fortune 1,000 companies illustrates the confusion that still exists concerning the nature of benefits organizationally.[3] No other function of business operations has experienced the degree of uncertainty that benefits has regarding where responsibility should be placed within the organization.

The survey drew a distinction between benefit insurance programs and retirement plans regarding the management functions responsible for day-to-day operations of the plans. The results are interesting primarily in three respects:

1. The distribution of responsibility between top management (officers) and middle management among the first 500 companies and the second 500 companies.
2. The variety of organizational functions with day-to-day or overall management responsibility for benefits.
3. In only 62 percent of the first 500 companies and 68 percent of the second 500 did the day-to-day management of pension plans also reside with the function responsible for benefit insurance plans.

There are 14 different officer titles in some aspect of personnel or finance, generally in finance, when top management has responsibility for benefits management.

There are eight different titles, almost entirely in personnel functions but also in risk insurance functions (no identifiable finance functions) where middle management has responsibility for benefits management.

The second 500 companies tend much more heavily toward top management responsibility for benefits than the first 500 companies. It is unfortunate that no similar subsequent survey exists for comparison. However, it is likely that a current survey taken now would show about the same result since, in general, the same uncertainty still exists between finance and personnel responsibility for benefits operations.

A new development, however, has been the very recent appearance of officers with specifically identified benefit responsibility—Vice

TABLE 2-1
Benefit Management in the Organization Structure

Day-to-Day Manager of Employee Benefit Insurance

	Top 500	Second 500
Top Management	**6%**	**28%**
Vice President—Industrial Relations, Personnel, Employee Relations	3	7
Vice President—Finance Administration	—	3
Secretary, Secretary-Treasurer, Treasurer, Controller	2	8
Assistant Officer	2	11
Middle Management	**87%**	**62%**
Director, Manager, Supervisor of: Employee Benefits, Employee Benefits and Relations, Compensation	50	28
Insurance	26	13
Personnel, Industrial Relations	4	20
Other department (not specified)	6	1
Other	4	6
No answer	3	3
(Base = 100%)	100% (157)	100% (180)

Title of Manager of Employee Retirement Plans (overall)

	Top 500	Second 500
Top Management	**16%**	**46%**
President	—	1
Executive/Senior Vice President	—	1
Vice President—Industrial Relations, Personnel, Employee Relations	4	8
Vice President—Finance	1	7
Other Vice President	1	2
Secretary, Secretry-Treasurer, Treasurer, Controller	3	19
Other Officers	1	—
Assistant Officer	6	9
Middle Management	**76%**	**44%**
Director, Manager, Supervisor of: Employee Benefits, Employee Benefits and Relations, Compensation, Pensions	54	21
Insurance Corporate risk	8	6
Personnel Industrial Relations	8	13
Other department	5	3
Other	4	5
No answer	4	5
	100% (157)	100% (180)

Note; Details may not add to totals because of rounding.
Portions reprinted with permission of Fortune Market Research.

President—Employee Benefits, Vice President—Employee Benefits and Services, Vice President—Employee Benefits and Administrative Services. While no hard survey data exists to validate any trend, and only a few such titles apparently are now in operation, it is highly significant that they exist at all!

What they indicate is the beginning of a recognition that employee benefits do not fit comfortably in either personnel or finance but broadly span both of these as well as other human resource functions, such as Industrial Relations. This development also reveals recognition that benefits management is far too complex to expect that it can be effectively managed by persons with other major responsibilities. Further, the cost implications of benefits and their effect on employees is vastly greater than a few years ago, and benefits management is now a highly technical function with the potential for significant organizational impact. It therefore bears a much larger load of responsibility than in the past.

The evidence is already apparent to justify a modest speculation that elevation of the top benefits position to assistant officer and full officer levels will be a significant benefit management development in the next two decades.

Benefits managers are sensing a higher level of responsibility even where open recognition by organizational change and salary is not yet a fact. The survey of benefit managers by the National Employee Benefits Institute revealed that almost one half of respondents indicated that corporate philosophy toward benefits was being developed in their own offices. Their comments contained frequent references to sensing higher levels of responsibility and involvement in benefit policy setting, as well as much greater direct exposure to top corporate management.[4]

Organizationally, then, the new role of benefits is forcing recognition that benefits functions do not fit comfortably either in personnel or finance and in fact span these and other functions of the organization. Benefits as a stepchild organizationally can no longer effectively serve the needs of employees or the organization. The result is organizational upgrading of the benefits operation.

The challenge to corporate management will be to bring benefits up in the organization despite the political ramifications attendant to long traditions of finance and personnel functions control over benefits. Territorial protection by entrenched interests will be a strong barrier to enabling benefit operations to meet the demands of their new role.

BENEFIT DEPARTMENT
ORGANIZATIONAL STRUCTURES

Specific functional structures of any department are very much a reflection of the management style of the responsible executive, the perceptions of the total organization regarding that function, and of course the size of the organization.

Smaller organizations customarily start with a simple structure of perhaps two persons, a manager (planning, control) and an administrator (claims, record-keeping, etc.). Heavy reliance is placed on outside advisors.

As the organization grows, the natural evolution is the manager and two administrators, pension and insured benefits, plus clerical support. More work is brought in-house as the staff size and competence increase. As organizational size continues to increase, natural structures expand with the manager becoming a director and managers being installed for retirement plans, insured (or health and welfare) plans, record-keeping and systems, and later on communications and retiree services and contacts.

The next evolution is to separate planning and design functions from administrative functions. Thus, the department structure has two distinct units, planning/design and administration. At some point, if the organization is corporate, an international benefits function comes into being and develops along the same structural lines, often going through a geographical-responsibility phase as well.

At this point traditionally the function has matured and this basic structure continues without significant change.

An organization may experience a decentralization, in which case some administrative functions (such as claims and record-keeping) may be spread down to other levels. However, the trend has been toward attempting commonality of benefits for all employees in similar circumstances, even as acquisitions are made, simply to ease mobility of employees between various subunits of the organization. Thus, a strong central planning, control, and administration function is necessary, even in decentralized organizations, so as to avoid chaos in benefit plans and coverages.

Of all the personnel functions, benefit operations are the most difficult to decentralize to any significant degree. Decentralization attempts may reveal the broad nature and scope of benefit operations and can be the point at which it becomes apparent that benefits should be established as an independent function, separate from, and on a par with, a central personnel function.

The expanded role of benefits points the way toward some changes in this traditional organization structure, such as inclusion of a legal and finance role within the Benefit Department. This change would occur at the point where the structure presently matures, so it is the larger companies that will be most affected.

The inhibiting factor in effectively structuring benefit operations for the new role will, of course, be the political protectiveness inherent in functions with traditional benefit responsibility (finance, legal, risk management, etc.) and the prevailing (but weakening) perception by management of benefit operations as an administrative subfunction of personnel.

The benefit executives coming to power in the 1990s will bear the responsibility for awakening the organization to benefits' new role and convincing the organization of the validity of a commensurate benefits department structure. Since the rest of the organization will also experience a new management generation with a different training background and perception of benefits operations than the past generation's, this change may be reasonably smooth. More likely, it will be slow and politically difficult to effect in most organizations because of the stable power base of entrenched interests.

The essential nature of the broader organizational structure of the future benefit department will be to enclose within it the entire span of disciplines necessary for the efficient management of benefit plans. Whereas traditionally benefit managers have had to rely upon other departments for a great deal of assistance (particularly legal, finance, risk management, and tax departments) the evolution of benefit structures will be that these functions as they pertain to benefits will come under one roof. The reason is simply that the new role of benefits will require such a degree of constant attention that they will demand the full time of staff members in these functions. Since it is much more efficient to have under the same banner persons who have the same objectives and who must cooperate closely and constantly, the natural evolution will be toward bringing them together under a single management structure. To the extent necessary, members will interact with their disciplinary counterparts in the total organization, but their perspective will be benefits management and their attention will not be divided between conflicting interests and loyalties, which is the cause of the present frustrations and costly inefficiences in benefits operations.

Figure 2-1 generally illustrates the evolution of benefit function organization structures in the new benefits role.

FIGURE 2-1
Evolution of Basic Organization Structures of Benefit Departments

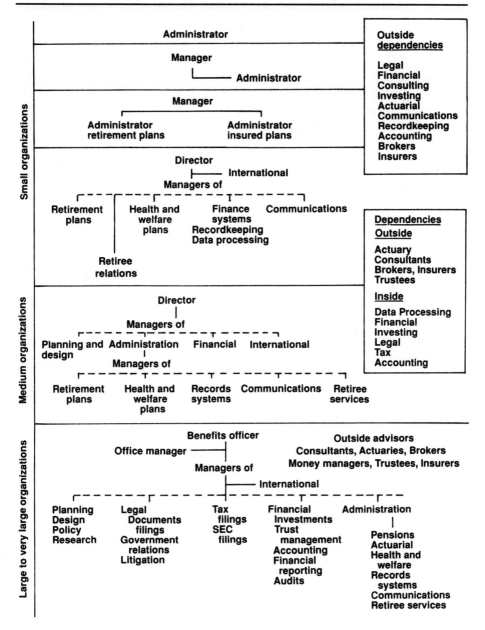

DECISION MAKING

Decisions about changes in benefits and new benefit programs have traditionally been made by the highest level of management, usually the president and/or a top management committee or board of directors committee. This is the proper level for such decisions because the impact of benefit program changes is far-reaching on the entire organization.

Benefit decisions made by management are, however, based on numerous factors, some rational and some irrational. An important factor is the emotional state of mind of management concerning benefits in general and the proposed change in particular, irrespective of the cost or merits. A particular benefit may be the pet idea of a member of top management, and the benefit thereby becomes reality, despite any evidence that for valid reasons it may be inappropriate to provide such a benefit.

The contrary often occurs when considerable evidence indicates the need and validity for a particular benefit action, but total opposition by a member of top management, based on their feelings about it, stops the implementation of the action. This is, of course, characteristic of the decision-making process and represents a major source of frustration for all managers. However, it seems to be a feature especially of personnel-type activities, including benefits, that everyone feels they intuitively know what is best for employees, irrespective of the facts.

Much of the reason for this type of decision making regarding benefits derives from years of low credibility with top management for personnel, including benefits. Dr. Hitchcock noted the credibility gap in pointing out that "personnel is primarily a paper shuffling activity that can only attract the attention of top management by recommending benefit changes contrary to corporate philosophy (which personnel usually had no part in determining)."[5]

The source of this weak credibility has been most often the inability of the benefits profession to factually validate the cost, value, and appropriateness of a benefits change or justify it on any basis except that (1) it had to be negotiated for hourly workers and now has to be extended to other employees, (2) it is necessary to be competitive in the labor market for employees, (3) the government has passed a new law requiring that the change be made, or (4) employees need (want) it.

The new role of benefits will cause some changes in this aspect of the decision-making process. The fast-growing complexity of benefit programs, combined with government intervention, the high cost of programs, and greater sophistication, interest, and demands from employees, is weakening the confidence traditionally placed by top management in the intuitive aspect of benefits decisions. The increased complexity of benefits has also weakened the traditional belief that benefits are largely administrative in nature, are easy to manage, and can thus be managed by almost any technician.

The result is a gradually developing new level of respect and greater credibility for the benefit manager. "At various meetings around the country and in private conversations, we have heard directors of benefit programs discuss their recent presentations of their company's benefit package to CEOs and boards of directors. For some, this has been a new experience which included directly making recommendations concerning both broad benefits philosophy and specific changes in programs."[6]

Besides the intuitive features that have characterized benefit decisions, there are many important factors that bear on a benefits decision. Basic assumptions about the purpose and role of benefits in the employment relationship have shaped greatly the informal and unwritten philosophical framework within which decisions have been made. Many of these assumptions, as discussed in Chapter 1, are under attack and some will pass into history during the 1990s. It is the transition from old to new assumptions that is creating the new role of benefits in organizations.

The restructuring of basic assumptions to meet changed conditions is a traumatic process. In the field of employee benefits particularly, benefit programs tend to become firmly fixed in place as an expected right of employment, not to be reduced in the level of benefits, let alone terminated entirely. A massive economic dislocation of the visibility and magnitude of the 1982 record unemployment and business failures is an example of an event that creates an environment in which reductions in salary and benefits are accepted by employees. Even under these conditions there is an expectation by employees that improved economic circumstances will result in restoration of the benefits that have been "given back."

The cost of changes in programs and of new programs always enters heavily into a decision. But who really knows the cost of a change, and what is that cost to be measured against? Is it too costly in actual dollars or relative to payroll? Sometimes cost is a convenient factor for either justifying or killing a proposed change based on other factors, usually intuitive factors previously mentioned. A benefit change costing $100,000 in a $10 million benefit budget may be killed because it is too costly in actual dollars or justified because it is only a 1 percent increase in the benefit budget. Alternatively, an expensive change will be implemented simply because a powerful member of top management thinks it is the action to take. Later a much lower cost change, perhaps of greater direct value, will be turned down because "benefit costs are already too high."

The development of cost data is fraught with uncertainty, unless the plan is very small and completely insured with definitely fixed premiums. As organizations grow and plans become experience rated then ultimately self-insured altogether, accurate advance determination of costs becomes increasingly difficult. The plan will cost whatever it takes to provide the benefit, except to the extent that the cost can be manipulated to some limited degree as in pension funding.

The tendency has been to look at costs of changes over very short spans of time, such as one or two years, often without considering apparent factors that may dramatically alter those costs only three or four years out. Thus, while the cost of a change is very important in a benefit decision, it can sometimes be manipulated because cost projections are so slippery and influenced by numerous factors that are not under complete control. Seldom will anyone look back five years to determine if a benefit actually cost what it was estimated to cost. If the cost of a given benefit balloons it is natural to think that the initial cost was underestimated or intentionally manipulated to justify the benefit. This is not usually the case. Instead some unforeseen or unfortunate event more likely has caused the cost increase.

Of course collective bargaining pressures often influence the decision regarding a benefit change, usually under intense time pressures that do not permit completely rational planning or consideration of the appropriateness of the change.

Surveys of employee's desires or of the practices of competing employers often generate the emotional pressure for a change. Such surveys are notoriously unreliable and also subject to manipulation to justify or oppose a particular viewpoint. Still they are an indispensable part of benefit decisions, but must be viewed more objectively and rationally within the context of the goals and existing benefit structure before judgments are made and actions based upon them are taken.

Given all these tensions and conflicting pressures, benefits considerations tend to drift to some sort of conclusion, and everybody is glad to simply get some sort of decision, right or wrong, just to get the matter resolved and behind them.

The key to effectively reaching a benefit program decision lies in

(1) having a formal philosophy that management agrees on and supports, (2) establishing an orderly planning process for benefits and a framework or rational basis for reaching decisions about changes, and (3) involving employees in some part of the decision process. Accomplishing this in a real world organization is going to be very difficult and will take years.

The coming generation of benefit managers must bear the responsibility for managing this change. They will need the informed support of a top management who understands the organizational and cost efficiencies of a strong benefit management structure. Many of the factors normally entering into a benefit decision will have a more rationally developed basis under this structure of positive benefits management. As a result the confidence level of top management in the the benefit function will rise, and the benefit department (as well as the benefits manager) will be strengthened organizationally.

POSITIVE BENEFITS MANAGEMENT: THE CONCEPT

Positive benefits management describes a process in which benefit decisions are made in an orderly fashion, based on planning that considers the relationships of various benefit and other personnel policies, within a philosophical and rational framework of reference points triggering benefit changes.

Positive benefits management encompasses correlation of benefit management with the planning process for the organization as a whole. Also, within its parameters are processes to maintain factual awareness of changes in the attitudes and needs of employees and changes in society that will impact on benefit decisions. Fortunately, changes in employee attitudes or expectations and changes in society generally occur slowly enough that there is ample time to plan ahead for what those changes will mean to benefit management. Still, traditionally there has been a resistance to actually taking action by planning benefit program changes, even when all the signs were clearly visible. Instead, the practice has been to ignore (or at least disparage) the signs and wait until the change is forced, usually by government action.

Examples of this are the Employee Retirement Income Security Act of 1974 and the 1978 Amendments to the Age Discrimination in Employment Act of 1967, which raised the legal mandatory retirement age to age 70.

In the early 1960s extensive activity in the form of government inquiries and publicity indicated that very basic changes in the operation of benefit plans were going to be forthcoming. By the late '60s and early '70s the shape of the changes were clearly visible. Still, when the Employee Retirement Income Security Act of 1974 became law, many plan sponsors and benefit advisors seemed to be caught off guard. A lot of expensive scrambling was necessary to bring benefit plans into compliance with the law within the 16-month period between September 1974 and January 1976.

The gestation period that led to the raising of the permissible mandatory retirement age from age 65 to 70 was also quite long, commencing with government actions and public pressure in the early and mid 1960s. The enactment in 1967 of laws concerning age discrimination indicated the direction of change. Still when the mandatory retirement age was raised by passage of the law in April 1978, plan sponsors seemed completely unprepared, and the period for compliance with the law was only nine months, to January 1, 1979. Again, very expensive scrambling and employee relation difficulties resulted as plan sponsors rushed to comply with the law.

If applied in these situations, the concept of positive benefits management would have had plan sponsors well prepared with contingency plans and perhaps even have had some actions already effected in advance of the legal requirements. The savings in direct cost and avoidance of errors in benefit plan and human resource management that occurred because of the need for urgent decisions would have been significant.

Controlled management of organization functions for most staff and production processes has been around for a long time. The application of controlled management to human resource functions has been slow in development. Despite some scholarly efforts, attempts to apply accounting techniques to accounting for the investment in human resources and to develop ways to measure return on investment in human resources have not been successful generally.[7] Without acceptable methods for attaching financial concepts and accountability to human resources, the controlled management of this great resource remains elusive.

Positive benefits management connotes controlled management of the benefits aspects of human resources. This is a first step, using the personnel function with the strongest financial connotations, as a starting point to practically apply management control techniques to human resource management.

The term *positive benefits management* is intended to draw a contrast with the customary reactive and defensive, even negative, manner in which benefits have been managed. One of the most significant returns from embarking upon a program of positive benefits management is to provide the organization with some genuine knowledge and experience in controlled management of human resources that can be applied in controlling other functions of personnel.

APPLIED POSITIVE MANAGEMENT

Positive management of benefits is the target that the benefits profession will be aiming at in the 1990s. It is a moving target, however, because real world operating conditions change constantly. Benefit programs must be changed to meet these conditions, and those changes will be made under the old rules even during the progression towards positive management.

Incongruities will result, with benefit plan changes made that will be inappropriate when the last pieces of positive management finally fit into place. It is a real-world fact that the process of managing programs cannot be halted while the positive management controls are put in place. However, as in the process of constructing a dam across a river, the changes can be channeled in an appropriate fashion even during the building process so that when the project is complete, those changes can be redirected to support the concept.

Simply sensitizing an organization and its management to the steps in implementing positive management immediately alters to some extent the manner in which benefit change considerations will be conducted. The initial step, therefore, in implementing positive management is for the benefit executive to insert the idea into the benefit management process as that process exists in the organization. There are any number of ways this can be accomplished, and the benefit executive will bear responsibility for strategically determining how best to do it in a given set of circumstances.

In many cases the stage is already set (or about to be set), and management is (or will be) ready for some fresh, innovative, and professional approaches. The stage has been set by skyrocketing benefit costs, onerous legislation and aggravating litigation, employee dissatisfaction with the work environment, and either (1) a seemingly endless inflationary spiral, (2) an economic recession requiring tighter controls, or (3) both.

Although it will take perhaps years to implement positive manage-

FIGURE 2-2
Positive Benefits Management System

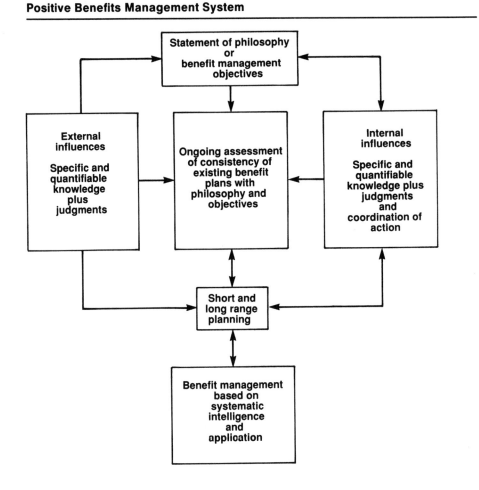

ment, it is necessary to have clearly in mind what the ultimate shape will be like. Figure 2-2 and the following discussion describe the components of a positive benefits management system.

A BENEFIT POLICY AND PLANNING SYSTEM (OR PHILOSOPHY)

The initial essential component of the system is an organizational benefit philosophy or (if the term philosophy is not acceptable) an organizational management statement of objectives concerning the purposes and reasons why the company maintains benefit plans and what the organization intends to accomplish by maintaining those plans. Probably some such unwritten overall philosophy presently exists informally in the thinking of the various persons involved in benefits management. In all likelihood, there is little conscious agreement on what this philosophy is, with the result that benefit management and decisions occur in an atmosphere of widely differing opinions and assumptions. Consequently, benefit programs are managed in a chaotic fashion, influenced to some degree by the philosophical viewpoints of all the competing forces.

Developing a philosophy at the outset that crystalizes, formalizes, and coordinates the wide variety of opinions and assumptions is essential to implementing real control over benefit management. Of course, this will be very difficult to accomplish because the process itself forces people to examine their intuition and assumptions and commit to an opinion. Generally, especially in the benefits area, there is a reticence to commit to a general principle that will appear in writing and perhaps be a limiting factor at some future point. However, order in controlling and managing benefits requires some formalized framework of assumptions. It is the lack of commonly agreed-upon ground rules that has permitted the unruly and uncontrolled development of benefit programs.

The starting point for drafting a benefits objective (philosophy) statement is with the informal and most often unwritten assumptions that are known to exist. The benefits executive has to take responsibility for preparing the initial statement that will become the discussion draft.

In many organizations there may exist some formalized policy statements that contain specific philosophical viewpoints concerning human resource management. Such policy statements are very helpful in isolating organizational philosophies and objectives that may guide benefit management. Using stated objectives that management is already committed to will give strength and support to the benefit philosophy statement, both during discussion stages and as it is finally formalized.

Usually, there also exists some formalized statement of total organizational goals as well. Very often this exists in the group responsible for the planning process. Such stated organization objectives may be part of short- and long-range planning. These objectives should be examined carefully for features that may affect, or be affected by, benefit management. Any such features should be incorporated into the benefit objective statement. This coordination will also add strength and support to the benefit philosophy and very importantly will demonstrate to management the professionalism and breadth of awareness of the benefit executive.

Using these references as a starting point—that is, informal and unwritten assumptions, formal human resource management policies, and organizational objectives—the benefit executive can begin to draft a set of assumptions and objectives for benefit management.

The components of a philosophy will vary depending on the nature and objectives of the organization and of course should reflect an approach to benefits that supports the objectives of the organization. The philosophy should include both a broad statement of benefit objectives and some statement also regarding the specific objectives related to each major economic risk; that is, illness, disability, death, and retirement.

A statement of general benefit objectives might address, for example:

1. The role and purpose of maintaining benefit programs—why are such programs provided?
2. General principles of plan design; i.e.,
    a. The relationship between employer and employee contributions.
    b. The extent to which income replacement plans should meet income needs.
    c. The distinction between benefit payments in events that are voluntary as opposed to events that are involuntary.
    d. The organization's attitude toward retirement.
3. Any general principles concerning the management of benefits; i.e.,
    a. Benefits plans shall support the equal opportunity and affirmative action goals of the organization.
    b. Benefits negotiated in collective bargaining shall be extended to employees not covered by collective bargaining.
    c. Benefit plans shall be integrated with legally mandated benefits to the maximum extent possible.
    d. When legal requirements are imposed on a benefit plan, only the minimum legal requirements shall be complied with during the first year following the compliance date.

The statement should also address specific objectives with respect to each major economic risk covered by benefit plans. For example:

Disability Benefits:
   To provide any employee who is unable to work due to temporary or long-term illness with income continuation at a level which recognizes the reduced taxes on such income, reduced expenses as a result of work-

related expense, and the income benefits payable during such a period of illness from any government programs.

Also included should be some statement of how programs will be measured against the objectives and how changes in programs will be validated. The following is a sample of planning guide that might be developed.

A PLANNING GUIDE FOR BENEFIT DESIGN AND MANAGEMENT[8]

I. General

Any benefit program is subject to a process of fairly continuous change arising from economic, competitive, and demographic factors. The purpose of this statement of benefits philosophy is to establish fixed general principles to control and shape this process of change. This statement is separated into three parts:
1. A statement of general principles of philosophy, purpose, and design.
2. An outline of a system to measure the benefit program against the real world.
3. A statement of the process to be followed to manage changes in the benefit program.

II. Statement of Purpose and Design Philosophy

A. Role of the Benefit Program

XYZ Company recognizes that it has a fundamental interest in the health and general welfare of its employees, which is partially given expression by its employee benefit programs. More specifically, the role of the benefits program is to:
1. Promote efficiency and safety in corporate operations by providing programs to maintain the employee's health and to replace income lost due to illness, death, or disability.
2. Maintain corporate vigor and energy by providing a program which enables an employee to retire when he or the company judges it the most appropriate time.
3. Attract employees.
4. Retain employees.

B. General Principles of Benefit Design
1. The major overall purposes of the program are:

   a. To replace the income lost as a result of the death, disability, or retirement of employees.

   b. To reimburse employees for major expenses incurred due to illness or injury.

   c. To maintain the health of employees.

2. The program will be designed around the needs of employees' family units.

3. The program should strike a balance between equity among employees and their individual needs.

4. The program should not meet the entire benefit needs of employees. It should:

   a. Be coordinated with, to the extent permitted by applicable laws, all benefits provided through governmentally mandated programs partially or fully funded by the company, such as the federal Social Security program, and state disability and workers' compensation programs, etc.

   b. Leave a role for the employees to provide a part of their own security.

5. As well as delivering benefits directly to employees, the program should also act as an intermediary to enable employees to supplement the company-paid benefits in order to meet their entire benefits needs.

6. Where an employee has control over the event giving rise to benefit payments, less than 100 percent reimbursement should be available.

7. Benefits which result from involuntary events (e.g., death and most disabilities, and illnesses) should be provided without extensive waiting periods and should be independent of an employee's length of service.

8. Benefits which result from voluntary events (e.g., voluntary termination or retirement) should be dependent upon length of service and should have elements of forfeiture.

9. The program should recognize the importance of tax implications by:

   a. Considering income replacement net of taxes.

   b. Recognizing differences in efficiency between company and employee funding of benefits.

   c. Recognizing the difference in tax treatment between alternative methods of funding benefits.

10. The program should ultimately provide a basic level of survivor, disability, retirement, and health care benefits for each employee; and then should permit each employee to select among a group of alternative benefit improvements as best fits his individual needs.

C. Goals for Specific Benefit Plans
  1. Retirement Benefit Program
    a. Pension Plan

PRIMARY GOAL: To enable an employee who has spent a full career to retire after age 65 with an income from the plan which, in conjunction with Social Security, will allow the employee and his dependents to enjoy and sustain the same standard of living after retirement as he enjoyed prior to retirement, using an ad hoc approach to making adjustments for inflation, after retirement.

SECONDARY GOAL: To provide an employee who has spent a partial career, or who wishes to retire before age 65, with an income from the plan proportionate to that provided to "full career" employees, with allowance for the facts that early retirement benefits will be paid for a longer period of time and that a shorter time will have been available to fund these benefits.

    b. Voluntary Savings Incentives

PRIMARY GOALS: To provide the employee with the opportunity and incentive to save from his own resources for:

(1) The medium term, to enable him to accumulate resources to meet large periodic expenses during his career.

(2) The long term, to enable him to supplement the benefits from the pension plan.

SECONDARY GOAL: To provide the employee with the opportunity to accumulate XYZ Company common stock.

    c. Profit-Sharing Plan

PRIMARY GOAL: To provide the employee with an indirect participation in the profits of the company each year.

SECONDARY GOAL: To supplement the benefits from the pension plan.

2. Survivor Benefit Program
   PRIMARY GOALS:
   *a.*To provide all active employees, as well as former employees in receipt of retirement income, with a lump-sum death benefit sufficient to wind up their personal affairs.
   *b.*To provide additional benefits to those active employees with dependents sufficient to produce a monthly income which, in conjunction with social security and workers' compensation benefits (where applicable), will be sufficient to support the deceased employee's dependents.
   SECONDARY GOALS:
   a. To provide additional protection to employees who die while traveling on company business.
   b. To offer employees the opportunity to purchase additional survivor benefit protection covering their lives and the lives of their dependents.
3. Disability Benefit Program
   PRIMARY GOALS:
   a. To provide an employee who is ill or temporarily disabled with a partial continuation of his income, as well as a continuation of health care benefits.
   b. To provide an employee who becomes totally and permanently disabled with a monthly income which, in conjunction with social security and workers' compensation benefits (where applicable), will be sufficient to support him in a reasonably similar manner to which he was accustomed while working for the company for as long as he remains disabled.
4. Health Care Benefit Program
   PRIMARY GOAL: To reimburse the employee for the major costs incurred as a result of illness or injury.
   SECONDARY GOAL: To promote the general health and well-being of the employee and his family.

III. Measurement of Benefit Program
A. General
   The goals of the program will be quantifiably measured using three separate approaches, as follows:
   1. A *relative* measurement, comparing the program with current business practice.

2. An *absolute* measurement, comparing the program to an optimum benefit program.
3. A measurement of the *perception* of the employees of the benefit program.

B. Comparison with Current Business Practice

A survey of the benefit program will be made to measure the benefit program against the programs of 12 other companies selected as follows:

1. Four other manufacturers, with whom XYZ Company competes.
2. Four industrial companies headquartered in Chicago.
3. Two companies that are regarded as employee benefit leaders.
4. Two other industrial companies about the same size as XYZ Company.

This survey will consist of:

1. A comparison of benefit plans, provision by provision.
2. A comparison of the dollar level of benefits produced by the benefit plans surveyed.
3. A benefit index, produced for each separate plan and for the total program, to rank the plans and the total program of the surveyed companies.
4. An analysis of benefit changes since the previous survey.

C. Comparison Against Optimum Program

The level of benefits from the XYZ Company program will be compared to those of an "optimum" benefit program that provides:

1. 100 percent continuation of income, insured against inflation, payable to the employee on disability and retirement and to his family upon his death.
2. 100 percent reimbursement of all health care costs.
   These measures will be calculated both before and after federal and state income taxes.

D. Employee/Employer Communications

A two-way system of communication with employees will be maintained whereby:

1. The dollar amount of an employee's benefits will be communicated to him through an annual benefit statement.
2. An employee attitude survey will be conducted periodically to determine the employee's perception of the program and perceived benefit improvement needs.

The employee benefit statement should assist in molding the employee's perception of the plan, and the employee attitude survey may suggest different communications approaches. The employee attitude survey will also provide essential input into the system for determining the priority and timing of benefit improvements.

E. Benefit Costs

The change in cost of each benefit plan, and the total program, will be analyzed annually to show how much of the change is due to:

1. Maintaining benefits to compensate for inflation.
2. Changes affected by utilization.
3. Real improvements in the quality of benefits delivered to the employees and their beneficiaries.

IV. Managing Benefit Improvements

A. Policy

XYZ Company's policy is to maintain an employee benefit program which:

1. Is competitive in the employment marketplace. This policy will be met by maintaining the program in the first quartile of benefit programs as measured by a benefit survey conducted biennially.
2. Utilizes a balanced approach to the real needs of the employees, as measured against the optimum benefit program.
3. Is responsive to the perceived needs of the employee, as reflected in the employee attitude survey.
4. Anticipates possible legislated benefit changes.
5. Takes into account tax effects on contributions, relative benefit levels, and benefit amounts.

B. Implementation

A five-year plan for benefit changes will be maintained consistent with the overall philosophy and policy set out above.

Any benefit change must be justified in terms of:

1. Consistency with the five-year plan.
2. A slippage in the desired ranking, as shown by the benefit survey.
3. Any pending or probable legislative changes.
4. A perceived necessary change as revealed by employee attitude survey.
5. A change in economic or demographic variables.

SUMMARY

Once having established a formal benefit philosophy statement, positive benefits management follows through the consideration of a number of other factors and a decision process that circulates around that statement (refer to Figure 2–2), all of which are discussed in depth throughout this book.

External influences, such as social changes, legislation, inflation, recession, competitor activities, and collective bargaining demands, must be evaluated and judgments made as to how these factors may affect benefit management.

Internal influences, such as changing employee attitudes, changing organization objectives, changes in management, rising or falling company fortunes, reorganizations, acquisitions/divestitures, and so on, must be evaluated and judgments made as to the effects on benefit management.

Plans must be assessed on an ongoing basis to determine continuing appropriateness of the benefit philosophy consistent with external and internal influences. From these evaluations follow short- and long-range benefit planning and decisions.

The result overall is a system of benefit plan management that is based on specific and quantifiable data, judgments within a known philosophy and objectives, planning that is orderly and provides a controlled environment for benefit management, and decisions that are rational and arrived at in an orderly manner based on specific intelligence.

This is positive benefits management.

REFERENCES

1. "The Second American Revolution," keynote presentation by J. F. Bere, Chairman and Chief Executive Officer of Borg-Warner Corporation, AMA 50th Annual Human Resources Conference, New York, March 5, 1979. Used with permission.
2. "Corporate Pension Decisions: Who Makes Them?" *Pension World,* October 1978. Reprinted with permission.
3. "How Major Industrial Corporations View Employee Benefit Programs," survey by Fortune Market Research, December 1974, pp. C–2 and C–5.
4. "Corporate Pension Decisions: Who Makes Them?" *Pension World,* October 1978.
5. "The New Personnel Professional: Responsive to Change," *The Personnel Journal,* January 1979. Reprinted with permission of *The Personnel Journal,* copyright January 1979.
6. "Corporate Pension Decisions: Who Makes Them?" *Pension World,* October 1978. Reprinted with permission.
7. Two works on the subject are Eric Flamholtz, *Human Resource Accounting* (Encino, Calif: Dickenson Publishing Company, Inc., 1974) and Ray A. Killian, *Human Resource Management: An ROI Approach* (New York: AMACOM, 1976).
8. Credit for some of the concepts in the balance of this chapter goes to David Gladstone, FSA, JD, of Hazlehurst & Associates, Inc., Consultants & Actuaries, Atlanta, Georgia, who developed the concepts under a contract with Levi Strauss & Co.

CHAPTER 3

BENEFIT PLANNING SYSTEMS

Ernest J. E. Griffes

THE COMPONENTS OF A BENEFIT PLANNING
SYSTEM
ASSESSMENT OF EXISTING BENEFITS
EXTERNAL AND INTERNAL INFLUENCES AND
CONSTRAINTS
EXAMPLE OF A SHORT-RANGE PLANNING CHART
THE FUNCTION OF THE BENEFITS EXECUTIVE
JOB DESCRIPTION VERSUS FUNCTIONAL ROLE
LONG-RANGE PLANNING
COMPONENTS OF LONG-RANGE PLANNING
PLAN SPONSOR LONG-RANGE PLANS
INFORMATION ABOUT DEVELOPING TRENDS
INTRODUCING LONG-RANGE PLANS INTO THE
ORGANIZATION
USING LONG-RANGE PLANS EFFECTIVELY FOR
SHORT-TERM ACTION
CONTROLLING BENEFIT CHANGES
CONCLUSION
CHARTS/DOCUMENTS
EXAMPLE OF DISABILITY INCOME BENEFITS
CHECKLIST FOR BENEFIT SHORT-RANGE
PLANNING
EXAMPLE OF SHORT-RANGE PLANNING CHART

POSITION DESCRIPTION FOR THE BENEFITS
EXECUTIVE
AUTHORIZATION FOR CHANGE

This chapter will discuss the process of planning as it applies to benefit management.[1] Implementing the policy and planning system outlined in Chapter 2 is one means of establishing an orderly planning process.

Benefits, as a human resource support system, enable the enterprise to meet its goals and objectives by contributing importantly to the employment environment. Properly planned, designed, managed, administered, and communicated, the benefit network of an enterprise will enhance the employment relationship and make a positive contribution to the attitude of employees and to productivity.

If, for example, the enterprise is growing very fast with a need for employees who are technically oriented and in short supply, the benefit programs must be aimed at attracting such persons, possibly through generous profit-sharing and the most futuristic benefit approaches, such as flexible benefits.

If the fortunes of the enterprise are on the wane, the goal may be to structure the environment so as to clear the enterprise of a no longer needed workforce.

A corporate goal, for example, of marketing its products based on the quality of workmanship and reliability of the product inherently contains the presumption that employees take pride in their workmanship and will produce high-quality products that are reliable. Supporting this goal requires an employment environment conducive to attracting and retaining the kind of employees who will take pride in their workmanship. Benefits are an important part of that environment. That business goal (and the success of the enterprise) will not be achieved if the employment environment is such that workers are discouraged or dissatisfied.

Benefits planning thus entails a high degree of awareness of the goals of the organization and integration into the planning process of the organization by which those goals are determined. Customarily, the planning process for design and management of benefits has been almost totally outside of the organization planning process. Only in the 1980s, as numerous new laws brought urgent attention to benefit matters, did planners begin to consider bringing benefits executives in on the organizational planning process.

Since planners for the organization are besieged with the variety of factors they must consider in developing plans, it remains incumbent upon benefits executives to seek out a role in the organizational planning process. Such a role is simultaneously aggressive and defensive.

The benefits executive, by the nature of the responsibility, is the repository of knowledge about developments that may influence the organization's planning. The impact of developing legislation, such as the potential for taxation of benefits, social security changes, and liabilities for pensions, may affect the organization's plans in significant ways, and the benefits executive must be aggressive in entering such knowledge into organization plans.

At the same time, organization plans will certainly influence benefit planning. The benefits executive must be aware of such plans so as to avoid benefit planning that is inefficient or unacceptable within the organization's plans or results in serious and costly errors in benefit management.

THE COMPONENTS OF A BENEFITS PLANNING SYSTEM

There is no great mystery about what constitutes a basic planning system—the mystery is why a formal benefits planning system is so seldom used in the benefit management process.

Recall from Chapter 2 the chart of a Positive Benefits Management System (see Figure 2-2).

The components of this system are:

1. The development of a set of benefit management objectives (a philosophy).
2. An assessment of existing benefits measured against those objectives.
3. Identification of external and internal influences and constraints that will impact on achievement of the objectives.
4. Short- and long-range planning resulting from the previous evaluations.
5. Benefit management and administration based on the plans that have been developed.

Such a system can be highly structured and formalized or relatively simple and informal, depending upon the needs of the organization, and is useful and appropriate to any kind or size of organization.

The first essential component for planning is setting objectives and goals. In Chapter 2 we discussed developing a "Statement of Philosophy," setting "Benefit Management Objectives." This statement is developed by examining the objectives and philosophies of the organization and translating them into benefit management objectives. Hopefully, this statement will be adopted formally by management so that benefit management can proceed in an orderly fashion within those objectives.

Equally as often, however, management may be unwilling to make such a formal commitment, be unconvinced of its usefulness, or be concerned that a commitment may box them in in the future or limit courses of action. Particularly in smaller enterprises with a central focus on economic survival, the fancy appendages of formal policies are frequently lacking.

For the management member responsible for benefits, the unwillingness of management to commit to a formal statement of benefit management objectives should not prevent development of an informal set of objectives, even of the simplest sort. Such an informal statement is essential to evaluating existing benefits and the directions of change those benefits should take as time goes on.

Such a statement of objectives must be perceived as the basic anchor for benefit management activities and once set should not be lightly or carelessly altered in major ways. Still, as with objectives for production of goods, when significant external changes occur there must be a willingness to alter the objectives to accommodate a new reality. If the market for a product doubles, production goals will be doubled. Similarly, if the reality of benefit needs changes in major aspects, the objectives of benefit management must be changed as well.

The important point is that the benefits executive and management recognize what they are moving from and what they are moving toward. This is preferable to simply drifting about with insufficient awareness of where a course of action will lead or what the impact of that action may be on benefit management as a whole.

So the first and a fundamentally essential component of any attempt to really control and manage benefits must be the development of a set of objectives, purposes, and goals for benefits in the enterprise.

ASSESSMENT OF EXISTING BENEFITS

The evaluation of the status of existing benefit programs relative to the objectives is more complex than it may seem when first considered, depending upon how detailed the objectives are in definition.

A benefit objective of always fully integrating with government benefit plans is quite definite, and therefore assessing existing benefits against that objective is very straightforward. Legally permissible integration limits for profit-sharing and pension plans with social security are carefully delineated in the Internal Revenue Code and regulations and fully understood by benefit practitioners. Integration of disability income benefits with social security disability income and workers' compensation is also quite straightforward, but does become a little more complex in deciding whether to integrate with the total of such benefits (including any payments from such programs for dependents), or to integrate with only the portion of such benefits attributable to the employees themselves ("primary" social security benefits, for example).

This represents a good example of how different objectives in benefit design and organization goals interact and must be planned for simultaneously. Use of disability income plans for this example is intentional since the costs of such benefits have been soaring in recent years, primarily because long-term disability is a condition subject to a wide range of definitions. Physicians increasingly are liberalizing their judgments of what constitutes a long-term disability, and increasingly disability income plans are used either consciously or unconciously as an alternative to pension income, particularly where a poorly performing employee at an older age is involved and disability is a more acceptable method of termination than "forced retirement" with its overtones of age discrimination.

The design and management of disability income plans involve major opportunities for cost control, therefore, as well as involvement with human resource management objectives of an organization; that is, clearing older, nonproductive employees from the workforce in a humane and socially acceptable manner. Obviously, controlling cost will be very difficult if the disability plan is intentionally used to meet this human resource management objective. It is necessary to be conscious of this trade-off and for management to be aware of the trade-off in order for benefit programs to be effectively managed.

Thus, long-term disability income benefits represent a good example for application of the concept of a benefits management/planning system.

In the "Planning Guide for Benefit Design and Management" set forth in Chapter 2, two separate objectives are:

1. Disabilities Benefit Program
   PRIMARY GOALS:
   a. To provide an employee who is ill or temporarily disabled with a partial continuation of income as well as a continuation of health care benefits.
   b. To provide an employee who becomes totally and permanently disabled with a monthly income which, in conjunction with social security and workers' compensation benefits (where applicable), will be sufficient to support him in a reasonably similar manner to which he was accustomed while working for the company, for as long as he remains disabled.
2. The program should not meet the entire benefit needs of employees. It should:
   a. Be coordinated with, to the extent permitted by applicable laws, all benefits provided through governmentally mandated programs partially or fully funded by the company, such as the federal social security program, and state disability and workers' compensation programs, etc.
   b. Leave a role for the employees to provide a part of their own security.

Benefit surveys in recent years indicate generally that the income replacement goal in the majority of long-term disability income plans is two thirds of basic pay during the year just prior to disability. This is one measure, in this case an "external influence," that may be applied in setting a specific goal for design of a long-term disability income plan.

To illustrate the point in a simple example, we will assume that a plan sponsor has decided upon an income replacement of 70 percent as the appropriate level in their plan based upon the rationale that:

1. Income taxes payable on salary but not on disability income and work-related expenses not incurred during a period of disability together constitute 20 percent of salary.
2. The employee should bear some part of the responsibility for his/her own financial security and have some incentive to recover and return to active employment, and the remaining 10

percent of salary not replaced by disability income will serve this
objective.
3. Future effects of inflation and cost-of-living adjustments will be
   dealt with on an ad hoc basis in the future. Thus, in replacing 70
   percent of income, the goals of providing a sufficient monthly
   income and leaving a role for the employee in meeting some part
   of his/her financial security have been met.

We now have a second goal to consider, and that is integration with
government income programs. In this case we shall use social security
disability income and workers' compensation income as examples.

Since we are evaluating an existing benefit against a defined objective, we shall presume that when this long-term disability income plan
was established many years ago, in the absence of any formal objectives
at the time, the integration with social security was simply set to use only
primary social security benefits payable. That is, the social security
disability income benefit payable for the employee only, irrespective of
any social security benefit payable for dependents of the employee.
Furthermore, assume that the present income replacement percentage in
the existing plan is at 60 percent of pay, an amount arrived at as a result of
increases from 50 percent of pay when plan was originally established.

There is yet one other aspect to consider, and that is the cost-of-
living increases that are automatic in the amount of the social security
benefits. Consistent with general practice, the existing plan provides that
as social security benefits are increased by cost-of-living adjustments,
the larger social security benefit results in a reduction of the benefit
amount paid from the plan so that the total income benefit remains the
same.

In our evaluation of existing benefits, it becomes apparent that if we
are to meet our stated objectives of full legal integration with government
benefits and our income replacement goal, changes are called for in the
provisions of the long-term disability income plan.

What are the consequences of this discovery? What is the significance of the integration only with primary social security, rather than all
the social security benefits a disabled employee receives? Let's look at
the example in Table 3-1.

What is really occurring? The actual disability income being received is now 77.3 percent of pay before disability, which is 17.3 percent
higher than the goal of 60 percent of pay intended by the present plan.
What's more, the 77.3 percent of pay is 7.3 percent higher than the 70

TABLE 3-1
Example of Disability Income Benefits from Present Plan

Income before disability	$1,000 per month
Total income replacement from benefit plans at 60 percent	$ 600 per month
Calculation of benefits from the plan at time of disability:	
1. Primary social security disability income	$ 300 per month
2. Workers' compensation income	$ 100 per month
3. Benefit payment from the plan	$ 200 per month
Total payments	$ 600 per month
Actual income benefits being paid now (2 years later):	
1. Primary social security with 10 percent cost-of-living adjustment	$330/mo.
2. Social security payments for dependents	$165/mo.
3. Workers' compensation	$100/mo.
4. Benefit payment from plan ($200–$30 SS COLA)	$170/mo.
Total income	$765/mo.
Total income as a percent of pay at disability	76.5 percent
Estimated income benefits next year:	
1. Primary social security with additional 5 percent cost of living	$347/mo.
2. Social security payments for dependents with COLA	$173/mo.
3. Workers' compensation—benefits have expired	-0-
4. Benefit payment from plan ($200–$47 SS COLA + $100 Worker Compensation)	$253/mo.
Total income	$773/mo.
Total income as a percent of pay at disability	77.3 percent

percent of pay income replacement objective we have set as the appropriate level under our new Benefit Management Objectives.

The evaluation of this existing benefit in relation to the Benefit Management Objectives indicates the following inconsistencies with the objectives:

1. The current income replacement percentage of 60 percent is less than our objective of 70 percent and less than prevailing practice of 66⅔ percent.
2. Current integration practice of using only primary social security is not consistent with the objective of full integration with government benefits.
3. The current plan is providing a level of income replacement (77.3

percent) that is greater than the intended objective of 70 percent of pay.

4. Disabled employees who have dependents are receiving a greater percentage of income replacement during disability than those without dependents.

5. As presently constituted the plan appears to provide in effect more net income during disability than is received during active employment.

There may be other inconsistencies as well, of course. This example is only intended to illustrate the basic process.

EXTERNAL AND INTERNAL INFLUENCES AND CONSTRAINTS

Having determined the differences between the existing benefit plan and the objectives, consideration next is given to the various influences that will come to bear in shaping the actual short- and long-range plan for moving toward the objective. External influences and constraints usually occur in the following areas:

1. Labor contract provisions and the need to negotiate changes in a benefit plan.
2. Competitiveness of a specific benefit or a total benefit program in seeking and retaining employees in a given labor market (national, regional, local).
3. Legal requirements, both those actually in effect and the status of proposed and pending laws or proposed regulations. It is necessary to be aware of many laws other than those specifically related to benefit plans.
4. General or specific trends developing in benefit practice relative to a benefit.
5. Tax laws and their impact on the taxability of a specific benefit to the employee.
6. Availability of the necessary vehicle for delivering the desired benefit; that is, insurance products, the flexibility of an insurer in accommodating the desired benefit provisions.
7. Social and economic trends that may have a bearing on the benefit changes under consideration.
8. Economic controls that may be in effect; that is, wage controls.

At the same time there are many influences and constraints within the organization that must be considered. Some of them are:

1. Financial aspects of the plan or changes in the plan.
2. Employee attitudes and perceptions about benefits, that is, desires and perceived needs, in particular with respect to the benefit change under consideration.
3. If the change entails considerable administration, the availability of staff support or data processing systems to handle the administration.
4. The relative importance of the change to other benefit change priorities.
5. Other internal pressures for or against a change; that is, affirmative action goals that would be supported by the change, the need for the improvement to support recruiting efforts, and so forth.
6. The opinion of other key functions with respect to the change; that is, industrial relations if the change involves union relations or financial functions if it involves liabilities or investments.
7. The availability of support from other functions if it is needed; that is, legal department, financial department, or payroll department support.
8. The timing with respect to the political atmosphere; that is, the appropriateness of the change given conditions in the organization at the time.

The process of developing a short- and long-range plan is actually the preparation of a strategy for reaching a benefit objective that factors in all these external and internal influences and constraints.

For that reason we will examine in some detail each of these influences and consider how they might fit into a strategy for reaching a benefit objective. For illustration purposes, we will use the case of the long-term disability income plan discussed earlier in this chapter as an example. In considering this example we will follow the checklist for Benefit Short-Range Planning, illustrating in detail the application of the entire process discussed throughout this chapter.

Checklist for Benefit Short-Range Planning
1. Benefit under consideration.
2. Summary of current plan.
3. Benefit objectives that affect this plan.
4. Possible changes for consideration.

5. External influences and constraints on this plan.
   a. Labor contracts.
   b. Competitiveness of present plan.
   c. Legal constraints.
   d. Developing trends.
   e. Tax laws.
   f. Availability of insurance or funding vehicles.
   g. Social and economic trends impacting this benefit.
   h. Economic controls.
   i. Other.
6. Internal influences and constraints.
   a. Financial considerations.
   b. Employee attitudes and perceptions.
   c. Administration.
   d. Relative priorities.
   e. Other.
   f. Viewpoints of other functions.
      (1) Labor relations.
      (2) Tax department.
      (3) Equal employment opportunity.
      (4) Personnel policies.
      (5) Operating managers.
      (6) Benefit recipients.
      (7) Other.
7. Availability of support functions.
8. Timing considerations.
9. Specific recommendations to management.

Example of a Short-Range Planning Chart for Benefit Plan Management

1. *Benefit Plan:* Long-term Disability Income Plan
2. *Summary of Current Plan:* After five months of short-term disability, a medical judgment that permanent and total disability is likely results in an employee being transferred to long-term disability status. Income continues until the earliest of death, retirement age 65, or until recovery and return to active employment. This income replacement level consists of primary social security income payments, workers' compensation payments, and a payment from the

companies' Long-Term Disability Income Plan, so that total income equals 60 percent of predisability income. (More could be added.)

3. *Benefit Planning Objectives That Affect This Benefit Plan:* (This section sets forth either the specific sections of the Planning Guide For Benefit Design and Management, or a summary of those sections.)

   The sections of the Planning Guide For Benefit Design and Management that have a direct bearing on this plan are summarized as follows:

   Section II.B. paragraphs 1, 4, 9, 10:
   A major purpose of the benefit programs is to replace income loss as a result of disability, fully coordinating with all government programs providing income during disability, and recognizing the different tax treatment accorded disability income.

   Section II.C. paragraph 3: Disability Benefit Program:
   This section sets the objective of continuing income during disability at a level, which in conjunction with all other government income benefits, will be sufficient to support the employee in a reasonably similar manner to which they were accustomed while actively employed with some adjustment for inflation.

4. *Possible Changes For Consideration*
   a. Raising the level of benefit from 60 percent to 66⅔ percent or 70 percent.
   b. Integrating with full social security.
   c. Offering employees an option to purchase at their own cost some additional disability income protection.
   d. Increasing benefits for inflation protection and requiring some employee contribution to the cost.
   e. Establishing a partial disability provision.
   f. Tightening up or liberalizing definitions of disability.
   g. Enhancing the incentives to rehabilitation.
   h. Liberalizing the provisions with respect to mental and nervous disabilities.
   i. Establishing an Employee Assistance Program to attempt to prevent problems that eventually become disability claims; (employee assistance refers to programs designed to assist employees with problems of alcoholism, drug abuse, adjustment to life problems, etc.).
   j. Self-insuring the benefits or changing insurance carriers.

5. *External Influences and Constraints Affecting This Plan*
   a. Labor Contracts: Not applicable to this plan because it covers only salaried employees.

b. Competitiveness of the Benefit Level: Surveys of benefits indicate that all of a selected group of 12 major companies maintain a similar plan, with income replacement levels ranging between 55 and 75 percent of predisability income, the median being 66⅔ percent. All of these plans coordinate with all government benefits, and nine of them coordinate with full social security benefits, i.e., all social security income for both the employee and the family. This survey indicates that costs of this plan range between 2 percent and 4 percent of payroll, and have been increasing as a percent of payroll by 8 percent to 12 percent per year for the last three years.

Other general benefit surveys indicate that generally three of five companies maintain such a plan with benefit levels averaging 60 percent of income prior to disability.

c. Legal Constraints: This benefit plan is covered as a welfare plan under the Employee Retirement Income Security Act of 1974 (ERISA). There are no constraints under ERISA regarding benefit levels, but certain communication requirements must be met and forms filed with the Federal Government.

In 1978 and 1979 legislation was considered to amend ERISA in several ways, one of which would prohibit the practice of using cost-of-living adjustments in social security to reduce benefit payments from the company plan. At the present this legislation is not under active consideration.

The Equal Pay Act was amended in 1978 to require that as of 1979, pregnancy must be included as a disability. Previously, pregnancy was not covered by most disability income plans.

In 1978 amendments to the Age Discrimination in Employment Act of 1967 (ADEA) set minimum alternatives to handling disability income for employees working beyond age 65, up to age 70. In general it is required that disability occurring during this period (65 to 70) must result in benefits under the disability plan until age 70 and may not result in retirement under the pension plan before five years of disability income or attainment of age 70, although an employer may be able to cost justify benefits of a shorter period.

d. Developing Trends: The major reason for fast rising disability income plan costs is a growing tendency to utilize such plans, either intentionally or unintentionally, as alternatives to early retirement for employees whose performance has declined. Particularly in the atmosphere of heightened awareness of age discrimination, older employees with poor, but inadequately documented, performance records may not be forcibly "retired" except at the risk of age discrimination suits. Since disability income is greater than pension income at retirement under most pension plans, disability becomes an attractive alternative if any reason at all can be found to justify the disability. This has resulted in physicians liberalizing their judgments on what constitutes disability, sometimes urged on by employers seeking to resolve a human resource management problem. This in turn has resulted in insurance companies who insure disability income plans sustaining losses in these plans, therefore raising insurance rates, and in many cases such companies have dropped this line of business entirely. Less than 10 major insurers will now take on new clients for disability income plans, and then only at high costs. This in turn has resulted in many employers who are large enough to do so, self-insuring their disability income plans.

While disability income plans for decades have grown slowly and been generally subordinated to pension, life insurance, and health plans, it seems apparent that in the future disability income plans will become a dominant factor in benefit plan systems and very expensive as well, perhaps rivaling pension plans in cost.

While it is logical to coordinate pension and disability income plans in benefit design, examples of how this coordination can be influenced and complicated by government regulation are the 1978 amendments to the Age Discrimination in Employment Act (ADEA). These regulations provide that for employees over age 60 eligibility for long-term disability income benefits must continue and in the event of long-term disability, disability income benefits must be paid for a certain period of time before the employee can be placed in pensioner status under the pension plan. In the past, disability at older ages traditionally was handled by providing for commencement of pension benefits rather than long-term disability income benefits. New ways will have to be found to efficiently coordinate benefit levels and costs between these two plans.

The prospect of the elimination of any mandatory retirement age in the next decade raises a further problem of determining at what point disability may convert to "retirement" with the higher benefit shifting from the disability plan to the lower benefit of a pension plan.

e. Tax Laws: The Internal Revenue Code provides that the first $100 per week of disability "retirement" income may be excluded from gross income during total and permanent disability prior to age 65. Workers' compensation, unemployment compensation, and social security payments are not taxable as income. If adjusted gross income exceeds $15,000 in a tax year, the excess of $15,000 reduces the exclusion dollar for dollar. Thus, if total disability income from a disability income plan or other earnings exceeds $20,200 the $100 week exclusion is nullified and such income is taxable.

Disability income benefits attributable to insurance policies purchased by an employee's aftertax income are not taxable income to the employee. Employee contributions toward disability income benefits also have the effect of voiding income tax on the portion of disability benefits attributable to those contributions.

f. Availability of Insurance (or Funding Vehicles): Many insurers have discontinued long-term disability income plans as unprofitable. Our current insurer has given some indication that they would like to discontinue this line of business since they are not accepting any new clients and have increased rates dramatically for current clients to attempt to make their current book of business profitable. We are large enough in employee population that we could self-insure this plan if necessary.

g. Social and Economic Trends Impacting This Benefit: The major social trend is work-related stress and pressure, or perhaps more accurately the stress and pressure of modern society as it reflects in work performance. Increasingly work stress is blamed for illness that impacts adversely on performance. The courts are increasingly willing to find in favor of an employee who claims stress on the job as a basis for workers' compensation. A seeming diminution of the work ethic and increasing availability of disability income benefits, combined with liberalized determinations of disability, is resulting in increasing utilization of disability income plans as an escape valve from the rigors of work. Combined with a wide range of government welfare plans that may be available to disabled persons (food stamps, aid to handicapped persons, etc.) there appears to be the encouragement to some types of employees to seek disability on the slightest pretense, perhaps even precipitate it intentionally.

A developing social trend is for employers to become involved in employee assistance programs or crisis intervention to help head off personal crisis situations that otherwise may lead to ill health and even disability. The availability of such a program, well managed, can be very effective in dealing with performance problems that might otherwise lead to disability and claims for disability income.

The major economic trends affecting this benefit are inflation and recession. In disability, social security benefits are indexed to inflation, so they continue to increase. In general, because one third to one half of a disabled employees income will be derived from social security, it will be inflation protected.

Recession always leads to increased claims of disability and thus more claimants for disability income benefits. Illness, perhaps long unattended, becomes the basis for a disability claim when the prospect of layoff or loss of job appears.

h. Economic Controls: Currently voluntary wage controls are in effect. Any changes in this plan that have increased costs for improved benefits are covered by these wage guidelines. The amount of the increased costs attributable to improved benefits must be included when determining compliance with these guidelines.

Internal Influences and Constraints

1. *Financial Considerations*

Since this plan was installed in 1960, there have occurred 135 disability claims, of which 106 continue receiving payments. Between 1960 and 1975, 75 claims occurred, an average of five per year. Between 1976 and 1980, 60 claims occurred, an average of 12 per year.

The cost of the plan in its first year was 1 percent of payroll, which provided an income replacement of 40 percent of pay. By 1975 the cost was at 2 percent of payroll for a benefit of 55 percent of pay. In 1980 the cost was 4 percent of payroll for a benefit of 60 percent of pay, having increased from 2.5 percent of payroll when the 60 percent benefit was implemented in 1976. Cost is related to increased utilization.

It is estimated that should the number of claimants continue at the same experience of the last five years, the cost will be between 6 percent and 7 percent of payroll by 1990 with no improvements in benefit levels.

The possible means of limiting this cost are: (*a*) installing an employee contribution feature; (*b*) reducing benefit levels and enabling employees to purchase additional benefits; (*c*) integrating with full social security; (*d*) reducing utilization and the number of claimants; (e) rehabilitating disabled employees; (f) self-insuring the benefit.

Possible factors that will increase the cost are:

a. Increased utilization.

b. Benefit improvements.

c. Changes in premium requirements of the insurer.

d. Inflation.

e. New laws or regulations expanding required coverage.

2. *Employee Attitudes and Perceptions*

A survey of employee attitudes in 1977 gave no indication of strong favorable or unfavorable attitudes toward this benefit. The measured responses was 75 percent "Good," 25 percent "Satisfactory"—no "excellent" or "poor."

There is generally little appreciation of disability benefits among young persons and persons with no dependents. Employees with dependents and middle-aged and older employees are very conscious of the need for this income protection, but since they have no expectation of using it, they are not too interested in exactly what the benefit provisions are. There is greater interest in sick-day benefits and short-term disability benefits than in long-term disability income benefits because their expectation of utilization is much greater.

A more detailed survey of employee perceptions of benefit values in 1979 indicated that 20 percent believed this benefit cost the company about 1 percent of pay, 50 percent believed 2 percent of pay, and 30 percent believed 3 percent of pay. Since it actually costs 4 percent of pay, the return on investment (in terms of employee perceptions and appreciation) is negative.

3. *Administration*

Most administration is handled by the insurance company. Internal administration is confined to explanation of the benefit and in almost every case considerable correspondence and sometimes controversy about the existence of "permanent and total disability." This plan requires disproportionate internal administration to the amount of utilization because of the complexities of each case. As utilization increases and the number of persons on disability grows, internal administration becomes more extensive. It is estimated this current plan requires about 500 hours of internal administrative time per year.

Possible changes to more effectively manage this plan all include increased internal administration and management time. Employee contributions and self-insurance represent the maximization of internal administration and would likely require one person full time with some clerical support.

4. *Relative Priorities*

Because of the potential for quickly rising costs and abuse of this benefit plan, changes in this plan should receive a high priority for attention spread across a moderate period of time, perhaps three years. While this benefit plan is not a high priority with employees, in terms of benefit cost control it is a high priority.

5. *Other Internal Nonbenefit Factors Relative To This Plan*

The disability income benefit plan is affected by nondiscrimination (particularly age discrimination) and equal pay policies. Increased utilization in the future will arise from the requirement to include pregnancy as a disability under the Equal Pay Acts as of 1979.

Avoidance of age discrimination complaints for "forced retirement" will likely involve increasing pressures for utilization of this plan as the escape mechanism for justifiable nondiscriminatory separation from the workforce of middle age and older employees with performance problems. Some evidence of this already exists in the greatly increased utilization of this plan in recent years.

6. *Viewpoints of Other Appropriate Internal Functions*

Industrial Relations is of the general opinion that this plan should be tightened up, restricted to its original purpose, and not be permitted to become the pressure-relief valve for performance related problems.

Risk and Insurance Management is of the opinion that the risk of large losses is high due to the risk of a major natural catastrophic event occurring at the main work location of most of the covered employees. It is their view that self-insurance of this program should be accompanied by a catastrophic loss protection umbrella.

The Tax Department is of the view that the exclusion of disability income from taxable income when paid for by the employee is a strong justification for employee contributions to this plan so long as the requirement for employee contributions is offset by reduced employee contributions elsewhere so that total employee contributions are not increased.

The Equal Employment Opportunity Department is of the opinion that this plan should provide for a less rigorous definition of "total and permanent disability" and should provide for partial disability benefits for cases that fall short of total and permanent disability. Their view is that disability should be more easily available to employees.

The Personnel Policy and Planning Function is of the view that some form of this benefit should be extended to permanent part-time employees engaged in job sharing and part-time work. The Equal Employment Opportunity Department shares this view since most such jobs are (or will be) held by women and older persons or handicapped persons.

Recipients of disability income benefits are of the opinion that a cost-of-living adjustment should be provided for the plan-paid portion of benefits and also that benefit levels should be increased.

Operating managers have expressed the view that the plan should be liberalized so that disability can more easily be justified and partial disability benefits should be provided.

The Direct Compensation Function expresses the view that under wage guidelines currently in effect there is very little room for benefit cost increases arising from new benefit improvements, that direct wage increases will consume practically all of the allowable wage increase.

7. *Availability of Support Functions*

This plan currently requires extensive support from the legal department as many cases involve potential age discrimination issues. Support is also required from the Risk and Insurance Department which handles workers' compensation claims.

Changes in this plan requiring employee contributions will require support from the payroll department.

Changes in the plan that involve self-insurance will require extensive legal support, data processing and systems support, treasurers department support, and controller department support as well as some support from the auditing department. Risk and insurance support would also be required. Public relations support will be required in communications.

Implementing employee contributions and self-insurance will require a full time Benefit Department staff member with part-time clerical support.

Staff time to support this plan is generally available from all required functions, except data processing, the legal department, and payroll department, who currently express uncertainty. Data processing expresses that support is generally not available unless other assignments are withdrawn or delayed, or additional staff are authorized.

Support within the benefit department is currently not available.

8. *Timing Considerations*

The long-range company plans anticipate a doubling of the salaried workforce by 1985. This would indicate that the sooner employee contributions are installed the easier it will be, since fewer employees are currently not contributing than will be the case at anytime in the future.

The anticipation of narrower profit margins and tougher competition in the next few years expressed in short-range plans indicate that controlling benefit costs is essential. Since this plan has the potential for being a major benefit cost-increase factor, control should be secured as quickly as possible.

The demographic shift to an older population, generally the highest utilization group for disability benefits, is under way and will begin being felt significantly towards the end of the 1980s. This plan should be solidly in place before that time.

With the current high rates of inflation, employees are very cost conscious. Increasing employee contributions currently will be an unpopular action and will require a maximum communications effort.

Summarization of This Example

This example illustrates the application of the first three components of the planning system:

1. The objectives with regard to a specific benefit plan.
2. An assessment of existing benefits measured against the objectives.
3. Discussion of external and internal influences and constraints.

Such a document should be prepared for each benefit plan and policy to serve as a "benefit catalog" for the final two steps in the planning system, developing a short- and long-range plan and specific benefits management and administration in accordance with that plan.

These last two steps are the genuine province of the benefits executive. Only he/she has the total perspective of benefit operations and the environmental awareness that is required in developing a plan and setting it in operation.

In the next sections we will consider the nature and functions of the benefits executive, and those qualities necessary to assimilate the knowledge and facts we have just reviewed so that they can be translated into long-range plans and short-term actions.

Development of long-range plans and short-term actions will be the last subjects of discussion in this chapter.

THE FUNCTION OF THE BENEFITS EXECUTIVE

The Wall Streeet Journal, April 24, 1979:

> *Positions Available*
> Benefits Manager
> Nationwide Organization needs Benefits Manager with (1) high-level intelligence, (2) technical skills, and (3) successful supervisory experience in group and pension operations. Ability to write and speak well about benefits is a must.

Technical skills and hands-on experience in benefits operations are understandable requirements for the position. Why is it necessary to actually specify a "high level of intelligence" and the "ability to write and speak well"? Because benefits management has now gone beyond the days of "benefits administration" when technical knowledge and experience were adequate to the job of handling benefits.

The function of the benefits executive requires the attributes of a highly developed intellect: logic, reasoning ability, capacity to grasp and relate apparently unrelated concepts and occurrences, a quick learning ability, the ability to read fast, to comprehend details and retain information accurately, a balanced mental state, self-confidence and self-control, good judgment, and common sense.

And beyond this the skills of education, explanation, persuasion, and compromise—the ability to write and speak well.

The successful candidate for Corporate Director of Benefits at a major international company in the fall of 1979 had the following educational and experience background:

B.S. Degree—Mathematics and Physics

M.S. Degree—Statistics

M.B.A. Degree—Accounting and Finance

L.L.B. Degree

Member of two State Bar Associations

Senior Benefits Consultant for major accounting firm[2]

JOB DESCRIPTION VERSUS FUNCTIONAL ROLE

The job description for a benefits manager sets forth the responsibilities and accountabilities associated with the job. This is not the same as describing the function of the benefit manager's role. A sample formal job description for the benefits management job appears at the end of this section. The duties and described responsibilities are well understood and widely accepted.

Not as well defined, understood, or accepted is the functional role of benefits management. *The Wall Street Journal* advertisement and the education and experience of the candidate just outlined begin to get at this functional role.

A functional role description might be as follows:

> The benefits executive has to attempt to keep the organization and the employees attuned to each other so that the benefit programs both meet the constantly changing needs and expectations of employees and simultaneously protect the interests of stockholders and the company by efficiently allocating resources among benefit purposes.
>
> He/she must be alert to changing conditions in the organization and changing attitudes of employees, changing social and economic conditions, and governmental activities. The awareness of what is happening must be assimilated and translated into useful knowledge. He/she must provide guidance and planning in the application of this knowledge to specific benefit management actions, properly coordinated with the goals and objectives of all the parts of the organization affected by these actions.
>
> He/she must inform management and employees of the meaning and effect of benefit plans and changes in a manner appropriate and acceptable to both groups. By the application of education, persuasion, and compromise he/she must bring about the implementation of achievable change and then assure acceptance in a cooperative spirit of the result.
>
> He/she must direct and coordinate the activities of all involved groups and persons in a manner that prevents any error from occurring and avoids dissident persons being able to sabotage the effective completion of the project and must assure that all follow-through is accomplished to deliver benefits in a manner that gains a return in appreciation, morale, and productivity that justifies the investment made.
>
> He/she must assess the impact of the various forces involved, set priorities for action and attention, evaluate what is ideal and what can realistically be achieved.
>
> He/she must provide the organization with a sense of direction in benefits management, with strategies, plans, and contingency plans and keep the competing forces moving together within those strategies and plans.

This functional role contains a number of personal characteristics that are difficult to provide through formal training—political astuteness, human relations skills of a high order, and a high level of personal integrity and credibility.

Still, this is the genuine role of the benefits executive. Job descriptions are too sterile to be able to convey this functional role in a meaningful way. Yet the successs or failure in benefits management rests on how well this functional role is played at least as much on how well the responsibilities in the job description are performed.

Job Description for the Benefits Executive

Position

The primary responsibility of this position is dynamic, results-oriented management of employee benefits plans to maximize the cost-effectiveness of expenditures for both company and employee. The incumbent develops and installs new or modified plans, administers existing plans, ensures optimum return on investment of pension and other benefits funds, and determines whether to "make or buy" group insurance. He also develops and, if they are approved, implements corporate benefits policies.

Responsibilities

1. *Research.* Conducts research into employee and company goals and objectives. Determines the effectiveness of all benefits plans in comparison with each other and with other forms of direct compensation. Identifies and forecasts the competitive position of company benefits compared with those of other employers by analyzing other plans, union demands, surveys, and other sources of information. Stays up-to-date and knowledgeable about technical, legislative, and tax developments.

2. *Development and design.* Develops innovative solutions to the problems of meeting employee and company needs within their ability to pay. Designs new plans or modifications of existing plans in a way that rationalizes, streamlines, and coordinates benefits with each other and with governmental programs. Prepares clear and complete specifications; develops asset, liability, and cost information; and determines the price to be charged to employees (contribution) and to operating departments or divisions (allocations).

3. *Installation of changes.* Installs plan changes by preparing announcement material, explanatory booklets, videotape presentations, and new releases for house organs and other media for communicating the new plans. Sets up employee meetings and arranges for the enrollment of employees in optional plans. Conducts seminars

for benefits administrators. Revises and reissues all communications material from time to time.

4. *Acquisitions and divestitures.* Initiates and executes the benefits aspects of corporate acquisitions and divestitures. Ensures the consolidation of funding and insuring arrangements to achieve minimum cost and maximum effectiveness. Redesigns and consolidates benefits provisions if necessary. Implements changes.

5. *Negotiation with unions.* Develops company bargaining proposals and positions and analyzes union demands. Negotiates with unions innovative and cost-minimizing settlements. Obtains cost data of initial, subsequent and final union and company positions. Prepares agreement language. Implements agreements.

6. *Implementation.* Instructs insurance carriers, trustees, and other administrative agencies outside the company to effect changes in benefits programs. Ensures prompt and accurate compliance.

7. *Documentation.* Prepares and executes benefits documentation such as original or amended plan texts, board of directors' resolutions, benefits agreements, insurance policies, and trust deeds. Files necessary reports and applications with government agencies, such as Internal Revenue Service, Department of Labor, insurance commissioners, and other regulatory agencies.

8. *Selection of suppliers.* Selects suppliers of services (insurance carriers, banks or trustees, consultants, actuaries, investment advisors, home purchase plan agencies, and the like) on the basis of quality service, compatibility with company needs, and competitive price. Supervises, audits, and maintains liaison with these suppliers on a continuing basis. Maintains liaison with government benefits agencies, such as social security, workers' compensation, and unemployment compensation.

9. *Administration.* Processes and updates membership records for all benefits plans. Processes applications of claims for benefits. Arranges for payment of insurance premiums and contributions and for payments to other suppliers of services to trust funds. Compiles and distributes required reports.

10. *Employee and management liaison.* Handles employee and management inquiries and complaints and ensures quick, equitable, and courteous resolution. Conducts preretirement and other employee counseling. Represents the company on administrative boards, deals with unions on routine benefits matters, and handles relations with government plan benefits offices.

11. *Quality assurance.* Audits the performance both of benefits administrators within the company and of outside suppliers.

12. *Systems and procedures.* Applies computer systems and management science techniques to the installation and administra-

tion of benefits plans. Develops total benefits information systems, including in-house preparation of actuarial valuations, insurance census data, personalized employee statements, financial reports, and statistics. Prepares simple-to-use procedure manuals.

13. *Financial planning.* Prepares or receives annual actuarial valuations, insurance renewals, and other cost, revenue, liability, and asset information. Assesses validity of assumptions and methods and ensures that these are appropriate and up-to-date. Analyzes and acts on control reports comparing actual experience with plans.

14. *Funding and insuring.* Handles investment of pension funds directly or through outside investment managers. Measures investment performance and maintains financial control of funds. Supervises investment managers and oversees safe-keeping function. Purchases insurance and evaluates and implements self-insurance possibilities. Performs investment research and portfolio management functions.

15. *Department management.* Sets up or reorganizes benefits department. Centralizes or decentralizes administration as appropriate. Trains and develops subordinates in managerial or professional roles. Carries on day-to-day management of department. Supervises and audits divisional, plant, and sales office benefits administrators.

Accountabilities

1. Managing benefits plan expenditures (totaling 13 percent of company sales) to maximize cost-effectiveness.

2. Managing benefits funds amounting to $XXX million or the equivalent of the depreciated book value of fixed assets to obtain performance 20 percent better than stock market averages. Maintaining such funds and reserves at a level that adequately covers present and potential liabilities while maintaining a balance between the needs of the benefits funds and the cash flow requirements of the corporation.

3. Developing and maintaining forward-looking, competitive, and understandable benefits plans and related systems and procedures that are within the means of the company and its employees and that meet corporate, employee, and governmental requirements as measured by company approval, employee participation, and government certification.

4. Ensuring that benefits are paid correctly, promptly, and courteously and that records are complete, accurate, and up-to-date.

5. Budgeting and controlling of time and money to ensure maximum return from both.

6. Selecting and developing competent and energetic subordinates who perform effectively as a team even though subject to time and work pressures; coordinating their efforts with those of consultants and suppliers.

7. Handling with foresight the complexities of benefits ramifications of acquisitions and divestitures quickly and effectively to avoid unexpected costs and liabilities.

8. Ensuring that all outside suppliers of services and internal administrators meet or exceed high standards of performance.

Source: Niels H. Nielsen, "The Employee Benefits Executive," *Compensation Review,* 2d Quarter (New York: AMACOM, a division of American Management Associations, Inc., 1972), pp. 35–38. Reprinted with permission.

LONG-RANGE PLANNING

Long-range planning for benefits is of course characterized by the same fallibility as long-range planning for any purpose: uncertainty about the future. Yet we all, as private individuals, do some degree of long-range planning for ourselves. Further, the employers for whom we work also develop various kinds of long-range plans to provide some degree of guidance and structure within which short-range plans and actions can be rationally applied.

In our considerations here we will focus on practical development and application of long-range plans and avoid entanglement in the many scientific techniques that have been developed for theorizing about obtaining greater certainty in setting long-range plans.

For this purpose, we will avoid defining long-range planning in any time frame such as 5, 10, or 15 years, because the time frame may well vary with each benefit plan. For example, long-range planning for pension liability may well span a time frame of 25 or 50 years. Long-range planning for implementing a program of flexible benefits, on the other hand, may span a time frame of five years or less.

COMPONENTS OF LONG-RANGE PLANNING

Long-range planning is much less structured than the process of short-range planning discussed earlier in this chapter. The factors to be considered are numerous and very much a part of the realm of knowledge, experience, and judgment of the planner.

At the minimum, however, certain basic components of long-range benefit planning can be identified.

1. The long-range plans, goals, objectives of the plan sponsor.
2. Information about developing or expected trends in many areas that may influence a benefit, or benefits in general.
3. The process by which such plans are developed and introduced within the organization.
4. The process by which such plans are actually and effectively applied for useful purposes in the present.

We will consider each of these components and how they might impact the long-range planning process.

PLAN SPONSOR LONG-RANGE PLANS

As previously pointed out, benefit management is a support function of realization of company objectives in that employee morale, employee attitudes, and even productivity are influenced to some extent by the level of benefit coverages and the management of benefit plans.

Benefit long-range planning, therefore, must consider the plans, goals, and objectives of the plan sponsor. Unfortunately, it is often difficult for a benefit executive to ferret out such information. There are many reasons for this.

Company long-range plans may often be kept secret; known only within a narrow group of key executives. The reasons for such security are obvious in that competitors and market analysts could use such knowledge to their own devious purposes.

In smaller companies, and even in large privately owned companies, the long-range plans may very well exist in only the head and files of the owner.

Even beyond these security constraints, long-range plans in a dynamic organization can also be very scattered in the sense that each functioning unit may have a plan and there is only one place all those plans come together. It is this one place where secretiveness most often occurs. The plans of any single functioning unit are usually more easily accessible than the combined single long-range plan.

The benefits executive needs to demonstrate considerable assertiveness, diplomacy, and political astuteness in uncovering these long-range plans. If it is not possible to convince management of "the need to know" of the overall plan, it still may be possible to obtain key components of the plan, such as the human resource plan that reveals expected growth (or decline) in the workforce, changes expected in the nature of the workforce (getting younger or older), or expected changes in location of the workforce (domestic or international).

As a practical matter, benefits executives spend a great deal of time simply talking with people in the attempt to secure insights into their plans that are needed to effectively manage benefits. This is especially true of the labor relations function where planning for negotiations is often secretive. And yet those plans may have sudden, major impacts on benefit management.

The classic example of difficulty in securing needed information about long-range plans has to do with plans for acquisitions or divestitures. The management of benefits in acquisitions and divestitures is very difficult, sensitive, and often confusing, and yet mismanagement of benefits can be so costly as to even negate the validity of the entire transaction. In real life, benefits executives constantly have their ears to the ground for such plans and when they get any intuition that such plans are underway seek immediate involvement in order to smooth the process and avoid costly errors regarding benefits.

Assuming, however, that benefits executives are given full access to company long-range plans, what should they look for as useful information for benefit planning and management?

In general, any information regarding the work force and expected changes in the work force is important. Factors to look for are changes in the size, age, location, or makeup of the work force. Planners often apply demographic data in attempts to identify where the human resources will come from to meet the needs of supporting growth in production and sales. Such data may reveal important insights for benefit management.

For example, if long-range plans forecast a need to increase the labor force in production skills where labor is in short supply, a benefit planner could conclude that reducing turnover in this group and holding such employees into later ages is going to be essential to meet the projected need. Benefits can play an important role in both reducing turnover, keeping the work force, and even in creating an attractive employment environment that can draw labor into the work force.

The other key essential data needed from company long-range plans is financial projections, particularly projected gross profitability. Within this data is contained projected benefit costs. The benefits executive can then evaluate, based on personal knowledge and judgment, the realism of benefit cost projections. If they are unrealistic, then the benefits executive must feed such judgments back into the planning process.

If it is expected that the plan sponsor's work force will be growing older in average age in order to satisfy labor needs (i.e., employees will be remaining to later ages and/or it will be necessary to hire older persons to meet work force needs), then some benefit plans and costs are affected—disability income, death benefits, and pensions, for example. By applying personal knowledge, experience, and judgment, the benefits executive may conclude that projected benefit costs are seriously overinflated or below what should be realistically expected. In large companies, millions of dollars can easily be involved with significant impact on long-range plans of the company.

Beyond information on the work force and financial projections, long-range plans may contain many other items of information useful to the benefits executive. Highly sophisticated long-range plans may contain carefully researched data on expected inflation rates or interest rates that can be used by the benefits executive in considerations of pension funding or forecasting pension contributions and liabilities.

Long-range plans also offer the benefits executive an overall feel for, and sense of, the expected future of the plan sponsor. This awareness of itself can be helpful in many ways over time as the benefits executive labors to keep benefit management in tune with the organization and the employees.

INFORMATION ABOUT DEVELOPING TRENDS

Benefits executives are deluged with information about developing trends, possible legislation, regulatory interpretations, and numerous other aspects of benefits management. It is virtually impossible for the benefits executive to read even a modest portion of this material in the benefits field, let alone to read important information in other fields that impact importantly on benefits management.

How can benefits executives engage in useful long-range benefit planning when they are so deluged with information, some of it contradictory and unrealistically speculative? How can they hope to sort out what is necessary, useful, and appropriate for their own needs? There are some techniques that can be applied to enable the benefit executive in this dilemma.

First, they can select for regular review a limited number of publications that are reliable and comprehensive in the benefits field as well as some in other key fields. A listing of such publications appears in the Reference Section at the end of the book.

Second, they can select a consultant as a personal advisor and meet with the consultant from time to time to recieve a briefing on developments in the field. Appendix 6 deals in depth with the issues surrounding selection, retention, and effective use of consultant services.

Third, various publications can be assigned to various staff members and occasional staff meetings conducted for the purpose of exchanging information.

Last, there are many conferences and seminars held throughout each year for the purpose of updating knowledge and providing an opportunity to exchange information with peers and other professionals. Equally as useful is direct participation in some of the many committees and organizations of benefits executives, several of which are described in the Reference Section.

Securing external information on developing trends that will affect benefit planning is one side of the equation. On the other side is securing information on developing trends within the organization.

The awareness of company long-range plans previously discussed is one aspect of internal developments. Another aspect of internal trends is what is developing in the minds and needs of employees.

Important pieces of information the benefits executive must have include: reliable information about the attitudes and expectations of employees about their benefits; an evaluation of how effective the benefits are in meeting the needs of employees; and whether or not the company is getting full value for its investment in benefits. Chapter 10 deals with the issues in evaluating the effectiveness of benefit plans.

Information about the needs and expectations of employees is developed through various kinds of employee surveys. The development, implementation, and evaluation of such surveys is a study of itself. Much has been written about such surveys, and there are many consultants who are able to assist very effectively in conducting a survey.

For purposes of this discussion it is only important to understand that such information is essential to any long-range benefit planning process. A sample survey actually used is displayed in Appendix 3.

The final essential ingredient in long-range planning is information about the benefits of other employers with whom the plan sponsor competes for employees. Over the years it has become common practice to follow the leader, so to speak, in benefit management. As we shall see in a later chapter when we consider benefit theory, this practice may become even more important as the basis for justification of changes in benefit programs.

It is essential to have knowledge of the practice of competitors, if only to be aware of differences and why those differences exist.

Many excellent surveys of benefit practice are available that can be subscribed to on a regular basis. A listing of some such surveys is available in the References Section. These general surveys are very useful in what they reveal about the general level of benefits, the new benefits that are being adopted, and how companies are changing benefits from year to year.

Much more useful are surveys that are generally identified as "indexing surveys." Such benefit indexing surveys overcome the major failure of general comparisons of benefits, that is the difficulty of relating the value of two benefits with differing provisions. In comparing two pension plans, for example, it is very difficult to equate all the various provisions so as to draw a judgment of the relative value of those plans.

One plan may provide a benefit of 2 percent of pay times years of service, while another provides only 1.5 percent of pay times years of service. Yet the plan with the apparently smaller benefit may provide death benefits with disability income benefits, while the plan with the apparently larger benefit may provide neither of these ancillary benefits. Which plan then is the better plan?

Benefit indexing is a very sophisticated technique for valuing all the aspects of two such plans and providing a judgment of the relative value of those plans based on all the provisions and ancillary benefits. Traditional company management is often greatly influenced by what competing employers are providing in the ways of benefits. Benefit indexing provides an important vehicle for the benefits executive in establishing solid and direct evidence to management of the relationship between their benefits and those of competing employers.

Several consulting firms provide service in developing such benefit indexing surveys.

Of particular interest to the benefits executive is the relationship between a survey of employees' attitudes toward their benefits and the results of a benefit indexing survey. Such a comparison can provide the benefits executive with very useful information for long-range benefit planning.

For example, an employee attitude survey may reveal that employees have little appreciation for their medical benefit plan, yet a benefit indexing survey of competitors may reveal that the plan ranks near the top of competitor plans, it is better in total than most such plans. The benefits executive then must examine why it is that such a good plan is so little valued by employees.

Perhaps the reason is that plan administration is poor, benefit payments are too slow or frequently improperly processed.

From this information the benefits executive can develop a plan for improving administration and restoring the plan to its proper value in the minds of employees.

INTRODUCING LONG-RANGE PLANS
INTO THE ORGANIZATION

Having assimilated the information in the company long-range plans and about developing trends, how is the benefits executive to utilize this information? Specifically, how can the long-range plans developed from such information be introduced effectively into the organization?

This process is very much the province of the judgment and political astuteness of the benefits executive.

Organizations have a personality of their own that develops around centers of influence, the focus of various power groups, the products, the policies and practices, and many other individual characteristics. The introduction of long-range benefit planning must be sensitive to these characteristics in order to be successfully integrated with company plans, accepted for various approvals, and ultimately realized.

The introduction of a flexible compensation program is a good case in point. To introduce the complex concept of individual choice in benefits, secure acceptance of the idea from all company operations affected, to prepare systems for handling administration and communication, to budget costs, to arrange for insurance coverages, test the program on employees, and finally implement the program for all employees—all this may take years to accomplish.

Along the way there will be many conflicting viewpoints to be resolved, many objections to be overcome, including legal hurdles and cost considerations. A carefully laid out long-range plan, managed by the benefits executive with diplomacy and sensitivity, is essential to bring the program of flexible benefits successfully to life. The variety of techniques for introducing long-range plans is endless and dependent on peculiarities of the organization.

Three techniques of general application are the "Discussion Paper," the "Benefit Catalog," and the "Annual Report."

The discussion paper technique involves circulation of papers that discuss the various subjects at some length, without recommendation. Their purpose is to initiate dialogue and discussion among all the people who may be involved in research, decisions, or implementation of a long-range plan.

An example of a discussion paper is included in Appendix 2. This particular example has as its subject "Flexible Compensation" and was actually utilized to introduce the subject for consideration in a multi-billion-dollar company in 1980.

Such discussion papers may circulate throughout an organization without action for a long time. They are intended to be educational, thought provoking, and to form the basis for further action as the idea catches hold. Equally as important, they are a demonstration to management of the creativeness and awareness of the benefits executive. Because management is usually impressed by careful, well-considered planning, such discussion papers often serve to create a degree of confidence in the planning skills of the benefits executive. This can be very important in securing cooperation and acceptance of ideas, particularly very complex ideas, where management is unable to take the time to understand technicalities and must rely on the benefits executive to be thorough and detailed in execution of the idea.

The Benefit Catalog describes a kind of compendium of possible changes in benefits plans. In the benefit philosophy statement outlined in a previous chapter, reference is made to maintaining a listing of all benefit plans, possible changes to those plans, and criteria of conditions that might trigger certain changes, such as falling behind competing employers in benefit levels.

The Benefit Catalog carries this a step further. In the Benefit Catalog for each benefit there is described a history of the plan, changes, and amendments over time, a year-by-year record of plan cost as a percent of payroll, general comments (such as references to that plan in employee surveys), notes on competitive position over the years from general survey data, notes on plan administration (such as who is involved in the process and why), comments on legislation affecting the plan, and general trends concerning that benefit.

All such information establishes important background information for the long-range planning aspect of the catalog, which is then to describe how the plan relates to other plans, what changes might be considered for the future and why, and under what conditions such changes might be appropriate for short-term action and implementation. As practical matter, actual development of such a benefit catalog may be a major undertaking—a long-term planning project, if you will—in itself. Benefit management is a young art, and in developing a catalog the benefits executive is likely to find the records are scattered or may never even have been maintained on some aspects of plan management in the past, that important historical knowledge was "lost" with the turnover of prior managers.

Such a compendium can be an extremely useful tool in many ways. It can be very important in quickly bringing up to date new staff members or company management. It can be most useful in relating changes in one plan to the impact of such change on other plans.

Most important, the process of considering future plan changes and considering what circumstances might make them appropriate for implementation is a valuable long-range planning effort.

A third useful technique for introducing long-range plans is the "Annual Benefits Report." The annual report as the name implies outlines the activities in benefit plan management during the previous year and plans for the coming year. Annual reports are accepted vehicles that management utilizes to keep informed of what is going on in the organization. Accordingly, they are good vehicles for introducing long-range benefit planning ideas into the stream of management thinking.

The annual report provides the benefits executive an opportunity to present thoughts on pending legislation, social and economic changes, and so forth, and what effect those changes may have on benefit management. Such information can be presented through this vehicle in a "noncommittal" form, or without specific recommendations, so that management can react with important feedback to the benefits executive. Such feedback from management is very useful to the benefits executive in formulating plans and proposing changes that would be acceptable to management.

The annual report is also a good vehicle for entering information about benefit management into the organization's long-range planning process. Planners of overall long-range plans, by reviewing the benefit annual report, can relate that information to their knowledge of other plans and observe important relationships that should be considered further for possible effects.

USING LONG-RANGE PLANS EFFECTIVELY FOR
SHORT-TERM ACTION

The purpose of long-range planning is of course to provide a rational frame of reference for short-term action. There are many short-term actions to be taken within any long-range plan, the objective being that each such short-term action is coordinated with other actions so that eventually the long-range plan is realized.

Long-range plans are most effective when they specifically contain a sequence of short-term actions to be implemented in an orderly manner. This process is the *systems approach* to management. Many scientific techniques have been developed by systems experts to try to assure that every short-term action is accomplished efficiently and then the long-range plan is realized precisely as planned.

While the systems approach has some application to benefit management, it is most useful in highly scientific and technological applications, such as landing a man on the moon. Benefit management is still much more an art than a science, so scientific planning methodologies are of limited use to the benefits executive in most cases, unless he or she has sophisticated planning resources readily available in the organization.

Effective short-term actions within a long-range benefit management plan have both a specific nature and a fluid nature. Certain short-term actions can be defined and predetermined, both in terms of the nature of the action and the time frame for completion. Management of such defined actions is not difficult, since for the most part the projects are clear and can be assigned to staff or consultants for completion.

The fluid short-term actions that can be taken often come in the nature of opportunities or threats to the long-range plans that could not have been anticipated. The opportunities are those unforeseen events that can advance achievement of long-range goals—such as legislation that breaks down a barrier formerly preventing movement toward the goal. Threats to achievement of long-range goals and plans can arise in the form of restrictive legislation, as well as from several other sources, such as changes in management, in direction of collective bargaining objectives, cost constraints, and so on.

Management of these fluid short-term actions is a key role for the benefits executive. Taking advantage of opportunities and warding off threats, or working around them, give rise to courses of action that require the judgment of the benefits executive.

A good example again lies in the process of approaching flexible benefits.

Let us assume that one long-range plan is to provide flexibility for employees in selecting benefit coverages. This has been accepted as a long-range goal on the basis that employee's attitudes toward work indicate a greater desire for participation in the decisions affecting them personally and also because it gives the employer a competitive edge in the labor market.

Clearly, along the way to achieving that goal, changes will be made in benefit plans each year. Short-term actions that could be taken along the way by the benefits executive would be to propose changes year by year that give employees more choices in participation in existing plans. An example might be installing a savings plan in which the employer matches employee contributions. Another example might be installing a cash choice option in an existing profit-sharing plan so that employees could elect each year to receive a portion of their profit sharing in cash instead of having it all deferred to some future date.

CONTROLLING BENEFIT CHANGES

The process of considering benefit changes, evaluating alternatives, securing input from all required interested persons, developing a plan, securing approvals, and finally implementing the plan obviously involves contact with many persons. In order to be sure that all appropriate persons have been contacted and signed off, it is very helpful to have a mechanism to facilitate this process. There follows such a form that can be used for this purpose. For lack of better terms we shall call it an "Authorization for Change."

Such a form can be as simple or elaborate as the benefits executive judges best fits the nature of the organization. The important objective is that use of such a form provides a control mechanism for the benefits executive. It assures that everyone who should be involved gets involved and must sign off, a process that gives them some share in the accountability for the change.

The form should be initiated by the benefits executive and his or her signature should be the final sign-off before it goes forward to management for their sign off and ultimately final approval by the proper authority.

This can serve a further very important purpose in large organizations. As an organization becomes very large and scattered, with decentralized benefit functions and widely scattered international operations, it becomes possible for such far-flung operations to initiate and implement benefit changes without the knowledge or consent of the central corporate benefit function. This can, and does in fact, lead to chaos in any attempt to control benefits within a design and cost philosophy that is intended to extend to the entire company. By use of this procedure, wherein it is required that the central corporate benefits executive sign off on any change, it is possible to restrict and constrain, in effect control, these scattered activities and make certain that overall benefits management stays within corporate philosophy, objectives, plans, and cost constraints.

The style, format, and application of this form can be easily adapted to the needs of a given organization.

Authorization For Change

This form is to be used for the proposal and approval of any change to any benefit plan anywhere in the Company worldwide. The final sign-off before the proposal is submitted for management approval is the sign-off by the Corporate Director of Benefits.

DATE _____   Person initiating proposed change _____
                  Location _____
                  Direct questions to _____ Ph # _____

BRIEF DESCRIPTION OF PROPOSED CHANGE (Attach additional materials)

REASON CHANGE IS REQUIRED (Attach materials as necessary)

COST OF CHANGE 1st yr _____ 2nd _____ 3rd _____ 4th _____ 5th _____
(after tax)
Basis of determining cost:
(assume 50% tax bracket in establishing costs above)

Identify administrative costs: communications, actuarial fees, etc.
Identify other resources required: staffing, equipment, etc., and their costs

APPROVALS

Initiator _____ Date _____

    This approval certifies that all diligence has been exercised in securing of all required consulting services, actuarial calculations, broker or insurer services and quotations of premium costs, that the proposal has been checked for legal issues and a plan developed for assuring proper implementation and communication.

PERSONNEL EXECUTIVE AT LOCATION

AFFECTED BY CHANGE _____
                                                            Date

CHIEF EXECUTIVE AT THIS LOCATION _____
                                                            Date

GROUP/DIVISION EXECUTIVE _____
                                                            Date

OTHER POSSIBLE SIGN-OFFS:

Legal _____ Tax Dept. _____

Industrial relations _____

Risk management _____

Corporate policy and planning _____

Treasurer's department _____

Benefits committees _____

Other—Specify _____

                              _____

CORPORATE BENEFITS DIRECTOR _____
                                                              Date

FINAL APPROVALS

    Executive VP/SR VP _____ Date _____

    Office of the President/President _____ Date _____

CONCLUSION

Employee benefits management has been characterized in the past by a focus on administration rather than planning. Changes to benefit plans have often arisen on an ad hoc basis in response to employee demands, competitive perceptions, or collective bargaining demands—too often without the time or opportunity to consider the effect of such changes in terms of any long-range planning.

The magnitude of the effect of benefit management on employees and employers alike is now such that planning is equally as important as administration, in some ways perhaps more important.

Planning is the province of the benefits executive. Devising short- and long-range plans, securing their acceptance in the organization, and nurturing them to achievement is the genuine function of the benefits executive.

REFERENCES

1. Although the material is not presented in a case study format, it represents a narrative of the benefit management process of a major growth company in the top of the *Fortune* 500 companies as the process was developed and implemented over a period of five years in the late 1970s.
2. *Business Insurance,* December 10, 1979, p. 95.

CHAPTER 4

THE HUMAN ASPECTS OF BENEFITS

Ernest J. E. Griffes

WHY DO EMPLOYERS PROVIDE BENEFITS?

PEOPLE PERCEPTIONS OF BENEFITS: EMPLOYEE EXPECTATIONS

EMPLOYEE APPRECIATION AND MOTIVATION

INDIVIDUALIZATION OF ATTITUDES TOWARD BENEFITS

ORGANIZED EMPLOYEE PERCEPTIONS OF BENEFITS

EMPLOYER PERCEPTIONS OF BENEFITS

WHY DO BENEFITS COST SO MUCH?

THE INFLUENCE OF BENEFITS ON PRODUCTIVITY AND WORK BEHAVIOR

THEORY OF THE BENEFIT PLAN LIFE CYCLE

THE SOCIAL ROLE OF EMPLOYEE BENEFITS

PRESENT SOCIAL PURPOSES OF BENEFITS

BENEFITS IN SOCIAL POLICY

DIAGRAM

LIFE CYCLE OF A BENEFIT PLAN

WHY DO EMPLOYERS PROVIDE BENEFIT PLANS?

Benefit plans are such a fundamental part of the work environment now that they are taken for granted and are often noticed by employees more for weaknesses and deficiencies than for the positive values they offer.

In planning and managing benefits, it is important for the benefits executive to have a clear understanding of why management has decided to provide benefits and what it expects to receive in the way of return on this investment in human resources.

The benefit philosophy statement described in detail in Chapter 2 is the planning mechanism designed to bring about clarification for a specific company of why it chooses to provide benefits for employees and how it expects those benefit plans to be managed.

As benefits expenditures grow larger and companies apply increasingly sophisticated techniques for measuring return on investment, managements increasingly ask what they are getting in return for benefit investments. This can be a very difficult question to answer in a practical way because the answer often relates to some intangible aspects of employee behavior—productivity, motivation, satisfaction from the work environment, reduced turnover, morale, and loyalty to the employer.

This chapter will examine a variety of reasons that have been, and are now being, presented as the theoretical basis for providing benefits. Also considered in this chapter is how the theoretical framework of benefits is changing and what it is likely to become in the future.

We will examine within the context of benefit theory what benefits mean from the perspective of employees and from the perspective of employers, since they are often very different perspectives. We will also examine the role of benefits in society.

PEOPLE PERCEPTIONS OF BENEFITS: EMPLOYEE EXPECTATIONS

Most employees can be expected to believe that a comprehensive package of benefits covering their security needs is a right of employment, part of their compensation reward for choosing to work for one employer rather than some other employer. Employees believe this because that is how benefits are promoted by employers—as part of total compensation and competitive with, or usually better than, the benefit plans of other employers with whom they compete for labor.

However, looking back only 50 years to the Great Depression era, it can be quickly observed that employees did not expect to receive much in the way of benefits upon taking a job. In fact, they were glad to have a paycheck at all, and any special considerations, such as a paid holiday for Thanksgiving and Christmas or a week of paid vacation, was a marvelous fringe benefit for which they were grateful. Most important was receiving income to house and feed their families. To consider going to work for one employer rather than another because of a better pension or profit-sharing plan was simply meaningless.

This time-related difference in employee perception of benefits illustrates a fundamental feature of benefit theory—employee perceptions of the value of benefits results from personal economic circumstances and personal social values. As these personal circumstances and values change over time, employee perceptions of the value of benefits changes—sometimes very dramatically.

This concept is fundamental to benefit planning and management. A benefit plan installed under a certain economic and social environment can become outdated and inappropriate as the socioeconomic environment changes. Reducing or eliminating benefits (like reducing salary or wages) is an event that seldom occurs because doing so is abhorrent to employees, union leaders, and management. Only the most dramatic negative socioeconomic conditions (such as the recession and massive unemployment of the early 1980s) create an opportunity to reduce or eliminate benefit programs in major ways, even though the logical rationale for such changes may have existed for some time before the negative conditions developed.

Of course, a benefit plan can always be improved to accommodate new needs and values, even if it cannot be as easily reduced in some way for the same purpose. This simple concept explains why benefit plans continue to expand and costs increase, yet employees seem to express diminishing levels of satisfaction with those benefits.

It is this feature of benefit theory that can lead planners to expect constant demands and expectations from employees for an endless stream of new benefit needs to be met by improved and new plans.

This personalization of the value of benefits is related to Maslow's *hierarchy of needs* theory. As basic-level physical needs are met, higher level self-actualization and psychological needs become more important and basic-level needs fade in importance.

Benefits are now a part of basic-level needs. Every employer of even modest size provides some form of the most basic and essential benefits, such as medical expense payments, life insurance, and some paid vacation. Larger employers, of course, provide any number of additional benefits that employees enjoy, are glad to have, and do appreciate.

However, in the employees' view, the larger in size the employer is, the more benefits are expected to be provided. Benefits are a given, so far as an employee or potential employee is concerned, and are more notable if certain benefits are *not* provided than if they are provided.

Employee perceptions of the value of benefits are also influenced by governmental action. ERISA in 1974 marked a watershed point in the history of employee benefits for many reasons. In terms of benefit theory, because of the wide publicity given to ERISA and its requirements for employee communications, the message to employees seemed to be that employers could not be trusted to keep benefit promises and therefore government would be increasingly involved to protect employee interests.

The expansion of government-provided benefits, such as social security, workers' compensation, and unemployment compensation, has further created a generalized impression that should an employee experience a serious problem in financial security as a result of illness or injury, somewhere there is a government benefit that will come to the rescue.

With government increasingly legislating over benefits and employees widely aware of what government is requiring, their perception can easily become a view that benefits provided by the employer to some large measure are the result of legal requirements, rather than a result of an employer's desire to motivate employees and help them in times of economic stress. Thus, an employer may receive little credit for improvements that employees believe (rightly or wrongly) are required by law.

Social security is the classic example. While employers may pay 6 or 7 percent of payroll for the benefits provided by social security, employees are generally of the view that they pay for most of it in deductions from their pay. Government gets credit for providing these benefits, not the employer who pays half or more of the bill.

Workers' compensation and unemployment compensation, as well as disability income in some states, are even more remote in employees' minds, since most employees have no idea that employer taxes paid on their behalf fund benefits for these programs. In their view, these are government-provided benefits. The employer receives no credit for paying for these programs.

EMPLOYEE APPRECIATION AND MOTIVATION

Benefits had their genesis in the largess of paternalistic employers early in the 1900s. The gold watch provided upon retirement at one time was viewed by employees and society as a generous act by a benevolent employer. Of course, in the light of current thought, the Gold Watch syndrome is now viewed sarcastically by employees in a society whose values are that forced retirement is immoral and retired persons have a right to expect generous pensions protected against inflation.

There can be no doubt that employees do appreciate the economic security and peace of mind that derive from the protection of benefit plans. The retiree in 1920 who received a gold watch certainly was appreciative, since most retirees in all likelihood received nothing at all. Modern day employees, while they view benefits as a matter of righteous entitlements they have earned, also appreciate the value of a pension since it is common knowledge that many employees do not enjoy an employer-provided pension. While employees do appreciate their benefits, the extension of that appreciation in the form of motivation, greater productivity, higher morale and job satisfaction, or employer loyalty, is not measurable in any real terms—at least not by any technique that would withstand a rigorous test of reliability.

Employees may be ecstatic, satisfied, or demoralized with their work environment—and benefits may play some part in their morale, motivation, and productivity, both positively and negatively. But numerous other factors are probably involved, some of which may have nothing at all to do with the work environment. A highly skilled and productive machinist or engineer may still abandon a generous benefit program and go to work for another employer because he cannot get along with his boss or doesn't like the employer's attitude toward environmental concerns or minority hiring.

Employee appreciation for benefits in individual cases has expression through the letter to the president declaring company loyalty as a result of the benefits paying for huge expenses connected with a serious illness, the cost of which, except for the benefits, would have destroyed the employee economically. Again, cost-of-living adjustments granted to pensioners invariably produce a number of letters of appreciation.

Such letters are often publicized in employee communications in an attempt to convey to other employees the value of their benefit plans.

At the same time, implementation of a costly vision-care program may produce immediate dissatisfaction among employees who sustained expensive bills for vision care only weeks or months before the new plan was installed.

Usually employee appreciation, which translates into assumed motivation, loyalty, and so on, is not readily apparent, and this is disappointing to business owners and managers who are accustomed to observing some real return on money invested in the business. Occasionally, a new and dramatic benefit, highly publicized at installation, will capture the imagination of employees, and measurable results become visible. Profit-sharing plans usually produce this effect as employees believe that reducing waste and increasing productivity will produce greater profits and thus more money for them personally. However, over time the interest may wane as the plan becomes an accepted part of the environment. Constant communication can be helpful in keeping employee interest high, but some event, such as a declining stock market or adverse business conditions over which they have no control, may undermine the value of their account or company profitability. Then employees may just as quickly feel that they have been cheated in some way since they did their part but they didn't receive their reward. The plan then becomes a dissatisfier as far as they are concerned, and appreciation or motivational value is diminished.

INDIVIDUALIZATION OF ATTITUDES TOWARD BENEFITS

As we have seen, attitudes about benefits are individualized by employees based on their own economic circumstances and value structures. Further, appreciation for benefits is most pronounced among employees who have actually experienced dramatic positive results from a benefit plan.

Within every organization sponsoring benefit plans, there are levels of employees whose financial conditions and values vary greatly, both as individuals and as classes within a social structure. A common benefit plan covering all such employees will be more meaningful to some than to others. A profit-sharing plan may mean a great deal to the manager or executive who can observe how his or her actions translate into greater profits and thus greater personal rewards. That same plan may be much less positive to an assembler in a plant who is a union member and believes that management manipulates the profitability of the company.

These differences in types of employees have resulted in the creation of differentials in benefits for various employee groups who are believed to have differing value structures. While there may have been, and may still be, some genuine reasons for providing different benefits to employees in various job groups, it is no longer valid to base that differential on any assumed class-structure mentality.

Different kinds and levels of benefits have an effect on employee perceptions of the benefit plans. Thus the creation of differentials in benefits must be carefully planned and managed so that the differences are seen as legitimate and rational on some valid basis.

Providing stock options to key managers and not providing such options to a press operator can be validated as legitimate—based on the job function. A key manager may well be motivated by a stock option. A press operator may, by the nature of the job, be more motivated by more frequent breaks from the routine work than by a stock option.

From the perspective of the employee where benefits are concerned, social trends toward equality of opportunity and treatment indicate that while the benefits in specifics may be different, at least the percentage of pay invested in benefits should be roughly the same for every employee whatever job function is fulfilled. The issue of "comparable worth" of jobs is likely to force in the next few years some equalization of the amount spent on benefits for various employee groups.

While trends in social justice and employees demands are for equality of treatment, employees also want individual recognition and attention and more control over every aspect of their lives, including the benefits provided by their employers. In benefit management, if employers are to derive whatever measure of motivation is achievable from benefits, techniques will have to be devised that satisfy these seemingly contradictory social forces.

As pointed out previously, employee appreciation for benefits (and hence the motivation by the benefit aspect of their work environment) is greatest in the employee who has actually had a real experience of value with a benefit plan. It is human nature to relate most strongly to positive events now or expected in the near future. Possible events in the distant future (retirement) or potential events of a negative nature (illness, disability, death) are not events that people want to think about or can relate to in a positive way. This fact of human character makes it difficult to create appreciation or motivation through benefits that are only of value to an employee in essentially negative circumstances.

Communications of benefits is one vehicle by which benefit managers seek to overcome this negative aspect in the attempt to secure motivation and positive, real returns from expensive benefit plans. A later chapter is devoted to the subject of benefit communications.

In the future, it will become ever more important to provide opportunities for benefit plans to produce more immediate positive results in order to derive greater motivation from benefits. While an employee surely senses greater security by the protection of medical, disability, death, and retirement benefits, it may be much more meaningful (and motivating) if a benefit plan enables the employee to buy a home at a reasonable interest rate on the mortgage or helps finance a low-cost vacation to Hawaii.

Offering some measure of individuality in the opportunity for benefits, and providing benefits with current positive values, may be the key to unlocking the motivational impact of benefit plans and responding to that aspect of human nature that constantly inquires "What have you done for me lately?"

ORGANIZED EMPLOYEE PERCEPTIONS OF BENEFITS

While it was originally the gratuitous act of a paternalistic employer to provide some employee benefits, the growth of unionization and government action favorable to unions in the early post–World War II years was the real impetus behind the explosive growth of benefit plans.[1] Collective bargaining for improvements in wages and a wide range of benefits were primary goals that attracted workers to unions. As the union members steadily won such improvements, very often the new plans and improvements were also extended to nonunion employees.

The need to bargain very hard, and sometimes even strike, over benefit issues made such benefits very important to unionized workers. At the same time, however, once obtained, such benefits in the perception of the employees became a hard-earned right of employment, an entitlement equal to wages since very often benefits were taken instead of wage increases.

Over time, this view of an earned right has become ingrained in the thinking of organized workers to the point that considerations of motivation and improved productivity related to improved benefits are almost irrelevant. Certainly organized workers appreciate the value of benefits, perhaps to a greater extent than nonunion employees who do not have to negotiate hard for such benefits. The appreciation does not generally extend to the employer or management, however, but instead to union leaders who are perceived as benefactors in securing such benefits.

To the extent such benefits are paid directly from the union through some form of trust fund, the relationship between the benefit and working for a given employer is even more remote.

EMPLOYER PERCEPTIONS OF BENEFITS

Motivation and Productivity

While employers in the early part of the century may have provided benefits out of some paternalistic impulse, clearly the expectations of management in recent decades has been that benefits would provide employees with a sense of security that would motivate them to company loyalty and thus improved productivity.

As we enter the 1990s there is evidence that employers no longer expect real motivation to result from most benefit improvements. A study of "Employer Attitudes toward Compensation and Productivity"[2] conducted among top executives by Mercer & Co. mentions only three benefit programs that are perceived as having an impact on productivity. They are Employee Stock Ownership Plans (ESOP's), Profit Sharing Plans, and Flexible Compensation or 'cafeteria' plans.

In terms of the potential for contributing to improved productivity, for Employee Stock Ownership plans, 37 percent of respondents indicated such plans "Very Important" (6 percent) as "Somewhat Important" (31 percent), while 33 percent reported actually having an ESOP in operation for employees.

For profit-sharing plans, 70 percent indicated such plans as "Very Important" (26 percent) or "Somewhat Important" (44 percent) while 34 percent reported actually having a profit-sharing plan in operation.

Most interesting was the response concerning flexible compensation packages, or cafeteria plans. While 65 percent of respondents indicated such plans as being "Very Important" (35 percent) or "Somewhat Important" (30 percent), only 5 percent reported actually having some form of flexible compensation actually in operation.

As the search for ways to improve productivity in the American workforce continues to build, it appears that flexible compensation plans will have a bright future. While managements no longer may expect a given benefit plan to generate a high degree of personal motivation among the workforce, it appears that packaging those benefits in a flexible compensation package may actually transform benefits into a motivational feature of the work environment.

Loyalty and Paternalism

Paternalism and its cohort, employee loyalty to the employer, are seldom observed any longer as management practices or expectations, except among small and medium-size family-owned and locally operating businesses.

Occasionally a large company with a strong ownership by one family, supported by traditions of familial concern for employees, will demonstrate some continuing traces of paternalistic behavior through benefit and other personnel practices.

Paternalistic ideals and loyalty concepts have fallen victim to changing social values and governmental actions. Paternalism depended on close personal relationships between workers and management to legitimize it as a management style. As unionization spread, separating management from the work force and building walls of formality between them, management's freedom of action to relate on a personal basis to employees was largely foreclosed.

Shifting social values that change employee attitudes about work and cast business as a naughty member of society, polluting the environment and mistreating employees and the public alike, erect more barriers between management and employees. Government, acting in response to demands from various segments of society, creates endless streams of laws and regulations formalizing the relationship between employer and employee to such a degree that a manager and employee now must pick and choose their words very carefully in many work circumstances or run the risk of being sued under one law or another.

The personal relationships essential to paternalistic management and concomitant employee loyalty have thus been largely removed in the work environment. Consequently, management can no longer expect that providing a good benefit plan will create employee loyalty. Benefit plans are constrained legally in so many aspects that while a company is not legally required to provide most benefits, if it chooses to do so, legal entanglements and suits by employees are possible.

Company loyalty has been an important concept in management perceptions because of the role it is presumed to play in employee turnover. A good employee, appreciative of management's concern for his welfare and therefore loyal to the employer, presumably is much less likely to be attracted away by job offers from other potential employers. Now that loyalty to an employer is anachronistic, almost viewed in derogatory terms by the modern workforce, management can no longer depend on it as a factor in controlling costly employee turnover.

Competitive Behavior

From management's perspective it is important—even essential—to be competitive in the labor market, to be able to attract and hold productive employees. As the cost of hiring and training workers has soared, the loss of an experienced and productive employee is a serious matter. The effect on production and profits of losing a good employee is a double effect—first, the additional cost of replacement and, second, the production lost during the period of training for the new employee.

Thus any action management can take to reduce turnover is viewed as very important.

Benefits have long been perceived by management as playing an important role in reducing turnover, but there is little evidence that benefits are the major influence in reducing turnover. Benefits are only one of many features in the work environment. An employee may leave for many reasons, one of which may be related to benefits. That reason may either encourage them to stay for a time (to fully vest in a pension) or to leave in order to receive a distribution from a profit-sharing plan (or similar plan) for some personal financial purpose (like purchasing a residence).

To the extent that an employer's benefit programs as a whole are not competitive, or specific plans are seriously deficient, an employee may be influenced to leave by the availability of generous benefits with another employer. This is no different than if salary levels are not competitive.

This feature of remaining competitive with other employers has influenced management perceptions and behavior regarding benefits more than anything else in recent decades. The first question most often asked when a new benefit is proposed is "What are other companies doing?"

To some extent, this focus on competitive behavior has almost a paranoia about it, creating a kind of race between employers to be always just a little better in benefit programs than other employers. A great deal of benefit communications activity with employees is directed at forming in their thinking the impression that the employer's benefits are better than those of competing employers. This has resulted in employee communications characterized by an advertising and sales approach, accenting the positive and avoiding any negative information. To some extent, it was this aspect of benefit management that created (in the 50s and 60s) employee expectations about pension benefits which they found were not to be fulfilled. While some employees may have thought they were promised a certain benefit by an expansive and enthusiastic benefit communication, they often were later disappointed to discover that no such promise had been made or that unspecified conditions not clear in the communication had resulted in their losing entitlement to the benefit. ERISA had its conception and birth out of these disappointments, traceable to union leadership and employer desires to present benefits in the best competitive light.

As the quest continues for improvements in productivity and as competition increases for high-quality employees, it seems possible that competitive forces may become an even more important factor in management's perceptions about benefit management. If this should become reality, then the trend to constant expansion of benefit programs is assured of continuation well into the future. As each employer seeks to gain a competitive edge by adding some new benefit, other employers are forced by their perceptions and competitive behavior to act in similar fashion.

As an illustration of the extremes to which this competitive behavior may be practiced, an electronics firm in the highly competitive Silicon Valley area of California advertised via public radio that they provided free checking accounts as a benefit of employment in the hope that this would help lure scarce labor away from competing electronics companies. Escalation of the "Benefits Race" may well be a major feature of benefit management in the future.

Return on Investment

The limiting factor to endlessly escalating benefit plans is the cost of providing these benefits. Company management must be cognizant of benefit costs and what effect those costs have on profitability and competitive pricing of the goods and services. Management and financial managers' perceptions are that benefits costs are getting out of hand and equally out of proportion to the return that can be expected on the investment.

There is no satisfactory technique for measuring return on the investment in benefits. Some remarkable attempts have been made to apply accounting principles and measuring techniques to human resource management and people assets. To date, however, genuinely useful applications are very limited.[3]

To begin with, what kind of return is management to expect? Increased productivity? Reduced turnover? Company loyalty? More satisfied employees? Higher employee morale? Letters of appreciation?

How is such return to be effectively measured? As we have already seen, most of these kinds of returns on the benefit investment are not measurable in specific ways, even if there is some identifiable return. (See Chapter 10.)

Ultimately, a work force is required to produce the goods and services. Many cost items enter into the recruitment, training, and maintenance of that work force. Benefits is one of them. Eventually, goods are produced and sold and a profit made or not made. If the profit is too low in terms of the investment in capital assets, management will seek to reduce costs and increase productivity with the same level of human assets.

Reducing benefit costs by genuinely significant amounts means cutting benefits generally, unless current benefits are being provided at higher cost than necessary and money is being wasted. Unfortunately, it seems probable that energetic and aggressive salespersons of many benefit plans and services have oversold plan sponsors who are anxious about their competitive stature in benefit programs. The future of benefit management portends ever greater emphasis on eliminating from the cost of benefits any expense that does not actually produce a payment to employees in the form of a benefit or is genuinely required to assure delivery of that benefit in a timely fashion.

The real measure of return on investment in benefits, then, is how much of the investment actually results in legitimate benefit payments. If $1 million is spent on benefits and only $600,000 finds its way into benefit payments while $400,000 is paid in commissions, sales expenses, errors, and various services, the return cannot be judged as very good.

Under competitive pressures and legal imperatives, management will provide the benefits it must to satisfy the perception that they must remain competitive. The question they should ask is "How much of our investment actually goes to employees?" in the attempt to answer the question "What return are we getting for the investment in benefits?"

The pressures on benefits executives will encourage them to measure how much of benefit costs actually provides employees benefits and to eliminate as much as possible of those costs that do not. Elimination of wasteful expenditures is of course a standard objective of any management. But where benefits are concerned, it has perhaps not been pursued in the past with the same vigor as in more easily measurable areas, such as the cost of materials and equipment.

A later chapter is dedicated to consideration of benefit cost management.

WHY DO BENEFITS COST SO MUCH?

In 1929 total benefit payments were 3 percent of payroll. By 1955 they were at 17 percent; by 1965, 21.5 percent; by 1975, 30 percent; in 1981, up to 37.3 percent, and in 1987, 39.0% of payroll.[4]

Actually, for many companies, benefit expenditures already exceed 50 percent of payroll, particularly if benefits are defined broadly to encompass all policies and programs other than direct wages that are "beneficial" to employees.

"If overtime and holiday premium pay, shift differentials, production bonus, and other miscellaneous payroll items are also considered benefits, the benefits . . . are 52.2 percent" of payroll.[5]

A benefits outlook survey conducted among members of the Council on Employee Benefits indicates that benefit executives expect benefit expenditures will be at 56 percent of pay by 1990.[6] These are for the traditional benefit programs narrowly defined as basic benefits, such as medical, life, disability, pension, and profit sharing plans.

The cost of benefits for any given benefit program is customarily defined by the formula:

> Benefit payments + Administrative expenses
> − Investment earnings and employee contributions
> = Employer benefit cost

A simple analysis of this formula reveals some of the reasons for increasing costs as a percentage of payroll. For any given benefit plan, such as a simple medical/hospital plan, once the plan is installed, real cost increases exceeding wage percentage increases arise from:

Benefit Payments

  a. Creeping minor plan improvements or major improvements (voluntary or legally required).

    b. Increased utilization by eligible participants as they become more aware of their entitlements.
    c. Excess payments beyond benefits provided by the plan made through erroneous interpretation of plan provisions or other administrative errors.
    d. Increasing cost of services rendered in providing the benefit (hospital costs).
    e. Adverse experience by a given group of employees; that is, a greater number of claims than normal.

Administrative Expenses

Administrative expenses in this sense refer to the cost of paying claims, insurer retentions, trustee fees, and other expenses generally charged directly to the cost of the benefit plan.

Seldom does a plan sponsor include the internal administrative costs of providing benefits to employees in computing total benefit expenditures. Such administrative costs for staff, office facilities, consultants, actuaries, attorneys, communications, and so forth, are very much a benefit expense but customarily are not charged against benefit plans or factored into benefit plan cost calculations. To factor such expenses into benefit plan costs can add 1 to 2 percent or more of payroll to benefit costs.

To the extent that administrative expenses are computed as a function of claims paid (e.g., 5 percent of medical claims paid) as claims increase faster than wages increase, a multiplier effect occurs in the administrative expenses that also pushes them upward faster than wage increases.

Investment Earnings

In plans that have reserve assets building against future claims, investment earnings serve to reduce total costs. If the earnings do not at least equal assumed investment earnings rates (and in many recent years they have not), then additional funds must be pumped into the plan to make up for investment losses.

Employee Contributions

Attempts to secure greater control over benefit plan costs have included a focus on requiring employee contributions toward the cost of their benefits. Section 401(k) Salary Deferral Plans and Section 125 Salary

Reduction Plans, both legislative developments in recent years, provide tax advantaged support for employee contributions in some plans.

Actually, the trend until the early 1980s was to eliminate employee contributions from plans. There was a very rational basis for eliminating contributions, which still holds true in any plan where Section 125 does not apply. Even in a 401(k) plan the tax is only deferred, so a tax is eventually payable. While requiring employee contributions may reduce the cost of a plan for the employer, it is really only shifting the cost to the employee, and not actually a reduction in the cost of providing the benefit. Furthermore, unless the required contribution can be funneled through a Section 125 plan to provide the employee some tax advantage, the cost shifting can be tax inefficient and costly to the employee, creating demands for higher wages to make up the reduced income.

An employee in a 25 percent tax bracket must earn about $1.33 in order to contribute $1 to the benefit plan after tax. Including social security and state and local income taxes this can easily become $1.40.

An employer in a 50 percent tax bracket can deduct the plan cost so that $1 of benefits costs actually only $.50. The employer can fund the benefit for only 40 percent of what it costs the employee.

During inflationary periods when salary increases can push an employee into a higher tax bracket that wipes out the salary increase, as well as during periods of wage controls that set limits on salary increases, one way of giving employees an effective salary increase is to remove required employee after tax contributions to benefits.

As we enter the 1990s, we may forget that in the last 20 years we have experienced both double digit inflation and wage controls. So the trend toward removing or reducing employee contributions was logical during the 1970s and early 1980s. However, in so removing or reducing employee cost sharing the employer picked up the expense, which was a real additional cost that added to benefit plan total costs as a percentage of payroll. The rise in benefit costs from 21.5 percent in 1965 to 30 percent in 1981 reflects to some extent the removal of employee contributions over that period. Now the cycle is coming full circle as cost control efforts incorporate employee required contributions.

Add to this the proliferation of additional benefit programs, both those mandated by law and those bargained by unions or voluntarily installed by employers. A completely new benefit plan obviously adds a real increase in cost that did not previously exist and therefore pushes benefits costs higher as a percent of payroll.

Legally mandated benefits to be paid for by employers have mushroomed in the last 30 years. More holidays, unemployment benefits, major social security improvements, safety equipment, private pension improvements, and maternity income payments are some of the major federally mandated benefits that have expanded in the last two decades.

Many states require minimum health benefit coverages and disability income plans.

Employers have created an upward spiral of benefit plans and improvements as they jockey to gain some benefit advantage over competitors in the labor market competition.

In the absence of a major restructuring of benefit management techniques and controls, and major philosophical changes in attitudes towards benefit plans, there are no foreseeable reasons for expecting real increases in benefit costs to level off. It will be surprising if benefit costs do not far exceed the Council on Employee Benefit projections of 56 percent of payroll by 1990. There is after all virtually no limit to the possibilities for new benefits.

If it is genuinely advantageous from an employer and employee taxation standpoint and satisfying to employees, what limitations (other than emotional and political) exist to prevent the investment in benefits from exceeding the value of direct wages? While no one is presently so brazen as to suggest that this is probable or even likely, neither is it impossible. Who would have thought in 1929 that benefit expenditures would be increasing over 1,000 percent in real terms in only 50 years?

In fact, "the Military Retirement System (MRS) required 57.3 percent and the CSRS (Civil Service Retirement System) required 39.9 percent of payroll in 1981 (to fund those retirement plans for that year). These contributions would not be adequate if federal plans were subject to Employee Retirement Income Security Act (ERISA) requirements. To comply with ERISA, the MRS would have needed over 159 percent and the CSRS would have needed over 92 percent of payroll in 1981."[7]

The recognition by the legislators that it is socially and economically desirable to encourage employee saving, as evidenced in Section 401(k) plans and Voluntary Employee Deductible Contributions (VEDCs), and equitable to allow them some tax advantage in benefit costs, as in Section 125 plans, indicates that there is understanding of the importance of benefits in supporting the socioeconomic structure of the nation.

Section 89, born in the Tax Reform Act of 1986 and intended to extend benefit coverages to more employees based on the extension of non-discrimination requirements to health and welfare plans, also indicates that the movement to require more benefit coverages is deeply founded in our political structure.

It appears there is nothing standing in the way of ever increasing real employee benefit costs as a percentage of payroll.

THE INFLUENCE OF BENEFITS ON PRODUCTIVITY AND WORK BEHAVIOR

We have examined employee perceptions of benefits and generally found that benefit plans and practices as they now exist are perceived by employees as a right and entitlement, part of their compensation reward for working in paid employment. As such, benefits generally are not an independent motivating factor that drives employees to improved productivity beyond their role as part of total compensation and other factors in the work environment.

Is it desirable or possible to attempt to structure and manage benefits in a way that would make them a more motivating factor in the work environment? If so, how could this be accomplished?

Of course, it is desirable to attempt the positive magnification of benefits in employee perceptions so that employees work harder and produce more, become more reliable, waste less time and materials, and become generally better employees. If benefit management could contribute to measurable real gains in productivity, it would earn the respect and admiration of plan sponsors, management, and stockholders. Certainly, the benefit profession would be enhanced and legitimized as a critical and key function of business management.

Because improving productivity is essential to social and economic stability worldwide, and also because the emerging benefit profession is steadily establishing higher standards of professional conduct, it is appropriate that benefits executives undertake concerted efforts to manage benefits so that they make contributions to productivity improvements. In considering how this might be accomplished, we must first examine the reality of benefits in the daily functioning of a given employee. What do they mean to the employee as part of all the many pressures and pleasures that come to bear as an employee considers, for example, whether to have a working lunch at the desk or go out for lunch. We must start by assuming that for an employee to be productive, he or she must be at work, actually producing something of value, and in a good condition physically and mentally to perform the assigned task.

Interestingly, benefits, by their very nature, come into play primarily when employees are not at work. For an employee to realize a paid sick day or vacation entitlement, he or she must take the sick day and vacation. In order to realize a medical benefit, the unfortunate connotation is that the employee is experiencing an illness that requires medical attention and inhibits the ability to perform work.

In this sense, benefits run counter to encouraging productivity since to collect a benefit the employee is in some condition that takes him/her away from the assigned task.

How often have we heard employees say "I haven't taken any sick days yet this year. I'd better take them soon or I'll lose them." This is the reality of the employees thinking as they go about their duties. Hence, around Christmastime, the incidence of sick days increases as employees use those days for shopping and other personal activities rather than lose the benefit.

Obviously, if employeees are seriously ill, they should not be at work because productivity would be low anyway and they could present a danger to other employees. The paid sick-day benefit is provided in the employer's self-interest as much as for the benefit of the employee's economic security.

Vacations are also intended to provide the employee with intervals of rest from the rigor of work so that productivity can be greater in between vacations. But how much vacation does an employee need? Does a 15-year service employee need five weeks vacation more than an employee with two years of service needs a two-week vacation? Some employees do not take a vacation for years at a time.

What this leads to, of course, is that employee *needs* vary considerably with the nature of the individual employee. A benefit structured to meet an employee need will have certain kinds of purposes. A benefit structured as a reward, such as an additional week of vacation for every five years of service, will have very different characteristics and purposes.

Benefits provided for needs should pay off only when the need actually exists and should be structured either to prevent a payoff under conditions of feigned need or translate the portion of benefit not needed into a reward. Need-type benefits, such as sick time, some vacation, medical benefits, disability benefits, life insurance, and pensions, do not inherently contain features that are adaptable directly to increasing employee motivation and productivity.

Reward-type benefits, or those aspects of need benefits that can be translated into rewards, do contain possibilities for motivating employees. The fundamental principle of motivation to change behavior is that the changed behavior will produce a reward.

Benefit theory has tended to confuse need benefits and reward benefits. While management may view a pension benefit as a reward for long service, an employee views the pension as meeting a serious economic need. The employee who works for an employer 6 years and 11 months and leaves without a vested pension needs that pension as much as the employee who works 7 years and 1 month and is rewarded with a pension.

In the employee's thinking, the pension reward is for surviving with one company for many years, not necessarily being highly productive during those years. In the employee's thinking, improved productivity beyond normal satisfactory performance will not affect receipt of that pension or the amount of the pension. Thus, an expensive pension plan is unlikely to have any motivational effect that will change employee behavior to greater productivity.

This is true of all need-type benefits.

The only feature of need benefits that is motivational is that when the employee actually has the usually negative experience that creates the need, the plan pays off handsomely—quickly and efficiently—with no hassle and trouble. This kind of positive experience in personally trying times conveys to the employee something of real economic and psychological value. This is worth working for—maybe even worth working harder for. Working harder is improving productivity.

Unfortunately, the theoretical confusion over needs and rewards has resulted in need-type benefits being encumbered with confusing restrictions most often because of cost constraints. If management views the benefit as a reward then employees should be appreciative of the benefit and not grumble if they must contribute to the cost or have a minor claim that is not covered for some reason.

From the employees' perspective, a benefit plan is of no use at all if they must help pay for it and then don't need to use it, or worse, find that when they do need it, it doesn't pay off for them. Thus, though employers spend millions on expensive need benefits, employees may not be motivated by those benefits to any appreciable extent.

Reward-type benefits do contain the possibility of actually changing employee behavior. Reward benefits are those that pay off under circumstances where a negative need is not involved and the employee in the normal course of events would survive quite well if the benefit were not provided.

Thus, the Silicon Valley employer who offered to pay checking account fees was offering a reward to employees. Furthermore, it was a reward that was useful, immediate, of some economic value, and imaginative.

If benefit management is to make a positive contribution to changed employee behavior, it will be in the following ways:

1. Identifying appropriate need benefits and managing those benefits so that when the need arises, the benefit pays off very well, very quickly, and very efficiently.
2. Establishing reward benefits that are positive, highly visible and useful in the life of the employee, with immediate or near term payoffs of real economic value that capture the imagination of the employees, get them involved and interested, and do not take them away from their work assignments in order to enjoy the reward.

Such reward benefits are tomorrows fringe benefits. Todays need benefits are now employee benefits, a standard and expected feature of total compensation in paid employment.

This challenge to the benefit profession will not be made any easier by the transition to a "postindustrial" or "superindustrial" society, as forecast by many sociologists, economists, and futurists. As Toffler describes it in *The Third Wave,* some traditional concepts of employment and productivity may be outmoded within 10 years as cheap computers and electronic communications make a resurgence of cottage industry possible. Many jobs associated with clerical types of work, financial-accounting functions, and data processing—generally any job in which employees work essentially by themselves processing some form of information—may be performed from cheap communications terminals located in the home. An employer may hire an entire family as "an employee," as all members of the family work together from the home performing some function, such as monitoring via television and computers some factory operation, or the security of a building during night hours.

What is the significance to employee benefits management of providing benefits to a "family employee" or an employee who comes to the office only one day a month for briefings or training? Toffler's answer is that "Within fixed limits, payment and fringe benefit packages will increasingly be tailored to individual preference."[8]

Thus we see that it is both desirable and possible for benefit management to develop a role for benefits in the worldwide drive to improve employee productivity.

THEORY OF THE BENEFIT PLAN LIFE CYCLE

Having considered benefit theory from the perspective of employees, employers, and motivation, let us shift now for a moment and consider the theory of a benefit plan life cycle.

Benefit plans are not static entities that are put in place and function on their own in a straight line. Benefit plans are dynamic systems that shift in purpose, function, and many other ways from month to month and year to year. It is helpful to the benefits executive to have a conceptual frame of reference for the life cycle of a given benefit plan in order to better understand what is occurring and what may occur in the future with respect to that plan. That conceptual frame of reference is the "Benefit Plan Life Cycle."

Consider for a moment the diagram in Figure 4–1.

Conceptually, there is an ideal benefit plan for a given purpose, either *need* or *reward*. The ideal plan meets employee needs or desires fully. It is motivational, easy to manage and administer, fully consistent with company philosophy, and meets every legal requirement and costs less than financial people expect. Of course, the ideal plan is almost never fully realized because numerous internal and external influences and constraints push and pull in different directions simultaneously. The resulting plan is less than perfect, therefore, and is somewhere off the center in the direction of the strongest influence that exists as the plan is installed or modified.

Competitive influence or some expressed but unsatisfied employee needs are usually the initiating forces that start a benefit plan idea in motion. As we have seen, increasingly there will be a third initiating force—the desire to motivate employees to greater productivity. Once the idea has been entered into discussions within the organization, political positioning commences as various viewpoints are expressed about the idea. Legal viewpoints are sought to clarify the legal considerations. Eventually, initial political and legal considerations are clarified and a plan design outlined. Often a consultant is invited in to offer suggestions, sometimes to satisfy a political consideration. Funding vehicles are considered and insurance agents, actuaries, brokers, or financial service representatives interviewed as appropriate.

A proposal to management is prepared and is subjected to internal political consideration, possible revisions in the proposal, and eventually the necessary approvals are secured. Implementation proceeds—administration is organized, communications distributed, and staffing

FIGURE 4–1
A Benefit Plan Life Cycle

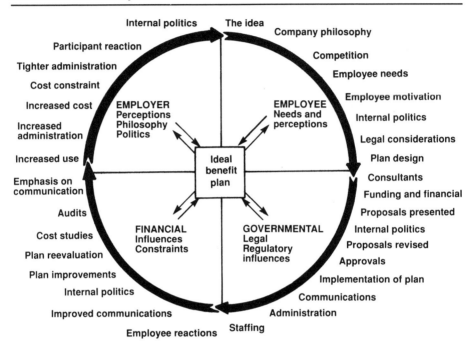

accomplished as necessary. Internal politics may enter into all these processes as various functions seek to influence some aspect of the plan management.

At some point, employee reaction is received or sought. Frequently, additional communication is judged as necessary to clarify the benefit or clear up misunderstandings. Sometimes, internal politics arise as a result of employee reaction, and adjustments or modifications are made in the plan. A reevaluation of the plan and costs is undertaken. In the desire to obtain maximum employee morale and appreciation for the benefit, more communications may be undertaken. This produces more utilization of the plan, increased administration, and higher costs.

The increasing costs draw the attention of financial managers, and frequently cost constraints are urged. This leads to tightening up administration in order to control costs better. Tighter administration often means closer scrutiny of claims and utilization with the result that more benefit claims are reduced or denied—within the plan of course, but denied nonetheless. Employees then may react negatively, and internal politics again comes into play as various factions express how the plan should be changed to work better.

The philosophy behind the plan is reviewed (perhaps social change or changed employee needs have outdated portions of the benefit), and the cycle begins again.

This life cycle varies for each plan and in each organization. A pension plan may have a very long cycle because utilization builds over a long period of time. A medical plan may be in constant turmoil because utilization is high. Quickly changing competitive positions or employee values may move a plan through the cycle very quickly or even short circuit some steps. Government action may force a plan through the cycle very quickly.

Given that a benefits executive is managing many different plans simultaneously, it is sometimes helpful in understanding what is occurring in the plans to conceptualize them in terms of the life cycle. It is also helpful in benefit planning if the executive can gain some insight into what phase may be expected to occur next.

THE SOCIAL ROLE OF EMPLOYEE BENEFITS

The benefits executive is not normally concerned about the macro role of benefits in broad social terms as he or she pursues their daily responsibilities. Yet, when planning for benefit management in the longer term, broad purposes for benefits in society can be expected to exert influence on possible courses of action that may be considered.

In the United States, the role of employee benefits in the social structure has not been clearly defined in an orderly way by government policy. This is in contrast to many other industrialized nations where goals for security of the employed population are set by government decree and employee benefit plans are the vehicles for providing this security.

However, a kind of ad hoc agglomeration of federal and state laws has developed that reveal very important purposes for benefit plans in the functioning of society.

In examining the social role of benefits we will consider first the current evidence and actual functions performed by employee benefits, and then consider briefly some of the debates now underway and what they may portend for the future role of benefits in American society.

PRESENT SOCIAL PURPOSES OF BENEFITS

An estimated 82 percent of the population is protected by one or more forms of private health insurance.[9] This remarkable level of security has been achieved through private enterprise and in the absence of a national goal for the provision of hospital/medical insurance against illness.

Group life insurance in force on employees exceeds $1,115,000,000,000—one trillion, one hundred and fifteen billion dollars.[10] Estimates are that perhaps more than 71 million employees are covered by some form of employer or private pension plan, possibly 50 million of them by private employer nongovernmental plans.[11]

Supplemental unemployment benefits and governmental unemployment income plans protect some portion of income for virtually all the workforce, as does workers' compensation programs.

Virtually every full-time employee, working for even the smallest employer will have some level of protection against medical expense, some employer-provided life insurance, income protection in event of unemployment, medical expense and income protection in event of work-related illness or injury, and ultimately at retirement, some income from social security and medical expense protection from medicare features of social security.

Generally, the larger the employer, the more generous are the levels of benefits provided under the privately sponsored medical expense, life insurance, disability income, and pension plans.

Obviously, employee benefits are an essential underpinning of the social structure. The existence of these vehicles of security for the American population makes it possible for our people to experience a good living standard, good health, a basic sense of economic security, and sufficient leisure time to enjoy pursuits of self-actualization, such as education, a high level of social and volunteer activity, political involvement in governmental affairs, and family activities.

Employee benefits have developed in support of society's goals—personal freedom and economic security.

The growth and development of benefits in American society has been largely free of governmental control because the market system has produced what people wanted and needed in the way of employee benefit coverage. The role of the government has been to attempt to provide for the economic needs of the total society what private companies could not address; for example, income maintenance of persons who are unemployed or have never been employed long enough to earn a pension with an employer. Minimum social security benefits, social security benefits for employees of companies that do not provide pension or disability income benefits, welfare benefits, and income maintenance during unemployment are examples of benefit programs that have been accepted as the responsibility of government.

In many nations, the security of the population has been provided for through government-sponsored or mandated benefit plans. In the United States, private enterprise has initiated and developed the benefit plans that meet a large part of society's need for protection and security.

Despite the success of private enterprise in providing such a high degree of economic security through private benefit coverages, there is considerable evidence that society is judging the adequacy and levels of benefit coverages to be deficient.

ERISA marked the initial public judgment, expressed through government, that private pension plans were not fulfilling the role society wants and expects.

Several debates are now underway that will define in major ways the role society will expect benefits to fill in the future.

BENEFITS IN SOCIAL POLICY

Major debates now in progress concerning the role of benefits in society are:

1. National health insurance.
2. The adequacy of private pensions and need for mandatory pension plans.
3. Funding and benefits under social security.
4. The role of benefits in work beyond age 65.
5. The role of benefits in sex discrimination.
6. The adequacy and funding of unemployment compensation.
7. The role of benefit plan assets in meeting social objectives.
8. Who should control these huge pools of assets.
9. The role of benefits in new work arrangements such as job sharing and part-time employment.
10. The adequacy of workers' compensation benefits.
11. Whether government or private enterprise should initiate and develop solutions to weaknesses in benefit systems.
12. The proper relationship between private pensions and social security.
13. Taxation of benefits for the highly paid.

Not yet widely debated but likely to become debates during the 1990s are:

1. The adequacy of death and medical benefits in retirement.
2. The role of benefits in productivity.
3. The meaning of "comparable worth" to benefit plans.
4. Benefit coverages for former families of divorced employees, extended families, and persons living together in a state of dependency but not married (different or same sex).
5. The extension of benefits to handicapped employees with preexisting medical conditions.
6. The extent to which benefits can be "tailored" or "individualized" to differing employee needs and desires.

While it isn't possible here to explore all the full arguments on these issues, it is useful to consider the general aspects of the debates.

National Health Insurance

The issue is whether or not we should have a national policy on what the minimum standards of health care should be and how that care should be financed. Over many years several proposals have been submitted to Congress and debated at length. None have been adopted because a consensus on what the standards should be and what the nation can afford has not been developed. Proposals range from complete care for every American financed by payroll taxes at a cost of billions of dollars— to a catastrophic plan covering only the most serious illnesses (cancer, organ transplants) financed by private employers through the private insurance system.

As medical care costs continue to soar and attempts are made to control inflation, it seems likely that the initial resolution of this issue will be some required minimum medical care plan to be provided by employers, financed through the private insurance system, with a national major medical plan to be provided by employers, financed through the private insurance system, through a national vehicle funded by payroll taxes, or general revenues. Coordination and integration of medical care benefit plans with government medical care plans will be a matter to occupy the attention of benefits managers.

Adequacy of Private Pensions

As government seeks to control the cost of social security and yet respond to public pressure for higher pensions to meet increasing living costs, some minimum level of private pensions to supplement social security combined with some required cost-of-living adjustment to private pensions seems likely. The enormous cost of such benefits is the issue.

The financing issue resolution may well come through encouragement of profit-sharing and savings plans sponsored by private employers. Such plans could serve as the vehicle for meeting cost-of-living adjustments in pensions as well as encouraging private savings and providing a pool of capital resources for the nation.

The macroeconomic issue is the transfer of profits from stockholders and employers to employees, as well as the reduction of tax revenues.

Social Security Benefits and Funding

The issue is high cost of funding even the present level of social security benefits and the transfer effect of moving income from workers to retirees.

Benefits in the future (near the end of the century) have already been reduced. It seems likely that the retirement age will be increased and encouragements offered to keep people working into older ages, thus meeting some of their living costs through wages and taking some pressure off the social security system. As these issues are resolved, it is likely that various changes will place additional cost burdens on private benefit plans. Reductions in social security benefits will increase the amount of private pension benefits in integrated pension plans. Encouraging work to later ages will shift some cost for medical, disability, and death benefits from social security and medicare to private benefit plans. A clear example of this shift is the change mandated by the Tax Equity and Fiscal Responsibility Act (TEFRA) that medicare is to become the secondary payor on medical benefits for employees working beyond age 65, instead of the primary payor.

The changes that will be made in the social security system to restore financial strength and public confidence will present private benefit plans with difficult design issues. On the one hand maximizing integration of private plans with social security benefits is a defensible and logical course of action to follow on the premise that private and public benefit plans should be coordinated fully to avoid duplication of benefits. On the other hand benefit plans integrated with social security are subject to a constant stream of changes every time social security is modified. These changes not only are difficult to communicate to employees but may also shift costs from social security onto the private benefit plan.

To escape from this dilemma some private benefit plan sponsors may well decide to abandon all social security integration in their private plans and provide a level of benefits that are judged adequate in their private plans, leaving social security benefits outside the private plans entirely.

The Role of Benefits in Work beyond Age 65

As people decide to continue working beyond age 65, either to meet income needs or in response to social and moral imperatives, it is to be expected that employee benefit plans will have to respond with full equality of benefit coverages for these employees with the same benefits provided employees under age 65. The Tax Equity and Fiscal Responsibility Act pointed employers in this direction with requirements that active employees over 65 must have the same medical plan benefits as workers under age 65 and the private plan medical benefits must be the primary payor ahead of medicare coverages.

This is a cost issue primarily since costs of benefits, such as medical and death benefits, are likely to increase (although some innovative work being done at the Andrus Gerontology Center in Los Angeles gives some early indications that benefit costs may not necessarily increase as age increases). However, it is also a benefit design issue, particularly with respect to disability income, which is usually greater than pension income. There are issues of real importance surrounding the question of at what point disability becomes retirement.

It is also likely that employers will be hiring people well into their 60s. Assumptions about costs of benefits, and particularly the assumption about when employees will retire that is so essential in pension funding, will have to be adjusted to consider the effects of employees being hired at older ages and working into their 70s.

Traditional benefit design has factored in reduced benefits after retirement, particularly medical and death benefits. Should such differentials continue, employees are encouraged to continue working if at all possible to participate in the larger benefits of active employment. Employers will have to consider narrowing these differentials in order to get employees to retire.

Phased retirements with periods of part-time work just prior to retirement are likely to become common. This points toward benefits for part-time employees adequate to provide some incentive to the employee to shift to such part-time status.

The Role of Benefits in Sex Discrimination

Traditional benefit design has been structured around providing benefits for the male family provider. Assumptions about pension plans and death benefits have also factored in experience differentials based on sex as developed in life expectancy tables.

As social and moral pressures build to eliminate the differences in employment status based on sex, already different funding and pension benefits have come under fire, and equal treatment is being required irrespective of decades of factual data indicating that women may expect to live longer than men. Benefit managers will be challenged further in the 1990s to eliminate any taint of benefit differentials related to sex in all benefit plans.

The Adequacy and Funding of Unemployment Benefits

Except for some SUB (supplemental unemployment benefits) plans of unions and a few employers, unemployment benefits are provided by federal and state plans. As the nation seeks to control inflation, unemployment seems to be an inevitable result. Since unemployment seems to fall unequally on various states, with midwestern and northeastern states suffering the most, the unemployment benefit funds of those states have become seriously depleted.

There is constant pressure to increase levels to benefits to cope with ever-rising living costs. Further, those states with funds in trouble maintain they should have funds transferred to them from the states with low unemployment and large reserves of funds. The federal government becomes the arbitrator of this debate and most likely will force such a transfer of funds since the alternative is an infusion of federal funds to states in trouble.

The likely result in the 90s will be significantly rising costs for unemployment benefits as well as pressures to extend some level of other benefits to employees laid off or forced out of work by plant shutdowns and other discontinuance of operations.

The Role of Benefit Plan Assets in Meeting Social Objectives

The huge pool of pension plan assets has drawn the attention of many groups who would like to see these assets applied to meet the capital needs of a variety of social objectives. In particular, the assets of union pension funds that are deemed to belong to union members are eyed enviously for application to purposes that serve those members—such as, providing them funds for mortgages on their homes and for financial support to modernize plants and equipment in industries threatened with job loss because they can no longer compete with more efficient competitors, particularly foreign ones.

Beyond these direct applications of pension funds to social purposes, many groups with special interests, such as human rights and environmental concerns, are inclined to apply pressure on managers of pension funds to avoid investing in businesses that they deem to violate their area of interest.

Those who oppose the application of such funds for social purposes point to the legal requirements that such funds be invested in the best interest of participants; that is, to secure their pension benefits. Their concern is that social purpose application of funds may endanger the earnings potential and security of the funds and thus the pension income benefits.

Benefits managers and plan sponsors, especially those involved in pension funds of unions, will be confronted with challenges to their custodianship of such funds from these social interest groups.

Who Should Control These Pools of Pension Assets?

A case is made by some individuals and groups that the funds held in pension trusts belong to the employees, and therefore, the employees should have considerable influence in where and how these funds are invested. Especially they maintain that there should be employee representatives on the investment boards who manage those assets. In some cases they maintain that employees should have proxy voting rights with respect to the holdings of the trusts.

Those opposing such employee influence over the management of funds maintain that uninformed and inexperienced employee members on such boards would do more harm than good and employees are not equipped to make decisions with regard to investments.

As the trend to participative management grows stronger and employees demand more involvement in the employment decisions that affect them, pressure for employee involvement in pension fund management will likely grow. Benefits managers will have to deal with the problems created by such employee involvement in fund management.

Benefits in New Work Arrangements

There is movement toward innovative work arrangements that allow employees more flexibility in the hours they choose to work. Such arrangements may even extend during the 90s to periods of leave of several months after specified periods of service, as well as work performed from within the home.

Benefit design will need to accommodate part-time employment and job sharing and benefit coverages during extended periods of paid and unpaid leave of absence. Many design and cost issues are raised by extending benefits to part-time employees, employees working from a home, or employees away from work for months at a time. Benefits managers will be confronted with the challenge of innovative benefit design to accommodate these new work arrangements.

The Adequacy of Workers' Compensation Benefits

As increasing attention is focused on the health costs of working, the tendency is to identify work-related reasons for illnesses that are related to stress, such as heart attacks. Also, more direct relationships are being identified between some illnesses and work performed many years before the illness becomes apparent.

The result is increasing worker compensation claims and challenges to the adequacy of the benefits. For benefit managers this means increased costs and a greater administration burden for such plans.

Who Should Develop Solutions to Weaknesses in Benefit Systems?

On the one hand many government officials and socially oriented groups maintain that the private benefit system is too diverse and scattered to be effective in voluntarily developing solutions to weaknesses, such as the provision of adequate private pensions to all workers, protected with cost-of-living adjustments.

On the other hand, those involved in the private benefit industry maintain that government involvement, legislation, and regulation is too onerous and more damaging than helpful to the provision of benefits to employees.

Benefits managers and plan sponsors, as well as all the many support groups involved in benefits (such as insurers and consultants) will be challenged in the 90s to prove that voluntary and coordinated effort is less costly and more effective than burdensome laws and regulation. While they are attempting to prove the point, government will continue to effect the laws and regulations it deems necessary. The objective will be to influence those laws and regulations so that they are helpful to the voluntary effort rather than harmful to it.

The Relationship between Private Pensions and Social Security

It has been traditionally accepted that the total pension income of a retiree is supported by the "three-legged stool" of social security, a private pension, and private savings. The soundness of social security is in question; private pensions are criticized as being inadequate and only covering half the population; and personal savings have suffered from low returns and the ravages of inflation. As a result, some observers have despaired that this triple whammy indicates that the only way to assure adequate pension income for the entire population is to fold all three together in a single federal plan. While this idea has not drawn a great number of supporters, it continues to generate discussion at some very influential levels of government.

There is likely to be considerable debate about how social security and private pensions fit together, how they work in support of each other, and how they work against each other. The existence of social security requiring almost seven percent of payroll contribution makes it very difficult for small employers to afford another five percent of payroll contribution to finance private pension plan for their employees. That is generally the reason that half the population working for small employers has no private pension.

Further, the process of *integration* (by which private pension plans factor the social security benefit into a total pension benefit) is often criticized as a means of providing larger private pensions to highly paid employees than are provided to lower-paid employees. The practice is defended as being fair because social security benefits are regressive, providing a smaller benefit as a percentage of pay to higher-paid employees than to lower-paid employees.

Integration was challenged at the time ERISA became law in that one remote provision in the late drafts of ERISA would have frozen the levels of social security integration for several years. It seems likely that similar challenges will be mounted in the 90s. Should the practice of integration be frozen or limited in some way, the costs of private pensions will increase substantially, and benefits managers will be confronted with serious issues of design in those plans.

The Adequacy of Death and Medical Benefits in Retirement

Traditional practice has been to reduce the level of death and medical benefits in retirement. There are sound cost and benefit design reasons for doing so. However, as people work to later ages and the lines between active employment and retirement become blurred by phased retirement practices, it is likely that pressures will build to narrow the differences between the levels of benefits during active employment and in retirement.

The Role of Benefits in Productivity

The search for ways to improve productivity is likely to include an examination of what role benefits can play. In general there is widespread opinion that benefits cannot make any significant contribution to improved productivity. Still, debates on the subject are likely to re-emerge and innovative attempts be made to determine if benefits can make any contribution to improved productivity.

"Comparable Worth" Applied to Benefits

The issue of comparable worth of jobs brings into question the relative value of various jobs and just how much more one job is worth to an employer than another. It is related to issues of equal pay and discrimination in pay. It is also related to challenges by the public and stockholders with regard to the levels of executive's pay, now required to be disclosed in public documents.

While good arguments can be made for paying employees differently based on the job they perform, in the quest for elimination of any taint of discriminatory practices, it is possible to conceive of pressures to provide equal percentages of pay for benefits among all levels of employees.

Benefit Coverages for Unusual Family Arrangements

As society increasingly accepts a variety of lifestyles and legal recognition is granted to unusual family relationships, it can be expected that employees will demand recognition in benefit coverages for relationships that they deem legitimate. Same-sex marriages, long-term unmarried cohabitation with written contractual commitments, former families of divorced employees, and extended families wherein an employee voluntarily accepts responsibility for dependency of persons not bearing any legal relationship—all present potential conditions wherein an employee may maintain entitlement of dependents to benefit coverages. Benefit design will need to consider the possibility of coverages for some such circumstances or at least prepare for defense against such claims.

Benefits for Handicapped Employees

The movement to extend special consideration in employment for handicapped persons will lead to an increasing number of persons being hired whose physical condition upon employment represents certain medical claims perhaps of very large amounts. Customary practices of delaying coverage of preexisting medical conditions for newly hired employees will have to be modified in order to accommodate such circumstances. If the design modification is to waive preexisting conditions and cover such handicapped employees fully from date of hire, it will be very difficult to maintain practices that delay covering preexisting conditions for non-handicapped employees.

Likewise, other conditions of employment, such as disability income plans, will need to be adjusted to accommodate the possibility of handicapped persons' conditions deteriorating and becoming long-term disability cases.

The Extent to Which Benefits Can Be Individualized

It is likely that interest in "cafeteria" benefit and compensation plans will increase in order to accommodate the changed social attitudes and lifestyles. The major deterrents to cafeteria-type plans are the possibility that employees will make inappropriate selections of benefits and later make claims that they were inadequately informed or misinformed about their choices. Plan sponsors desiring to approach cafeteria benefits in response to employee needs and demands will find themselves engaged in debates with actuaries and insurers about the extent to which benefits can be tailored to individual needs within established actuarial and risk control practices. Consultants will be challenged to devise communications that will avoid misunderstanding and misinformation.

From this brief glimpse of issues confronting the benefits field in the 90s it is apparent that there is sufficient controversy and challenge to keep benefits professionals interested and busy for the decade and beyond.

Taxation of Benefits to the Highly Paid

In the Tax Reform Act of 1986, the efforts to find sources of tax revenue led to the introduction of Section 89 of the IRC. This addition to the tax law requires employers to prove that basic benefit plans, such as health insurance, do not discriminate in favor of the highly paid employees, and if they do, to include the value of the discriminatory portions of the benefits in the taxable compensation of the highly paid employees.*

The concept of nondiscrimination in the workplace was initially extended into the benefits area with ERISA in 1976. It was further extended with the elimination of mandatory retirement in ADEA, and in 1986 with Section 89.

As the political leveling of society has proceeded, attention has focused on the prequisites that are often provided to higher paid employees, on the premise that all employees should be treated equally and benefits that are tax deductible to an employer (thus supported by the taxpayers overall) should be extended equally to all employees.

Section 89 is of limited application, applying initially and primarily to health benefits, but it signals the attention that is being focused on the differentials in benefits between employees generally and highly paid employees. As we enter the 1990s the debate is already expanding to include direct discussion about taxation of benefits for highly paid employees.

---

* Note: At press time Section 89 was about to be repealed by Congress. This may result in even more direct attempts to tax benefits of highly paid employees.

REFERENCES

1. Jost and Sutherland, *Guide to Professional Benefit Plan Management* (Brookfield, Wis.: International Foundation of Employee Benefit Plans, 1980), pp. 1–9.
2. *Employer Attitudes toward Compensation and Employee Productivity* (New York: William M. Mercer, Inc., November 1980), p. 17.
3. See Eric Flamholtz, *Human Resource Accounting* (Encino, Calif.: Dickenson Publishing Co., 1974); and Michael Mercer, "Turning Your Human Resources Department into a Profit Center," Amacom, 1989.
4. "Employee Benefits 1988," U.S. Chamber of Commerce, Table 17, p. 33, and Table 5.
5. "Employee Benefits 1981," U.S. Chamber of Commerce, p. 24. Statement Not Updated in 1988 Survey.
6. *Employee Benefit Plan Review Research Reports,* (Chicago: Charles Spencer & Associates, November 1978).
7. *Employee Benefit Research Institute Issue Brief 13* (Washington, D.C.: EBRI, December 1982), p. 3.
8. Alvin Toffler, *The Third Wave* (New York: Williams Morrow & Co., 1980), p. 370.
9. "Benefit Spotlight on National Health Insurance," (New York: Johnson-Higgins, November 5, 1980).
10. *Life Insurance Fact Book 1978* (Washington, D.C.: American Council of Life Insurance), p. 22
11. *Pension Facts, 1978–1979* (Washington, D.C.: American Council of Life Insurance), p. 8.

CHAPTER 5

ADMINISTRATIVE SYSTEMS AND SERVICES

By Joel F. Levy

INTRODUCTION

EFFECTIVE ADMINISTRATION

USES OF ADMINISTRATIVE MANUALS

PREPARING STEP-BY-STEP PROCEDURES

THE IMPORTANCE OF RECORDS

KEEPING PARTICIPANTS INFORMED

KEEPING GOVERNMENT INFORMED

KEEPING CALCULATION METHODS UP TO DATE

CHECKLISTS CAN HELP

REVIEWING THE ADMINISTRATIVE PROCESS

LOOKING AHEAD

LISTS AND CHARTS

A STEP-BY-STEP PROCEDURE FOR ADMINISTERING
A PENSION PLAN

ERISA REPORTING AND DISCLOSURE
REQUIREMENTS TO EMPLOYEES

REQUIREMENTS FOR REPORTING AND
DISCLOSURE TO GOVERNMENT AGENCIES

CHECKLIST FOR TERMINATING EMPLOYEES

CHECKLIST FOR RETIRING EMPLOYEES

CHECKLIST FOR REVIEW OF BENEFIT
  ADMINISTRATION
SAMPLE PLAN ADMINISTRATION MANUAL
RECORD-KEEPING REQUIREMENTS

INTRODUCTION

The purpose of this chapter is to chart a course through the mounting complexities of administering employee benefits. For the sake of directness we shall focus on one aspect of the function—the administration of pension plans, which has become the most complex assignment for corporate benefits administrators. But the concepts we shall discuss apply as well to the administration of other employee benefits.

The complexities of employee benefits have been gathering force from a number of sources: from the action of organized labor, from government legislation and regulation, and from shifts in the American economy.

There was a time when employee remuneration was a simple act. Employees were paid so much an hour or so much a week. It was direct and uncomplicated. Each employee was responsible for saving to pay doctor bills, for retirement income, and for other needs. Then, gradually, pay was supplemented by other forms of compensation—now called employee benefits. Pensions first came into the picture as early as 1885. Over the years other benefits were added: group life insurance, savings plans, medical benefits, disability plans, dental plans, and so forth.

The federal government got involved when it passed the Social Security Act. Then, starting with ERISA in 1974, Congress commenced serious and intense involvement in benefits administration. ERISA has been followed by major benefits legislation every three to four years. The major burden of benefits administration derives from requirements of all of this legislation and the volumes of regulations it has spawned.

Further complicating the administration of employee benefits are economic trends. Periods of inflation have brought on demands for cost-of-living increases in benefits at a time when cost containment is a major corporate necessity.

Meanwhile, the very size of the cost of employee benefits has mushroomed. Today it often makes up as much as 30 to 40 percent of payroll cost, making it more important than ever to administer benefit programs efficiently.

A Source of Frustration

In view of all of these gathering forces—more and larger benefits, more regulation complications, inflation, and so forth—is it any wonder that many a benefits administrator has become frustrated and bogged down by the ever-mounting challenge presented by the task of administering employee benefits?

We have reached a time when it is essential to systematize the benefits administration function, to develop a plan, to establish set procedures, to apply controls, and to make periodic reviews of the function.

EFFECTIVE ADMINISTRATION

So we come to the crux of the problem—the effective administration of pension plans and other employee benefits. How can it be accomplished? How can responsibilities be set forth? How can the job be broken down into logical parts? How can it be effectively controlled? How can the process be kept up-to-date and efficient?

Organizing the Function

The first step in the effective administration of benefit plans, and pension plans particularly, is proper organization. This usually involves a review of the benefit plans and a visit to the plants, offices, and other locations of the company to examine the administrative and record-keeping procedures and needs.

Then administrative procedures may be charted or diagramed to show the flow of steps in the process, the forms and reports required, and who is responsible for each step in the process. It should be clear which steps are to be performed at the plants and field offices and which at headquarters.

Some steps in the process are initiated by the employees themselves; some by the administrative staff in the field, some by the plan administrator, and others by the government. When these steps have been identified, responsibilities can be assigned. Throughout this process, the objectives of proper organization should be kept in mind. Major among them are these:

To make sure the company's benefits objectives are being achieved.

To make sure the plan is administered in a cost-effective manner.

To make sure that communications with employees—brochures, forms, letters, and audiovisuals—suitably inform employees so they can make informed decisions on their own behalf and can fully appreciate the value of the company's programs.

To make sure that the plans conform with government requirements.

TABLE 5–1
A Step-by-Step Procedure for Administering a Pension Plan

Events	Administrative Steps
Upon employment	Verify accuracy of employment date. Determine if previously employed by the company or an affiliate. Start maintaining records to determine when the employee is eligible to join the plan.
When employee meets plan membership requirements	Give Summary Plan Description to employee. Notify employee of opportunities for contributions to an individual retirement account, either individually or through company participation. Notify payroll department so that employee's W-2 Form can be properly prepared to indicate that the employee is a participant in a qualified plan.
Meeting age and service requirements for preretirement spouse's coverage	Send application form if plan provides that employees must elect preretirement joint and survivor coverage. Notify employee of the postretirement joint and survivor provisions of the plan before reaching early retirement age (required by IRS regulations). Employee has to receive this information even if in-service death benefit is provided free.
Retirement	Identify participants eligible for retirement in near future and counsel participant about benefits available and how to apply for them. Prepare applications and other forms needed to process the participants' paperwork.
Calculation of benefits	Establish a detailed set of procedures for calculation worksheets and verification. It may be necessary to obtain past earnings history for the period of time before employees joined the company if benefit formula is integrated with social security.

TABLE 5–1—Continued

Events	Administrative Steps
Election of benefits	Notify participants of their rights to elect benefits within time frames required by government regulations. Provide participants with opportunity to request estimates of amounts payable under each payment arrangement. Review rights of the spouse in community property states.
Participants working beyond normal retirement date	Explain benefit formula and spouse protection coverage provisions of plan. Also, advise participants of status of welfare benefits, including retirement for applying for Part B of Medicare. If pension payments are not to begin until the participant retires, inform him or her about the suspension of pension payment provisions of the plan.
Termination of employment	Notify participants of amount of deferred vested benefit, if any, and enter name and amount on Schedule SSA of Form 5500. Return employee contributions if plan is contributory and employee is not otherwise vested.
Reemployment	Determine whether employee worked for the controlled group of companies to ensure that he is properly credited with pre-break service. If pension payments stop upon reemployment, notify employee of suspension of benefit rules of the plan.
Death	Notify beneficiary of any benefit payable and obtain proof of death. Obtain state estate-tax waiver certificate, if applicable.
Follow-up on participants currently receiving benefits	Identify when payments to retired employees change so that the trustee or paying agent can be notified, for example, in the case of social security leveling options. Verify participant's continued eligibility for benefits, such as in the case of disability retirement, by arranging for physical examination or completion of medical questionnaire. Establish procedure to verify that the participants are still living.

TABLE 5–1—*Concluded*

Events	Administrative Steps
Participants requesting documents or information about the plan	Make available for inspection copies of plan documents, SPDs, annual reports, books and financial records, etc. ERISA has created new rights for participants to obtain this information.
Participants requesting statement of accrued benefits	Provide information required by regulations. Annual benefit statement generally satisfies this requirement.
Appeal of denied claims	Write claims procedures and forms. Participants, beneficiaries, or their representatives can bring appeals. Regulations require responses be given within designated time frame.
Retirement board meetings	Prepare procedures for meetings and record minutes.
Annual recording of service and pensionable earnings	Develop procedures that meet the requirements of government regulations and provisions of the plan document. Submit data to actuary for valuation purposes.
Government reporting	Collect census data for all employees in controlled group. File or distribute such items as: Annual Return/Report of Employee Benefit Plan (Form 5500) PBGC Premium Payment Summary Annual Report.
Plan amendment	Prepare appropriate amendments and board of directors resolutions. Obtain approval from the IRS and maintain determination letter for plan's qualification. Distribute announcement letters, Review all administrative procedures to insure they conform to new plan provisions. Hold training sessions for benefits personnel.

Note: This procedure is for a typical plan. In every case, the procedure must be tailored to the plan it refers to.

TABLE 5–2
ERISA Requirements for Reporting and Disclosure to Employees

Type of Report	Due Date
Summary Plan Description	Within 90 days of the date when employee becomes participant
Summary of Material Modifications to Plan	Within 210 days after the end of the plan year in which the change was adopted
Summary Annual Report	By the last day of the ninth month after the end of each plan year

USES OF ADMINISTRATIVE MANUALS

Once the organization is established, steps must be taken to maintain the proper functioning of the staff under the organization. One of the best ways to accomplish this is by preparing an administrative manual.

TABLE 5–3
Requirements for Reporting and Disclosure to Government Agencies

Type of Report	Government Agency	Due Date
Annual Return/Report (Form 5500)	Internal Revenue Service	Last day of seventh month after end of plan year
Annual Registration Statement (Schedule SSA)	Internal Revenue Service	With Annual Report
Annual Premium Payment (Form PBGC-1)	Pension Benefit Guarantee Corporation	Within seven months of beginning of plan year
Summary of Material Modifications to Plan	Department of Labor	Within 210 days after end of plan year in which change was adopted
Notice of Plan Termination	Pension Benefit Guarantee Corporation and IRS	For PBGC, 10 days before termination date
Notice of Reportable Event	PBGC and IRS	Within 30 days of knowledge of occurrence for PBGC

EXHIBIT 5–1
Checklist for Terminating Employees

Name _____ Soc. Sec. No. _____

Last day worked_____ Severance from Service date _____

( ) Complete *Calculation of Service Worksheet*
Does the member have at least 10 years of vesting service?
( ) No   ( ) Yes
If "No," the member is not entitled to a deferred vested benefit and no further action is required.
If "Yes," proceed as follows:

( ) Review with the member his eligibility for a vested benefit and the forms of payment available under the plan.
Does the member have 15 or more years of service?
( ) No   ( ) Yes
If "Yes," inform the member that pension payments may begin as early as age 55.

( ) Verify member's full name, Social Security number, and date of birth.

( ) Obtain proof of member's birthdate.

( ) Advise the member of any other company benefit programs which may be affected by his termination, e.g., medical or life insurance.

( ) Give the member a copy of the latest Summary Plan Description booklet, if he/she does not already have one.

( ) Complete *Calculation of Final Pension Worksheet.*

( ) Complete the *Deferred Vested Benefit Letter* and send it to the member with the *Application for Retirement & Election of Benefits* and the *Example of Effect of 50% Joint and Survivor Annuity.*

( ) Enter the appropriate information on *Schedule SSA* (Form 5500).

( ) Notify the secretary of the Pension committee that the member has terminated employment with a vested benefit and forward all pertinent information, forms, letters, and worksheets to the secretary. The secretary will arrange the payment of the pension when the member applies for it.

Note: It should be noted that this checklist will not apply to other pension plans. It must be tailored to conform with a plan's provisions and the employer's administrative organization.

EXHIBIT 5–2
Checklist for Retiring Employees

Name _____Soc. Sec. No. _____
Location _____Prepared by _____
Preretirement Counseling Session   (Held on _____ by _____)

A. FOR ALL RETIREMENTS
( ) Verify the employee's full name and Social Security number.
( ) Obtain proof of birthdate of the employee and his spouse and proof of marriage.
Type of Proof of Birth for employee _____
Type of Proof of Birth for spouse _____
( ) Suggest that the employee contact the Social Security Administration concerning information about Social Security and Medicare benefits at least 90 days before reaching age 65.
( ) Advise the employee of any other Company benefit programs which may be affected by retirement, e.g., medical or life insurance.
( ) Give the employee a copy of latest Summary Plan Description booklet, if he/she does not already have one.
( ) Was the employee previously covered by this or any other Company Pension Plan?
( ) Yes   ( ) No
If "Yes", advise the employee how this will affect the benefit he is going to receive and contact the Plan Administrator for instructions.
Does member intend to work past age 65?
( ) Yes   ( ) No
If "Yes", give member the *Election Form For Spouse's Death Benefit* which he/she must complete and the *Example of Effect of Spouse's Death Benefit Election on Your Ultimate Retirement Benefit.*
( ) Explain to the member the suspension of benefit information contained in the above form.
( ) Review with the employee his eligibility for benefits and the forms of payment available under the Plan.
( ) Complete a Request for Benefit Computation Form so he can be provided with an estimate of his/her pension under the payment arrangements available under the plan.
( ) Date sent to HQ _____ Date received from HQ _____
( ) Give the retiring employee an Application for Retirement & Election of Benefits and explain use of this form.
( ) Upon receiving the Benefit Estimates from HQ send the employee a Payment Information Form.
date sent _____

EXHIBIT 5–2—*Concluded*

( ) Advise the employee that federal law requires the withholding of taxes from pension payments and distributions from profit sharing and other IRS qualified plans, unless the employee elects not to have any taxes withheld. Provide employee the form for electing not to have taxes withheld or the W-4P form if they wish to have taxes withheld.

( ) Advise the employee that he may have his pension checks deposited directly into his own bank account. If he does, give the employee a Direct Deposit Agreement form.

B. PROCESSING ACTUAL RETIREMENT

( ) Obtain a completed Application for Retirement and Election of Benefits.

date received _____

( ) All proofs of birth and marriage, as applicable, are received. Has plan date of retirement, earnings, option tables, or any other data changed since the Request for Benefit form was received from HQ? Yes _____   No _____

If yes, complete a new Request for Benefit Computation Form.

If data or Plan changed, contact the Plan Administrator to determine the effect on the employee's retirement.

C. ADDITIONAL ITEMS FOR EARLY RETIREMENT

( ) Advise the employee retiring on early retirement that he/she may have the pension paid at the time of retirement or may defer receipt to a later date (but not later than age 65).

( ) If the employee intends to defer payment of early retirement pension, give him the *Election Form for Spouse's Death Benefit* which must be completed and submitted before his early retirement date, and the *Example of Effect of Spouse's Benefit Election on Your Ultimate Retirement Benefit* and explain its use.

( ) Inform the employee that he can elect to receive a larger benefit from the plan until he reaches age 65 at which time he will receive a smaller Plan benefit.

D. ADDITIONAL ITEMS FOR DISABILITY RETIREMENT

( ) Report of the Company's Examining Physician(s)

( ) Copy of Social Security Award if issued

( ) Has insurance company waived life insurance premiums because of disability?

cc: file

EXHIBIT 5–3
Checklist for Review of Benefits Administration

(This checklist summarizes the major steps to be
taken for a systematic administrative review.)

( ) Examine the various benefit programs being administered and
how the responsible personnel are organized to administer
these programs.

( ) Evaluate current systems and procedures in terms of the requirements of the plans, the fiduciary obligation of the sponsor,
and the need to meet government reporting and disclosure requirements.

( ) Review procedures to follow in administering each plan, based
on the provisions of the plan, on current administrative practices, and on availability of personnel.

( ) Review the administrative forms needed to communicate specific provisions of the plan to participants on an accurate and
timely basis.

( ) Review the operating manual for the benefits staff that incorpo-
rates all procedures and forms to be used from the time employees are hired until they are no longer employed, or until their
benefits cease. In the manual, identify individuals or groups
responsible for each aspect of administration.

( ) Review records which should be maintained to administer the
benefit programs effectively and to facilitate the calculation of
benefits. Include illustrations and instructions on maintaining
the required data and identify those items which should be
recorded at the time of hire and upon each actionable event in
the employee's working life with the company. Recommend how
long each record should be maintained.

Note: This checklist is typical only. Any checklist must be tailored to fit its specific pension plan.

A part of the complication of retirement income plans is that many different plans may be involved. Salaried employees are often covered under a single plan, whether they work at headquarters or at some other company location. Hourly employees may be covered under a number of plans depending on where they are located and/or with which union they are affiliated.

That and other complications in administering retirement income plans call for safeguards to insure that employees are informed of their benefits and that all who qualify for benefits are uniformly treated.

The administration job is so big that most of the day-to-day steps must be performed by clerical people. If they are to administer the plans uniformly, efficiently, and effectively, it is essential that they have basic written information to follow each step of the way and be well trained.

To maintain this uniformity and efficiency, many companies use detailed procedures set forth in an administrative manual that is distributed to all personnel who handle steps in the administrative process. It is detailed enough to give the administrative personnel the necessary guidelines, procedures, forms, and checklists they will need. The manual can also serve as a training tool, setting down the responsibilities of each position on the administrative staff.

To get some idea of the scope and detail that is often included in an administrative manual, see Table 5–4. Notice that this is just for a pension plan, but the process applies to other benefits plans as well.

PREPARING STEP-BY-STEP PROCEDURES

The benefits administrator always is faced with the problem of making sure that the plans are suitably, effectively, and uniformly administered throughout the organization by the various personnel assigned to the job. This can be difficult unless the administrator sets up a system to be followed by all parties to the administrative process.

Administrators must identify all the steps to be followed in administering the plan and communicate the findings to all personnel involved in the administrative process. Table 5–1 is a typical step-by-step procedure for a pension plan. The purpose of the chart is illustrative only; it will not apply to a company without some tailoring to the company's plan and organizational framework.

Procedures can, of course, be made more detailed than shown in the chart. For example, under "Upon employment or meeting membership requirements of plan," such details as these can be added to further standardize the procedure:

Based upon employee's age and date of hire, was eligibility determined correctly? Were the hours of service counted correctly?

Did the employee become a participant of the plan on the correct entry date?

TABLE 5–4
Pension Plan Administration Manual

TABLE OF CONTENTS

		Page
SECTION 1:	ACTION INDEX	1–1
	A. ERISA Reporting and Disclosure Requirements	1–1
SECTION 2:	ENROLLMENT OF NEW EMPLOYEES	2–1
	A. Procedures at Hiring	2–1
SECTION 3:	RECORD-KEEPING REQUIREMENTS	3–1
	A. Purpose of Maintaining Accurate Records	3–1
	B. Type of Records to Be Maintained	3–2
	C. Length of Record Maintenance	3–2
SECTION 4:	SERVICE	4–1
	A. Service for Eligibility for Retirement Benefit	4–1
	B. Service for Computation of Retirement Benefits	4–2
	C. Service for a Leave of Absence with the Armed Forces of the United States	4–2
	D. Service during Disability Leave	4–4
	E. Breaks in Service	4–4
	F. Reemployment	4–5
	G. Exhibit 4–1. Eligibility Employee Listing	4–9
SECTION 5:	COMPENSATION	5–1
	A. Plan Year	5–1
	B. Salesperson's Compensation	5–1
	C. Account Executive Compensation	5–2
	D. All Other Employees	5–3
	E. Final Average Compensation	5–3
SECTION 6:	TERMINATION OF EMPLOYMENT BEFORE RETIREMENT	6–1
	A. Eligibility for a Vested Benefit	6–1
	B. How to Determine If an Employee Is Vested	6–1
	C. Vested Benefit Statement	6–1
	D. Vested Benefit Payable	6–2
	E. Benefit Computation	6–3
	F. Payment of Vested Benefits	6–4
	G. Information to Be Sent to the Trustee	6–5
	H. Payment of Pension Benefits by the Trustee	6–5
	I. Examples of Manual and Machine Benefit Calculations	6–6
SECTION 7:	PRERETIREMENT COUNSELING	7–1
	A. Benefit Computation Procedures	7–1
	B. Exhibit 7–1. Listing of State Mandatory Retirement Laws	7–4
SECTION 8:	EARLY RETIREMENT	8–1
	A. Eligibility	8–1
	B. Notification to Eligible Employees	8–1
	C. Early Retirement Benefit	8–1
	D. Maximum Benefit	8–1
	E. Benefit Computation	8–2
	F. Information to Be Sent to the Trustee	8–2
	G. Examples of Manual and Machine Calculations	8–4
SECTION 9:	NORMAL RETIREMENT	9–1
	A. Eligibility	9–1
	B. Normal Pension Benefits	9–1
	C. Maximum Benefit Provision	9–1
	D. Benefit Computation	9–2
	E. Information to Be Sent to the Trustee	9–2
	F. Examples of Manual and Machine Calculations	9–4

TABLE 5–4—Concluded

SECTION 10:   DISABILITY BEFORE RETIREMENT   10–1
     A.   Disability Pension Benefit...   10–1
     B.   Benefit Computation   10–1
     C.   Information to Be Sent to the Trustee   10–1
SECTION 11:   DEATH IN ACTIVE SERVICE..   11–1
SECTION 12:   DEATH AFTER RETIREMENT   12–1
SECTION 13:   CLAIM DENIAL AND REVIEW PROCEDURE...........................   13–1
     Exhibit 13–1. Denial of Benefit.....................................   13–3
     Exhibit 13–2. Notice of Extension of Review   13–4
SECTION 14:   CHANGE IN MEMBER'S STATUS..   14–1
     A.   Change in Name   14–1
     B.   Change in Marital Status...   14–1
     C.   Misstatement of Age   14–1
     D.   Change in Address   14–2
SECTION 15:   REPORTING TO PLAN MEMBERS, PENSIONERS, AND
     BENEFICIARIES..   15–1
     A.   Penalties..   15–1
     B.   Summary Annual Plan...   15–1
     C.   Summary Plan Descriptions...   15–2
     D.   Summary of Material Modifications   15–3
     E.   Employee Benefit Statements   15–4
     F.   Documents Requested by Members................................   15–5
SECTION 16:   REPORTING TO THE SECRETARY OF LABOR   16–1
     A.   Summary Plan Description (Employee Booklet)...............   16–1
     B.   Summary of Material Modifications (Inserts)   16–1
SECTION 17:   REPORTING TO THE SECRETARY OF THE TREASURY..........   17–1
     A.   Annual Report Form 5500   17–1
     B.   Preparation and Filing Responsibilities   17–1
     C.   Records and Data   17–2
     D.   Schedule SSA—Annual Registration Statement...............   17–2
     Exhibit 17–1. 1980 Form 5500 and Instructions......................   17–4
     Exhibit 17–2. Schedule A (Insurance Information) and
     Instructions   17–5
     Exhibit 17–3. Schedule B (Actuarial Information) and
     Instructions   17–6
     Exhibit 17–4. Schedule SSA and Instructions........................   17–7
SECTION 18:   GOVERNMENT REQUIREMENTS REGARDING REPORTABLE
     EVENTS   18–1
SECTION 19:   FILING FOR IRS DETERMINATION   19–1
     A.   Submission of Forms to the IRS   19–1
     B.   Notification to Interested Parties.....................................   19–1
     Exhibit 19–1. Form 5300 and Instructions   19–2
     Exhibit 19–2. Form 5302 (Employee Census) and Instructions   19–3
     Exhibit 19–3. Form 5303 and Instructions   19–4
EXHIBITS
PLAN DOCUMENT
SUMMARY PLAN DESCRIPTION

Was the employee notified that he/she became a participant of the plan?

Did the employee receive a Summary Plan Description of the plan within 90 days?

Were the plan records updated to reflect when the employee became a plan participant?

THE IMPORTANCE OF RECORDS

One of the most important aspects of the administration of a pension plan is keeping records. And it has become much more essential since ERISA created new rules for crediting service.

Before ERISA, most companies measured service from the date of hire to the date of termination. Some companies recorded hours for certain employees including union members. Part-time employees who worked less than 20 hours a week or five months a year could be excluded from plans and therefore from record-keeping for pension purposes.

The ERISA created minimum participation standards as to age and service for employees joining a pension plan. A company could set a waiting period of three years or a one-year waiting period with an age-25 requirement. To exclude part-time employees, a company had to use the new ERISA hours-of-service rules. This meant that the company had to actually record hours in accordance with detailed Department of Labor regulations or use certain equivalency methods.

So record-keeping has become more complicated and more essential than ever before, and more attention must be devoted to it to be sure to satisfy ERISA regulations for determining length of service on which to base eligibility, vesting, and ultimately the size of pension benefits. To give you an idea of the broad scope of ERISA requirements for keeping records, see the listing in Table 5–5.

The ERISA rules are many and complex, covering elapsed time of service, hours of service, and breaks in service. There are also rules to determine eligibility, vesting, and the accrual of benefits. Each company must identify the types of records it needs to maintain in order to effectively administer its benefit programs and to facilitate the calculation of employee benefits.

TABLE 5–5
Record-Keeping Requirements

A. *General*

The Employee Retirement Income Security Act (ERISA) requires that employers keep records "sufficient to determine the benefits due or which may become due to . . . employees." This will require permanent records on all employees, past and present, including those who terminate employment.

B. *Purpose for Maintaining Accurate Records*

Proper maintenance of accurate pension records are needed to:

1. Accurately calculate the service for each employee.
2. Administer the plans as they relate to:
   a. Eligibility for membership.
   b. Eligibility for death benefit payable to spouse.
   c. Eligibility for and computation of vested pension benefits.
   d. Eligibility for and computation of early pension benefits.
   e. Eligibility for and computation of disability pension benefits.
   f. Computation of normal pension benefits.
   g. Service bridging of rehired employees.
3. Respond to employees' written request for accrued benefit calculations within the 30-day limit established by ERISA.
4. Calculate the amount of nonforfeitable accrued benefit earned by vested members who terminate employment.
5. Make the necessary reports to government agencies.
6. Provide plan actuary with accurate membership and service information for plan evaluation purposes.

C. *Type of Records to Be Maintained*

The benefits data center is responsible for maintaining the following records.

1. Employee name and address.
2. Company location.
3. Social Security number.
4. Sex.
5. Date of birth.
6. Marital status.
7. Date of marriage.
8. Birth date of spouse.
9. Dates of employment, reemployment, and transfer.
10. Beneficiary:
    a. Name and address.
    b. Social Security number.
    c. Sex.
    d. Date of birth.
    e. Relationship to member.
    f. Date of designation of beneficiary.
11. Period of, and reason for, absences.
12. Normal retirement date.
13. Early retirement eligibility date.
14. Vesting eligibility date.
15. Termination dates.

TABLE 5–5—Concluded

16. Reason for termination.
17. Compensation.
18. Earnings history.

D. *Length of Record Maintenance*

ERISA requires that all records used to meet reporting and disclosure requirement and ". . . which will provide in sufficient detail the necessary basic information and data from which the documents thus required may be verified, explained, or clarified, and checked for accuracy and completeness, and shall include vouchers, worksheets, receipts, and applicable resolutions . . ." will be maintained for a minimum of *six years*.

Based on this requirement, the following purge procedures may generally be applied to the maintenance of records:

1. Information used to prepare reports to the Secretary of Labor and Secretary of Treasury—six years after reports are made.
2. Vested terminated employees—five years after final benefit payment to member and/or spouse.
3. Nonvested terminated employees—after the terminated employee is beyond the mandatory retirement age in the plan.
4. Retired employees or survivors receiving benefits—five years after final benefit payment to member and/or beneficiary.

KEEPING PARTICIPANTS INFORMED

An important element in the success of pension plans (as well as other employee benefit plans) is the communication of information to employees. As a matter of fact, many forms of communication are required by ERISA, as outlined in the accompanying table.

Forms and form letters are among the important means of keeping employees informed about their retirement income plans. They serve as a reliable backup to the verbal communications and help eliminate misconceptions. Forms also offer an opportunity for employees to request information about the provisions of their retirement plans so they can make informed decisions about the payment options best suited to their needs.

All information forms should be carefully reviewed to make sure they properly conform with the detailed provisions of the retirement plans. Then they should be incorporated into the administrative manual to serve as a continuing reference for administrative personnel.

KEEPING GOVERNMENT INFORMED

In addition to the requirements for keeping employees informed about retirement income plans, there are many requirements for keeping various government agencies informed. A summary of the many requirements is presented in Table 5–3.

KEEPING CALCULATION METHODS UP TO DATE

Methods of calculating pension benefits must be kept up-to-date, so they will be done efficiently, at the right time, and in compliance with government regulations. Changes in the Social Security Act and other government requirements often have an impact on the procedures for calculating benefits.

Compensation records and service records should also be reviewed periodically to make sure they are being maintained to conform with the provisions of the pension plan and with government regulations.

Perhaps the calculation process can be speeded up and made more cost effective by the use of computers with remote terminals or by some alternate automation process.

And More

There are many other steps in the administration process for retirement income plans as outlined in the Step-by-Step Procedure. It is necessary to:

- Identify and track the coming retirees.
- Handle election of benefit options and rights.
- Notify employees of preretirement joint and survivor coverage.
- Deal with employees who work beyond normal retirement age as well as those who separate before retirement and those who rejoin the company.
- Follow up with retirees concerning benefit payments.
- Follow through concerning payments after the death of an employee.

CHECKLISTS CAN HELP

Throughout the process of administering pension plans, many companies make effective use of checklists to better control the financial and personnel aspects of the process. See the examples of two typical checklists: one to use for terminating employees, one to use when an employee is retiring. In each case, the list serves as a reminder of the detailed steps that must be taken to properly administer an important aspect of a pension plan.

These checklists should be incorporated in the administrative manual, which can also explain each person's role in filling out the checklists.

REVIEWING THE ADMINISTRATIVE PROCESS

After the administrative function has been organized, and after all the procedures have been established and a manual prepared and distributed, all the personnel trained, and necessary checklists developed and put to use—after all this, there is still more.

To maintain vital and effective administration of a pension plan, the administrative process must be regularly reviewed to make sure it is continuously carried out as intended.

Some Questions to Ask

In the process of reviewing administrative procedures there are many questions to be asked. Here are some of them:

1. Is the organization of the benefits staff suitable to handle the changing pattern of benefits administration effectively?
2. Are plan documents well understood by those administering the plan?
3. Is the administrative staff adequate to handle the job?
4. Have areas of responsibility been appropriately delegated?
5. Are the manuals up to date?
6. Is full advantage being taken of computerized systems?
7. Are records being properly kept to meet internal needs as well as government requirements?
8. Are there suitable controls to assure that benefit payments are in the right amount and are paid in accordance with the plan documents?
9. Do participants receive the information they need and the information required by the government?
10. Is the reporting to the government agencies properly and efficiently handled?
11. Is there a procedure in force to make sure the plans are periodi-

cally reviewed and modified in keeping with changing needs and with changes in legal requirements?

Again, checklists are helpful as a guide for the personnel assigned to keep tabs on the effectiveness and the suitability of the plans.

A typical general checklist for reviewing the administrative process is shown here.

We usually find that the careful scrutiny of an administrative review can provide a number of benefits, such as:

Higher efficiency and lower costs in administering the plan.

Improved control over operations, procedures, work flow, quality, and service. As a result, employees have a greater appreciation of the value of the programs being offered to them.

A realignment of administrative work functions to better correspond with operating requirements.

An improvement in the capability of the staff to administer the plan.

LOOKING AHEAD

As we look ahead to the future, we can see even more reason for establishing orderly and effective administration of benefits. Among the added complications in the future may well be such matters as accelerated vesting, portability of pensions, required accrual of benefits after age 65, and indexing of benefits.

Furthermore, if the recent past is any guide, we can expect even more government regulation, more careful scrutiny by auditors (both internal and external), more interest in benefits administration by shareholders and investors generally, added bargaining pressure from unions, and increasing concern by participants and beneficiaries.

So, to steer an effective administrative course, avoiding the cost of incorrect benefit payments, the loss of taxes, and the injured morale of employees, a careful, thorough, and orderly approach to benefits administration is essential.

CHAPTER 6

COMMUNICATIONS

---

*By William O. Shearer
and Ernest Griffes*

EFFECTIVE BENEFITS COMMUNICATION
PLANNING
PRODUCTION
IMPLEMENTATION
EVALUATION
FUTURE TRENDS
BENEFITS STATEMENTS
SOCIAL SECURITY BENEFITS STATEMENT
FINANCIAL EDUCATION

An effective employee benefits program requires effective employee communication. Period.

At first, that statement may sound a little too black and white. But think about it a moment. It really is nothing more than common sense, not to mention good business sense. For even the best designed, most comprehensive benefits package is of little value to the employer—or for that matter, to the employee—if the employees don't realize what they are receiving. And you can bet they won't, unless you tell them—on an ongoing basis and in terms they can understand and appreciate. Let's face it, most people don't think much about their benefits—that is, until they need a benefit or think another employer offers better benefits.

Your benefits program represents a substantial investment. It only makes sense to get the most for that investment. And the only way you can do that is by communicating—by making every effort to see that your employees not only know about and understand their benefits, but appreciate their value.

Indeed, in today's business environment, where productivity and motivation have become so vital to survival, the question is no longer whether to communicate with employees but how to communicate more effectively. That is what this chapter is all about.

EFFECTIVE BENEFITS COMMUNICATION

The key word here is *effective*. Effective benefits communication is more than just distributing a summary plan description (SPD) or meeting the minimum communication requirements of the Employee Retirement Income Security Act (ERISA). It's also more than simply spending money—even a lot of money—on brochures, slide shows, or other communication tools. Why? Because effective benefits communication—like any other form of employee communication—is not an event or a product, but a process . . . an ongoing process.

First, there's *planning*. What do you want to say, why, and to whom? What are your objectives, your priorities? How are you going to go about it? What is your strategy? What image do you want to portray? What media should you use? What about timing? How much money can you spend? And don't forget, how are you going to measure your success?

Next comes *production*. This is where you "package" your message—where you write, design, and print your brochure; script, photograph, and produce your audiovisual; plan, organize, and prepare your meeting. The message comes first, but proper packaging is crucial to getting that message across—to the right people, at the right time, at the right price.

Then comes *implementation*. Having the right communication tools and the right packaging is important. But unless used effectively, even the best written brochure, most professionally produced audiovisual, or most organized meeting will do little real communicating. For a communication tool is just that: a tool, a means to an end, not an end in itself. It's not the tool, but how well the tool is used that counts.

Finally, there's *evaluation*. How did you do? Did you achieve your goals? What worked? What didn't? Why? What should you change?

And that brings you back to planning. For effective employee communication, remember, is an ongoing process. It is not something you can turn on and off to suit you—not if you expect your employees to believe what you have to say. Without credibility, the tools and techniques of communication are just so much wasted effort.

One other point. When it comes to their benefits, employees basically only want to know two things:

"What do I get?"

"How do I get it?"

That's just normal human nature. But it's an important fact to keep in mind as you plan, produce, implement, and evaluate your benefits communication program. Because the success or failure of your effort really boils down to how effectively you answer those two key questions.

OK, enough introduction. Now, let's look at this communication process in more detail and in terms more specific to communicating employee benefits.

PLANNING

Know Your Product

An effective benefits communication program starts with knowing your product—your benefits package. What are its strengths and weaknesses from both the employer's and employees' points of view? How is it likely to change? Why is it designed the way it is? What is your benefits philosophy? What are the real reasons behind your benefits—to stay competitive in your industry? To keep the union out? To attract and retain top talent? What? Be candid and honest in this evaluation. For only then can you design a realistic communications strategy, one that will reinforce your basic benefit goals. But beware: Do not expect a razzle-dazzle communications effort to substitute for or cover up a deficient or poorly designed benefits program. It simply won't work. And if you try, you'll do more harm than good.

Know Your Audience

Next, you must know your audience—your employees. Who are they? What are their interests, needs, and concerns?

The first question is relatively easy to answer. It's mainly a matter of collecting demographic data—age, sex, education, marital status, income, job type, length of service, geographic location—whatever audience breakdown will help you focus your communication efforts and better understand your audience's interests, needs, and concerns.

The second question is more difficult to answer. Here, you must determine not only what your employees *actually* know about their benefits, but what they *think* they know and what they *want* to know. You must also assess how they feel about their benefits—good, bad or indifferent, for how they perceive the value of their benefits (right or wrong) is the *reality* with which you must deal (and try to mold) in your communication efforts.

How you go about answering these questions could be a whole book in itself. Surveys, focus groups, and communication committees are three of the most frequently used methods, and there are many "variations on a theme" within these approaches to audience profiling. The point here is simply that you cannot have effective benefits communication without first knowing who you are talking to and what their interests are. Only by presenting your message in terms your audience can understand and appreciate can you even hope to have them listen to what you have to say.

Know Your Objectives and Set Priorities

The next step is to clearly identify your objectives and set priorities. Don't confuse objective with message. You must know what you hope to accomplish (objective) before you can decide what you need to say (message) and how best to say it (strategy and media).

The basic purpose of benefits communication is to help acheive the goals of the benefits program. Typical communication objectives might be to attract good employees; boost employee morale; reduce turnover; increase job satisfaction; motivate employees; increase employee awareness, understanding, and appreciation of benefits; promote more cost-effective use of benefits; and the list could go on. On a more specific level, however, you should express your objectives in terms of what you want your target audience to do, or not do, think or not think in response to a given communication.

Determine Your Strategy

You know your product. You've defined your audience. You've identified your objectives and set priorities. Now, it's time to consider strategy. What image do you want to convey? What style or tone should you use? Answers to these questions will depend largely on the philosophy behind your benefits program and your organization's general character and management style.

Define Your Message

Now—in light of your audience profile, your objectives, and the strategy you've chosen—you are ready to define your message. Specifically, what do you want to say? What information or ideas do you need to get across to meet your objectives? Actually, if you've set clear objectives and taken a good hard look at your target audience, your message should be fairly self-evident.

Select Your Media

The big question is: How you are going to get your message across? You must decide what communication tools (media) you are going to use, how you are going to use them, when, and how often.

You could, of course, simply publish a summary plan description that meets the minimum legal requirements and let it go at that. But that's not communicating. That's merely reacting. Effective benefits communication requires:

A basic reference source.

Regular and ongoing communications.

Special-purpose communications.

Person-to-person contact.

The *basic reference source* might be your SPDs, a handbook, a booklet package, or individual booklets. Whatever the format, its purpose is to provide a single place where employees can go to look up just about everything they need to know about their benefits.

You need *regular and ongoing communications* to keep in touch with your employees and to provide the continuity and repetition so necessary for successful communication. Remember, effective benefits communication is not a single-salvo proposition, but an ongoing effort to keep employees apprised of their benefits.

You have a number of communication tools at your disposal to do this. If you have an internal magazine, for example, consider doing a regular feature on benefits. Most company magazine editors are hungry for good editorial material, and it's relatively easy to prepare a question-and-answer-type column—especially if you're keeping a file on typically asked questions.

Another effective tool for ongoing communication is a simple benefits bulletin, published on a regular basis and on benefits-program letterhead. You can use such a bulletin to expand on particularly complex or sensitive benefit issues, such as making employees wiser consumers of health care or more aware of the advantages of a second opinion on surgery. But keep your bulletin brief and to the point. It should contain only short, easy-to-digest messages about topics of current interest.

Other media to consider include pay-envelope stuffers, poster campaigns, regular employee meetings, and one of the best benefits communication tools of all: the personal computerized benefits statement. The annual benefits statement undoubtedly is the single most effective communication tool for relating a person's benefits to his or her individual needs and circumstances. Its physical presence alone provides tangible evidence of the employer's commitment to the employee's well-being. And in doing so, the benefit statement can be an extremely powerful tool for shaping the employee's attitudes not only toward benefits, but toward the employer and employment itself.

Special-purpose communications, as the name suggests, are needed to handle special problems—and opportunities—in benefits communication. For example, you may want to develop a slide show and collateral print material to announce and explain major benefit-plan changes. Or you may need special materials for use in employee orientation, recruitment, preretirement counseling, or supervisory training. Employee attitude surveys are another type of special-purpose communication.

With a little preplanning, you can use special-purpose communications to personalize the benefits program and often at very little cost. For instance, when an employee brings a new baby home, send a combination congratulatory letter and update of his or her revised coverages and options as a result of the new arrival. Similarly, you might want to send a letter to employees that have just become vested in the pension plan, notifying them of their eligibility and reminding them of what it will mean to them when they retire.

Finally, you need *person-to-person contact.* All the modern techniques and technologies of communication are wonderful and should be exploited to the fullest by the benefits communicator. But they can never replace the most effective—and difficult—communications vehicle of all: personal communication directly between real people.

Why is this type of communication so difficult? Because other types of communication generally move in a single line from your office to your intended audience. How direct this line is and how sharp or fuzzy, of course, depends on the overall quality of your efforts. But person-to-person contact has many lines of communication. Your employees quite rightly will discuss their questions and concerns among friends and co-workers. Thus, prejudices and misunderstandings on the part of a few can quickly spread throughout the entire group. It is important, therefore, to establish your own avenues of person-to-person contact—both to keep tabs on what employees are thinking and to clear up any confusion or misunderstandings that may arise.

How can you do this? Primarily, by recognizing the importance of having well-informed managers and supervisors with positive attitudes toward the benefits program. These are the people, after all, that deal with employees' day-to-day benefit questions and concerns.

Keep them informed. How? Perhaps by conducting periodic benefits workshops or by providing them with special benefits binders containing the information they need to answer their employees' questions—accurately.

In addition, certain communication devices lend themselves particularly well to fostering one-on-one communication. The ordinary telephone is a prime example. If practical, set up a benefits hotline and include the number in all benefit communications. Equally important, encourage employees to use the number to ask their questions and express their concerns. The overhead projector and flip chart are other examples. They may seem rather clunky and old fashioned, but they work, they are generally quite economical, and they require face-to-face communication.

The point, again, is that effective benefits communication requires the use of more than one medium. Bulletins, brochures, basic reference sources, audiovisual presentations, posters, magazine articles, telephone hotlines—they all have their place. Examine them all. Weigh their value in relation to your audience, objectives, and message. Then choose the mix that's most appropriate for your program, schedule, and budget.

Establish a Schedule and Budget

How much time and money you need for benefits communication depends on your objectives and the number and complexity of communication tools needed to meet those objectives. Only by having a clear understanding of the goals to be achieved and methods to be used can you determine a realistic schedule and an adequate budget.

Start by examining your existing communication efforts. How much time and money are you now spending on communicating benefits? How is it being spent? In light of current objectives, can existing communication dollars be used more effectively? You really can't lose in this type of evaluation. At the very least, you will establish a sound basis for why you need more time or a larger budget—and in terms directly related to stated objectives.

Another approach is to estimate how much your organization spends on employee benefits and then use a percentage of that figure as the basis for your communications budget. As a general rule of thumb, many benefits experts consider 2 to 3 percent of total benefits cost to be a reasonable amount to devote to communicating. Actually, when you consider the sizable investment your benefits package represents and the fact that effective communication is the only practical way to gain a return on that investment, the cost of a benefits communication program is quite nominal.

Another important point. The time to plan and budget for communications is right up front—when you are designing your benefits program. Benefits communication deserves the same thoughtful preparation and attention that goes into benefits planning itself. Indeed, how you are going to communicate the benefits to employees should be a major selling point in getting management to buy the benefits program in the first place.

Pick a Measuring Stick

Finally, how will you know if your communications program is working? Even if you've conscientiously analyzed your audience, defined clear messages to meet clear objectives, and carefully chosen your communication tools—you can't simply assume that your message will get across—that your communications program will work the way you planned. You must have a predetermined "measuring stick" with which to monitor your progress and measure your success. More on this later.

PRODUCTION

Fight the temptation to jump too quickly into producing communication tools—at the expense of proper planning. It's a natural tendency. After all, you can point to a brochure and say, "See, I've done my job, I'm communicating.'' But of course, you're not. You're mistaking the tool for what the tool is supposed to do. Or perhaps you're simply being lazy. Communication planning is not that easy.

Content

When you *are ready* to start producing your communication tools, however, the first thing to consider is content. Here, there are two general rules:

Keep it simple.

Make it specific.

How many times have you read or listened to benefits material that sounds like it was written by a benefits expert for a benefits expert, even though the intended audience supposedly was the employee? Right. It doesn't work.

To get your message across, use simple, easy-to-understand language, with no jargon or legal terms. Also, don't be tempted to try to cover up a weak spot in your benefits package by resorting to formal language. That trick rarely fools anybody. More often it backfires by raising suspicions that might not otherwise have been there. And once you've lost credibility with your audience, it takes a long time and an awful lot of effort to earn it back again.

You'll also be more effective in getting your message across if you're specific—not only in terms of the information you present, but in how well you organize and relate that information to the employee's interests, needs, and concerns. Take your basic reference source, for example. You could organize it strictly according to benefit plan. But it would be more effective if organized from the employee's point of view; that is, if it were organized to answer the questions: ''What do I get? And how do I get it?''

More specifically, organize your basic reference source by event; that is, to answer the questions: ''What if I get sick? Die? Become disabled? Retire?'' Following this events approach, you would divide your reference source into the following major sections:

Health care.
  Medical.
  Dental.
Death.
  Group life.

Supplemental life.
Accidental death and dismemberment.
Business travel accident.
Spouse's benefit.
Disability.
Salary continuance.
Short-term disability.
Long-term disability.
Retirement.
Pension.
Capital accumulation.
ERISA.
Legally required information.

Further, you would need to answer the following questions for each benefit plan within each event:

1. What are the eligibility requirements?
2. How do I enroll?
3. What does it cost?
4. When does coverage start?
5. What does the plan cover?
6. What doesn't the plan cover?
7. How do I apply for benefits?
8. When or under what circumstances does coverage end?
9. Can I convert coverage? How?

Packaging

People say: "Never judge a book by its cover." But we all do. Indeed, our perception of the adequacy of a program or product quite often is heavily influenced by the texture, design, and color of the communication materials about it. Your benefits program is no exception. So recognize that fact and take advantage of it.

Legally, you could produce nothing more than photocopies or mimeographed material. But is that really the kind of image you want to portray? Neither do you have to go to the other extreme of super sophisticated, super expensive communication tools. That can be just as harmful—prompting employees to ask why so much money is being spent on fancy advertising instead of better benefits.

There is a middle ground. And the way to find it—surprise, surprise—is to know your audience, your objectives, and your priorities. Ugh! More planning? Yes.

By this time, you should have identified your communication objectives and determined the relative importance of each. You should also have decided on the media you want to use. But you're not done planning quite yet.

For each communication tool you're considering, list all of the requirements for meeting your objectives. Brainstorm. List everything you think should be in the final product. List all factors you think will or should affect production. Not editorial content, but production requirements and considerations. Not *what* you're going to write, for example, but who's going to write it. What can be done in-house? What will have to be done outside? The length and detail of this list will depend on how directly you or your staff will be involved in the actual production. The more directly involved, the longer and more detailed the list.

Now divide your list in two by looking at each requirement and deciding if it is critical to the success of the project or something that would be nice but could be sacrificed. Then prioritize each of these sublists in descending order of importance to meeting your communication objectives.

At last, you're ready to set production goals and allocate budget, time, and personnel. Having established specific priorities, you now know where your emphasis must be and where cuts can be made if necessary.

The worst mistake you can make is to not go through at least some kind of preproduction goal- and priority-setting exercise. And don't think you can make these kind of decisions "as you go." That's not only foolhardy, you can bet it will cost you dearly in production problems and wasted time and money.

Now before moving on to a discussion of *implementation,* consider some other production tips.

First, there's a lot of free advice out there, but you have to ask for it. Start at home—in your own public information or advertising departments, for example. Printers and graphic designers also can provide information and suggestions that can improve your product as well as save you time and money. But you must be specific in your questions and not make a pest of yourself.

Second, collect samples. Study your competition. Always be on the lookout for communication tools that you think work. Keep a file and then use these samples when explaining your needs and wants to a writer, designer, or printer. *Show* them what you mean.

Finally, beware of false economies. Simply saving money is not the same as being cost-effective. Packaging your message is important. It can make the difference in whether or not your audience picks up and reads your brochure or stays awake during your slide show. And if they don't, you really haven't been cost-effective no matter how much you saved on production.

IMPLEMENTATION

Here, we're basically talking about two things: training and follow-through.

You have to do more than just plan and produce good communication tools. A tool, if you recall, is only as good as how well it is used. And for communication tools, that means how effectively they are used in opening up and maintaining channels of ongoing, two-way communication with employees. That often takes training; training in how to run a meeting, how to write clearly, how to be a better listener, how to be a better speaker, how to run a slide projector—you name it.

Follow-through simply means doing what you say you're going to do and doing it well. And that often boils down to paying attention to details. An example: You say you're going to establish a benefits hotline. Do it. Then make sure you've taken adequate steps to tell people about it and, equally important, that you've encouraged them to use it. But that's not all. Have you made sure the people manning the telephone know what they're talking about? If they don't know an answer, do they know how to find one? Do they understand and agree with the reason behind the hotline? Are they truly interested in providing helpful, accurate answers? Do they have or have they been trained in good telephone manners? Granted, some of these concerns may seem a bit minor, but it only takes one "less-than-positive" telephone response or goofed-up answer to destroy the project's credibility with a caller. What's more, you know that person is going to spread the word.

Another example: There's no better way to get a person's attention than putting his or her name on a sealed envelope and mailing it. Your mailing, however, will only be as good as your address list. If the list is inaccurate, incomplete, and out of date, much of your hard work and good intention (not to metion postage) will wind up in the dead-letter office or back on your desk. Pay attention to detail. Assign someone reliable to maintain your mailing list.

The examples could go on, but I think the point is made. Your communication program will only be effective if it is implemented well. Too many overlooked details, too many cases of "I just assumed," and too many instances of not knowing (or perhaps not caring) how to use communication tools effectively will spell failure for what otherwise should and would have been a successful program.

EVALUATION

This is where you step back and use that measuring stick you identified earlier to see how you've done . . . to see what worked, what didn't, and why? Be advised: Not everything will work as well as you expect no matter how well-planned and executed it may have been. Communication means dealing with people, and dealing with people is not by any stretch of the imagination an exact science. That's why your communications program must have a built-in evaluation system—a way of keeping tabs on whether or not your message is getting through and, if not, what you must do to remedy the situation.

Actually, you'll want to use several different measuring sticks— some formal, such as employee attitude surveys; others informal, such as keeping track of the number and types of inquiries you receive and the areas in which they are generated. Effective mechanisms for this latter type of feedback are the benefits hotline and a self-addressed, postage-paid reply card, which employees can use to ask questions. The front-line supervisor can also be an invaluable conduit to the interests, needs, and concerns of employees.

An important point to remember here is that the more people know, the more they generally want to know. So don't judge your communications program a success because you haven't received a lot of questions from employees. This doesn't mean they understand the program. More likely, it means they're totally confused by it. Understanding benefits will generate lots of *specific* questions. A few *general* questions, on the other hand, suggests inadequate communication. And a large number of similar questions indicates a high level of awareness but a correspondingly low level of comprehension.

The main point, again: Communication is a two-way process—the sending and receiving of information. If your benefits communication program is one-way only—that is, you're sending out information, but don't have any idea whether or not it's being received—you're just wasting your time, money, and effort.

FUTURE TRENDS IN BENEFIT COMMUNICATIONS*

The two essential activities of communications about benefits are (1) dissemination to the employees of factual information about their benefit entitlements and (2) explanation of that information so that the employees understand what it means to them.

Future trends in benefit communications focus on the delivery systems that facilitate accomplishing these two essential activities.

Communications techniques for *providing* factual information to employees increasingly are dominated by the application of data processing and computer technology. Data processing and electronic information display devices are the ideal vehicles for easily and efficiently storing data about an employee, processing that data to calculate benefit entitlements, and then displaying the results for review.

Communication techniques for *explaining* the factual information will increasingly utilize face-to-face interaction between the employee and communications specialists who understand the benefit plans. The underlying trend among employees for more personalized and individualized attention requires that plan sponsors develop the means for providing both easy access to personalized interaction in benefit communications and a broader spectrum of information about benefits and financial planning.

The future of benefit communications focuses on the way that plan sponsors bring together these two essential activities.

The Benefit Information Center, the benefit communications vehicle of the future, is a centralized communications operation, staffed by persons completely knowledgeable in all the details of every benefit plan and personnel policy, who have access at their work location to all the information stored in the data processing facilities. As a result they bring together the dissemination of factual information and the opportunity for personalized interaction with the employee.

Also available thru this communications center will be information

---

* The remainder of this chapter was written by Ernest Griffes.

for employees on personal financial planning and many other aspects of money management, such as individual retirement accounts, IRA rollovers, credit union facilities, preparing a will, estate planning, the process of investing in the market, and so on. The communications specialists staffing the operation will be carefully trained in providing full information to employees without straying into the legal trap of "giving advice."

The centralization of the communications process will provide both the employer and employee several advantages. For the employee it will provide access to personal interaction with staff who can bring together all the various aspects of benefits information at one time and in one place, as compared to the traditional situation in which an employee must speak to one benefit staff member about medical plan questions, another benefit staff member about pension plan questions, a third about death benefit questions, and so on. The centralized operation will also assure an employee that when he or she calls with a question someone will be there to respond, as compared to the common situation in which an employee calls and the benefit staff member who can respond is on the phone, out to lunch, or out sick.

For the employer there are even more advantages. There is assurance that the information being given to employees is accurate and is being explained by well-trained and knowledgeable employees, so that the risk of giving advice or bad information is greatly reduced. The productivity of both the benefits staff and the employee seeking information can be improved—the benefits staff can concentrate on their work free from distracting calls, and the inquiring employee can have questions answered right away instead of having to make several calls or visits to get an answer.

Equally important is the ability through an electronic network to assure that employees in work locations distant from the main location get accurate information, as compared to the common situation in which such distant employees are often served on benefit questions by a local personnel assistant who has many duties besides benefits and often does not have current or accurate information about the employee or the benefit plans.

At the Benefit Information Center employees will be able to directly access the data base of their own benefit information in an atmosphere of privacy, calling up for electronic display their record on various benefit plans, projecting based on their own plans, for example, pension benefits at various ages, checking on the status of a medical claim that has been filed, checking on their beneficiary designations, and so on. And at the press of a button they will be able to produce a hard copy of the information to take with them.

Audiovisual programs will be available that explain various benefit plans so an employee can call up, for example, a 10-minute film on the employee savings plan, what the process is for creating a will, or how the employee assistance program can help them deal with an alcoholic spouse.

All the written communications about the benefit plans will be available at the Benefits Information Center, as well as all the forms necessary in the administration of the plans—so the employees will need to go to only one place to get all the information they want and need.

Benefit communications in the past have been characterized by very imaginative applications in written and audiovisual materials but often ineffective systems for interaction with the benefits staff on individual personal questions.

In the future, communications specialists will have available an entire new vehicle in addition to written and audiovisual aids—the virtually unlimited capabilities of data processing and electronic display. The possibilities are very exciting for using these new tools in imaginative communications and at the same time satisfying employee desires for individual attention.

BENEFIT STATEMENTS

The Annual Benefit Statement has become the primary means of employer efforts to organize and present individual employee benefit information in a comprehensive yet easily understood way. The benefit statement brings together, in one place, essential information about all of the benefits coverage for the individual employees and their dependents.

Sometimes it also includes information about compensation and bonuses paid during the period covered by the statement, as well as estimates of the cost of employee benefits for the individual. When utilized in this manner it becomes the ultimate in communicating total compensation.

Through the courtesy of Bank of America NT & SA, the "Personal Compensation Statement" presented to employees is reproduced in the following pages. This statement presents an excellent example of how to communicate total compensation in a way that secures maximum employee understanding of their benefits. This statement was produced for

Bank of America NT & SA by David M. Gladstone of Hazlehurst & Associates.

Mr. Gladstone offers the following insights into the complexities of production of such a benefits statement:

The production of an annual employee benefit statement or total compensation statement involves the following steps:

1. *Design of the Statement.*   The statement design should be compatible with the plan sponsor's benefits logo and benefits communication philosophy. It should cover all areas of benefits and compensation provided by the plan sponsor in order to provide employees with an accurate conception of their total compensation.

2. *Transmittal of Data and Development of a Comprehensive Database.*   Data is provided on magnetic tape, floppy disk and/or hard copy. The data is merged into a comprehensive generic database. The format of the database allows flexible manipulation and query capabilities for the current year and subsequent years.

3. *Development of Detailed Set of Data Audit Specifications.*   Every input data field in the database must be audited. Detailed audit specifications are developed which list specific values or a range of potential values, as well as any special data auditing applicable to the particular statement being developed. Once all the finalized data has been provided, it is subjected to an audit and reconciled prior to statement production.

4. *Development of a Comprehensive Statement Methodology.*   The methodology describes in detail what will be done with each data item, and how and where it will be displayed on the statement, including special messages applicable to, for example, employees not eligible for a particular benefit or employees who have elected not to participate in a specific benefit program. This methodology forms the set of guidelines used for checking that all calculations and interpretations used in the statement have been performed according to the plan sponsor's specifications.

5. *Data Testing.*   In addition to data testing for audit specifications, the data and calculations are also sampled by the plan sponsor selecting a crossection of employees with different characteristics for producing test statements prior to actual production of the statements for all employees.

6. *Production Process.* During the actual computer/laser printing of the personalized information on the statements, quality checking is performed to make certain that the preprinted material lines up with the computer printing, that there are no ink smudges on statements developed during the preprinting process, and many other checks to ensure the quality of the statements. When all the statements are printed and checked for accuracy and quality, then they are assembled, saddle stitched or stapled, folded, stuffed and finally mailed to the individual employees.

The complexties described by Mr. Gladstone make it clear that producing a benefit statement is not an easy task. The consequences of even a simple error are of considerable magnitude. A simple error could destroy much of the value of all of the useful and correct information contained in an individual's statement. Further, incorrect information, in the current litigious environment, could become the basis for some claim to the benefits that are incorrectly set forth in a benefit statement.

SOCIAL SECURITY BENEFIT STATEMENTS

In 1988 the Social Security Administration began a new benefit statement process, recognizing that it too, like corporate benefit plan sponsors, must undertake extensive communciation efforts if there is to be real understanding and appreciation of the benefits being provided for participants.

The new statement is titled Personal Earnings and Benefit Estimate Statement. A mock-up example is reproduced in the following pages. Also reproduced for comparison is an example of the Statement of Earnings that the Social Security Administration provided for decades prior to commencement of the new statement, in response to requests for a statement of benefit entitlements.

The difference is dramatic. In the past only a list of annual earnings was reported. To compute an estimate of their benefit, an individual was required to go through all the mathematical calculations and intricacies of the social security laws.

Now the estimated benefit is clearly stated in terms that can be easily understood. Given the massive data base of information that the Social Security Administration must work with, clearly it is only the advent of modern data processing technology that has finally made it possible to communicate an individual's estimated benefits in an understandable manner.

FIGURE 6–1

Your Compensation
Package

This Personal Compensation Statement
Was Prepared Especially For: **TAILOR D SAMPLE**

Social Security Number: **123-45-6789**

Your Compensation Package

```
$63,000 ANNUAL SALARY RATE
 13,000 PIP INCENTIVE AWARD RECEIVED IN 1988
  5,000 AMIP AWARD RECEIVED IN 1988
----------
```
$81,000 Cash Compensation
 14,098 Estimated BankAmerica Cost of Your Benefits

$95,098 Your Compensation Package

The information presented in this statement is based on personnel
data as of **DECEMBER 31, 1988.**

AS OF DECEMBER 31, 1988, YOUR DEFERRED COMPENSATION
BALANCE WITH ACCUMULATED INTEREST, AMOUNTED TO
$153,000.00. THE COMPONENTS OF YOUR BALANCE ARE AS
FOLLOWS: AMIP DEFERRALS $100,000.00 AND BASE SALARY
DEFERRALS $53,000.00.

YOU ARE ENTITLED TO A FINANCIAL COUNSELING ALLOWANCE
TO DEVELOP AND MAINTAIN A COMPREHENSIVE PERSONAL
FINANCIAL PLAN. AS OF DECEMBER 31, 1988, YOUR ACCUM-
ULATED UNUSED ALLOWANCE AMOUNTED TO $4,000. IF YOU
HAVE ANY QUESTIONS, PLEASE CONTACT EXECUTIVE PROGRAMS
AT 622-2946.

TAILOR D SAMPLE
HAZLEHURST AND ASSOCIATES
BELLEVUE, WA 98004

FIGURE 6–1—*Continued*

Health Care
Benefits

BankAmerica's health care program is flexible enough to let you select the medical, dental, and vision care coverage that best fits your needs. In general, you may choose from two kinds of health care plans:

- Fee-for-service plans such as the BA Medical Plan, and
- Prepaid plans such as those sponsored by a "health maintenance organization."

BankAmerica offers more than 40 medical plans, three dental plans, and one vision care plan to our salaried employees. Each of these plans is summarized in the comparison chart entitled "1989 Summary of Health Care Plans."

```
IN 1988, BANKAMERICA PAID $3,036 ON YOUR BEHALF
FOR MEDICAL AND DENTAL COVERAGE.
```

Medical Care Coverage

```
IN 1989, YOU HAVE ELECTED TO PARTICIPATE IN
GROUP HEALTH MEDICAL FOR YOURSELF AND YOUR
ENROLLED DEPENDENTS.
```

Dental Care Coverage

```
IN 1989, YOU HAVE ELECTED TO PARTICIPATE IN
BA DENTAL.  YOU HAVE NO DEPENDENTS ENROLLED
IN THIS PLAN.
```

Vision Care Coverage

```
IN 1989, YOU HAVE ELECTED NOT TO PARTICIPATE IN
ANY BANKAMERICA-SPONSORED VISION CARE PLAN.
```

Benefits Plus — This program consists of Health Care and Dependent Care Reimbursement Accounts, both of which allow eligible employees to pay for certain expenses with pre-tax dollars.

```
IN 1989, YOU HAVE ELECTED TO CONTRIBUTE ON A PRE-TAX
BASIS $3,000 TO THE DEPENDENT CARE REIMBURSEMENT
ACCOUNT AND $2,000 TO THE HEALTH CARE REIMBURSEMENT
ACCOUNT.

EXECUTIVE HEALTH PROGRAM

AS A PARTICIPANT IN THE EXECUTIVE HEALTH PROGRAM, YOU
ARE ELIGIBLE FOR AN INITIAL COMPREHENSIVE PHYSICAL
EXAMINATION, AND SUBSEQUENT EXAMINATIONS, WITH RE-
IMBURSEMENT OF UP TO $500 EACH, EVERY TWO YEARS.
A SUMMARY OF THE PROCEDURES RECOMMENDED TO BE COVERED
IN THE EXAMINATION APPEARS IN YOUR "EXECUTIVE PROGRAM
SUMMARY" BOOKLET.
```

FIGURE 6–1—*Continued*

Disability
Benefits

Our disability benefit plans provide you and your family with income and financial protection if you become ill or are injured.

Disability income protection includes:

- BankAmerica's Sickness Benefits for short term disabilities for salaried employees,
- BankAmerica's Long Term Disability benefits for salaried employees, and
- Workers' Compensation for all employees.

Short Term Disability
Each day you are absent because of illness or injury, you will receive your accrued Sickness Benefits equal to the difference, if any, between your current salary rate and any other disability benefits payable to you, such as Workers' Compensation or state disability insurance benefits.

    4.0   Sickness Benefit days were used in 1988.
    57.0   Sickness Benefit days were available on December 31, 1988.

Long Term Disability
Your BankAmerica Long Term Disability (LTD) Plan provides benefits for disabilities that continue for more than 90 days.

    $2,625   is the monthly amount that you may be eligible to receive from the LTD Plan in combination with certain other disability benefits. Benefits may be payable to the earlier of recovery or upon certain other events described in *Your Employee Handbook,* or **AGE 65 (MAXIMUM AGE).**

The LTD benefit is reduced by any available state disability benefits, Workers' Compensation, and third party settlements. The LTD benefit will also be reduced by one-half of any Social Security benefits you may be eligible for, based on your earnings history under your Social Security Number, **123-45-6789.** Social Security disability benefits may be available after five months of disability.

FIGURE 6-1—Continued

CareerAccounts
Current Balances

Our retirement program at BankAmerica is made up of two plans—BankAmeraccount and BankAmerishare. Together, they are called CareerAccounts.

CareerAccounts can provide financial security in your retirement program. At retirement, you may elect to transfer your BankAmerishare balance into BankAmeraccount in order to receive it as an annuity (a monthly payment). You may also receive a lump sum distribution from both plans.

Current CareerAccounts Balance AS OF DECEMBER 31 1988

```
$6,100.00  YOUR SUPPLEMENTAL BANKAMERACCOUNT BALANCE
 5,230.00  YOUR SUPPLEMENTAL BANKAMERISHARE BALANCE
76,245.48  is your BankAmeraccount balance *
15,456.65  is your BankAmerishare balance
           (INCLUDING YOUR TRASOP BALANCE)
$103,032.14  is your CareerAccounts total balance
```

```
YOUR BANKAMERISHARE BALANCE IS 100% VESTED.  AS OF
JANUARY 1, 1989, YOU WERE 100% VESTED IN YOUR
BANKAMERACCOUNT BALANCE.

* YOU MAY ALSO BE ELIGIBLE FOR GRANDFATHERED BENEFITS.
```

Projected CareerAccounts Balance

In response to employee requests, this year we have included, in addition to the regular 5% salary growth assumption, a projection using your current salary rate only. This new projection should help you consider some of the impact of inflation on your purchasing power when you retire. Also, to show you how your CareerAccounts balance can grow, your current balance is projected using two investment assumptions. These projections are for illustration only. The assumptions may be different from what actually happens in your individual situation.

BankAmerishare is intended to provide a significant part of your retirement income. You can help to ensure retirement security by participating in BankAmerishare throughout your career with the company. The investment rates of return for BankAmerishare will vary over time, depending on the rate of return for the funds in which you decide to invest.

For recent rates of return for the BankAmerishare investment funds, look on the fund performance summary sent to you with each CareerAccounts quarterly statement. See the assumptions on pages 11 and 12, which form the basis for the following calculations.

```
THE FOLLOWING PROJECTIONS INCLUDE YOUR ESTIMATED
SUPPLEMENTAL BANKAMERACCOUNT BENEFITS AND YOUR
ESTIMATED SUPPLEMENTAL BANKAMERISHARE BENEFITS.
```

FIGURE 6-1—*Continued*

CareerAccounts
Projected Balances

Your Projected:	BankAmeraccount Balance	BankAmerishare Balance	CareerAccounts Balance
If the rate of return on your balance is			
8% per year to...			
11/30/90 (AGE 45)	$115,430	$28,211	$143,641
11/30/00 (AGE 55)	$810,212✳	$113,047	$923,259
11/30/10 (AGE 65)	$1,530,234✳	$291,355	$1,821,590
If the rate of return on your balance is			
8% per year, and your salary			
increases 5% per year to...			
11/30/90 (AGE 45)	$115,563	$28,291	$143,854
11/30/00 (AGE 55)	$847,010✳	$129,402	$976,412
11/30/10 (AGE 65)	$1,780,776✳	$382,513	$2,163,295
If the rate of return on your balance is			
6% per year to...			
11/30/90 (AGE 45)	$114,296	$27,502	$141,798
11/30/00 (AGE 55)	$810,212✳	$95,485	$905,697
11/30/10 (AGE 65)	$1,530,234✳	$213,648	$1,743,882
If the rate of return on your balance is			
6% per year, and your salary			
increases at 5% per year to...			
11/30/90 (AGE 45)	$114,429	$27,581	$142,010
11/30/00 (AGE 55)	$847,010✳	$110,640	$957,650
11/30/10 (AGE 65)	$1,730,778✳	$291,865	$2,072,643

THESE PROJECTIONS ARE BASED ON YOUR CONTRIBUTION
RATE, WHICH IS LESS THAN 6%. BY NOT CONTRIBUTING
6% OF YOUR PAY TO BANKAMERISHARE, YOU ARE LOSING
SIGNIFICANT MATCHING BANKAMERICA CONTRIBUTIONS
($2,040 IN 1988). FOR EXAMPLE, IF YOU CONTRIBUTED
6% OF PAY TO BANKAMERISHARE UNTIL 11-30-2000, YOU
COULD INCREASE YOUR BANKAMERISHARE BALANCE TO THE
FOLLOWING AMOUNTS:

           AT 6% INTEREST: $231,767
           AT 8% INTEREST: $265,270

✳ YOUR GRANDFATHERED BENEFIT IS SHOWN BECAUSE IT IS
  PROJECTED TO BE GREATER THAN YOUR BANKAMERACCOUNT
  BALANCE ON THIS DATE. YOU NEED NOT RETIRE BY
  JULY 1, 1990 TO TAKE ADVANTAGE OF THE
  GRANDFATHERED BENEFIT.

FIGURE 6–1—*Continued*

CareerAccounts
Monthly Retirement Benefits

When you become eligible for benefits from BankAmeraccount, you may elect to receive your account balance either in a lump sum payment or as monthly income.

Projected Monthly Retirement Benefits at Age 65

$29,215 is your estimated monthly retirement benefit from your projected BankAmeraccount balance. ✱

4,019 is your estimated monthly benefit from your projected Bank-Amerishare balance if you transfer it into BankAmeraccount at retirement. (INCLUDES SUPPLEMENTAL)

2,221 is your estimated monthly Social Security benefit.

$35,459 is your estimated total monthly retirement income. This amount is approximately 194% of your projected salary at age 65.

These projections use the lump sum accumulated balance in the chart on the previous page, using an 8% per year rate of return and a 5% per year salary growth rate, projected to 11-30-2010.

✱ YOUR GRANDFATHERED BENEFIT IS SHOWN BECAUSE IT IS
PROJECTED TO BE GREATER THAN YOUR BANKAMERACCOUNT
BALANCE ON THIS DATE. YOU NEED NOT RETIRE BY
JULY 1, 1990 TO TAKE ADVANTAGE OF THE GRANDFATHERED
BENEFIT.

SEE THE ASSUMPTIONS ON PAGES 11 AND 12, WHICH
FORM THE BASIS FOR THE CALCULATIONS ON THIS PAGE.

FIGURE 6-1—*Continued*

Survivor
Benefits

Our survivor benefits provide your family or other beneficiaries with financial protection if you should die while employed at BankAmerica.

Lump Sum Benefits

In the event of your death, your beneficiary could receive:

$63,000   BankAmerica-paid Basic Group Life Insurance (BGLI)
126,000   Employee-paid Voluntary Group Life Insurance (VGLI)

$189,000   Total Life Insurance Benefits

Upon accidental death or disability, you and/or your beneficiary may be eligible for:

$63,000   Accidental Death and Dismemberment (AD&D) benefits, and
$189,000   Business Travel Accident benefits.

```
YOUR BGLI BENEFICIARIES ARE JOAN SAMPLE,
KEVIN SAMPLE AND BEVERLY SAMPLE.

YOUR VGLI BENEFICIARIES ARE JOAN SAMPLE,
KEVIN SAMPLE AND BEVERLY SAMPLE.
```

In addition, your survivors may be eligible for benefits in the amount of
$103,032   (your current combined CareerAccounts balance).

Monthly Benefits

Social Security may provide for your eligible dependents up to:

$744   for each eligible child under age 16, and
$744   for your spouse if caring for a dependent child under age 16.

The maximum monthly benefit payable upon your death from
Social Security is $1,738.

Life Insurance Coverage For Your Eligible Dependents

BankAmerica provides life insurance coverage for your eligible spouse and dependent children. You may purchase additional life insurance on your dependents at group rates lower than what you would pay on your own.

```
YOU HAVE ELECTED $50,000 OF ADDITIONAL LIFE
INSURANCE FOR YOUR SPOUSE AND $25,000 FOR YOUR
DEPENDENT CHILDREN.
```

FIGURE 6–1—*Continued*

Compensation
Summary

```
$63,000  ANNUAL SALARY RATE
 13,000  PIP INCENTIVE AWARD RECEIVED IN 1988
  5,000  AMIP AWARD RECEIVED IN 1988
----------
$81,000  Cash Compensation
 14,098  Estimated BankAmerica Cost of Your Benefits

$95,098  Your Compensation Package
```

THE VALUE OF PAID TIME OFF (VACATIONS, A PERSONAL CHOICE DAY, AND HOLIDAYS) WORTH $7,996 IS INCLUDED IN YOUR CASH COMPENSATION.

Other benefits of significant value may include:
- Preferred Employee Loan and BankAmericard/Visa Rates
- Various Banking Services
- Tuition Assistance
- Service Award Program
- Adoption Assistance
- Unemployment Insurance

The following data was used to prepare parts of your statement:
- Date of Birth: **11–14–1945**
- Most Recent Date of Hire: **12–01–1965**

For more information on these and other BankAmerica benefits, please see the 1989 *Your Employee Handbook* (Exec-40), and any updates. Your manager can answer questions regarding your cash compensation. For answers to benefit questions, you may call:

CareerAccounts—BankAmerinet 624-2314
Health and Group
   Life Insurance—BankAmerinet 624-3705
Long Term Disability—BankAmerinet 624-4785
Short Term Disability—BankAmerinet 624-4675

FIGURE 6–1—*Continued*

How Your Statement Was Prepared

In preparing this Compensation Statement, we assumed that:
- your December 31, 1988 salary rate and scheduled hours will remain the same through 1989;
- each of the benefit programs outlined in this statement, including Social Security, continues in effect and is not changed; and
- other factors affecting your individual circumstances will remain unchanged.

Your Annual Salary Rate was determined by multiplying your monthly salary rate as of December 31, 1988 by 12 (and thus may not be the same as your W-2 wage statement).

Group Life Insurance

The Basic Group Life Insurance benefit was set equal to your annual earnings; it includes the average of certain commissions earned over the past two calendar years.

If your Basic Group Life Insurance benefit shown is greater than your annual earnings, it was calculated based on the assumptions that:
- you were eligible for Basic Group Life Insurance on June 1, 1981; and
- you had eligible dependents at that time.

This amount will remain frozen until the earliest of the date:
- you no longer have eligible dependents;
- you no longer are eligible for the plan; or
- your salary is more than the frozen amount.

If any of these events occur, your Basic Group Life Insurance benefit will be reduced to the amount of your annual earnings.

If the Basic Group Life Insurance amount shown for you is less than your annual earnings (or less than the frozen amount of life insurance described above, if you were eligible on June 1, 1981), it was calculated based on your age as of January 1, 1989, as follows:

Age	Benefit Amount
65–69	65% of your pre-age 65 amount
70–74	45% of your pre-age 65 amount
Over 74	30% of your pre-age 65 amount

Social Security

To compute your estimated Social Security benefits, it was assumed that:
- you qualify for the Social Security benefits described in this statement;
- you have participated continuously in Social Security since first becoming eligible;
- your past and future salary rates increased at an average rate of 5% per year, compounded annually over your career. Note that your previous salary history may be completely different from this assumption. If that is true, your actual Social Security benefit may vary significantly from what is shown; and
- the Social Security taxable wage base ($48,000 in 1989) increases at the rate of 4% per year, compounded annually.

CareerAccounts Projected Balances

Your projected BankAmeraccount balances assumed that:
- your salary will grow at average rates of either 0% or 5% per year, compounded annually over your career;
- the Social Security taxable wage base ($48,000 in 1989) will increase at average rates of either 0% or 4% per year, compounded annually; and
- transition credits will be added to your account (if applicable).

Your projected BankAmerishare balances assumed that:
- your salary will grow at an average rate of either 0% or 5% per year, compounded annually over your career; and
- you will continue to contribute at your December 31, 1988 rate, or the contribution rate in effect just before you reached the $7,313 annual limitation in 1988.

FIGURE 6–1—*Continued*

How Your Statement
Was Prepared (continued)

Changes in the law and/or amendments to BankAmerishare and BankAmeraccount may result in actual benefits being significantly different from the projected balances shown in this statement.

Neither the projections shown on page 7, nor the monthly retirement benefits shown on page 8, take into account IRS limitations on either benefits from BankAmeraccount, or annual contributions to BankAmerishare (except for the $7,313 annual limitation, indexed for future increases in the cost-of-living, on pre-tax contributions to BankAmerishare). Certain reductions because of the IRS limitations will be made up in a separate non-qualified plan.

If an amount is asterisked in the BankAmeraccount column on page 7, the amount shown was based on an estimated calculation that your grandfathered benefit from the BankAmerican Retirement Plan will be larger than your projected BankAmeraccount balance. That calculation assumes you will retire from BankAmerica. The grandfathered benefit from the BankAmerican Retirement Plan has been converted to a lump sum using a 10% "Level Annuity Interest Rate" under the BankAmeraccount Plan. The actual lump sum may be more or less than the amount shown, depending on the Bank-Ameraccount Level Annuity Interest Rate when you retire. Upon retirement, you will receive the greater of either your grandfathered benefit or your regular BankAmeraccount balance. Additional information regarding grandfathered benefits is available from BankAmeraccount (#3007).

CareerAccounts Monthly Retirement Benefits

Estimated monthly retirement income was based on the BankAmeraccount and BankAmerishare projected balances using an 8% per year rate of return. The BankAmerishare balance was assumed to be transferred to the BankAmeraccount Plan. The balances were converted to a monthly income amount using an assumed BankAmeraccount Level Annuity Interest Rate of 10% per year. The actual monthly payment may be more or less than the amount shown, depending on the BankAmeraccount Level Annuity Interest Rate in effect when you retire.

Cost of Your Benefits Program

We calculated the cost of your benefits as follows:

- the sum of BankAmeraccount pay-based and transition credits (based on your salary rate and the 1988 Social Security taxable wage base) was used for the estimated BankAmerica cost of your BankAmeraccount benefits;

- the matching contribution made on your behalf to BankAmerishare was used for the estimated BankAmerica cost of your BankAmerishare benefits;

- for Social Security benefits, 7.51% of your 1988 salary rate (up to $45,000) was used;

- for plans (such as the LTD Plan) that have neither a defined premium nor a defined contribution amount, the dollar total of benefits paid in 1988 was divided by the number of employees eligible to participate; and the result was used for the estimated BankAmerica cost of these benefits per employee; and

- for plan benefits that have an identifiable "per employee" premium or "per employee" contribution, the actual cost of premiums and contributions was used for the estimated BankAmerica cost of these benefits.

Planning for Your Family's Financial Security

The individualized information in this statement is BankAmerica's effort to assist you in protecting your financial security. However, you also have a responsibility in taking care of that security; in particular, keeping your beneficiaries and other parts of your security program up-to-date and coordinated with the benefits shown in this statement.

Information Accuracy

While every effort has been made to report information accurately, the possibility of error always exists. If you believe that the information on your statement is incorrect, please see your manager, or call the appropriate number on either Page 10 or the inside back cover. In addition, *Your Employee Handbook* provides more details about each benefit. Finally, the information furnished is subject to the provisions of the plan documents regarding each benefit, which control benefit availability and amount.

FIGURE 6–1—*Concluded*

If you want to make a change in any of your plans after reading your Personal Compensation Statement, here is information you may use:

If you want to	Use form number	Information phone number
Enroll in BankAmerishare	Exec-650	624-2314
Change your BankAmerishare contribution	Exec-650	624-2314
Transfer funds in BankAmerishare	Exec-5090	624-2314
Make an ordinary BankAmerishare withdrawal	Exec-652	624-2314
Apply for a BankAmerishare hardship withdrawal	Exec-902	624-2314
Enroll in or change voluntary life insurance coverage	*	624-3705
Enroll in or change dependent term life insurance	*	624-3705
Enroll in or change health coverage	Exec-183	624-3705
Change your BankAmeraccount beneficiary	Exec-5087	624-2314
Change your BankAmerishare beneficiary	Exec-906	624-2314
Change your basic life insurance beneficiary	Exec-173	624-3705
Change your voluntary life insurance beneficiary	*	624-3705
Change your dependent term life insurance beneficiary	*	624-3705

*These are insurance carrier forms. If not available in your department, call Employee Insurance Plans #3995 at the number shown.

In all cases, be sure to check *Your Employee Handbook* to see if any special rules apply.

© 1989 Bank of America NT & SA

FIGURE 6–2

SOCIAL SECURITY ADMINISTRATION
Personal Earnings and Benefit Estimate Statement

This is the earnings and benefit estimate statement that you recently requested. It lists your Social Security earnings history, and gives you an estimate of the benefits for which you and your family might qualify now and in the future. On the back of this statement is information about how the Social Security program works.

Many people believe that Social Security works like a bank. But, Social Security is not a savings or checking account. Rather, it is a pipeline. Most of the taxes collected from today's workers flow into one end of the pipe and out of the other end in the form of payments for today's beneficiaries. The remaining taxes are building a reserve that will be needed to help pay future beneficiaries, when the number of workers paying taxes compared to the number of beneficiaries receiving benefits will be less than today.

In addition, many Americans think of Social Security as only a retirement program. However, it is much more than that. Social Security also protects you and your family if you become severely disabled or die. But, keep in mind that Social Security was never intended to do it all. That is why I encourage you to build a complete financial package by supplementing your Social Security with private pensions, savings, other insurance, and investments.

I hope that this statement gives you a better picture of what Social Security has to offer and helps you plan for your financial future. Social Security is currently financially sound and we are committed to making it work for you.

DORCAS R. HARDY
Commissioner of Social Security

FIGURE 6–2—Continued

HOW YOU EARN SOCIAL SECURITY CREDITS
Before you can qualify for benefits and hospital insurance, you need credit for a certain amount of work under Social Security. In 1988, you earn one credit (previously called a "quarter of coverage") for each $470 of your covered wages or self-employment income. You can earn no more than 4 Social Security credits a year when you work in a job covered by Social Security.

MILITARY AND RAILROAD SERVICE
Any basic pay you earned from active duty or active duty for training in the military since 1957 is shown on this statement. Inactive duty payments count as wages beginning January 1, 1988. In addition, if you served in the military after September 15, 1940, you may qualify for free earnings credits for that service. These credits do not appear on this statement. We decide if you qualify for these free credits when you apply for benefits.

This statement does not show any wages you earned from a railroad employer. But, if you worked less than 10 years in the railroad industry, we considered any railroad wages when we estimated your Social Security credits and benefits.

ABOUT SOCIAL SECURITY BENEFITS
Social Security benefits are based on your earnings over your working career, up to the maximum amount, not on taxes you paid. When we figure your benefits, we update your earnings to take account of changes in the national average wage from the time you started to work, until you reach age 60, become disabled, or die. These adjusted earnings are averaged together and a formula is applied to the average to arrive at a benefit amount. This amount may be reduced at the time you apply if you receive workers' compensation, a public disability benefit or a pension based on work not covered by Social Security. The amount your spouse receives may also be reduced if he or she receives a government pension.

Social Security retirement benefits will replace part of your pre-retirement earnings. The replacement rate ranges from about 60 percent of pre-retirement earnings for a worker who has always earned the minimum wage to about 26 percent for a worker who has always earned the maximum covered by Social Security. At the beginning of 1988, the average monthly cash benefit paid to a retired worker at age 65 or older was $523. The value of Medicare benefits was an additional $202 (39% of the cash benefits), for a total value of $725 per month.

ESTIMATED RETIREMENT BENEFITS
The estimates on this statement are based on your earnings record and any information you gave us. We used current dollar values for these estimates. We adjusted all retirement estimates to account for average wage growth in the national economy by increasing your benefit by 1% for each year between now and when you turn age 62.

If you qualify, you can start receiving reduced retirement benefits as early as age 62: However, we now pay full, unreduced retirement benefits at age 65. **Starting in the year 2000, this full retirement age will be increased in monthly steps until it reaches age 67 in 2027.**

FIGURE 6–2—*Continued*

ESTIMATED BENEFITS

RETIREMENT You must have 40 Social Security credits to be fully insured for retirement benefits. Assuming that you meet all the requirements, here are estimates of your retirement benefits based on your past and any projected earnings. The estimates are in today's dollars, but adjusted to account for average wage growth in the national economy.

If you retire at 62, your monthly benefit in today's dollars will be about. . . . .$ 825

The earliest age at which you can receive an unreduced retirement benefit is 65 years of age. We call this your full retirement age. If you work until that age and then retire, your monthly benefit in today's dollars will be about. $1,055

If you continue to work and wait until you are 70 to receive benefits, your monthly benefit in today's dollars will be about $1,460

SURVIVORS If you have a family, you must have 29 Social Security credits for certain family members to receive benefits if you were to die this year. They may also qualify if you earn 6 credits in the 3 years before your death. The number of credits a person needs to be insured for survivors benefits increases each year until age 62, up to a maximum of 40 credits.
Here is an estimate of the benefits your family could receive if you had enough credits to be insured, they qualified for benefits, and you died this year:

Your child could receive a monthly benefit of about . . . .$ 645

If your child and your surviving spouse who is caring for your child both qualify, they could each receive a monthly benefit of about . . . .$ 645

When your surviving spouse reaches full retirement age, he or she could receive a monthly benefit of about. . . . .$ 865

The total amount that we could pay your family each month is about. $1,520

We may also be able to pay your surviving spouse or children a one-time death benefit of. . . . .$ 255

DISABILITY Right now, you must have 29 Social Security credits to be insured for disability benefits. And 20 of these credits had to be earned in the 10 year period immediately before you became disabled. If you are blind or received disability benefits in the past, you may need fewer credits. The number of credits a person needs to be insured for disability benefits increases each year until age 62, up to a maximum of 40 credits.

If you were disabled, had enough credits, and met the other requirements for disability benefits, here is an estimate of the benefits you could receive right now:

Your monthly benefit would be about. . . . .$ 850

You and your eligible family members could receive up to a monthly total of about $1,275

IF YOU HAVE
QUESTIONS If you have any questions about this statement, please read the information on the reverse side. If you still have questions, please call 1-800-937-7005.

FIGURE 6–2—*Continued*

ABOUT YOUR EARNINGS AND BENEFIT ESTIMATE STATEMENT

YOUR EARNINGS RECORD
The Social Security Administration keeps a lifetime record of the earnings reported under your name and Social Security number. When you apply for Social Security benefits, we check your earnings record to see if you worked long enough to qualify, and use your earnings to determine the amount of your monthly benefit.

This statement includes any wages from employment as well as any self-employment income. Wages were covered under Social Security beginning in 1937, and most self-employment income was covered beginning in 1951.

MAXIMUM EARNINGS
The maximum amount of yearly earnings covered by Social Security is set by law. You and each of your employers only pay Social Security taxes on earnings up to this maximum. If you pay taxes on more than the yearly maximum, you can ask the Internal Revenue Service (IRS) for a refund if you are within the time limit, usually your last 3 tax years. (Contact your local IRS office with questions about refunds.)

YOUR SOCIAL SECURITY TAXES
You and your employer each pay an equal share of Social Security (FICA) taxes. If you are self-employed, you currently pay taxes at twice the employee rate, but with a 2 percent credit. These taxes finance both Social Security and Medicare hospital insurance benefits. The following tables show the tax rates for 1988 through 1989 and for 1990 and later.

TAX RATES FOR YOU AND YOUR EMPLOYER—Percent of Covered Earnings

Years	For Retirement, Survivors, and Disability Insurance		For Medicare Hospital Insurance		Total Employee and Employer Rate (Each)	Combined Total
1988-1989	6.06%	+	1.45%	=	7.51%	15.02%
1990 and later	6.20%	+	1.45%	=	7.65%	15.30%

TAX RATES FOR SELF-EMPLOYED PEOPLE—Percent of Covered Earnings

Years	For Retirement, Survivors, and Disability Insurance		For Medicare Hospital Insurance		Total
1988-1989	12.12%	+	2.90%	=	15.02%*
1990 and later	12.40%	+	2.90%	=	15.30%

*A 2% credit reduces the effective tax rate to 13.02 percent.

On this statement, we estimate the amount of Social Security taxes you paid for any year in which you had Social Security covered earnings. If you had earnings from both employment and self-employment in a single year, this statement shows a tax amount as if all your earnings were from employment.

FIGURE 6-2—Continued

FACTS ABOUT YOUR SOCIAL SECURITY

September 30, 1988

THE FACTS YOU GAVE US	Your Name.....................................
	Your Social Security Number ....
	Your Date of Birth..................................
	1987 Earnings $20,000
	1988 Earnings $45,000
	Your Estimated Future Average Yearly Earnings ....Over $45,000
	The Age You Plan To Retire............................Not Provided

We used these facts and the information already on our records to prepare this statement for you. When we estimated your benefits, we included any 1987 and 1988 earnings you told us about. We also included any future estimated earnings up to age 62.

If you did not estimate your future earnings, we did not project any future earnings for you.

| YOUR
SOCIAL
SECURITY
EARNINGS | The chart below shows the earnings on your Social Security record. It also estimates the amount of Social Security taxes you paid each year to finance benefits under Social Security and Medicare. We show earnings only up to the maximum amount of yearly earnings covered by Social Security. These maximum amounts are also shown on the chart. The chart may not include some or all of your earnings from last year because they may not have been posted to your record yet. |

Years	Maximum Yearly Earnings Subject To Social Security Tax	Your Social Security Taxed Earnings	Estimated Social Security Taxes You Paid	Years	Maximum Yearly Earnings Subject To Social Security Tax	Your Social Security Taxed Earnings	Estimated Social Security Taxes You Paid
1937-1950	$ 3,000	$ 0	$ 0	1970	$ 7,800	$ 7,800	$ 374
1951	3,600	0	0	1971	7,800	7,799	405
1952	3,600	0	0	1972	9,000	9,000	468
1953	3,600	594	8	1973	10,800	10,800	631
1954	3,600	1,102	22	1974	13,200	13,200	772
1955	4,200	1,223	24	1975	14,100	14,100	824
1956	4,200	762	15	1976	15,300	15,300	895
1957	4,200	829	18	1977	16,500	16,500	965
1958	4,200	1,083	24	1978	17,700	17,700	1,070
1959	4,800	1,436	35	1979	22,900	22,900	1,403
1960	4,800	1,596	47	1980	25,900	25,900	1,587
1961	4,800	3,059	91	1981	29,700	29,700	1,975
1962	4,800	4,084	127	1982	32,400	32,400	2,170
1963	4,800	4,800	174	1983	35,700	30,515	2,044
1964	4,800	4,800	174	1984	37,800	37,800	2,532
1965	4,800	4,800	174	1985	39,600	39,600	2,791
1966	6,600	5,729	240	1986	42,000	20,010	1,430
1967	6,600	6,565	288	1987	43,800	27,912	3,433
1968	7,800	6,880	302	1988	45,000	0	0
1969	7,800	7,800	374	1989		0	0

| YOUR
SOCIAL
SECURITY
CREDITS | To qualify for benefits, you need credit for a certain amount of work covered by Social Security. The number of credits you need will vary with the type of benefit. **Under current law, you do not need more than 40 credits to be fully insured for any benefit.** (See "How You Earn Social Security Credits" on the reverse side.) |

Our review of your earnings, including any 1987 and 1988 earnings you told us about, shows that you now have at least 40 Social Security credits.

FIGURE 6–2—*Continued*

BENEFITS FOR YOUR FAMILY
As you work you also build up protection for your family. Some of your family members who might qualify for benefits are listed below.
o Spouses and some divorced spouses of retired or disabled workers. Benefits are paid as early as 62, or at any age if the spouse is caring for your child who is under 16 or disabled and is receiving benefits on your record.
o Widows and widowers, including some divorced spouses. Benefits are paid at age 60, at age 50 if disabled, or at any age if the widow or widower is caring for your child who is under 16 or disabled and is receiving benefits on your record.
o Unmarried children under age 18 (under 19 if in high school) or at any age if disabled before age 22.

MEDICARE
The two parts of Medicare, hospital and medical insurance, help to protect you from the high costs of medical care. Hospital insurance helps pay the cost of inpatient hospital care and certain kinds of followup care. Medical insurance helps pay the costs of physicians' services.

You may qualify for Medicare hospital insurance when you turn 65. You may also qualify for hospital insurance before age 65 if you are disabled or have permanent kidney failure. Almost anyone who is 65 or older or eligible for Medicare hospital insurance can enroll for supplementary medical insurance, although you must pay a monthly premium for it. You may also buy hospital insurance at 65 if you do not have enough credits to be eligible for it.

IF YOU THINK OUR RECORDS ARE WRONG
If your earnings records do not agree with ours, please call the 800 number shown on the reverse side. We can usually help you by phone. Have available any W-2 forms, payslips, tax returns or any other proof of your earnings. You also will need to refer to this statement to help us correct any problems with your earnings record.

You should report any errors right away because the law only allows us to correct a Social Security record within a limited period of time. This is usually 3 years, 3 months, and 15 days after the year in which an error occurs, but there are some exceptions. To ensure the accuracy of your earnings record, we recommend that you request this statement every 3 years.

A REMINDER
This statement is not a decision on a claim for Social Security benefits. You do not qualify for any of these benefits unless you apply for them, have all the Social Security credits you need, and meet all other requirements. The actual number of Social Security credits and the benefit estimates shown on this statement may change. We will determine the exact amount of your Social Security benefits, if any, when you apply.

If any of the information you submitted is wrong, the Social Security credits we show and the benefits we estimated in this statement may also be wrong. We base your benefit estimates in part on your future average yearly earnings. How accurately you predict your earnings will affect the accuracy of your benefit estimates.

SSA-7005 (06-88)

FIGURE 6–3

DEPARTMENT OF
HEALTH, EDUCATION, AND WELFARE
SOCIAL SECURITY ADMINISTRATION
BALTIMORE, MARYLAND 21235

SOCIAL SECURITY NUMBER

We are pleased to furnish you information about your social security earnings account. Shown below are the earnings now recorded for you.

PERIOD	EARNINGS
1937 THRU 1950	$ NONE
1951 THRU 1964	21,084.70
1965	4,160.45
1966	4,462.27
1967	5,050.70
1968 THRU DEC	5,489.71
TOTAL – 1937 THRU DEC 1968	$ 40,247.83

Our records may not show all the earnings a person had in the last calendar year because of the time required to receive and process reports.

If this statement does not agree with your own record, please write or visit your nearest social security office, or write to us. This statement should be enclosed if you write us, or take it with you if you visit one of our offices. Unless you report an error within 3 years, 3 months, and 15 days after the year in which you were paid wages or after the taxable year in which you derived self-employment income, correction of our records may not be possible.

The enclosed booklet contains a brief summary of the social security program, information about your social security account, and a further explanation of the action you should take if you do not agree with this statement of your earnings. Answers to any specific questions you have asked will be found on the pages checked in the booklet index. The people in your local social security office will be pleased to answer any other questions you have about the social security program.

Sincerely yours,

William E. Hanna, Jr.

William E. Hanna, Jr., Director
Bureau of Data Processing and Accounts

Enclosure

FINANCIAL EDUCATION

The essence of core employee benefits is that they provide some economic and financial value to the employee during a time of income need or economic adversity.

Over decades, employee benefits have become an integral component of the social and economic structure of the nation. So much so that in some ways employees have come to rely so heavily on pension plans, social security, and medical plans that they believe they will be provided for in adversity or retirement, one way or another, by government or an employers plans.

The long decline in personal savings combined with increases in personal spending and use of credit are indicators of how attitudes have shifted from a self-reliant society in which individuals planned and saved for their own retirement needs to the present state of reliance on employers and government to provide for retirement needs.

Government has taken note of this trend with some alarm and encouraged programs that enable personal savings, such as 401(k) plans, IRAs, and ESOPs, deeming it socially desirable and economically important that individuals take a greater role in planning for and saving for their own retirement needs. The precarious position of social security, with benefits being limited and even reduced in the future, has been one source of this government interest in personal financial savings for retirement.

Employers, in the quest for reducing costs of doing business so as to be more competitive in world markets, have done surgery on benefit plans, cutting out pension plans, and taking excess funds back into cash flow. They have generally shifted from pension plans with promised benefits to defined contribution plans where the risk is borne by the employee.

In the process it has become clear that employees must change their expectations about retirement income security and where it will come from. Personal financial planning and savings will play a greater role in retirement security in the future than has been the case in the last 40 years.

For decades retirement income has been predicated on what has been called "the three-legged stool" of private pensions, social security, and personal savings. Personal savings was the first leg to weaken, then social security, and now defined benefit pension plans. The stool is a little shaky at the moment.

One result of this shift has been that employers are considering and adopting programs of financial education for employees to sensitize them to the need for a greater sense of self-reliance and better personal financial planning for their future security. These programs take many forms, but at the heart of all of them is the communication of benefits— particularly the benefits from pension, profit sharing, savings, and similar plans.

Financial education means providing information about personal financial management, investment risks, inflation and its effects, setting personal financial goals, and so on. Financial planning means using that knowledge to manage personal assets toward achieving those personal financial goals. Financial planning for employees is offered by many investment firms and brokers, usually as a business development tool since they hope that as employees enter into investing they will select the firm or broker as their investment advisor.

Some employers are reticent to expose employees to this type of financial planning program, based on a concern that should an investment program not go well for the employee the employee may blame the employer for exposing them to the investment firm or broker. In other cases, the employer may be unable to introduce a particular investment firm or broker because there are several who would like to do business with the employees and the employer cannot choose one over the others for political reasons.

As an alternative, employers are seeking out programs of pure financial education that avoid any implications about using a particular investment firm or broker or any particular investment approach. Many such programs are available, but in the context of employee benefits communications, one such program, based on an application of software, is outlined here, as an example of the kinds of programs that are available.

This particular program is called FINDPRO©. It is a financial education program designed to be used by employees to set a future financial goal and by entry of data into the software program to be able to see immediately, in real time, what the effect of various assumptions will be on achievement of their goal.

The program functions from data provided about pension, profit sharing, and other similar benefits as provided in a benefit statement. The software and related workbook materials are customized to the benefit plans of the employer so that employees can observe the role of the employer's benefit plans in their future financial security. Thus, it becomes a very important benefits communication tool for gaining understanding and appreciation of the benefits provided. It is also useful in building participation in a 401(k) plan by lower paid employees.

The program is implemented by offering employees a brief workshop about the program, how it works and how they can use it, usually presented by in-house benefits staff, thus avoiding the costs of bringing in a trainer. The software disk and manuals are licensed to the employer so the cost of materials is minimized. All the information an employee needs to use the program is self-contained in either the workbook or the benefits statement.

Following the workshop, each employee completes one or more Information Input Forms (example reproduced herein) containing their data for various personal financial scenarios, for use in the software program. The employee may process the data using the software on company computers, or may submit the forms to the benefits staff for processing and return of the reports to them.

As data is entered into the program, the employee can see immediately how each item of information affects the achievement of his or her goal. When all the data is entered, a hard copy print-out may be made for the employee to review and consider and discuss with family members.

A copy of the Retirement Income Projection Report is reproduced in Exhibit 6–1, based on the data provided on the Information Input Form also reproduced herein.

A sample of the explanatory workbook that explains each line item in the report is also reproduced herein.

The result of providing such a program for employees is that the employees gain an understanding of various aspects of financial management, set their own financial goals, and come to understand what is necessary in terms of personal action to achieve those goals. At the same time, they get a clear conception of the role of the employer's benefits in enabling them to achieve their financial goals.

EXHIBIT 6–1
Financial Independence Education Program
Client Retirement Income Projection Report
Content Reference Manual © FIES, INC 1986

This Reference Manual is intended to assist in the interpretation
of the information contained in the report

Table of Contents

	Page
What the Program Is and How It Works	1
Sample Input Information Form—Completed	2
Sample Retirement Income Projection Report Based on Sample Input Information Form	3
Detailed Description of Information in the Report	4

What The Program Is and How It Works

The Financial Education program provides employees the knowledge
and motivation for setting a future financial objective. Employees also
gain understanding of what is required to realize that objective.

By providing their own financial data for processing in a software
program, they receive personalized reports that inform them of what
they need to do financially to achieve their goal.

The software program, personal reports, and explanatory material are all customized to the specific benefit plans of the employer so
that employees can understand the role of those benefits in their
financial security and in achieving their personal financial goals.

A workshop is conducted for employees in which financial concepts and education are presented, and the personal financial goal-
setting process is explained. Participants then complete a simple form
with personal financial information that is processed, and personalized reports are provided to them for use in setting and moving toward
their goals.

Providing this program for employees:

- Conveys to them real understanding of the role of the benefits
  in their future financial security.
- Illustrates in real terms the values of the benefits.

EXHIBIT 6–1—*Continued*

- Communicates effectively the values and features of pension and savings plans.
- Enhances employee interest in the benefit plans.
- Provides them a directly useful means of planning their financial security and retirement.
- Motivates them to take action to achieve their goals and shows them what they need to do.
- Teaches responsibility for personal financial planning and action.

INFORMATION INPUT FORM: COMPLETE BLANK SPACES

Name ___KENNY___

Present Age   ___45___ Prepared: _1_ Month _89_ Year
Desired Age of Retirement ___65___ Retirement Year   0
Normal Life Expectancy ___86___

Years for Accumulation   0   From   0   to   0
Years of Income   0   From   0   to   0
Present Annual Salary $_75,649_
Assumption About Future Salary Increases   ___5.5___ %
Assumption About Average Annual
  Inflation Rate   ___5___ %
Average Interest Earnings on Income Producing
  Assets   ___7___ %
Annual Income Desired After Taxes and In Current $_50,000_
  Dollars
Equivalent Annual Income at Retirement $0
  (Inflation Adjusted)
Income Producing Assets Required at
  Retirement to Provide That Amount of Annual
  Income Using Principal and Interest $ 0
    Projection of Future Values of Personal Investment
      Assets
      Present Value of Your Investment Assets $_265,498_
      Tax Rate on These Assets   _20_ %
Projected After Tax Value of These Assets at   0 $0
  Projection of Future Values of Pension Plans

	Currently	At Age\ /	After Tax
Tax Rate on Pensions _20_ %		0	\ /Value\ /
Projected Monthly Pension	$_673_	$0	$0
Vested or Frozen Future	$_150_	$0	$0
Pension Income Monthly			

EXHIBIT 6–1—*Continued*

Projected Monthly Social Security	$ 924	$0	$0
Projected Value of Profit Sharing and Savings Plan Balances at 0	Current Balance		
Profit Sharing Account	$ 25,461		
401 (K) Plan Account	$ 31,587		
Savings Plan Account	$ 12,432		
Other Accumulation Plan Accounts	$ 15,467		
Total Value Current Accounts		$0	$0

Projected After Tax Value of Future Contributions to These Plans
Your Assumptions About Future Contributions as a % of Pay Each Year

Yours as % of Pay Each Year	6 %	$	0
Company Match as a % of Pay	3 %	$	0
Company Profit Sharing Contribution	4 %	$	0
Other Plan Contributions (IRA)	1 %	$	0
Total After Tax Value of All These Plans at	0	$	0

>>>>>> Summary <<<<<<

Total of Investment Assets and Pension Plans Available	$	0
Total Needed	$	0
Shortage (−) or Surplus Projected at Retirement Age	$	0
Additional Savings Required to Meet Goal (As a % of Salary/ A Minus Sign Indicates a Surplus)	0%	

EXHIBIT 6–1—*Continued*

EMPLOYEE RETIREMENT INCOME PROJECTION

Name _____ Mr. & Mrs. Kenny _____

Present Age	45	Prepared: January	1989
Desired Age of Retirement	65	Retirement Year	2009
Normal Life Expectancy	86		
Years for Accumulation	20	From 1989 to	2009
Years of Income	21	From 2009 to	2030

Present Annual Salary $75,649

Assumption About Future Salary Increases   5.5 %

Assumption About Average Annual Inflation Rate 5 %

Average Interest Earnings on Income Producing
  Assets   7 %

Annual Income Desired After Taxes and In Current $50,000
  Dollars

Equivalent Annual Income at Retire- $132,665
  ment (Inflation Adjusted)

Income Producing Assets Required at
  Retirement to Provide That Amount of
  Annual Income Using Principal and
  Interest $2,321,996

Projection of Future Values of Personal
  Investment Assets

Present Value of Your Investment Assets $ 265498

Tax Rate on These Assets   20 %

Projected After Tax Value of These Assets at 65 $821915

Projection of Future Values of Pension Plans

		At Age\ /	After Tax
Tax Rate on Pensions 20 %	Currently	65	\ /Value\ /
Projected Monthly Pension	$673	$1,964	$204,261
Vested or Frozen Future Pension Income Monthly		$150	$15,603
Projected Monthly Social Security	$924	$1,373	$142,823

	Current Balance	
Projected Value of Profit Sharing and Savings Plan Balances at 65		
Profit Sharing Account	$25,461	
401 (K) Plan Account	$31,587	
Savings Plan Account	$12,432	
Other Accumulation Plan Account	$15,467	
Total Value Current Accounts	$84,947	$262,974

EXHIBIT 6–1—*Continued*

Projected After Tax Value of Future Contributions to These Plans
   Your Assumptions About Future Contributions as a % of Pay Each
   Year

Yours as % of Pay Each Year	6 %	$ 230,454
Company Match as a % of Pay	3 %	$ 115,227
Company Profit Shar-ing Contribution	4 %	$ 153,636
Other Plan Contribu-tions (IRA)	1 %	$ 38,409
Total After Tax Value of All These Plans at	65	$1,163,388

>>>>>> Summary <<<<<<

Total of Investment Assets and Pension Plans Available	$1985303
Total Needed	$2321996
Shortage (−) or Surplus Projected at Retirement Age	$−336693
Additional Savings Required to Meet Goal (As a % of Salary/ A Minus Sign Indicates a Surplus)	7%

No warranties, guarantees or assurances of any kind are made by anyone with respect to the accuracy, use, results or application of this program for any specific purpose. The user takes full responsibility for the results and how this information is used.
Copyright <C> Fies, Inc 1986

Detailed Description of Information in the Report

This section provides a narrative discussion of the information on each line of the Client Retirement Income Projection Report.

IMPORTANT NOTE: This planning process necessarily looks ahead over a period of many years, during which it is impossible to project accurately such factors as salary increases, inflation rates, interest rates, and so on. Ideally, so as to stay more accurately on the plan, the program should be redone each year, when new salary levels, new benefit plan information, and other information can be updated. In this way, as the actual planned year of independence

EXHIBIT 6–1—*Concluded*

approaches, the planning becomes more accurate and more dependable.

Furthermore, it is generally useful to use conservative assumptions, meaning smaller numbers for such factors as salary increases, interest rates, future company contributions to benefit plans, and so forth, and a higher inflation rate. The result of the planning then, could be expected to be more conservative, meaning that any differences in the ultimate outcome should be more favorable—rather than a disappointing surprise that might result from unrealistically overstated expectations. Such a disappointment may come in the form of reaching the age of intended financial independence only to discover that unrealistic expectations in the assumptions have undermined the entire process and the goal cannot be achieved as hoped.

present age   Using your next nearest age will provide more conservative planning than using your present age.

desired age of retirement   This will be the age at which you desire to retire or be financially independent. Retirement and financial independence are not the same, however. Financial independence means being able to make more choices about your life, whether to work or not work, or to work part time, or to be able to retire or semiretire, to be able to start a business, and so on. Retirement generally means to withdraw from work.

retirement year   This is computed as the actual year of retirement, based on the present age and the desired age of retirement.

normal life expectancy   This is the age to which you expect to live. For a married couple it may be the age to which you expect a spouse to live, since statistically women do live longer than men, and you may want to factor that into your planning. A standard life expectancy table is included in this manual for reference.

years for accumulation   This is simply the number of years between now and the planned age of financial independence—these are the years remaining in which to accumulate additional savings for financial independence.

years of income   These are the years between the age of financial independence and life expectancy, and are the years during which the accumulated assets and benefits will be paid out to you as income from the various sources of accumulations of investments or income sources.

present annual salary   This should be your base pay only, on the premise that standards of living are based on base salary, and bonuses are extra income. For a two earner family, it may be the base pay of both workers but to do so will distort some of the calculations and thereby distort the planning process. The reason is that some benefit calculations in the program, such as profit sharing plan and savings plan contributions, depends on this number for projecting future contributions. Most benefit plans base such contributions on base pay only, so using a combined base pay or including bonuses will substantially overstate the result. Also, the projection of future savings to achieve your financial goal uses this number for computing future savings and this will also be distorted by use of combined salaries or bonuses.

assumption about future salary increases   This is whatever realistic annual increase you believe you may expect during the period of accumulation. If you choose to redo the program every year it would be the increase you expect during the next year, since the planning process the next year will then adjust each year for actual experience. If you do not plan to redo the program, it should be the average increase you expect during the remaining accumulation years.

assumption about average annual inflation rate   This is your own personal guess as to the average inflation rate during the period of remaining years of accumulation as well as during the years of payout as income. Obviously this is anyone's guess, as are the interest rates you expect in the future. No one can really offer firm guidance on selection of inflation or interest rates, because no one really knows. Simply use a best guess, and it can be adjusted from year to year as the program is redone. A chart of historical inflation rates is included in this manual for reference.

average interest earnings on income producing assets   This is the average interest rate you expect to earn before taxes on personal investments during the remaining years of accumulation as well as during the years of payout as income. It is a best guess, as with inflation rates. A chart of historical interest rates is included in this manual for reference.

annual income desired after taxes and in current dollars   This is the amount of income you want to receive annually when you become financially independent. In general, it is the amount you desire to maintain a certain standard of living. This amount is to be in current dollars, as the program automatically adjusts for inflation between now and the time of financial independence and during the years of payout.

In arriving at the amount of annual income desired, you may wish to go through an exercise of expenses as you expect them to be when you are in fact financially independent in the future. Try to visualize what you expect your expense needs will be at that time, but in current dollars. This amount is only what you expect to need in addition to any other income you expect, such as income from a business or part time work, or income from rental properties, and so on.

It is important that some allowance be made for taxes you may expect to be payable on any such income. Some parts of such income may not be taxable, and some part of it may be taxable.

A simple method of approaching this amount, although by no means as precise or as useful as going through the actual exercise of projecting your expected needs, is to use some percentage of current income, such as 65 percent, 75 percent or 80 percent, or some other amount.

equivalent annual income at retirement (inflation adjusted)   This is the amount of income that would be required in the future, at the age of retirement, that would be the equivalent of the annual income desired based on adjustments for inflation between now and the time of retirement.

income producing assets required at retirement   This is the total present value of funds from all sources—investments and benefits—that would be required at the time of financial independence to provide the income level computed on the previous line. This presumes that both principal and interest are used to provide income in retirement.

present value of investment assets   This is the current market value of personal investment assets that you own. It is not the same as net worth, which includes items such as a home, household goods, cars, and so on—items that you will need during retirement and would not liquidate in order to provide income.

Investment assets are such things as stocks, bonds, savings accounts, IRAs, and other similar holdings that you would be willing and able to liquidate, if necessary, in order to provide income during financial independence.

tax rate on these assets   Since some or all of your investments will have taxes payable if liquidated (such as real estate or stock holdings that you plan to sell) this entry provides an opportunity for you to make an allowance for the effect of taxes on such personal assets. This number may be 0 percent if all such assets are expected to be in the form of a savings account that will be drawn down, on which taxes on the accumulated interest have already been paid.

If assets are a combination of holdings, such as stocks, real estate and savings accounts, or IRAs, the tax rate entered here will have to be simply some estimate of the overall tax rate expected for such holdings.

This is of course a very imprecise number that cannot be actually known until the taxes are paid under the tax laws in effect at that future time. Simply enter some reasonable assumption, 10 percent, 15 percent or whatever number seems reasonable, so that the total value of these assets will not be overstated. If the assets are overstated, that will of course distort the planning process.

projected after-tax value of these assets at age ____   This is the projected after-tax value, at the retirement age, based on your interest assumption.

projection of future values of pension plans   This identifies that the following section refers to income or asset values that have been, or will be in the future, accumulated in pension, savings, or other similar benefit plans, all of which will be part of the assets necessary to provide income in retirement.

Information about current pension or other benefit plan values will come from benefit statements or other reports provided by an employer.

tax rate on pensions   As with your personal assets, there will be taxes payable on some distributions from benefit plans. The tax law may be different at the time of independence than at present, and often, depending on how the accounts are withdrawn, different tax rates will apply. These tax laws are very complex and the taxes payable will depend a great deal on decisions made at the time of withdrawal of the accounts.

Use here whatever number seems to you to be reasonable for this tax allowance, 10 percent, 15 percent, 20 percent, or whatever other number seems reasonable. It will of course be imprecise, but some allowance for such taxes will bring more dependability to the planning process.

projected monthly pension currently   This is the current projected pension benefit usually shown on a benefit statement, based on past earnings and total years of service to some age such as 62 or 65.

In the case of monthly income pension plans the current benefit, based on past and current earnings, will be projected in accordance with your salary increase assumption and the resulting projected benefit is shown on the report as the Projected Monthly Pension at Age ____.

after-tax value   This is the calculated present value, at the age of retirement after taxes, based on the interest rate assumption. This will actually be paid out as monthly income, but the present value is calculated here to be applied as part of the total assets required to provide the income desired in retirement.

vested or frozen pension income monthly   This refers to a monthly pension that may be payable at the age of independence, such as a vested pension with a former employer, a spouses pension, a veterans pension, or similar item. Other items that might be entered here are such things as alimony, an annuity from an insurance company under an insurance policy, rental income from property (if you do not plan to sell the property at the time of independence) and so on.

projected monthly social security   This is the current projected monthly social security benefit sometimes shown on benefit statements. If such a number is not shown on a benefit statement, it may be estimated from social security tables provided at local social security offices. Such a table of estimated income is included in this manual for reference.

This number should be included only if financial independence is targeted for age 62 or above when social security benefits are actually available.

In the case of social security, the current benefit, based on past and current earnings, will be advanced by 2% per year to project the benefit at the age of retirement.

projected value of profit sharing and savings plan balances at age ____   Refers to the following lines which project after tax future values of current balances in these accounts, at the age of retirement, using the interest rate assumption.

profit sharing account   This is the current balance in a profit sharing plan.

401(K) plan account   A 401(k) plan refers to a salary deferral plan in which employees can contribute savings on a pretax basis. Employee contributions are often matched on some basis by the employer.

savings plan account   This refers to a plan to which employee savings contributions are matched by a contribution by the employer. This may be the same plan as the 401(k) plan, or it may be a separate plan.

other accumulation plan accounts   This provides a place to include an account in some other type of plan that doesn't fit into profit sharing or savings plan. Such a plan may be an ESOP, TRASOP, TSA, deferred compensation or similar plan.

total value current accounts   This illustrates the total value of all of these current accounts and calculates the future after tax value of all of these accounts at the retirement age, based on the interest rate assumption.

projected after-tax value of future contributions to these plans   In addition to current pension and other capital accumulation plan values that you have earned, should you stay with the employer you would probably expect future contributions to be made into such plans, and those future contributions (yours and the company's) will also be an important part of the total assets you need to accumulate.

Therefore, a section is provided for you to estimate what the future contributions will be worth, by entering an assumption about future company contributions and your own future contributions. These are entered as percentages of base pay and then they are mathematically adjusted for your assumptions about future salary increases and interest earnings, so as to project an estimate of the value of such future contributions at the time of your financial independence.

yours as a percent of pay each year This refers to contributions you may make in the future into a savings plan, TSA, or similar plan. This is a percentage of your annual pay each year as it increases in accordance with your salary increase assumption.

company match as a percent of pay This refers to any company matching contribution that may be made under a savings plan, based on the employees contribution to the plan. This is the percentage of your base pay that you expect the company to contribute on your behalf.

company profit sharing contributions This refers to your estimate of future company contributions to a profit sharing plan, as a percentage of your base pay.

other accumulation plan contribution This provides a place to recognize anticipated future contributions to some plan not already described. An IRA contribution would be an example.

total after-tax value of all these plans at age ____ This is the total of all after tax accumulations shown on each line for pensions, social security, and accumulation type plans. This total value is part of the total investment assets required to provide the level of income desired at retirement.

summary This section simply summarizes how much in investment assets will be available from the prior calculations, compares that to how much would be required, illustrates the difference (a surplus or a shortage), and offers a calculation of how much would have to be saved as a percentage of salary in the future to make up the difference (if there is a shortage).

total of investment assets and pension plans available This is total of the future after tax value of prior calculations for personal investment assets, pensions, social security, and accumulation plans.

total needed This is the previously calculated amount of assets that would be required at the retirement age to provide the income desired.

shortage (−) or surplus projected at retirement age This is the difference between what would be required as compared to what is projected to be available.

additional savings required to meet goal This is the percentage of future salary that would need to be saved each year to accumulate the difference if there is a shortage (this will be a positive number). If there is a surplus, or more assets than will be needed, this will appear as a minus number.

7

CLAIMS ADMINISTRATION

By Robert Griffith

INTRODUCTION
IMPORTANCE OF EFFECTIVE CLAIMS
ADMINISTRATION
PLAN COSTS
EMPLOYEE SATISFACTION
ELEMENTS OF EFFECTIVE CLAIMS
ADMINISTRATION
TYPES OF CLAIMS ADMINISTRATORS
SELECTING CLAIMS ADMINISTRATORS
ASSESSING THE CLAIMS OFFICE
EVALUATING CLAIM SYSTEMS
NEGOTIATING PERFORMANCE AGREEMENTS
FUTURE TRENDS IN CLAIMS ADMINISTRATION

INTRODUCTION

The purpose of this chapter is to discuss the importance of effective claims administration in the overall management of employee benefits programs. The primary focus is on the claim payment process for medical and dental health plans since these two areas account for most benefits plan contact for employees and the greatest cost to employers. We also must consider several other areas which influence the claims payment process to put claims administration in the proper context of benefits plan management. Specifically, the proliferation of managed care programs such as utilization review (UR), preferred provider organizations (PPOs), health maintenance organizations (HMOs), and employee assistance programs (EAPs), as well as increased government reporting requirements, creates a need for effective integration of all components to ensure optimum plan performance.

This perspective of integrating administration components will assist in:

- Evaluating current administrative arrangements.
- Selecting future administration vendors.
- Anticipating future trends in claims administration.

IMPORTANCE OF EFFECTIVE CLAIMS ADMINISTRATION

Claims administration strongly affects plan cost and employee satisfaction—through the quality of services provided by the administrator.

Plan costs are influenced by:

- Administrative fees.
- Benefits payments.
- Plan utilization.

Employee satisfaction is determined by:

- Claims payment accuracy.
- Timeliness of processing.
- Responsiveness to claimant inquiries.
- Quality of communication with claimants.

PLAN COSTS

Administrative Fees

Funding method, employer size, and type of administrator clearly influence the cost of plan administration.

A 1988 employer survey by Foster Higgins revealed that administrative fees range from 4.6 percent, of paid claims for employers of 40,000 or more employees, to 6.5 percent, for employers with under 500 employees. The average for all employers was 5.7 percent (see Figure 7–1). The same survey found that employers using Blue Cross organizations as claims administrators experienced higher administrative costs (6.7 percent of paid claims) than employers using commercial carriers. Some of the difference may lie in the Blue Cross organizations' fees for discount arrangements or in lower percentages of self-funding with Blue Cross clients. Employers using third-party administrators (TPAs) or processing claims internally, reported the lowest administrative costs (4.7 percent of paid claims for TPAs and 4.5 percent for self-administration). Note, however, that services such as actuarial forecasting, medical consultations, and so forth, often are purchased separately when using a TPA.

Benefits Payments

Actual benefits payments to claimants obviously represent the major expense to employers who finance health plans through self-funding or minimum premium arrangements. Benefits dollars paid out also determine premium rates for conventionally insured and experience-rated

FIGURE 7–1
Administrative Expense, by Employer Size

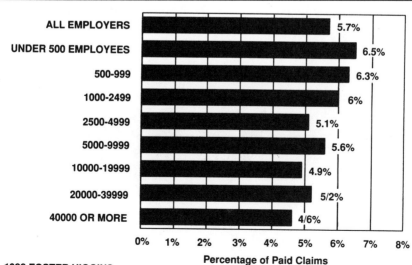

Source: 1988 FOSTER HIGGINS
HEALTH CARE BENEFITS SURVEY

plans. Studies show that larger employers favor self-funding (65% of employers with 1,000 employees or more self fund) and that smaller employers use insured funding arrangements (59% of employers with under 1,000 employees have fully insured or experience-rated plans) (see Figure 7–2). To counteract the potential impact of shock claims, self-funded employers are increasingly sharing risk through stop-loss coverage or reinsurance. This increase is in response to the AIDS epidemic and the increasing numbers of high-cost catastrophic cases from such factors as improved technologies and transplant skills.

Regardless of the funding method, dollars paid out for health care claims are the major expense of an employer's benefit program—no matter how significant an administrative fee is for self-funded employers or how low a premium rate for more traditionally insured programs. The dollars paid out will be a function of two key variables:

- Plan utilization.
- Accuracy and effectiveness of the claims administration process.

FIGURE 7–2
Method of Funding

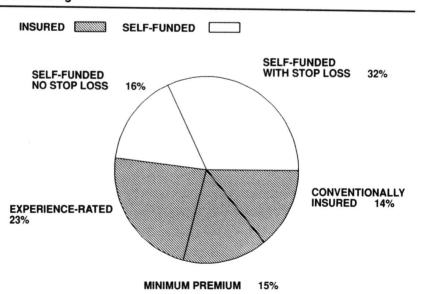

INSURED   SELF-FUNDED

SELF-FUNDED
WITH STOP LOSS   32%

SELF-FUNDED
NO STOP LOSS   16%

CONVENTIONALLY
INSURED   14%

EXPERIENCE-RATED
23%

MINIMUM PREMIUM   15%

Source: 1988 FOSTER HIGGINS
HEALTH CARE BENEFITS SURVEY

Plan Utilization

Plan utilization is defined as the amount of benefits consumed by the covered employee population. It is a function of benefits plan design and utilization control mechanisms in that design. Applying both factors is the substance of the claims administrator's responsibility. The administrator is primarily concerned with determining which health care services are covered under a particular benefit program and is, in varying degrees, expected to assess the medical necessity of particular services. In many instances, this responsibility is delegated to separate UR specialists at the claims administrator or to outside vendors of these services.

EMPLOYEE SATISFACTION

Claims Payment Accuracy

Claims payment accuracy is critical to the employees' satisfaction with the program. Because of the high cost of benefits today, employers strive to ensure positive perception of their benefits plans by the employees. Inaccurate claims payments reduce employee satisfaction through the adjustments needed to correct errors. Obviously, overpayments also mean unnecessary costs. Bill collectors may also dun employees for late payments that result from mistakes, and an employee's credit rating may be negatively affected. These consequences can be particularly distressing to employees who may already be experiencing anxieties associated with illness.

The accuracy of payments will be a function of the claim processing staff's expertise and quality in the claim payment processing system.

Timeliness of Processing

How quickly the claims administrator processes a claim is another key determinant of employee satisfaction with the benefits program. If the employee has paid the bill, funds should be quickly reimbursed. When the administrator is to pay the service provider through assignment of benefits, quick payment will avoid straining the employee/provider relationship. In some instances, prompt-pay discounts may be available to help keep plan costs down. PPO arrangements may contractually require claim payment within a specified period.

Responsiveness to Claimant Inquiries

When employees have questions about claim payments or benefit provisions, the claims administrator must be responsive. Many administrators have toll-free numbers to handle such inquiries. How quickly employees can get through, as well as the courteousness and helpfulness they receive, are consistently rated as important by employees when evaluating satisfaction with an administrator.

Quality of Communication with Claimants

The primary vehicle of communication between a claims administrator and a claimant is the Explanation of Benefits (EOB) form sent to the claimant with notice of payment. Therefore, this must be clear and complete when describing the action that the claims administrator has taken. If the description is unsatisfactory, the employee will be forced to make inquiries to the employer or claims administrator lowering employee satisfaction with the plan.

ELEMENTS OF EFFECTIVE CLAIMS ADMINISTRATION

To accomplish plan objectives of providing payment for medical and dental services in a cost-effective, positively perceived way, a claims administrator must perform certain key functions:

- Eligibility determination.
- Benefit adjudication.
- Financial and utilization data capture and reporting.
- Check and EOB generation.
- Servicing claimant and provider inquiries.

In addition to these classic responsibilities, controlling and monitoring unnecessary utilization is increasingly becoming part of many claims administrators' duties.

Eligibility Determination

The claims administrator must pay only claims for eligible employees and dependents under an employer's health plan. Eligibility may be certified either claim by claim by the employer or by the claims administrator from listings or enrollment forms.

Employer certification, which involves individual verification for each employee's claim by the employer's designated representative, has both advantages and disadvantages. On the positive side, eligibility verification is most current when the employer directly certifies each claim as it is submitted for payment. This method of eligibility determination ensures that only claims eligible for payment are forwarded to the administrator. Additionally, large claims and those with potential for case management can be identified by the employer. Some employers also certify to prescreen claims for completeness, which improves the chances a claim will be processed to completion with initial submission. Employers also can hold small claims that may apply to plan deductibles until sufficient expenses have been incurred. This practice can reduce claim processing costs by limiting the number of zero dollar and small claim payments.

Negative consequences of employer certification involve confidentiality, expense, and timeliness issues. Employees may be inhibited from submitting sensitive claims if an employer representative will be reviewing the claim. This situation can adversely affect employee satisfaction. The costs associated with having staff certify and review each claim as well as answer questions on submissions can be substantial. An administrator usually can perform those functions more efficiently. Employer certification generally adds time to the overall claims payment process, but where screening for completeness is performed, claims payment is actually facilitated.

Eligibility certification by the administrator for claims submitted directly by employees has become the predominant form of eligibility determination. Improved computer capabilities have spurred the movement in this direction. Methods of providing information to the administrator range from copies of enrollment cards to computer tapes; the latter is the preferred method because accuracy of data transfer is enhanced. Whichever method of transferring the eligibility information is used, the most important issue is the administrator's timely receipt. This minimizes the claims rejected for insufficient eligibility information and limits the claims paid after coverage is canceled.

Other issues to consider when using a claims administrator to certify eligibility involve what information will be supplied to the administrator and who will update changes in the database. Employers usually provide employee names and social security numbers, effective/termination dates of coverage, and whether or not the employee includes coverage of dependents, but not dependents' names and employee addresses. This information is usually obtained from claim submissions because it changes frequently. With the increased focus on costs and fraudulent claims, many employers have begun to collect dependent, coordination of benefits (COB), and address information and then provide it to their administrator. As more employers install improved human resource computer systems, this will become easier.

Benefits Adjudication

The actual application of benefits plan provisions and calculation of allowances are known as benefit adjudication. Claims administrators are responsible for this function as part of the administration process. In the past, this process was handled by clerks who referenced coverage information and manually calculated benefits. Paper claims files were maintained and updated as subsequent claims were received. As expected, the accuracy and speed of processing varied greatly. Tracking claim expenditures and utilization was also difficult in such an environment.

Today, most administrators use computerized claims payment systems with differing sophistication in adjudication capabilities as well as for data capture and reporting. The best of these systems are highly automated and can adjudicate complicated claims with various pricing conventions in a fraction of the time required for manual adjudication.

Financial and Utilization Data Capture and Reporting

Today's benefits manager needs extensive financial and utilization data to effectively manage a plan. Collecting and reporting this data are responsibilities of the administrator because the data is contained in individual claims submissions.

An effective administrator must capture complete data for the benefits manager to assess plan performance, and it must be collected with high specificity and accuracy. At a minimum, the administrator must collect employee or dependent name, age, sex, type and number of services, date incurred, provider name, diagnosis, and cost. Diagnostic and type of service (procedure) data should be collected using the standard ICD9–CM and CPT–4 coding conventions for comparisons with established utilization and financial norms.

The actual reporting of financial and utilization data should use summary formats rather than voluminous printouts of each claim detail. Financial data should summarize expenses by specified plan types, employee populations, and cost centers. Utilization data should highlight major diagnostic categories (MDCs), lengths of stay for inpatient admissions, admission rates and outpatient utilization patterns. High utilization—by employees and providers—also should be evaluated. This data will allow the benefits manager to measure effectiveness of current benefits design and consider alternatives to support company cost and benefits objectives.

Check and Explanation of Benefits

Successful adjudication of a claim will result in generation of an EOB and, if appropriate, a claim check. The administrator produces checks and EOBs either daily or according to agreement with the employer. If the payment is going to a provider, the administrator will issue a second EOB to the covered employee.

When checks or other financial instruments are used, security is critical. The claim administrator is responsible for maintaining adequate security over check generation and stock. Procedures are necessary to account for checks issued and returned/refunded and to return credit to an employers' plan.

The EOB is a critical communication vehicle in the benefit plan administration process. It details what services were considered for payment, what benefits were paid, and if plan maximums have been exhausted. An effective EOB will detail these items in an easily readable format. For employers with significant non-English speaking populations, some administrators are offering EOBs in other languages.

Servicing Claimant and Provider Inquiries

Some claims involve unusual circumstances or require additional information. Other claims payments may be delayed or be incorrectly adjudicated. In all these situations an employer, employee, or provider will contact the claims administrator to ask a question or provide an answer to a request for information. How the claims administrator handles these inquiries contributes significantly to effective administration of the benefits program.

Today, most claims administrators use sophisticated telephone systems to distribute calls, track waiting times, deliver prerecorded messages, and provide servicing reports to management. These systems are critical to effectively managing customer inquiries. Once the call reaches a customer service representative, the representative's skill determines the inquirer's satisfaction. Specifically, courteousness, ability to understand the problem, and willingness to provide information or make payment adjustments will determine the effectiveness of the interaction. Claims administrators are responsible for providing this service effectively with minimum waiting times for both initial contact and problem resolution.

Monitoring and Controlling Unnecessary Plan Utilization

While some facets of monitoring and controlling plan utilization are part of claims adjudication, their importance has forced major components of these activities to Utilization Review (UR). This function is a recent development that has become widely accepted. Over two thirds (68 percent) of all responding employers to a recent benefits survey require participants to certify elective hospital admissions for medical necessity (see Figure 7–3). These services are provided by UR departments of claims administrators as well as stand-alone UR vendors. Related services included under UR include continued stay review, discharge planning, and large case management. These activities complement the claims administration process. Many companies have penalties for not complying with hospital precertification requirements; the claims administrator is responsible for applying these penalties. Data transfer must occur between the UR and claims adjudication processes which can be complex, particularly, if separate mental health and/or substance abuse UR functions are used.

TYPES OF CLAIMS ADMINISTRATORS

Claims administration has traditionally been provided by four major types of organizations:

- Commercial insurance carriers.
- Blue Cross/Blue Shield organizations.
- TPAs.
- Self-administration.

The type used by an employer is determined by several factors:

FIGURE 7-3
Growth in Use of Precertification Programs

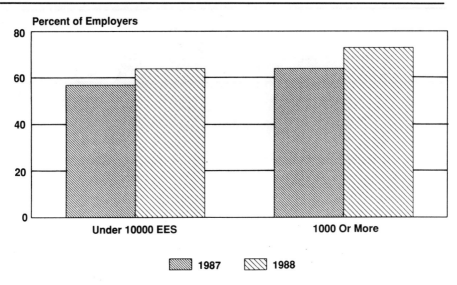

Source: 1988 FOSTER HIGGINS
HEALTH CARE BENEFITS SURVEY

cost, employer philosophy, tradition, and Blue Cross/Blue Shield discounts.

Most employers rely on third parties to adjudicate health claims. According to the 1988 Foster Higgins survey, only 7 percent handle these functions in house; the rest use commercial carriers, Blue Cross/Blue Shield organizations, or TPAs to administer their plans. Employers with insured programs, including minimum premium arrangements, generally rely on their insurers for administrative services, giving TPAs only an 8 percent share of their business. Self-insured employers tend to spread the business across commercial carriers (41 percent), TPAs (35 percent), and Blue Cross/Blue Shield organizations (20 percent) (see Figure 7-4).

Commercial Insurance Carriers

The insurance carrier is a popular option for administration because, in most instances, it offers comprehensive services. The employer can package life insurance, disability, and various other benefit options with

FIGURE 7–4
Type of Administrator Used—All Employers

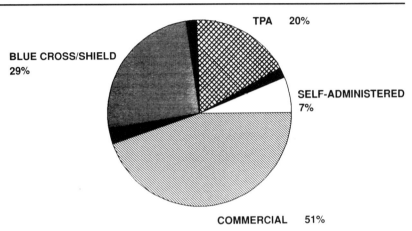

Source: 1988 FOSTER HIGGINS
HEALTH CARE BENEFITS SURVEY

health benefits. Multiple funding options are available. As health care moves in the direction of managed care, commercial carriers are also offering UR services and provider networks. These trends have positioned the largest of the commercial carriers as the most appealing handlers of multiple-option plans for many employers.

From a claims administration perspective, commercial carriers tend to have mainframe payment systems with high capabilities and sophistication. Financial and utilization data reporting has improved to the point where meaningful analysis can be done from many standard report packages. The commercial carriers also tend to have large regional claim payment facilities. Some carriers have combined their indemnity health plan claims administration with managed care claims processing. This trend results in more standard reporting formats and greater ability to assess both the managed care and indemnity pieces as a single entity.

Blue Cross/Blue Shield Organizations

Unlike commercial carriers, Blue Cross/Blue Shield organizations began with strong ties to providers, including negotiated arrangements with hospitals in many parts of the country and participating arrangements in the physician community. These situations have favored Blue Cross and Blue Shield organizations in terms of costs. In some parts of the country, discounts on the hospital side have been so favorable that commercial carrier major medical plans were "wrapped" around a Blue Cross hospital plan. Depending on plan design, this could cause claims administration problems, but hospital discounts have diminished in recent years so the issue is not as compelling.

Blue Cross/Blue Shield plans belong to a national association of plans. From a claims administration perspective this has several implications. The national association promulgates quality standards for all plans—a positive feature. Also, because of the nature of discounts, claims tend to get paid by the Blue plan with jurisdiction over the location where services are rendered. Employers' claims charges are billed back to the plan the employer has contracted with through an Interplan Data Reporting (IPDR) system. Generally this arrangement works well, although some coordination problems do occur.

Because of their strong ties to providers, Blue Cross organizations are more likely to have electronic interfaces with providers, facilitating claim submissions.

Where provider discounts are less of an issue, Blue Cross organizations tend to be less competitive and have less market share. This may be due to a less comprehensive products offering than commercial carriers, as well as a perceived lesser degree of flexibility in product design options.

Third-Party Administrators

As self-funded plans have increased, so has the use of TPAs. This correlation is not surprising; just as self-funding is a way to reduce health plan costs, so is the use of a TPA.

TPAs vary greatly in size, geographic presence, and sophistication. Some are small, stand-alone organizations while others are divisions of large insurers or managed care companies. Common to almost all TPAs, however, is a focus on providing claim payment services only. Services such as underwriting and actuarial services traditionally provided by large commercial carriers need to be purchased elsewhere. Limiting the services TPAs provide has allowed them to be less costly claims administrators. TPAs also are often able to offer more flexibility in benefit design.

Until recently TPAs had less sophisticated claim systems; this no longer appears to be the case. Some of the smaller TPAs are still plagued by fluctuations in service quality, due mainly to fewer resources to handle staff turnover or increased work. The Foster Higgins study shows that approximately 20 percent of all employers and 35 percent of self-funded employers use TPAs exclusively or in conjunction with some other administrator (see Figure 7–5).

Self-Administration

As an administrative option, paying claims internally has been a less popular alternative than using a third party. Current data indicates only 7 percent of all employers and 11 percent of self-funded employers administer their own claims—for several reasons:

• A certain critical mass of employees is required to make self-administration economically feasible. Staff must be hired and trained, claims payment hardware and software needs to be purchased or leased, and provisions need to be established for medical and/or dental profes-

FIGURE 7–5
Type of Administrator Used—Self-Funded Employers

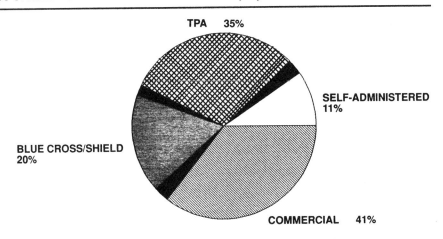

Source: 1988 FOSTER HIGGINS
HEALTH CARE BENEFITS SURVEY

sional review. Most employers cannot justify these costs on a per claim transaction basis when compared with a third party, who can spread costs across a much larger base of covered lives. A minimum of 5,000 lives seems to be necessary to justify self-administration.

• Many employers prefer to maintain a buffer between employees and the claim payment process for confidentiality as well as liability concerns.

• If done poorly, self-administration can be particularly damaging to employee relations and potentially expensive if significant claim backlogs occur.

Despite the negatives of self-administration, in the right circumstances, it can make a great deal of sense. If an employer is sufficiently large, this alternative can be less expensive than a TPA and offers greater control over claim turnaround time, benefit determination, and financial and utilization reporting. Today's claim payment software also makes this alternative more realistic than in the past. Costs are also much more attractive.

SELECTING CLAIMS ADMINISTRATORS

In selecting a claims administrator, a structured process is best to find one who meets an employer's cost and employee relations objectives. Generally, a bid process is used consisting of a Request for Proposal (RFP) which is issued to selected administrators. The RFP usually includes a structured questionnaire which covers pricing, system capabilities, staffing resources, and other pertinent information. Once proposals are received, spreadsheet analysis is performed so that the respondents can be ranked. The top-ranking administrators make presentations and answer additional questions. From the administrator presentations, finalists are chosen. Visits are then made to the administrators' claim offices. This step is critical because many of the important elements of effective claim administration cannot be ascertained from either proposals or presentations, for example, whether the employer believes they can work with the claims office staff. Since day-to-day contact will most often occur with this group, the employer's comfort with these individuals is important. No matter how impressive the proposal responses, presentations, and visits, reference checks of other clients are advisable to see if the service promised is delivered.

Preparing the RFP

Before preparing an RFP, clearly defined benefit plan objectives are necessary. An employer will be most successful in selecting an appropriate claims administrator after determining which goals are primary—cost, systems sophistication, customer service, comprehensiveness of products, administrator flexibility, and data reporting capabilities. Once priorities are set, questions specific to an employer's objectives can be devised. Depending on level of importance, questions and evaluations will focus on the areas below.

ASSESSING THE CLAIMS OFFICE

The administrator's claims office is where most activity of the benefits plan administration will take place. It is important then to evaluate key elements of that claims office. The critical elements to evaluate include:

- Location.
- Size and experience levels of staff.
- Organization structure.
- Ability to coordinate with vendors of adjunct services.
- Flexibility and responsiveness.
- Quality control and security.

Location of Claims Office

Depending on the physical dispersion of the employer's staff across the country, the location of proposed claims offices becomes important. With commercial carriers and larger TPAs, the trend has been away from small, local claims offices toward large, regional service centers. Blue Cross organizations can provide centralized services, also, but often use participating arrangements between plans.

Determining the numbers and locations of claims offices needed will depend on the employer's particular needs. The favored approach is as few claims offices as possible because more dedicated staff in one place allows for better knowledge of an employer's plan and more influence with claims office management on the employer's behalf. Time zone differences may be an issue for some employers and must be balanced against the advantages of a single claim payment office.

Size and Experience Levels of Staff

Quality claim service is mainly determined by the number of experienced claims-paying staff at the office. No matter how sophisticated the administrator's system, if the staff is not competent and experienced, quality claims service is impossible. Sufficient staff to handle growth and seasonal variations of claims submissions is also necessary.

Organization Structure

How a claim office is structured influences the level of service an employer receives. Key contacts for employees and benefits staff need to be ascertained. Also, a separate customer service unit, as opposed to claims processors who also handle telephone inquiries, is better for many employers. On-site UR will be important to some employers, as will walk-in customer services centers for others. If the administrator also provides a preferred provider organization (PPO), a separate client services department needs to be integrated into the claims process to ensure smooth functioning.

Ability to Coordinate with Vendors of Adjunct Services

Managed Care is quickly becoming the norm in health benefits plans today. As this trend continues, the need to effectively integrate options such as EAPs, PPOs, UR, and point-of-service options where employees choose provider options each time they use a service, becomes critical. Administrators have differing capabilities, flexibilities, and philosophies regarding these programs. Employers must carefully assess their objectives in these areas and determine if a good fit exists between potential claims administrators. Since these programs will be a departure from traditional ways of claims administration for many employers, the potential for employee dissatisfaction is high if the various entities do not integrate well. Furthermore, the cost savings expected from these programs cannot occur without effective integration.

Some employers may be tempted to accept an administrator's packaged set of services to avoid these pitfalls. This may not achieve maximum effectiveness, mainly due to unevenness in some administrator's cost containment products and geographic differences in many provider networks. A separate evaluation of these adjunct services is in the employers best interests in most instances.

Flexibility and Responsiveness

Administrators differ markedly in their ability and willingness to be flexible in administering a plan, based on claims systems, pricing strategies, and attitude. The need for administrative flexibility must be evaluated by an employer in light of their particular employee population. In some instances, inflexibility may be desired for bargaining situations. In others, such as those with high numbers of retirees or professional employees, greater flexibility will be better. Responsiveness to inquiries also will vary in importance. In general, responsiveness is viewed as a positive, but for special degrees of responsiveness, for example, separate dedicated customer service representatives, added costs may be significant.

Quality Control and Security

Ensuring the accuracy of claims payment and preventing unauthorized use of plan assets are critical to the financial integrity of a benefits plan. The claims administrator is responsible for establishing procedures in the areas including:

- A formal internal audit program to test claims for accuracy on an ongoing basis.
- Benefit calculation, examining claims for completeness and medical necessity, and claim coding checks.
- Specialized audits for fraud and high-dollar payments.
- Monitoring office and claim system security measures.
- Logging and securing check stock and returned checks.
- Passwords for claims systems access, to be issued by management and changed periodically.
- Reports of system overrides, for review by management to ensure against unauthorized transactions.

All these should be stated in the RFP and, during the visits, proposal responses compared to actual setups. Where discrepancies exist, probe further to establish the administrator's actual situation and capabilities in these areas.

EVALUATING CLAIM SYSTEMS

The claim payment process has benefited greatly from computerization. The myriad of benefit plan options, plan maximums, and data elements lend themselves especially well to the capabilities of today's sophisticated software. While some claim administrators still adjudicate claims manually, most use computers. Some administrators have developed software themselves, while others rely on vendors to design the system. As one would expect, there are significant differences that can affect the claims payment process. Each employer should carefully evaluate capabilities and regularly update their knowledge base of the various systems before choosing an administrator. To assess a claims payment system from an employer's perspective the following areas should be reviewed:

- **Input**   What files are maintained in the system? What degree of specificity in data capture exists?
- **Adjudication capabilities**   Is the system flexible enough to accommodate various benefit designs?
- **Output**   Are reports, EOBs, and inquiry functions user friendly and responsive to employee needs?

Input

To meet the processing, reporting, and customer service needs of today's employer, software must be capable of accessing a great deal of data. The system must track eligibility information on an employee and dependent basis. Information on effective dates of coverage, breaks in service, ages and sexes of covered participants, work division, and presence of other insurance is maintained by the more sophisticated systems. Most will accept this data from employers on magnetic tape as well as in paper formats. Some will even allow direct entry via terminal hookup.

Necessary provider information is also to be maintained on-line. At a minimum, provider names, addresses, and tax identification numbers (TIN) need to be stored in data files for IRS 1099 reporting and checking credentials.

If an employer participates in a managed care network, provider files may also contain or interface with pricing files which detail negotiated fee levels. Pricing files will exist for benefit plans that pay on a reasonable and customary, scheduled, or managed care basis. The degree of updating will vary by administrator, customer requirements, and provider contracting. It is important that pricing be system controlled to ensure accuracy and consistency in claims payments.

The employer's benefits plan is loaded into the software in the plan description file. This file contains most plan features for a particular set of benefits. The more benefit provisions that can be loaded into this file, the greater the accuracy and consistency of adjudication.

Adjudication Capabilities

The benefit plan calculation logic available in a claims system determines its adjudication capabilities. Issues to be evaluated include the amount of manual intervention necessary to pay a claim, the degree that special payment routines (i.e., COB and medical necessity) are programmed, and system prompts to assist claim processors. Batch processing may be of interest to some employers who choose to release benefits at specific intervals rather than continually.

Output

Output is largely a function of input and adjudication capabilities. Assuming the proper data elements are in the database; appropriate financial, utilization, and management reports will be available to the employer. These reports should be reviewed in light of overall business objectives. Clarity and completeness of data output are critical.

If a review of available reports indicates deficiencies, several options are available:

• Request custom reports, which may be available if the systems captures necessary data elements. (Confirm the cost of these reports; they vary greatly among administrators depending on ad hoc report-generating capabilities.)
• Obtain raw data and have a utilization or financial data analysis performed by a consultant.
• Some administrators make data access available to clients on-line or down loaded in formats that allow manipulating data into desired report formats (this requires specific technical knowledge and can be costly).

EOBs, benefit checks, and requests for additional information are other important output items and also should be reviewed for clarity and completeness. The better claims systems have extensive communications capabilities, including free form and customization options.

Claims systems continue to evolve as technical advances occur and requirements of plan administration change. Reviewing recent and planned enhancements to an administrator's system will give an employer a sense of the relative sophistication of one system when compared with others.

NEGOTIATING PERFORMANCE AGREEMENTS

A growing number of employers with Administrative Services Only (ASO) and minimum premium arrangements are negotiating performance standards with their claims administrators. Foster Higgins' survey indicates that 10 percent of responding employers with these funding arrangements have negotiated performance standards and another 11 percent plan to do so (see Figure 7–6). Larger employers are generally more successful in securing such agreements. In the survey sample cited, only 5 percent of employers with fewer than 5,000 employees had negotiated performance agreements compared with 25 percent of employers with more than 5,000 employees. For the very large employer, performance agreements are becoming the rule rather than the exception; 46 percent of survey respondents with 40,000 or more employees had implemented performance standards in 1988 with another 23 percent planning to do so soon.

Standards usually focus on timeliness of payment, financial accuracy, and data capture accuracy. Less frequently, minimum COB savings are prescribed. Many performance agreements include financial penalties and/or incentives for the administrator.

Determining results under a performance agreement can be a problem, however. It is important at the outset to define clearly what will be evaluated and the specify methods that will be used to test for the results achieved. This is important so that both administrator and employer accept the validity of any audits or other performance measures. For example, if data entry, timeliness, and/or accuracy will be measured, a simple random sample of claims paid during the period can be selected for audit, based on the size of claim population. If overall financial accuracy will be evaluated, more sophisticated sampling techniques, such as stratification, will be necessary. The key point is that attributes to be measured will decide the appropriate sampling method. Failure to

FIGURE 7–6
Negotiate Performance Standards, by Employer Size

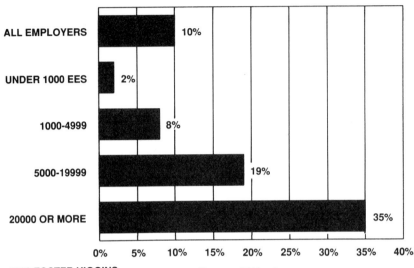

Source: 1988 FOSTER HIGGINS
HEALTH CARE BENEFITS SURVEY   Percent Of Employers

specify items to be evaluated and how they will be measured when entering a performance agreement can cause disagreements on results.

Generally accepted financial accuracy standards range between 98.5 percent and 99.5 percent for dollars paid out correctly by an administrator without error. This standard includes both overpayment and underpayments on a *non*-netted basis. Most administrators set financial accuracy standards at 99 percent. In terms of numbers of errors (rate or occurrence), payment error rates should not exceed 5 percent; most administrators are willing to commit to rates less than this, however. Nonfinancial error rates also are generally limited to 5 percent.

A complicating factor is how error rate percents are determined by various administrators, who differ in what constitutes an error and how errors are counted. Some use line items or services rendered to calculate error rates while others count data entry incidents to measure accuracy. Some administrators have devised weighted error classifications. These examples underscore the need to define terms first and avoid disagreements later.

FUTURE TRENDS IN CLAIMS ADMINISTRATION

As in most other areas of employee benefit programs, claims administration can be expected to change and evolve. Government action, continued cost increases, and changing attitudes will move claims administration into new areas. Major trends follow.

More Managed Care

Continued cost increases will accelerate the current trend to more managed care-oriented health benefits plans. The traditional fee-for-service indemnity health plan will decrease in prominence during the 1990s. With this greater emphasis on managed care, claim administration will shift in focus to the provider. Employees still will be involved but it will be far more limited. Direct claim submission by providers—either electronically or on paper—will be part of most provider contracting. This should improve control over the claims administration process.

Better Software

Improved claims payment software also will bring about more control over the claims payment process. Treatment protocols will be integrated with provider profiles to control health plan utilization. This will be monitored by the claims payment process. Improved software also will allow higher customization in benefit design, reporting, and EOBs.

Integrated Processing

As HMOs improve their claims systems and data reporting capabilities, integration with other managed care options and indemnity plans becomes possible. Several major commercial carriers have combined claims payment operations for these health plan options. This trend will accelerate as employers seek greater control over all health plan offerings.

Direct Employer Access to Administrator Systems

Employers are increasingly interested in direct access to their administrator's claims systems. Direct eligibility input into an administrator's system by an employer eliminates delays in claim processing and allows for immediate updates. Claim status inquiries can also be handled by on-line access, and financial and utilization experience data can also be made available. As administrators become more adept at providing on-line access, new applications will undoubtedly become available.

Technological Advances

Some administrators are experimenting with public claim submission terminals similar to bank automatic teller machines. The idea has appeal given today's computer-oriented society and wider application is expected. Optical scanning of claims also is being investigated by some administrators. If successful, this should improve productivity for claims administrators. This will help to control processing costs. Other technological advances include voice activated telephone inquiry systems and improved electronic data transfer between various suppliers of managed care services.

CHAPTER 8

COST MANAGEMENT AND CONTROL

By John W. Barton

INTRODUCTION BY ERNEST J. E. GRIFFES
MANAGING BENEFIT COSTS
WHAT IS COST CONTROL?
HOSPITAL-MEDICAL BENEFITS
USE OF THE 501 (C) (9) TRUST IN MANAGING PLAN COSTS
LONG-TERM DISABILITY BENEFITS
DEFINED BENEFIT PENSION PLANS
COST CONTROL AND PLAN ADMINISTRATION
COST CONTAINMENT

INTRODUCTION*

Controlling the rising cost of employee benefits has been of concern to company management and benefits executives for many years. In earlier chapters we have reviewed how these costs of doing business have increased steadily and what we can expect in the future. In this chapter, we will examine what benefit costs consist of and how those costs might be managed.

---

* By Ernest Griffes

Control Versus Reduction of Benefit Costs

It is common to confuse *controlling* costs with *reducing* costs. There are some actions that can be taken to manage the cost of benefits; that is, control when the cost is recognized, how it is recognized, where in the accounting functions it is recognized, who absorbs the cost, and so on.

These accounting aspects of benefit costs are very significant because they affect profitability, shareholders' earnings, and thus, market price of the stock—depending upon how and when the costs are "booked."

Controlling costs, then, involves close coordination between the benefits executives and financial units of the organization. The benefits executives inform the financial people of what the costs are expected to be, when they will have to be actually disbursed in the form of payments, what part of the costs constitute current direct cost, and what part of the costs may be of a *liability* nature, (that is, a future cost but not a current expense).

It then rests with the financial function to decide how and when to book these expenses, how to accrue future liabilities, whether to actually set these aside in a trust or to only recognize these on the company's books, who to charge for the expenses, and so on.

We will explore throughout this chapter some of the accounting ramifications of managing plan costs.

Cost *reduction,* on the other hand, is a very different matter from cost management. Cost reduction encompasses the actual changing of benefit costs to lower costs than in the past. However, it also includes the concept of reducing costs in the future, that is to say, reducing the expected increase in costs in the future. Some level of increasing cost is virtually a certainty, short of actually reducing benefits, a reversal in inflationary trends, or shifting costs to employees.

In discussing reducing benefit costs, then, we must think in two frames of reference—the means of reducing actual current benefit costs and the means of acting to reduce the increases in future benefit costs.

What Exactly are Benefit Costs?

The first reaction to considering what benefit costs are is to think of them as the dollar cost booked as a benefit expense each year. For a medical-hospital plan, for example, the cost might be thought of as the dollar amount of premiums paid to the insurance company and thus charged as an expense against earnings. In fact, this may not be the "cost" of a benefit because of a number of factors we shall consider in this chapter.

As we discussed in earlier chapters, the cost of a benefit has been simplified into the formula:

Cost = Benefits paid + Administration expense − Earnings on assets

To get at the possibilities for reducing costs requires a much more careful examination of each benefit plan, what expenses enter into the cost of that plan, and what can be done to change those expenses to lower levels, either now or in the future. This exercise can lead us into some almost mystical realms as we pry into how insurers develop premium rates and actuaries develop pension costs.

As pointed out in previous chapters, the cost of a benefit is also a function of where the benefit expense falls; that is, who is charged for the expense. An employer may well reduce the company's cost by requiring employees to pay more for the benefit. Such a course is obviously not reducing the cost but is only shifting it—and in an inefficient way at that—since the employer can deduct the cost but the employee must pay taxes on the earnings to pay for their part of the cost.

Cost shifting to employees has become a more viable and practical strategy for employers as a result of the pre-tax treatment of employee contributions in 401(k) salary deferral plans and 125 flexible spending account plans. Still, even with the employee pre-tax treatment, the net result is a reduction in take home pay—and that leads to pressure for salary increases. If competition for skilled employees results in concessions to these pressures for higher pay, the end result is that the employer has only shifted the cost from benefits into direct compensation.

The benefits executive, in considering how to reduce benefit costs, must be thinking not only about how to reduce the employer's share, but also about how to reduce the employees' costs as well.

The net of this is that reducing costs, actually defined, means providing the same benefit at lower cost for all cost-sharing units or providing more benefits for the same current cost to all cost-sharing units. The corollary to this definition of cost reduction is to provide the benefit at the most efficient cost to all cost-sharing units—that is, the cost that fully capitalizes on all legal and tax opportunities to bring each related expense to its lowest possible point for whomever is paying the expense.

Benefit Costs Overall

In considering the management and reduction of benefit costs, it is true that the sum total of the expense of each plan is equal to the "expense for benefits" for a given organization. It is also true that the whole cost of benefits is greater than the sum of the expense of each benefit. The reason for the whole being greater than the sum of the parts is that the expenses for designing, administering, and communicating benefits overall is also a benefit cost, often an expense ignored in evaluating what the total expenses are for benefits in a given organization. These expenses for managing benefit plans are, however, a cost of benefits that the benefits executive needs to be very conscious of, even if the financial management of the company is willing to consider these as something other than a benefit expense.

This point is made because managements tend to think in total concepts; that is, the cost of benefits in total is "too high," or benefits are "costing too much." Benefits executives, who must explain the cost of benefits to management, must think in terms of the total cost and the detail components of that total cost. By explaining the cost of each component benefit as related to the competitiveness of that benefit in the labor market, the benefits executive can participate in judging if, in fact, benefit costs are too high and why the costs are what they are.

Another reason that the whole is greater than the sum of the parts is that there is a cost associated with *not* providing a benefit or certain benefits. Earlier chapters examined the question of benefits as a tool for competing for labor and motivating employees. If a benefit program in total cannot be marketed to employees as competitive or specific parts of the program are significantly deficient, then the organization is hobbled in competing for labor and motivating the workforce. This produces costs in human resources management—in recruiting and retaining employees and in morale and productivity. These are benefit costs though they do not appear on the books of the company as a benefit expense.

In examining the management and reduction of benefit costs, the benefits executive must maintain a balanced perspective between benefit costs overall and the actual expense of each specific component of the benefit program.

In order to make real progress in reducing benefit costs, each benefit program must be examined and acted upon in separate ways. Moreover, in this examination of the expense of each program, it may become discouraging to find that only a very small reduction in cost can be effected. If the cost of a $5 million medical plan can be reduced $250,000, that is a savings worth the effort. But viewed in terms of total benefit costs—that is, as management views benefits costs—this savings makes virtually no difference whatever. Hence, it is the fate of benefits executives to struggle with reducing benefit costs in meaningful dollar amounts as a result of painstaking effort only to face the ultimate fact that total benefit costs are not significantly reduced.

The point is that the benefits executive should make note of these cost reductions and point them out clearly to management in dollar terms, in order to attack the impression that nothing is being done or can be done to reduce benefit costs. Since management only sees benefit costs as a budget line or expense line in some complex financial statement, they have only the difference in those line items from year to year on which to judge the effectiveness of managing those costs.

And that line item for benefits usually increases every year, even when the benefits executive has effected significant dollar reduction in some benefit expenses.

What to Include in Benefit Costs

It is common practice to compare benefit costs in surveys as a percentage of payroll. The annual survey of employee benefits by the U.S. Chamber of Commerce is one of the most reliable comparative surveys of benefit costs because it has been conducted on the same basis since the 1950s. The 1988 report illustrates that benefit costs as a percent of payroll increased from 17 percent in 1955 to 39 percent in 1987.

However, behind such dramatic information lies the question to be asked—"What benefits are included in these percentages?"—and beyond that "What expenses are classifiable as a benefit expense?"

For example, are social security payments by the employer a benefit expense or a tax expense? Is a contribution to governmental workers' compensation plans, unemployment compensation plans, or state disability income plans, a benefit expense or a taxation expense? Is a vacation allowance or a paid holiday a benefit expense or simply a part of salary expense? Such questions beg the issue of what really is a benefit in the employment context.

What to include as benefit expenses is a very important matter to decide for any given organization, however, simply because from year to year management is interested in measuring its benefit costs and this is difficult to do if there is no clear definition of what is to be included for this measurement.

Best illustrating this point, perhaps, are employee product discount plans by which employees may purchase the products (or services) of the employer at discounted prices. Certainly, employees think of this as a benefit of employment with that company. Yet there may be no cost at all to the employer if the products are sold to employees at the wholesale price at which they would otherwise be marketed to a retailer. If the employees save 50 cents on the dollar or get the product for half retail price in a store, certainly this is of benefit to the employee. But should this savings be included in benefit costs inasmuch as it doesn't actually cost the employer at all?

Accordingly, it is necessary for the benefits executive to lead the organization into a definition of what is to be acknowledged as a benefit in evaluating from year to year the cost of benefits.

This is also very critical to the benefits executive for guiding the organization in planning and budgeting for benefit expenses. Confusion in management over what benefit costs actually are is often traceable to the difference between what benefit costs are as projected in the budgeting process, as against what those costs are as described in employee communications or reports to management. For example, consider only vacations and holidays, which may alone constitute 5 to 6 percent of payroll. These are not generally budgeted as a benefit expense separately since they are masked within the salary budget. But they are generally considered a benefit. Thus, the budget process may project benefits costs at, say, 20 percent of payroll (for pensions, medical insurance, etc.), but in this case, benefits may be described as being worth 26 percent of payroll when nonbudgeted vacations are included.

Again, if the value of employee product discounts is 3 percent of payroll to the employees, this may be added to a description of the worth of benefits to employees, making the percentage 29 percent of payroll. But such a value is not budgeted as a benefit cost or recorded as a benefit expense.

In this simple (but valid) example the described value of benefits is almost 50 percent greater than the budgeted benefits expense. Such a difference can be confusing to management in evaluating benefit costs, and it rests with the benefits executive to clear up or avoid such confusion. (See the extensive listing of programs and plans that may be considered as benefits in Table 8–1.)

TABLE 8–1
Partial Listing of Benefit Plans and Programs Offered by Employers

Accidental death and dismemberment insurance	Matching educational, charitable contributions
Adoption benefits	Nurseries
Birthdays (time off)	Nursing home care
Business and professional memberships	Outside medical services
Cash profit sharing	Paid attendance at business, professional and other outside meetings
Civic activities (time off)	
Club memberships	Parking facilities
Company medical assistance	Pension
Company provided or subsidized automobiles	Personal accident insurance
	Personal counseling
Company provided housing	Personal credit cards
Company provided-for subsidized travel	Personal liability insurance
Credit unions	Physical examinations
Day care centers	Physical fitness programs
Death leave	Political activities (time off)
Deferred bonus	Preretirement counseling
Deferred compensation plan	Price discount plan
Deferred profit sharing	Professional activities
Dental and eye care insurance	Psychiatric services
Discount on company products	Recreation facilities, sports activities
Discount on other products	Resort facilities
Education costs	Retirement gratuity
Educational activities (time off)	Sabbatical leave
Employment contract	Salary continuation
Executive dining room	Savings plan
Financial counseling	Scholarships for dependents
Free or subsidized lunches	Severance pay
Group automobile insurance	Sickness and accident insurance
Group homeowners insurance	Social Security
Group legal insurance	Social service sabbaticals
Group life insurance	Split-dollar insurance
Health maintenance organization fees	State disability plans
Holidays	Stock appreciation rights
Home health care	Stock bonus plans
Hospital-surgical-medical insurance	Stock option plans (qualified, nonqualified, tandem)
Interest free loans	
Layoff pay (SUB)	Stock purchase plans
Legal, estate planning, and other professional assistance	Survivors benefits
	Tax assistance
Loans of company equipment	Training program
Long-term disability benefit	Travel accident insurance
	Vacations
	Weekly indemnity insurance

Components of Benefit Costs

In the balance of this chapter, the components of cost for each of the four major benefit plans will be examined and discussed—namely, medical benefits, long-term disability benefits, life insurance benefits, and pension benefits. This process will provide the basic guidance concerning how to go about examining the cost components of any given benefit plan.

MANAGING BENEFIT COSTS*

The cost of benefits has been increasing dramatically in recent years. The reasons for the increase are several:

Inflation.

The lag between increases in inflation and the rates of investment return on plan assets.

Benefit improvements—agreed upon in negotiations—provided as a result of competition in the job market to meet other human resource objectives or extended as an alternative to direct compensation because of the income tax implications for employees and the payroll tax costs for employers.

Increased utilization of many forms of benefits.

Controlling the cost of benefits is an important management function and will become more so if, as is expected, costs continue to increase—both in nominal terms and as a percentage of pay.

This chapter will review the component parts of the cost of different types of benefits and discuss the principles of managing costs.

The basic functions in plan financial management are to account for costs so that they are recognized as being incurred when appropriate, to control the timing and volume of cash disbursements, to allocate costs between employee and employer, and to fund plans so that the costs incurred are minimized.

Because benefit costs have a direct impact on a corporation's ac-

---

* The rest of this chapter was written by John W. Barton.

TABLE 8–2
Benefit Costs: A Model

Benefit costs should be considered as consisting of three parts:
1. The value of benefits under the plan provisions
                              plus
2. The cost of administering those benefits
                              less
3. Earnings on investments (for plans which accumulate assets).

The following should be the benefits executive's objectives in managing plan finances:
1. To minimize the cost of administration without losing administrative controls which are necessary to assure that the benefits payable are consistent with plan provisions.
2. To assure that the benefits received are of the appropriate type, which is accomplished by good plan design.
3. To control the obligations for benefits, to the extent possible so that costs are incurred at a time consistent with the employer's broader financial objectives.

counting for profitability, plan management involves close coordination between benefit and financial managers. Although the accounting for benefit costs, the investment of plan assets, and incorporating projected benefit costs and cash disbursements into the long-term plans of the company are generally financial functions, the benefits executive's expertise is a vital part of the process. The benefits department must advise financial managers what cash will be disbursed and when, what portion of incurred costs must be or can be recognized for accounting purposes as a form of liability, and what the pattern of incurred costs and cash disbursements is likely to be in the future.

The benefit cost model and its components (see Table 8–2), in conjunction with the objectives in managing plan finances, form the framework for considering management of benefit plan costs throughout this chapter.

WHAT IS COST CONTROL?

To establish the objectives for plan financial management, it is first necessary to balance the direct cost, which is represented as a budget expense, against the broader objectives that led the company to provide benefits in the first place. If the benefit plan provisions are necessary to recruit and retain employees—especially if the employees needed are highly skilled or for other reasons in great demand elsewhere in the job market, then controlling plan costs by changing benefit design or allocating some additional portion of the expense to the employee may be shortsighted and have an impact on the company's profitability (i.e., create additional costs which can or should be related to benefit management decisions).

It is also important to restrict the cost control effort to those benefits over which the company has control and which otherwise have a negative impact on profitability.

For example, social security tax rates are beyond the control of the employer. Thus, management need only be concerned with the extent to which the social security tax rate will increase in the future, to incorporate expected tax increases into its long-range financial plans, and to anticipate the impact of increasing benefits on the cost of the company-sponsored plans. If the company-sponsored plan benefits are integrated with social security, the projected costs of the company plan should anticipate the changing level of benefits under the social security system's dynamic (or indexed) benefit formula. And the formulas for social security integration in the pension and long-term disability plans should be reevaluated periodically in light of expected changes in social security benefits to assure that the company is receiving the maximum, or appropriate, value for its share of Social Security taxes.

Plan management also requires recognition of the cost of administering plans. Record-keeping systems, accounting, communications, and management decision making have a direct impact on the cost of doing business and are charged against the benefits executive's budget. While this aspect of benefit costs is important, this chapter will restrict itself to controlling *plan costs* (that is, the portion of expense that is a part of the direct cost of any particular plan). In the case of an insured plan, the direct cost is premium dollars paid to an insurer. For self-funded plans (including pension plans) it is the charges made directly to the budget because a particular plan exists; in the case of a pension plan, for instance, it would be contributions made to the pension trust.

Cost control is not necessarily cost reduction. The effect of cost control may be to minimize cost increases or to reduce the cost of some features of plan design, administration, or underwriting so as to make additional money available for benefits of another kind. Nor is cost control a process or reallocating costs from the employer to the employee, unless, as is sometimes the case in cost containment for health

TABLE 8–3
Five-Year Experience Accounting for a Group Hospital-Medical Benefit Plan

	Year 1	Year 2	Year 3	Year 4	Year 5
Paid premium	$8,000,000	$9,000,000	$9,600,000	$9,700,000	$10,000,000
Incurred claims	7,800,000	8,300,000	8,450,000	8,850,000	9,400,000
Retention:					
Administration	300,000	310,000	330,000	360,000	390,000
Risk charges	140,000	140,000	150,000	160,000	165,000
Premium taxes	100,000	110,000	125,000	125,000	130,000
Commissions	20,000	22,000	23,000	23,000	24,000
Total expenses	8,360,000	8,882,000	9,078,000	9,518,000	10,109,000
Surplus (deficit)	(360,000)	118,000	522,000	182,000	(109,000)
Dividend (cumulative deficit)	$ (360,000)	$ (242,000)	$ 280,000	$ 182,000	$ (109,000)

care benefits, the objective is to make the employee more sensitive to costs and/or to provide economic incentives to utilize benefits differently.

The techniques for controlling costs depend on the type of plan, on how the plan is financed (for example, whether it is insured, self-insured, or a combination of the two), and on the type of benefit provided. There are methods to control or change patterns of benefit utilization that can have a substantial impact on the timing and amount of cash disbursements. This chapter will explore these techniques for four standard types of benefits—hospital-medical, life insurance, long-term disability, and pension. For each plan, the components of plan cost will be discussed, the risk implications and long-term costs of various financing methods will be reviewed, and techniques for cost control will be described.

HOSPITAL-MEDICAL BENEFITS

Traditionally hospital-medical benefits plans were fully insured. In recent years many plans have become self-funded (most commonly referred to as *self-insured*). Self-funding does eliminate some of the cost of an insured plan, but the savings must be considered in light of what the insured cost should be if it is well managed and in light of the risk implications of not being insured. Insurance companies have also introduced "minimum premium" contracts that offer some of the advantages of being self-funded without the risk. This section will discuss the cost implications of each financing method and standard cost management methods that apply to all health benefit plans.

Insured Plans

Table 8–3 shows the experience accounting for a relatively large insured hospital-medical benefit plan over a five-year period. The model assumes that the premium for the first year was arrived at by some realistic method. Underwriters of hospital-medical plans use the demographic characteristics of the covered population (age, sex, number of dependents, and geographic location) and the underwriting experience for the group. The underwriting experience includes the volume of claims paid by type (hospital, surgery, laboratory, etc.), a history of changes in the benefit plan, and a history of the group's size and demographic characteristics. If the plan is new the underwriter relies on demographic characteristics and applies the insurance company's experience for groups of a similar size with similar characteristics and benefit coverage to establish the first-year rates.

Once the initial rate has been established, annual reviews (including rate adjustments when justified) are required under most insurance contracts. Changes in the demographics of a group and its utilization patterns can have a significant impact on the risk. Inflation in the cost of medical services also necessarily affects the underwriter's estimate of the required premium. The primary measure of the premium required is the volume of claims paid and the trends in payment—by amount, volume, and type. If the experience is reasonably consistent from one period to the next, the underwriter is able to estimate the pattern of future claims payments, determine a premium which is reasonable, and minimize the risk charges. An analysis of the annual experience accounting requires a review of the following categories of expense.

Incurred Claims

Incurred claims include those actually paid and those incurred during the policy year and either filed but not yet paid as of the end of the year *or* not yet reported. Often there is a lag—of a few weeks for hospital billings to several months for minor expenses such as prescription drugs—between the time services or goods are received and the time a claim for reimbursement is filed. In most plans, the amount of incurred but unreported claims at any time is between 20 and 30 percent of the amount of claims paid during the preceding year.

The reserve requirements for incurred but unreported claims should be tested periodically to assure they are correct. Most insurance companies and plan administrators keep records of the month in which claims are incurred and when they are paid. Then several months after the end of a policy year, a record is available of the precise amount of claims paid since the end of the year but incurred before that time.

Retention

Retention charges consist of the following elements:

- The insurance company's cost of managing the benefit plan—which includes contract preparation, general advice on benefit revisions and other actuarial services, data processing reports about trends in claims payment, and accounting analyses of the experience.

- Claims administration costs.
- Risk charges—which in most cases vary between 1 and 4 percent depending on the unpredictability of future claims payments or the level at which the premium has been set.
- Premium taxes.
- Commissions payable to the broker or consultant—which are most often paid on a sliding scale as a percentage of the total premium.

There are not standards by which to judge the appropriate retention charges for an insured plan of group hospital-medical and life insurance benefits. They vary by the extent to which the premium rate or type of benefit coverage puts the insurance company at risk; (1) depending on the amount of claims administration necessary to adjudicate the claims for the policy, (2) depending on whether or not commissions are payable and the level of commissions payable, and (3) depending on state premium taxes. Retention charges also vary substantially because of the interest credits some insurance companies make available and by which they reduce their retention; in some insurance companies it is still the practice not to credit interest against retention or to credit only modest investment earnings on policy reserves.

In view of the many ways in which insurance companies charge retention and because it is also sometimes difficult to assess the appropriateness of the premium rate for an insured arrangement, the most effective way to test whether retention charges and the premium rate are competitive is to request proposals from various insurance companies in response to a letter of specifications. Exhibit 8–1 outlines the questions that should be asked in the standard letter of specifications and the information that should be provided under ideal circumstances with the letter of specifications. One of the questions asked about retention charges is the difference between those expected in the first year of the contract and for subsequent years. An insurance company incurs additional expense for the preparation of the original policy and the development of a plan booklet and for other start-up costs associated with training claims staff and developing procedures for the proper administration of the benefits. After the first year, these costs are no longer being incurred, and the retention charges should be reduced accordingly.

Assessing the appropriateness of the retention charges proposed by carriers and monitoring them after a carrier has been chosen requires careful judgment. The judgments should be made by category of expense.

EXHIBIT 8–1
Description of a Letter of Specifications for Group Life and Hospital-Medical Benefit Proposals

A detailed letter of specifications assures that the plan sponsor (or the consultant) will be able to compare proposals and determine if the proposals meet the plan sponsor's standards. The letter should include exhibits which describe the program of benefits underwriters are being asked to insure, changes to the program of benefits which have taken effect in recent years, and the following additional information which helps the underwriter to develop premium rates appropriate to the group:

1. A description of the employee population—including ages, sex by age category, and family composition, preferably by age category.
2. Paid claims by type of coverage for three years.
3. The number of eligible employees covered each year during the three years preceding the effective date of the insurance proposal.
4. Salary data if any portion of the coverage (e.g., life insurance) is related to the amount of the employee's salary. Salary information should be provided by age, and sex, which are fundamental determinants of life insurance risk.

Questions to be asked:

1. Premium rates, assuming that coordination of benefits would apply to all medical coverages.
2. All projection of the insurance company's retention charges in three categories: taxes, commissions, and all other expenses. In order to compare the insurance company retention charges, the proposal letter should ask the insurers to project their retention charges on a specified level of incurred claims which represents the sponsoring company's best estimate of the claims liability. *The request for retention projections should also specify what services will be provided by the insurance company and what services will be provided by the sponsoring company's internal staff.*
3. With respect to life insurance coverage, the following questions are appropriate:
   a. What is the amount charged by the insurance company for substandard mortality conversions?
   b. Is the amount charged to claims or retention? (Note: State laws require that employees who become disabled or for any other reason leave the service of the employer must have the privilege of converting their life insurance and paying their own

EXHIBIT 8–1—*Continued*

premiums for the continuation of coverage. Because individuals who continue coverage are often substandard mortality risks, and because of the risk of adverse selection against the insurer, most companies charge an extra premium—or "substandard mortality charge" against the plan sponsor to fund their pooled assets so as to cover these high risks.)

   c. What is the method for setting up reserves for the waiver of premium benefits?
   d. Are there any reserve requirements for unknown premium waiver claims and/or for unrevealed life insurance claims and, if so, what are the amounts of these reserves?
   e. By what formula will reserves for incurred but unreported claims be developed?
   f. What other charges will be made against the policy other than those already mentioned?

4. The insurance company should be asked to specify that any unused premium in excess of incurred claims *plus* retention will be returnable to the policyholder or in the event of policy cancellation after claims runout has elapsed.

5. Explain how both an on-anniversary and an off-anniversary cancellation would affect the timing and manner in which the final settlement of the underwriting experience would be accomplished.

6. What rate of interest is credited on reserves and cash flow? Insurers should be asked to explain their formulas for determining the interest payable and explain whether the interest credit is used to offset retention charges or is returnable directly to the plan sponsor.

7. Specify that the benefit coverage the insurer proposes to underwrite matches that described in the attachments to the letter of specifications and, if not, in what ways it will differ.

8. Explain to what extent the premium rates and retention charges are guaranteed and for how long.

9. How frequently should the insurer be allowed to renew its premium rates?

10. Explain to what extent any of the coverages would be pooled (that is, would not be subject to the experience rating process).

One of the principal advantages of a minimum premium arrangement is that the insurance company, in most cases, permits the plan sponsor to hold policy reserves. However, in order to confirm what contract variations are available, the insurance companies should also be

EXHIBIT 8–1—*Concluded*

asked the following questions if the minimum premium concept is under consideration:

1. Would you allow the company to hold the reserves for incurred but unpaid claims?
2. Assuming that your company holds the incurred but unpaid claim reserves, what formula would be used to credit interest? Would the interest be an offset to retention or returned to the company as a separate transaction?
3. Would your company place any restraints on the account established to pay claims? For example, could the account be credited monthly by the company or would a daily transfer be required? Would your company have to choose the bank where the money is to be deposited?

The retention charges for *contract administration* should be directly related to the amount of service required. If the insurance company is issuing a standard form of contract, which requires little if any tailoring to the specific needs of the plan sponsor, then the cost of developing the contract is reduced. Likewise, if the service provided by the group representative of the insurance company is minimal, that, too, should minimize the charges for management services. On the other hand, if the insurance company is being asked to prepare and distribute plan booklets, if the benefit plan has unusual eligibility or contract provisions which require careful attention by the insurance company's legal staff and underwriters, and if the requirements for claims data produced are different from the insurance company's standard format for data, then the administrative fees can be substantial.

The expense for *claims administration* should be analyzed not only as a percentage of the premium paid but also in dollar terms. One appropriate test for the charges is to relate them to the number of individual claims processed during a year and to compare the number against the number paid in previous years. The complexity and type of claims also has a bearing on the cost of processing. For instance, surgical claims are more difficult to process and more time-consuming than prescription drug claims; dental claims require a great deal more attention than the typical hospital claim.

Risk charges are related to both the stability of the claims experience and to the premium rate. There is a trade-off between the level of total premium, which determines how much money is available to cover claims costs, and the extent to which the insurance company is incurring risk.

Premium taxes are charged by states against the premiums of profit-making companies. They are charged on a sliding scale and in many states are as much as 2 percent of the volume of premium paid. In some states nonprofit insurers are also taxed but at a lower rate than insurance companies.

Most states do not require that *commissions* be paid, and in those states where they are required, the mandated level is minimal. There are various sliding scales in the industry governing commissions. The volume of commissions should be directly related to the quality of the service provided by the broker or consultant receiving them. The policyholder, not the broker, should determine what commissions, if any, will be paid.

On small policies commissions are generally provided because of the difficulty of obtaining coverage and of negotiating the appropriate premium with an underwriter. However, on large policies the volume of commissions often substantially exceeds the value of services received.

One aspect of a letter of specifications outlined in Exhibit 8–1 that is particularly valuable in controlling retention charges is the projected retention. Because retention charges are not fixed or guaranteed and vary from year to year depending on the amount and number of claims paid and the level of service provided, the charges should be compared each year to the originally projected level. The underwriter should be asked to justify the differences.

Underwriting Gains (Losses)

Underwriting gains are the amount, if any, by which premium charges exceed claims incurred *plus* retention charges. If the insurer experiences a gain it should be recovered by the plan sponsor. It is not uncommon for underwriters to suggest, especially for smaller groups, that gains be maintained in a "premium stabilization fund" to offset future premium increases. Leaving the gains in a premium stabilization fund reduces the plan sponsor's control over the underwriter and allows the insurer to use the stabilization fund to offset subsequent underwriting losses. If such an arrangement is being considered, the plan sponsor should ensure that the rate of investment yield credited to amounts held in the premium stabilization fund is competitive with rates that could have been earned by the plan sponsor if those monies had been invested elsewhere.

Underwriting losses are carried forward on the underwriter's books, and subsequent experience gains are first used to offset losses incurred in previous years; the net amount is the dividend.

Self-Funding

Self-insurance is a misnomer; *self-funding* is the appropriate terminology. There is no insurance involved. The cost of benefits is funded directly by the employer with none of the protection of an insurance contract.

If the insurance company's premium rates have been appropriate, self-funding is attractive because it eliminates three of the costs of an insured plan: risk charges, state premium taxes, and commissions, if any. Together, these expenses can represent as much as 4 to 5 percent of the total amount of premium paid.

The other principal advantage of self-funding is that the benefit expense is not realized until claims are actually paid, whereas under a fully insured contract, premiums are paid monthly whether claims are payable or not. Self-funding gives the plan sponsor control over the cash flow.

The plan sponsor should assess the cash flow advantage by comparing the rate at which the insurance company credits interest on the reserves it holds to the rate the plan sponsor could earn on the cash. Interest is credited by most insurance companies, either directly or indirectly as a reduction in what would otherwise be the retention charges.

Risk Implications of Self-Funding
There is a degree of risk in the direct payment of benefits under any circumstances. There are two basic types of risk—*ordinary* and *catastrophic*.

Ordinary risk means the danger of high rather than normal or average utilization of claims. Ordinary risk also includes inflation in the cost of claims. Even very large and otherwise reasonably stable groups experience fluctuations in utilization. No group is immune from recent steady inflation in the cost of hospital-medical care. Even if utilization does reach a plateau, inflation will continue to add liability each year for a given group.

Catastrophic risk is associated with sudden and unusual increases in claims experience and may be due to an epidemic or other catastrophe.

An insurance carrier generally provides ultimate protection only against catastrophic risk. The losses suffered from ordinary risk are, under normal conditions, ultimately expected to be paid for by the policyholder. When a catastrophe occurs, the insurance carrier—assuming that it has reasonable assets—can be counted upon to absorb the losses involved. However, when poor claims experience occurs as a result of ordinary risk, the insurance carrier generally:

  a. Increases its rates in order to cover the newly estimated risk.
  b. Recovers its losses in future years through various techniques depending on the specific terms of its contract with the plan sponsor.

In the absence of a catastrophe, a plan sponsor must expect that it will ultimately pay to the underwriter the full amount of all claims losses plus that underwriter's expense of doing business, unless the sponsor changes to a new carrier while the old carrier has a substantial underwriting deficit on its books.

Stop-Loss Insurance

Some plan sponsors with self-funded programs obtain so-called stop-loss coverage to insure against the risk of aggregate losses for the group exceeding the level of ordinary risk and/or individual losses exceeding a certain level.

The cost of stop-loss insurance is directly related to the extent of protection provided by the insurance. For example, the premium will be lower if the stop-loss underwriter is insuring claims above 150 percent of the normal claims level anticipated, than if they are insuring claims above 125 percent of normal claims. The premiums paid generally can be anticipated to offset partially or altogether the savings that result from eliminating the carrier's risk charges for an insured plan. There is, of course, variability in the cost of this protection as compared to risk charges depending on the actual experience of the group and the extent of the stop-loss protection. If there have been no extraordinary losses for the group or if claims have been reasonably predictable over a period of several years, the premium charges for stop-loss insurance can be minimized.

When considering stop-loss coverage the plan sponsor must assess its value in terms of the degree of protection it provides and in comparison to what the risk charges realistically should have been under a fully insured arrangement. Many companies obtain coverage that is overly expensive in comparison to the protection and that is more expensive than the risk charge for a fully insured policy. Of equal concern to the sponsor is the way in which the stop-loss policy pays. Many policies cover claims *paid* in excess of the policy threshold only after the end of the policy year, in which case the plan sponsor must be able to cover the claims costs before they will be reimbursed by the underwriter.

Reserve Requirements
When a plan sponsor self-funds, it must plan for risks. Risks can be covered either by depositing in a trust account (created under Section 501(c)(9) of the Internal Revenue Code) funds sufficient to cover the risk or by anticipating as a contingency expense the volume of claims that might be payable in excess of the budgeted level of benefit costs. In either case, the company should anticipate the risk of loss whether the potential cost is funded in advance or not. The funded reserves are generally of two types: reserves for pending and unrevealed claims and reserves for claims fluctuations.

Reserves for pending and unrevealed claims represent an estimate of the liability outstanding at the end of any period for:

   a. Claims that have already been presented to the claims administrator by the end of the period on which payment has not been made or determined to be due.
   b. Claims that actually occurred before the end of the period but that have not yet been presented for payment at the end of the period.

These reserves are accumulated and maintained by an underwriter and are available to pay claims when and if the policy is terminated.

Under a self-funded program it is not necessary to fund this reserve requirement. During the first few months of a self-funding arrangement, very few claims will be paid. Within a short time, the plan sponsor should have established sufficient reserves to cover its liability for pending and unrevealed claims or have "saved" that amount which is then invested elsewhere.

The risk of claims fluctuation is not insignificant. It is not uncommon for the level of claims costs to vary between years—apart from the impact of inflation—by as much as 25 percent. The precise amount of claims fluctuation reserve which should be maintained depends on the nature of the benefit covered (the extent to which it covers the type of expense that can fluctuate and the degree to which the expense can fluctuate) and the experience for the group as whole. After the reserve is established, it can then be increased or decreased each year depending on the extent of change in the claims experience.

A suggestion that there should be some understanding of the reserve requirements does not mean that the reserves would actually be spent. It is only a recognition of the risk that the reserves would be required. A later section of this chapter discusses the management and funding of a 501(c)(9) trust.

Minimum-Premium Contracts

Some of the advantage of self-funding can be achieved without losing the protection of insurance. Minimum-premium contracts, which also go by various other names, have become available only in recent years, primarily as an alternative to self-funding.

The precise terms of these contracts can vary considerably among insurance companies. Under the typical arrangement the premium payable monthly covers primarily the retention charges the carrier would ordinarily apply to the case; this includes the cost of administration and the risk charges. Most of what would have been paid as premium under a conventionally insured arrangement is instead held by the plan sponsor. Claims payments are funded as they clear the bank from an account maintained by the policyholder in its own name. The payments are usually made by wire transfer to the insurance company's bank. Any claims exceeding the policy's liability limit (which is the difference between the total conventional premium and the amount actually paid directly to the insurance company for the policy) are the responsibility of the insurer, just as is the case with conventional underwriting. Any losses are carried forward and charged against the experience in subsequent years. In addition to having an annual limit on liability, there is usually a monthly limit on the policyholder's expense; surpluses that develop during the year are carried forward and are recoverable by the insurance company.

The advantages of this type of contract are the following:

- Premium taxes are not payable on the amount of expense funded from the policyholder's own bank account. However, the taxability of this amount is now under challenge in some states.
- The policyholder has the advantage of using the cash flow for other purposes if it so wishes or at the very least of managing the investment of the cash until it is used to fund claims payments.

(Control of cash flow is one of the basic reasons that many companies prefer to self-fund their benefits.)
- Predictability—the policyholder has all of the advantages of a fixed-premium rate, including a fixed maximum cost of coverage.

GROUP LIFE INSURANCE BENEFITS

Most employers provide some form of life insurance benefit. Usually the coverage is for the term of the employee's service. Some employers use a whole life arrangement or a combination of term and whole life coverage —especially for executive survivor income benefits or as an optional form of supplemental benefit available to employees at their own expense (group rates are often less than individual rates because of volume discounts from the insurer). The employer-sponsored benefit usually is a fixed amount per employee or some amount equal to the salary or a multiple of the salary up to some maximum. The value of insurance in excess of $50,000 that is financed by the employer is considered taxable income to the employee. The IRS determines the rate at which the coverage is taxed.

Most group life benefit plans have a feature that provides for extra payment (usually double) in case of accidental death or some additional amount, defined as a percentage of the accidental death benefit, for dismemberment (i.e., loss of eye or limb). The cost of this accidental death and dismemberment benefit is generally only a very small part of the cost of regular life insurance.

Most policies are experience rated. The premium rate is based on the claims experience of the group, with modifications for major changes in the demographic characteristics, *plus* retention. And the principles of controlling the cost of insurance are similar to those for hospital-medical plans. In many group programs, the experience-rated life and accidental death and dismemberment coverages are combined with the hospital-medical coverages into one contract.

Because of the risk that large benefit payments will cause the premium rates to increase substantially and/or result in substantial losses to the insurer, many underwriters and plan sponsors pool the risk for claims in excess of some level—most often between $50,000 and $100,000. Pooled premiums are paid into the insurance company's general assets for this risk. Benefits are also paid from the pool and are not charged against the group's underwriting experience.

Life insurance policies may also contain provisions for premium waiver, which allows or extends coverage to employees who are permanently and totally disabled—so long as they remain so. Under this arrangement the disabled employee pays no premium. The most common practice is to assume that most of the claims will be paid and to charge against the experience accounting 75 percent of the face value of the coverage. Investment earnings, generally at some assumed rate of return consistent with actuarial practice for funding long-term liabilities (often between 7 and 8 percent), are generally credited on these reserves and used to offset retention charges. Charging this amount against the experience allows the carrier to accumulate reserves it retains if the policy is cancelled and to pay the benefit to the disabled employee even if the death occurs many years after policy termination. When the claim is actually paid, the other 25 percent of the face amount is charged against experience. If and when the employee recovers, the reserves are credited to the underwriting experience for that year.

Because of its substantial impact on premium rates many employers have chosen to self-fund their premium waiver coverage. Many companies have concluded that the true present value of the benefit for most qualifying employees is less than the 75 percent reserve requirement levied by most insurers, particularly because most carriers credit interest on those reserves at a lower rate than plan sponsors can expect to earn on conservatively invested assets. This present value calculation takes into account the probability of death for disabled individuals and a reasonable rate of return on invested capital. Because the benefit is funded on a pay-as-you-go basis in most cases, most companies assume that the rate of return will be higher than that credited to policy reserves by most insurers.

Self-funded death benefits in excess of $5,000 are taxable income to the beneficiary. For that reason the self-funded premium-waiver coverage is usually insured but only to the extent that the company pays premium on the disabled employee at the same rate as is paid for nondisabled employee coverage. When the disabled employee dies, the benefit is charged against the underwriting experience. The premium is adjusted periodically (usually annually) and will slowly increase to the appropriate level, which is, in most cases, lower than the premium that would have been payable if the underwriter had created reserves. Under this arrangement, when the policy is terminated, the premium-waiver liability is not retained by the terminated insurance company. The liability is instead transferred to the new underwriter.

USE OF THE 501(c)(9) TRUST IN MANAGING PLAN COSTS

Section 501(c)(9) of the Internal Revenue Code grants exemptions from federal income tax to certain trust funds established to provide life and health benefits to employees. Employer contributions to the fund are tax deductible, and the fund's assets may be invested tax-free. The trust fund may be used to self-fund a particular coverage or to pay premiums to an insurance company. In either case a corporation will establish a trust for two reasons:

1. Use of the trust lowers the net cost of the benefits program.
2. It allows a corporation much greater control over a portion of its cash flow.

The benefit, insurance, funding, and tax implications of the trust arrangement are an important part of plan financial management.

IRS regulations specify that the benefits provided through the trust must be in the nature of life, sickness, accident, or other related coverages which are similar. Similar benefits must satisfy one of the following two conditions:

1. The benefit must be intended to safeguard or improve the health of a participant or a participant's dependent.
2. The benefit must protect against factors that interrupt or impair a participant's earning power.

Permissible benefits include:

- Vacation benefits.
- Child care.
- Financial grants in times of disaster.
- Unemployment compensation benefits.
- Education or training benefits.

The benefits can be insured, self-funded, or partially insured. Earlier in this chapter the advantages and risks of self-funding group hospital-medical and LTD benefits were discussed. Use of the 501(c)(9) trust eliminates state premium taxes and federal income taxes on the investment earnings of the assets (reserves) held in trust. In addition the trust can be used to prefund postretirement medical and death benefits. Usually the actual postretirement coverage is purchased on a renewable term basis, but the fund from which premiums are paid is created during the employee's lifetime. The corporation is allowed to put money aside now to cover known future obligations; this prefunding reduces the ultimate net cost of benefits by the yield on the invested assets.

Unlike pension plans, where annual minimum and maximum contribution levels are explicitly dealt with in the Internal Revenue Code, the contributions to a 501(c)(9) trust are relatively discretionary. Aside from the amounts needed to pay current benefits, there is no minimum amount which must be in, or contributed to, the fund. The maximum amount that may be held in the fund is the full actuarial reserve requirement. The deductibility of contributions into a 501(c)(9) trust is governed by the general rules applicable to ordinary, necessary, and reasonable business expenses. However, within this "reasonable" spectrum is a broad range of contribution possibilities. The reserves may be built up more rapidly in years when the corporation's need for cash is not that great or when it appears that the fund will achieve a much better return than the corporation. In years when the corporation's cash needs are acute, the reserve accumulation may be decelerated, and if desired, the amounts already accumulated in the fund for reserves may be used for benefit and premium payments. This could eliminate a potential cash flow problem for the corporation.

Despite the flexibility in accumulating reserves and the corporation's ability to modify the growth of reserves in conjunction with its cash needs, it is generally felt that the reserves in the fund (however rapidly or slowly built up) cannot exceed a level that may be justified actuarially. The IRS has given very little guidance with regard to what constitutes actuarial justification.

Although the funding requirements of the trust may be unclear, the use of the funds is quite clear. Money put into the fund becomes an asset of the plan and may never revert to the corporation. This money must be held for the exclusive purpose of providing benefits to participants. Therefore, the employer who "overfunds" a 501(c)(9) trust by accumulating reserves at a rapid rate runs the danger of not being able to recapture those assets if benefit payments become unnecessary (for example, because of plant shutdown, large layoffs, or legislation such as national health insurance).

The regulations governing 501(c)(9) trusts require that such trusts meet a number of standards. The most significant of these standards include the following:

- Individuals covered under the trust must share an "employment-related common bond."
- The program must be controlled by employees. Such a trust meets

this requirement if it is subject to ERISA's reporting and fiduciary standards.

- The trust may only pay life, sickness, accident or similar benefits to participants, their dependents, and their beneficiaries. Benefits cannot be paid for retirement, stock bonuses, or profit-sharing.
- The trust may not discriminate in its rules for eligibility, and it may not provide disproportionate benefits. However, if benefits such as life insurance or disability are provided to all eligible employees as a uniform percentage of pay, they are not considered disproportionate just because higher-paid employees receive higher benefits.

LONG-TERM DISABILITY BENEFITS

A somewhat more complicated type of risk is presented by long-term disability (LTD) benefits. For a fully insured long-term disability program the model is the same as for hospital-medical benefits: the cost represents the sum of claims incurred *plus* the insurance company's retention. However, in anticipating the probable level of claims, the insurance company underwriter must also consider not only what is a reasonable probability of disability for each employee covered but also the severity of the disability (i.e., whether the employee will recover and, if so, when and, if the employee is not expected to recover, the probable length of his life unless it is reasonable to expect he will live longer than the period for which benefits are payable). Benefits are commonly payable after a few months of disability to age 65; the benefit is usually some percentage of salary, most often between 50 percent and 66⅔ percent.

Anticipating the probability of disability requires that the actuary apply disability assumptions to the population of covered employees. These disability tables usually assess the average number of people who will become disabled at each age. The probabilities can be based on the underwriter's experience with other similar plans or on some standardized table.

After a period of two to three years, the underwriter's experience with a stable group of employees is sufficient to allow him to predict with reasonable accuracy the probability of disability. In many cases, the premium rate is determined not only by a reasonable expectation of the probability of disability but also by calculating the liability incurred during the underwriter's experience with the group with the expectation that future experience will be reasonably consistent with past experience—allowing for growth in the company's payroll and changes in the characteristics of the employee population with respect to age and sex.

To calculate the incurred claims liability, the underwriter must first assume for how long benefits will be payable. He then discounts the future stream of payments by the assumed yield on invested reserves under the policy. This lump-sum present value is the value of *incurred claims* charged against the experience during the year in which the disability benefits commence.

Self-funding long-term disability benefits is risky. The present value of a large part of the salary payable for a disabled employee's life is substantial, and an unusually large number of claims can result from a catastrophe. For these reasons most companies continue to insure their disability coverage, though partially self-insured arrangements are widely used.

Under the traditional partially self-insured arrangement for LTD, the underwriter assumes the liability for the claims payable after the first year or two of an employee's disability. Because the longer-term disability has the greatest present value, the coverage gives protection from catastrophic losses. The self-funding of shorter-term losses gives the company more control over the cash flow necessary to fund these claims, reduces risk charges, and eliminates a part of premium taxes. The primary disadvantage is that a catastrophic event can result in a dramatic increase in the self-funded benefit costs which are not the liability of the carrier.

Another alternative to the fully self-insured long-term disability plan is a *limited liability* arrangement. Under this type of contract payments are fully insured for the first one or two years of an employee's disability. Thereafter, they are paid from a 501(c)(9) trust under an administrative services only (ASO) contract, with the insurance company continuing to administer and adjudicate claims as an independent third party.

The principal advantages of the limited liability arrangement are:

1. It eliminates risk charges, commissions, and premium taxes on the payments after the first one or two years, which is one of the principal advantages of self-funding.
2. Investment earnings on funds accumulated in the 501(c)(9) trust for benefit payments after the first one or two years are tax-free.
3. The company controls the build-up of the reserves.

The principal disadvantage is that the risk of a large loss is borne by the sponsoring employer. However, because LTD benefits are not subject to the large lump-sum losses characteristic of life insurance, the contribution requirements for losses can be spread over several years.

DEFINED BENEFIT PENSION PLANS

A defined benefit pension plan provides retirement income payable many years in the future. Most plans typically require that an employee work for a specified number of years and live to a certain age. The benefit amount generally depends on the length of service and the level of compensation—though other factors can be used as well.

Developing the cost of a pension plan first requires a projection of the amount of retirement benefits payable in the future to employees currently participating in the plan. Once the projection is made it is then necessary to determine how plan assets will be accumulated. The calculation of projected benefits and the funding options available is the subject of this section.

The Actuary

An actuary is a professional charged with the responsibility to cost a plan initially and to measure its funding progress periodically once the plan is operating. The initial cost is calculated by combining the probabilities of continued participation in a plan and estimating the benefits to be provided. Allowing for income on invested contributions, the actuary then develops a schedule of payments for the plan which should support the estimated benefit payments.

In determining the cost of a pension plan, the actuary projects benefits expected to be paid under the plan given the characteristics of the employees and the plan provisions. By combining his assumptions about future salary increases and rates of investment earnings and the various probabilities of death, disability, termination, and retirement at each stage of the employee's career, the actuary develops the lump sum present value of future benefit payments. This lump sum is calculated by discounting the future income and benefit payments at the assumed rate of investment yield. The process of deriving a lump sum and of developing a schedule of payments to accumulate sufficient assets to pay those benefits is called the actuarial valuation.

The funding progress and the appropriateness of the actuarial assumptions must be tested periodically. ERISA requires that valuations be conducted at least once each three years. In addition to testing the appropriateness of assumptions and the funding progress, the periodic valuation also recalculates the lump sum present value of benefits for the population of covered employees as of the date of the valuation. A change in the demographic characteristics of employees will affect the cost of the plan.

Actuarial Valuation Report

The results of the valuation are presented in a written report, which includes the following:

1. A description of the employee population summarized by age, sex, length of service, and salary levels. The report should also comment on any inadequacies in the data provided to the actuary and explain any assumptions made about the characteristics of the population if the data were inadequate.
2. A summary of the assets of the plan, showing both book and market value as well as an explanation of the values used for valuation purposes.
3. An outline of the benefit provisions.
4. The results of the valuation, including the employer contribution requirement.
5. A summary of the actuarial funding method and a description of the actuarial assumptions used as well as the justification for any changes in assumptions.
6. Any items the actuary believes require the attention of the plan sponsor, including a discussion of any emerging trends that could affect future cost calculations.

Actuarial Assumptions

In determining the appropriate probabilities of death, disability, termination, and retirement at various ages, the actuary must consider the characteristics of the employee population—including active employees, former employees who have rights to benefits, retired employees, and any beneficiaries of retired and deceased employees. The characteristics of this plan population that have a bearing on the actuarial costs are the number, sex, age, length of service, and salary, if salary is a determining factor in the benefit formula.

The actuary's objective is to compute the lump sum present value of future benefits accurately. Some assumptions may be too *conservative*, which in actuarial terminology means that they produce some costs higher and some more *liberal* than the actuary believes are fully justified. Under the provisions of ERISA, the assumptions chosen must, *in the aggregate*, be the actuary's best estimate of experience.

Terminations

The termination assumption is a measure of the probability that an employee will leave service before retirement, death, or disability. The rates of termination are usually higher at younger ages than at later ages. Often the actuary will use what is known as a *select and ultimate* set of assumptions. The select and ultimate assumptions assume that the probability of termination for a short-service employee is greater than for a long-service employee. Some tables are designed to apply select rates (which vary by length of service) up to a certain age and to apply rates which vary only by age after that time.

The impact of an employee's termination on the cost of the plan varies depending on how long he or she has been employed and the value of benefits accrued. Because the probabilities of termination are an important part of the calculation, actuaries generally adjust the rates for each plan. Usually after the actuary has worked with a plan for several years, experience allows him to develop a termination schedule and to adjust that schedule as time passes. However, adjusting the termination assumptions for a smaller employer may be difficult if the population is not large enough to give a reliable indication of the experience.

Mortality

The mortality assumption is a measure of the probability of death. The mortality assumptions usually are developed so as to show an expected rate of death per thousand individuals at each age. Although there are standardized mortality tables, actuaries often adjust the tables to fit their expectations for each plan, which can vary depending on the industry and the characteristics of the employees (because women on the average live longer than men).

The two mortality tables most commonly used are the 1951 Group Annuity Table and the 1971 Group Annuity Mortality Table. Because the 1951 table was developed many years ago, actuaries often adjust the ages of the covered population to account for improvements in mortality since then. For instance, when applying the probability of mortality to a male employee, age 35, the actuary may assume that, for purposes of mortality, he has the same characteristics as a 33-year-old male in 1952.

Because mortality improved after 1951, a new table was developed in 1971. This table uses the experience for individuals who retired between 1964 and 1968 as reported by life insurance companies as well as the experience under several group deferred-annuity contracts and a municipal employee plan.

Disability

Disability tables indicate the probability of becoming disabled at various ages before retirement. The rates should vary depending on the standards for disability benefits under the pension plan. For instance, if the definition is not very restrictive and the employee does not have to wait long to receive disability benefits after first becoming disabled, then the rates of disability probably should be higher.

Retirement Ages

Under most retirement plans employees may retire early, and many employers do not require retirement at whatever age may be legally permissible. An actuary must assume at what age employees will retire. The assumption may be an average age or may be a scale that varies by length of service. A table of probabilities that varies by age is also often used.

Social Security Benefits

One of the assumptions the actuary must make in any plan that integrates the benefits with, or offsets pension payments by, all or some portion of social security is to predict the level of social security benefit that will be payable. The predictability of social security benefits is problematic.

Because social security benefits are based on career average covered earnings and are indexed, the benefit amount payable at retirement depends on the individual's salary progression during his or her working career. The formula for determining the benefit is intended to result in a stable *replacement ratio* (which is the percentage of earnings during the last year of employment replaced by the benefit) in future years for employees in the same situation relative to prevailing wage levels. The stability of the replacement ratio depends in part on the relationship between increases in an individual's earnings and national average earnings. If the individual's earnings increase more rapidly than national average earnings, the replacement ratio will be lower.

Economic Assumptions

There are three basic economic assumptions: future salary increases, investment earnings, and plan expenses.

Salary Increases
Many plans provide benefits based on an employee's salary at retirement or the average of the salary during the last few years preceding retirement. Expected salary increases take into account both cost-of-living adjustments and merit and promotional increases. Some assumptions are select and ultimate in the sense that they expect an employee will receive larger salary increases early in his or her career and lower salary increases after reaching a particular level within the organizational structure. Because in most plans the benefit payable at retirement is directly related to the level of pay, the projected salary should anticipate all merit increases, increases resulting from promotion, and cost-of-living increases.

The merit component of the "salary scale," as this assumption is often called, can be developed by analyzing the development of employees' salaries by age. If, for instance, the average salary of employees age 30 is one half of the average salary of employees age 40 and one third of the average salary of employees age 50, then the salary scale should anticipate this rate of progress. The salary scale often is refined to reflect differences among various types of employees (for example, between clerical employees and senior management).

Investment Yield
The investment yield assumption has a direct bearing on the cost of the plan. Because the valuation process measures the value of future payments, the higher the assumed investment yield, the greater is the rate at which future payments are discounted. Generally an increase of 1 percent in the assumed investment yield without a corresponding change in the salary scale can reduce the cost of a pension plan by about 15 to 20 percent.

The actuary's calculation of the investment yield will also be affected by the way in which unrealized gains or losses in the portfolio are treated in the valuation process. Under the requirements of ERISA, there must be some recognition of the difference between book and market value for equity investments.

Actuaries consider that although the investment yield assumption is very sensitive, equally important is the relationship between the investment yield assumption and the salary scale. For instance, if a flat salary scale is used or if the average expected annual increase in the salary scale is developed, most actuaries agree that the difference between the two should be no greater than 1½ to 2½ percent. The difference is modified depending on the expectations for salary increases and the degree of risk in the investment portfolio.

In recent years concern about the relationship between the investment yield assumption and the salary scale has increased. Higher rates of inflation have had a direct impact on salary increases but have had a slower impact on the yield from plan portfolios because many long-term plan investments were made when the average yield was less than the yields currently available, and because the rates available on new long-term investments have not always been equal to (let alone in excess of) the rate of inflation. In recent years it has not been uncommon for an actuary to provide the results of a valuation on a plan in which the average salary increases was 10 percent during the year and the investment yield as calculated by the actuary was only 6 to 7 percent. Whether this is primarily a function of the rate at which investment yield changes in response to changes in the rate of inflation has not been tested. In any case, it is appropriate for a plan sponsor to discuss with the actuary the sensitivity of the relationship between the two for purposes of costing the pension plan.

The Importance of Asset Valuation

A method that combines cost and market values is preferable. Actuarial valuations will utilize such methods as writing up (or down) some part of the difference between cost and market value, amortizing bond costs, averaging market values, and making implicit assumptions as to return and ignoring actual return. Whatever method is actually chosen, ERISA requires that the market value be reflected in the asset valuation and that the overstating or understating of value be within 80 to 120 percent of the market value unless average values are used.

Expenses

To the extent that expenses for the administration of a pension plan are deducted from the assets of the pension plan, the actuary must assume what the expenses will be. This expense can be related to general record-keeping, the value of investment advice, actuarial services, legal advice, and communications.

After all assumptions are chosen, the projected benefits are calculated. Projected benefit calculations take into account the ages of employees, the benefit formula, and the eligibility rules. The sum of the values for all individual employees is the total amount needed currently to pay an anticipated pension to all present participants.

A company can plan to pay the present value of benefits in a lump sum or as a stream of payments into the future. Arguments in favor of paying in the future are many. They include the fact that a company would have the use of more money over a longer period of time. Paying off the full amount immediately is an unnecessary drain on a company's capital resources, and in any case, neither the IRS nor ERISA will allow the full payment amount to be deducted for income tax purposes. Finally, as with other benefit coverages, it is generally considered appropriate to allocate the cost of a pension benefit to the year in which it is earned. If a decision is made to pay the cost of pension benefits as a stream of payments in the future, the company must decide the method to be used to allocate costs to each year.

Actuarial Funding Methods

There are two features that distinguish actuarial funding methods. First, the different cost methods determine the pattern of funding and, thereby, the portion of the ultimate plan cost that will be met by contributions and the portion that will be met by investment earnings. For example, if the cost method produces higher contributions in the early years, lower contributions will be required in later years. Conversely, if the cost method produces lower contributions in the early years, higher contributions will be required in the later years.

Actual experience inevitably deviates from the actuarial assumptions to some degree. The effect of these deviations is to create *actuarial gain or loss*. If experience is more favorable than predicted, a gain results, and there is a decrease in the calculated cost of the plan. If experience is less favorable than predicted, a loss results, and there is an increase in the calculated cost of the plan. The way in which the actuarial cost method reflects these gains and losses is their second important feature. Some cost methods automatically spread the effect of actuarial gains and losses over the future working lifetime of plan participants. Other cost methods determine the actuarial gain or loss explicitly and then amortize it over a specific number of years.

Actuarial funding methods can also be divided between *accrued benefit* and *projected benefit* methods. Accrued benefit methods reflect the benefits earned to date. Projected benefit methods reflect both the benefits already earned and those to be earned in the future. Table 8–4 compares the various funding methods described hereafter.

Accrued Benefit Method
The accrued benefit method is generally called the *unit credit cost method*. The annual cost under the accrued benefit method is the cost of the benefit earned that year for each plan participant. Under this method, the same benefit accrual becomes more expensive each year of age because there is less time for the money to accumulate interest and because it is more likely the benefit will be paid. The accrued liability is the cost of all benefits earned to date for all plan participants. The accrued liability is increased or decreased by the effect of plan amendments and actuarial gains and losses. The unfunded accrued liability is the excess of the accrued liability over plan assets. That amount is amortized in yearly installments.

Projected Methods
There are several projected cost methods. The fundamental characteristic of projected cost methods is that they project benefits to retirement and develop an annual or normal cost which is either a level percent of payroll or level dollar amount.

Under projected cost methods, normal cost becomes the anticipated benefit at retirement spread out over the future working life of the employee or spread over the employee's whole career from date of employment to retirement. The past service liability (like an accrued liability in the accrued benefit method) is the accumulated value of the normal cost that would have been contributed up to that point if the plan had always existed. There are several different projected benefit cost methods.

Aggregate Cost Method. Under the *aggregate cost method,* the annual contribution is determined by spreading the lump sum cost of all projected benefits—including those attributable to past service—over the future payroll of all employees combined. The combining of the cost of all benefits into a single number is both the advantage and disadvantage of the aggregate method. The disadvantage is the lack of flexibility in the allowable contribution level for a given year. Under other methods, contributions made toward amortization of a separately calculated past service liability can be varied depending on the number of years over which it is to be funded. Under the aggregate method there is no separate liability and therefore no flexibility in funding. The aggregate method's advantage is that there is a single contribution covering the cost of all benefits which decreases gradually as new entrants with no past service enter the plan until all employees who originally had past service credit have retired; thereafter, the cost remains level.

Entry Age Normal.   The entry age normal cost method calculates separate costs for each employee covered by the plan in two parts. One cost reflects currently accruing benefits (normal cost), and the other reflects benefits earned in the past (past service or accrued liability). The annual contribution under this method is the normal cost *plus* the payment required to amortize the past service liability over a selected number of years. Gains and losses that arise from experience different from what was predicted under the actuarial assumptions are reflected in the past service liability, which allows flexibility with respect to contributions.

Frozen Initial Liability Method.   A variation of entry age normal cost is the frozen initial liability method. This method calculates the same initial past service liability, but normal cost is not calculated individually for each employee. Instead, normal cost is determined by calculating the total value of all future benefits exclusive of past service liability and dividing the net result by the future payroll of all employees combined. Gains or losses from experience are included in the normal cost, while the initial past service liability is paid off by a level dollar amount over the amortization period. As with the entry age normal method, there is a degree of flexibility with respect to contributions.

Individual Level Premium.   The individual level premium method is based on projected retirement benefits and an individual calculation. There is no past service liability; the cost of each individual's projected benefit is funded over his remaining working lifetime. This amount, totaled for all employees, is the plan's normal cost. Under the traditional method, actuarial gains or losses are determined separately and amortized over a period not exceeding 15 years. Under variations of the

TABLE 8–4
Comparisons of Funding Methods

Method	Benefit Valued	Normal Cost	Past Service Liability	Total Contributions	Gains/Losses	Flexibility
1. Unit credit	Accrued benefit	Cost for benefit earned in year of valuation for every individual member	The normal cost for the current year times years of past service	Normal cost and amortization of unfunded liability	Reflected in past service liability and amortized over period remaining	Yes
2. Aggregate cost	Benefit projected to retirement	Level annual cost for all members to fund all benefits over remaining working lifetime	None	Normal cost	Spread over future working lifetime of participants in normal cost	No
3. Entry age normal	Benefit projected to retirement	Level annual cost for individual member	Lump sum accumulated value of all missing normal cost contributions	Normal cost and amortization of unfunded liability	Reflected in past service liability and amortized over period remaining	Yes
4. Frozen initial liability	Benefit projected to retirement	Level annual cost for all members	Lump sum accumulated value of all missing normal cost contributions	Normal cost and amortization of unfunded liability	Spread over future working lifetime of participants in normal cost	Yes
5. Individual level premium	Benefit projected to retirement	Level annual cost for individual member to fund all benefits over remaining working lifetime	None, or alternatively accumulated actuarial gains or losses	Normal cost, or alternatively normal cost and amortization of gains or losses	Spread over future working lifetime or alternatively amortized over specified period	No, or alternatively limited

method, gains or losses are spread over each employee's remaining working lifetime through the normal cost. This method is generally used for small plans where it is important to have the cost determined by individual. It is also advantageous for a small plan in which one or two individuals with substantial benefits are close to retirement because the method will allow the amounts necessary to fund benefits to be accumulated by their retirement.

Selecting the Funding Method

Each of the actuarial funding methods has certain essential characteristics. For example, the aggregate method will tend to produce the highest initial cost and does not provide any flexibility in the required annual contribution. Alternatively, the accrued benefit cost method will tend to produce the lowest initial cost and does provide flexibility. (It should be noted that there are restrictions on the use of the accrued benefit method for final pay plans under IRS regulations.)

A plan sponsor would examine what factors are important in funding its pension plan. With these factors in mind, the most appropriate funding method can be selected.

There are several important factors that can influence the choice of funding method. First, it is generally considered advantageous to determine, to the extent possible, the annual pension cost as a level percentage of payroll (or as a level dollar amount for a plan with benefits unrelated to salary). Most cost methods are intended to do this, at least for part of the cost. The entry age normal cost method, for example, produces a normal cost that remains level as a percentage of payroll. The part of the total cost that represents the amortization payment of the past service liability, however, may decline as a percent of payroll because it is a fixed-dollar amount on a generally increasing payroll. The accrued benefit method under certain circumstances may be an exception, with a tendency for the annual cost to escalate. However, where salaries have been projected using a relatively conservative salary scale that projects salaries higher than emerging experience, the cost might start to decline with this method as well.

Second, flexibility in the required annual contribution is important. The methods that have a past service liability determine a range of acceptable contributions since the past service liability can be amortized over 10 to 30 years. On the other hand, under the aggregate and individual level premium methods, the cost determined must be contributed; no range of permissible contributions is produced.

Third, a plan sponsor may wish to fund rapidly so that accrued benefits are fully funded as quickly as possible. This can be especially important where a new plan is started with a substantial past service liability. In this situation, with many employees close to retirement and no assets accumulated to meet the cost of their pensions, the employer may wish to accumulate funds as rapidly as possible. On the other hand, where the financial situation is temporarily tight, an employer may wish to start out with as low a funding requirement as is sound yet that meets government requirements. This often leads to the choice of the accrued benefit method.

Open Population Method

The valuation methods described thus far have viewed the employee population as a closed group. The open population method, on the other hand, views the labor market as a dynamic environment—sensitive to shifts in population and economic forces like investment return, volatility, and inflation. The open population method is theoretically suitable for both annual valuations and projected valuations. However, ERISA does not currently allow open population valuations for filing purposes.

In any event, the open population method is helpful in company planning. For example, open population projected valuations take into account a selected time horizon and, allowing for probable changes and economic shifts, apply all the actuarial assumptions in successive valuations to estimate future annual costs. The method requires sophisticated, costly data processing procedures to produce the most accurate results, but the results can be useful in planning pension benefit increases to conform with company growth plans.

In general, this method is a planning tool for management. An analysis of the impact of various combinations of possible experience helps the company to determine what variations it can anticipate and withstand. Based on the sensitivities that are uncovered, the company can, for example, forecast the likelihood and predict the consequences of selling fixed-income investments before maturity. As another example, a company can also determine its ability to sustain swings in the equity market by testing the impact of inflation on its assets, liabilities, and cash flow.

COST CONTROL AND PLAN ADMINISTRATION

Claims administration—especially for health care benefits—is a complex process. Although accurate and efficient administration is a standard management objective, the quality of administrative systems varies widely. The effectiveness of administrative procedures has a bearing on the cost of a benefit plan. For a group of 10,000 employees, as many as 30,000 medical and dental claims may be filed each year. The average claim for most groups is in excess of $100, and some individual claims will exceed $100,000. Inaccuracies in the payments will have an impact on the cost of coverage. Overpayment will increase the cost of benefits; consistent underpayments will lead to employee dissatisfaction. The objectives in plan administration are to assure that

- Claims are paid only for eligible individuals.
- Plan provisions governing benefits are properly applied.
- For health care benefits, the appropriate fees are recognized as covered expenses.

It is especially difficult to apply the plan provisions and to determine what fees should be covered. For example, most policies and self-insured plans cover treatment necessary for the treatment of illness or injury; there is often doubt about the therapeutic value of treatment, as in cases where a patient is hospitalized for days after he should have recovered sufficiently to be discharged and where there is no indication that the extended hospitalization was justified.

Plan provisions are usually too generalized to cover all interpretations that must be made in benefit claims processing. Most administrators have claims manuals that explain claims standards in detail. The most difficult provisions to apply are those for hospital-medical and dental claims.

Because costs for health care services have been increasing dramatically in recent years and because changes in technology cause the standards for quality care to change continuously, many plans cover expenses that are "usual, customary, and reasonable." This requires careful monitoring of the charges for services and a definition of what is meant by usual, customary, and reasonable.

Most plan sponsors, underwriters, and administrators define usual and customary fees as being those charged by 85 to 90 percent of providers in a geographic area, most often defined as a group of ZIP codes or counties; fees vary markedly from one metropolitan area to the next and between metropolitan and rural areas. Administration of usual and customary charges is often complicated by an individual patient's needs. A surgical procedure performed on an otherwise healthy patient will be less expensive than one performed on a patient whose medical condition complicates and prolongs the surgery and follow-up treatment. For this reason expenses exceeding the usual and customary norms are usually referred to the more experienced claims examiners or medical consultants for their review and analysis.

Other standards by which medical and dental claims should be processed include the following:

- For dental claims, is the treatment appropriate, or would some alternative and less expensive treatment have been appropriate?
- Was the length of hospital stay justified by the condition of the patient, or was the stay extended for convenience, custodial care, or some other noncovered reason?
- Are the frequency and type of treatment appropriate or necessary? Experimental procedures and fad therapies should not usually be covered.
- Were the X ray and laboratory tests necessary given the symptoms or condition on which the claim is based?
- Were the expenses for prescription drugs, and was the dosage necessary or appropriate?

This list is not exhaustive, and appropriate claims standards are subject to change as medical technology or modes of treatment change.

Another important administrative control is the application of coordination of benefits plan provisions. Coordination of benefits (COB) eliminates duplicate payments. Group policies and self-funded plans should specify the primary and secondary liability where two plans cover the same claimant; these provisions are governed by state laws. Because the number of families with two workers is increasing, it is especially important, and will be more so in the future, to identify claims on which there is overlapping coverage so that the benefits from all sources do not exceed 100 percent of allowable expenses. Cases where expenses are the legal obligation of a third party should also be identified in claims processing. By the legal process of subrogation, the plan may recover expenses reimbursed by the third party or its insurance company. Subrogation allows the plan to recover those reimbursed expenses directly.

The most effective way to test the adequacy of health care claims administration is to conduct periodic audits. The audit program should cover a representative sample of each type of claim (e.g., medical, dental, drug) and test the following:

1. The claimant's eligibility for benefits.
2. The appropriateness of services in light of the diagnosis.
3. Interpretation of the plan provisions with respect to covered and uncovered expenses.
4. Application of usual, reasonable, and customary standards for fees.
5. The calculation of benefits.
6. The application of deductibles and plan maximums.
7. Proper coordination of benefits and/or third-party subrogation.
8. Payment to the appropriate party.

COST CONTAINMENT

In recent years the increase in cost of most benefit plans has made it necessary for managers to be concerned not only with assuring that plans are properly financed and administered but also with the fact that benefit costs are often increasing at a rate that exceeds inflation. Cost containment is best defined as the effort to change patterns of benefit utilization in the health care field and to control the liabilities for benefits in pension plans. Some techniques for achieving these objectives are new and experimental, especially in the health care field, and some have been available for many years.

Cost Containment for Pension Plans

The costs of most defined benefit pension plans are increasing. The primary causes have been dramatic increases in salaries and yields on investments that are not consistent with recent rates of inflation. Other causes include ERISA-imposed funding, vesting requirements, new eligibility standards, plan termination insurance, fiduciary responsibility, and reporting and disclosure requirements, all of which had some impact on the cost of pension plans (the impact varied depending on the plan provisions in force and funding method used before ERISA's passage). The increase in the number of women workers, who are expected to live longer than men, has also increased the value of benefits that will be paid to many workers. Another contributing factor in many industries is that the average salary enjoyed by employees (especially at entry levels) has been increasing, apparently as a result of the improved higher educational attainment. Finally, a recent trend toward early retirement has increased the number of years over which benefits will be paid on the average.

Ultimately the cost of the pension plan depends on two factors: the characteristics of the population covered under the plan and the benefit formula. Controlling the cost of the pension plan can be most effectively accomplished by changing its design.

There are no standard plan provisions that can help to control costs. The impact of various design options on a particular group of employees must be tested by the actuary for its cost implications. The plan sponsor should also consider if alternative design is consistent with the objectives of the corporation. Some factors influencing the objectives in designing a pension plan include the corporation's type of industry, its position in the labor market (or markets) in which it competes for employees, the extent to which it is able to use pension benefits to control turnover, its willingness to incur costs for benefits, and the pattern of costs it can afford consistent with other financial plans.

One effective method for controlling plan costs is to use a defined contribution arrangement or a profit-sharing program. These benefit formulas fix costs as a percentage of payroll or as a percentage of profit.

- Money purchase plans, which fix the contribution rate as a percentage of the employee's salary or as a fixed dollar amount. Fixed contributions are credited to the employee's personal account so that he understands the value of the accrued benefit.
- Profit-sharing plans, which share a percentage of profits with employees. The formula for determining the percentage of profits allocated to employees can be fixed or discretionary. Benefits are usually allocated in proportion to salary and are held in trust until retirement, total disability, or death. Vesting is usually achieved over a period of time. Some plans also allow employees to make voluntary contributions. The two advantages to a sponsoring company are that the benefit costs are directly related to the ability to pay. In an unprofitable year contributions need not be made to the profit-sharing plan. In addition, the profit-sharing plan may serve as an incentive to encourage employees to help the company perform well.
- A combination of a defined benefit pension plan, which provides

benefits consistent with an employee's final salary, and a profit-sharing or defined contribution arrangement. The most cost-effective design is to provide a defined benefit plan, which provides benefits based on some fixed salary amount, most commonly the social security wage base, and provides profit-sharing contributions on the amount of salary in excess of that level.

- Thrift and savings plans, which reward employees by matching, most often on a 50 percent basis, contributions made by the employees.

A particularly important part of any cost containment strategy for a retirement plan involves integration with social security benefits. Usually the intent in designing retirement income benefits is to relate the amount of retirement income to the standard of living established during working years. However, the extent to which social security benefits replace preretirement income varies by an employee's salary; and because the social security benefit formula is sensitive to inflation, the extent to which the formula replaces an employee's preretirement income will inevitably change depending on the relationship between an employee's salary increases and the general salary increases for all individuals covered by social security. For these reasons, it is important to design the company's retirement program so that its benefits are integrated with the social security benefit formula in such a way that the company receives full value for the social security contributions made.

Through integration, a company's retirement program can adjust for the lower replacement income from social security payable to the higher paid employees. A company may also wish to maximize retirement benefits for higher paid employees so that it can compete favorably in the marketplace for top executive talent. A small, closely held corporation may find social security integration advantageous in order to make large contributions to the retirement program on behalf of the company's principals, thereby creating a tax shelter for the owners.

Cost Containment for Health Care Plans

Medical care costs have been increasing dramatically in recent years. During the last decade, health care costs increased more rapidly than the consumer price index (CPI).

The medical care component of the CPI is not, by itself, an adequate measure of the impact of inflation on an employer-financed plan. The CPI measures consumer spending habits, but because so many Americans have generous hospital-medical coverage through their employment, the CPI does not measure the impact of inflation for hospitalization on an employer's cost of benefits. Moreover, inflation in the cost of services is only one factor affecting an employer's cost of benefits.

The other reasons for increase in the cost of care generally are:

- Population growth, which is responsible for approximately 10 percent of the increase in the last decade.
- Increases in utilization, which is responsible for approximately 33 percent of the increased cost.

Inflation in the prices of medical services accounts for approximately 50 percent of the cost increase.

The increase in the cost of services can be traced to the following factors:

1. The removal of health care price controls in 1974.
2. Inflation in the general economy.
3. Increased expenditures for new equipment and supplies because of greater technical sophistication.
4. An improved quality of care.
5. Higher labor costs, which were a contributing factor because the health care industry is labor intensive.

Higher utilization of health care services is the result of the following:

1. Higher family income (families with higher incomes tend to spend more heavily for health care).
2. An increase in the average age of the population (older age individuals need more medical attention).
3. An apparent increase in the demand for services, most particularly surgery.
4. Noncost effective utilization of facilities (for instance, utilization of hospitals when out-patient services are sufficient).
5. Increases in the supply of physicians (utilization increases as the supply of service increases).
6. Increases in the portion of expense covered by third-party payment.

This last factor is important. The fact that benefit payments are retrospective and often reimburse most if not all of the expense incurred does not encourage economizing by providers and patients. The design of some plans tends to encourage utilization of facilities that may not be the most appropriate for the treatment of a patient's condition. For instance, chronic and degenerative diseases (for example, cancer and heart disease) will likely be the chief problems of the 1990s. They are the most expensive because they require the most extensive treatment. The leading causes of hospitalization, disability, and substantial expense are heart disease, cancer, stroke, gall bladder disorders, ulcers, arthritis, diabetes, and hypertension. These conditions develop gradually, usually over a period of many years, and their care requires long-term therapy and/or maintenance rather than the short-term treatment and cure characteristic of hospitalization and the nature of the health delivery system.

The objective in developing a hospital-medical benefit plan design appropriate for the 1990s, is the balance the employee's need for protection against the ever-increasing cost of care where care is necessary and to control utilization by accomplishing the following:

- Preventing unnecessary and inappropriate care.
- Encouraging employees to seek cost-efficient forms of care by making the employee more cost sensitive without substantially increasing his or her risk of major expense.
- Encouraging early detection and treatment of conditions that would otherwise lead to major expense.
- Encouraging good health habits and fitness to prevent degenerative disease.

Preventing Unnecessary Care

It is not possible to measure accurately the extent to which unnecessary care is now being rendered. Whether treatment is required and the intensity of the treatment required is a judgment not subject to quantifiable terms. Efforts such as federally funded Peer Review Organizations have been made to measure the extent of inappropriate or unnecessary care provided to publicly supported patients, but the results of such studies are often disputed.

Physicians do generally agree that their judgments are improved by consultation with colleagues. Such consultation often encourages alternatives forms of care less radical than what otherwise would have been prescribed; the alternatives are often less expensive. Consultation and review has the additional advantage of directing patients to the appropriate form of care, which in any case helps to assure better quality.

The area in which consultation is the most useful is in testing the need for nonemergency surgery. Many plans cover the expenses of a consultation by another physician and the cost of any laboratory tests and X rays he orders. Some plans offer a financial incentive to obtain the second opinion by agreeing not only to cover in full the expenses for the consultation and necessary tests but, in addition, by reducing the employee's out-of-pocket expense if the second opinion is obtained and the employee proceeds with surgery. If the second opinion recommends against surgery, it will discourage the patient from proceeding. A second financial advantage of second-opinion surgery programs is that if the second opinion confirms the surgery, the patient will be encouraged to proceed with the operation instead of postponing it and allowing the condition to become more serious.

Traditionally benefit plans have reviewed the necessity for care only when the claim for expenses is presented for reimbursement. This retroactive review process has the disadvantage of leaving the covered employee and his dependents at risk for expenses not allowed if the treatment is deemed unnecessary. The denial of a claim also leads to dissatisfaction among employees. The more effective form of utilization review takes place when the treatment is being rendered.

Second-opinion surgical programs review the necessity for surgery, but reviewing the necessity for hospitalization is equally important. The review tests the need for inpatient services for both surgical and non-surgical cases and reviews the length of stay on a continuing basis after the patient has been admitted to assure the length of stay is minimized. Peer review organizations were created in many metropolitan areas to review the necessity of care for medicare eligibles and other publicly supported individuals in metropolitan areas. Where work of these publicly financed agencies is supported by the local medical community, they can help to control utilization and improve the quality of service. But funding is no longer available for many Peer Review organizations. Those that are funded and that make their services available to private plan sponsors have been able to demonstrate substantial savings to corporate sponsors.

Some hospitals and private groups are also providing utilization review services. In some areas private utilization review satisfies a demand for the service and is organized on a profit-making basis. Some nonprofit hospitals are now providing utilization review in response to the concern of the public about overutilization. In rare circumstances the service is available to employers who encourage their employees to use particular facilities; this marketing arrangement works in metropolitan areas where hospitals are competing to attract patients.

The effectiveness of peer review can be tested only if the peer review process captures data. The data is useful if it compares utilization of services to the norms of the community as a whole for the following:

1. The average length of hospital stay.
2. The number of days of hospital care per 1,000 employees enrolled.

The data base should be used to produce review criteria that focus the peer review process on the lengths of stay exceeding norms and on particular physicians or institutions whose practices differ from the community norm or from some other reasonable standard of care.

Cost-Efficient Forms of Care and Preventive Measures

Plan provisions which should be considered as ways of reducing costs incurred are described here.

Preadmission Testing
Plans which provide full reimbursement for inpatient care and not for outpatient testing encourage hospitalization for diagnosis. Full reimbursement for outpatient tests before admission will eliminate some room and board charges and the higher charges made by hospitals for tests that can be made more cheaply and just as reliably by outpatient clinics.

Ambulatory Surgical Coverage
Many surgical procedures can now be done safely in facilities that allow the patient to return home within hours of treatment. These facilities are less expensive, less frightening to the patient, and often safer because there is greater risk of infection inside a hospital than elsewhere. Plans should cover the fees of outpatient facilities on the same basis as charges made for in-hospital care so that there is no financial incentive to be hospitalized.

Coverage for Alcoholism
Many plans exclude or reduce reimbursement for the treatment of alcoholism. Left untreated, alcoholism can result in serious deterioration of the digestive system and the heart, which can lead to expensive forms of treatment covered by most plans. Employees and their families should be encouraged to seek treatment for alcoholism. Employee assistance

programs help; plan design can also encourage treatment. The coverage can be limited so that repeated treatments are not covered in full.

Plan sponsors should consider the implications of benefit design on employees' decisions about care. Apart from the plan provisions already discussed, many sponsors are also considering ways to make employees more sensitive to the cost of care—by increasing the annual major medical deductibles or otherwise changing the reimbursement without leaving the employee at risk for catastrophic expenses. Among the more innovative changes in plan design in recent years has been the introduction of financial rewards for not utilizing health care services. While this is being experimented with on a limited basis, its effectiveness has not yet been fully tested. The most common design is to provide employees with a cash incentive contribution to a tax-deferred plan of up to $500. The $500 can be used to reimburse medical expenses or left on deposit in the tax-deferred plan. The experiments are testing two assumptions:

1. That there is a great deal of unnecessary utilization for minor services, such as office visits and routine laboratory tests, and financial incentives will encourage individuals to be more selective in engaging health care services.
2. That the financial incentives will give employees reason to modify their health habits so as to stay healthy and continue qualifying for the tax-deferred cash rewards.

Whether in fact employees will change their health habits, whether the change will necessarily be beneficial or will result in a postponement of necessary care, and whether this type of incentive will be widely accepted by employees as a suitable alternative to otherwise generous health benefit plans is not yet known.

The importance of preventive care and good health habits must be considered in any cost containment strategy. Periodic physical examinations should be covered—as often as annually for employees over age 50, less often for younger employees—so that degenerative conditions will be detected early. Employees need information to help them prevent degenerative disease. Especially needed is information about:

- The need for moderate exercise.
- Good nutrition.
- Stress control.
- The risks of smoking and alcohol abuse.

Cost containment in the health care field is a subtle process. The appropriateness of the various techniques to any one plan depends on a number of factors—the characteristics and attitudes of employees, their patterns of utilization, and the structure of the local health care delivery system and its impact on the cost of services. Not all cost containment techniques are appropriate to every setting. The cost containment program must, like the benefit plan itself, be coordinated with the employer's broader benefit objectives.

CONCLUSION

Managing benefit costs is a painstaking process. Each type of plan has its own cost implications, and each type has several cost components that require continuous control. Some cost components are small in the scheme of a plan. For example, some benefit provisions have a minor impact on the total cost of a program. But the effectiveness of a manager is measured by his impact on the sum of the parts. Taken together, the component parts of a benefit plan represent a major financial commitment by a company. If the plan costs are mismanaged, the additional costs incurred represent a loss of valuable money that can be spent elsewhere. If the plan is unnecessarily generous, the additional expense incurred may not have as much effect on employees as would the same amount of money spent in another way. If the plan is perceived as too restrictive by employees because of design or financial management techniques designed to reduce incurred costs, the negative impact on productivity and turnover may be greater than the value of the money saved. Sound financial management requires a careful balance between the organization's desire to minimize expenses as a means to maximize profitability and the human resource objectives of maximizing profitability by recruiting, motivating, and retaining valued employees.

CHAPTER 9

MANAGING PLAN ASSETS

By William C. Kuehne

INTRODUCTION BY DOUGLAS A. LOVE
THE SIZE OF EMPLOYEE BENEFIT PLAN ASSETS
HISTORICAL ANSWERS
NEW SERVICES FOR TRUSTEES
ERISA SECTION 404—FIDUCIARY
RESPONSIBILITIES
CUSTOMARY MANAGEMENT TECHNIQUES
SELECTING INVESTMENT ADVISERS AND
DEALING WITH THEM
OTHER INVESTMENT FUNCTIONS
PERFORMANCE AND RISK MANAGEMENT
FUTURE INVESTMENT TRENDS

INTRODUCTION[1]

Taking Pension Liabilities Out of the Footnotes

Corporations—and their accountants—will have to wake up to the fact that pensions have a major impact on their financial health.

If one believes what pension administrators report, pension finance

---

[1] Douglas A. Love, Chairman, Buck Pension Fund Services, Inc. Extracted from *International Investor Magazine,* December 1979. Reprinted with permission.

still takes a back seat at most companies. In spite of the huge dollar amounts involved and the frequent recitation of the impact of funding on earnings, senior management remains unimpressed. Why?

I believe that senior management acts responsibly given its perceptions of the way the world works today. And the perception is that pension finance is not a legitimate component of the corporation's major financing and planning activities. In the view of the great majority of senior managers, pension contributions are simply a part of wages, and unfunded pension liabilities are not a real liability. Otherwise, the accountants would put pension liabilities on the balance sheet. As for plan assets, it is the accountants' opinion that they are not the "property of the corporation."

Top management consequently views pension finance as being "outside" of the firm or segregated. Economic reality, however, is precisely at odds with accounting opinion on this point. The economic reality is that defined benefit plan assets are, in fact, corporate property.

I am convinced, therefore, that pension finance is an integrated part of corporate finance, though the fact will be obscured as long as pension issues are segregated in the footnotes. Most corporate financial executives behave, publicly at least, as if the security markets actually believe accounting statements, unadjusted and uninterpreted. If nothing else, Moody's incorporation of pension financial considerations in its bond rating formula has spoken eloquently to the point that investors are not so naive.

Accepting the Facts

But let us suppose that the 1990s finally bring a revelation, that economic realities prevail, and that top corporate management accepts the fact that pension finance and corporation finance are united. What then? What will they do differently?

First, the reconstruction or augmentation of their corporate balance sheets will result in management's having a better understanding of the financial condition of their own companies.

Second, it will become clearer with the advent of integrated financial statements that the opportunity cost of investing money in plants and equipment is what could have been earned in pension assets.

Third, it will become obvious that pension plan contributions are not an expense. They are merely a tax-advantaged transfer of assets from one pocket (working capital) to another (plan assets), which, unless the firm insists on buying overvalued assets for its pension plans, does not alter the value of the company.

Fourth, management, within limits set by actuarial standards and IRS maximums and ERISA minimums, will learn to contribute to their pension plans with more flexibility in order to maximize the ability to manage the corporation's finances.

The desegregation of corporate finance and pension finance that I hope will occur in the 1990s will change corporate financial reporting and planning considerably. The old distinctions between investment management and corporation finance will blur. In the process, the demands made by corporate management on actuaries, investment managers, and pension consultants will also force those professionals to modernize the economic and financial content of their models. As a consequence of increased sophistication on the part of financial officers and those who serve them, there will be a significant improvement in financial planning and hence in the use and value of America's scarce capital resources.

THE SIZE OF EMPLOYEE BENEFIT PLAN ASSETS*

The size of the problem of pension asset money management is impressive. Pension assets of private trusteed plans nearly doubled from $655 billion in 1982 to $1,274 billion in 1988, a 12 percent average annual growth rate, according to research by the Employee Benefits Research Institute (EBRI).

Such a huge pool of liquid and growing assets attracts many interested parties. Bankers want the deposits of cash, real estate developers want money for their projects, and stockbrokers want money for stock and bond investments. Cities want cash to bail themselves out of bankruptcy or for social programs. Indeed, a wide variety of political entities talk of "productively" utilizing this huge pool of money in amazing and, from the pensioners' viewpoint, often alarming ways. Special interest groups abound who would invest the money to create "jobs now for workers," help the poor or other needy groups, or create more jobs for minority workers. In fact the list is nearly endless of those eager to put employee benefit plan money into their schemes. Sometimes special

---

* The rest of the chapter was written by William C. Kuehne.

interest groups want to keep investments out of corporations whose policies seem to disregard ecological considerations or whatever someone finds fault with, or out of political entities such as South Africa.

The first problem of any newly established fund is how to put the new contributions of money to work to meet the actuarial assumption of rate of return. Should it be socially directed or invested for the pensioners? Should it be *in-house* (investment decisions made by the corporation or other funding organizations) or *externally managed* (investments made by investment advisers, banks, insurance companies, or other professionals)? Should investments be made with safety of principal the key factor or with some risk to obtain growth of asset value as a hedge against inflation? And what is risk? How do you hedge against it or measure it to get some idea of whether it falls within the loss tolerance of your fund?

HISTORICAL ANSWERS

First, let's look at history to see how these questions have been handled by pension funds in the past. One of the very first union pension funds began with all its money going only into U.S. Treasury issues (e.g., Treasury bonds, certificates, notes, bills). This was very conservative in the sense that maturity risk was nil. It was also nearly the worst possible investment at the time in terms of total or real rate of return since Treasury bills were sometimes paying under 1 percent and Treasury bonds less than 3 percent. Even now the present market value of these bonds bought long ago is only 70 cents on the dollar.

This was to be the first of many investment "answers" for pension investment that proved to offer negligible or negative return. From investments in governments only, many funds moved to investments in corporate bonds. Again most funds did so at the wrong time—wrong in the sense that once they invested in long-term corporate bonds they faced nothing but increasing interest rates and declining market values for the bonds they held. While maturity value of their investments was safe, market value surely was not. Investing in corporate bonds became a way of losing market value "prudently," although results were better than for government issues.

Comparisons to returns available from common stock (9 percent average but with considerable variability) to corporate bonds (less than 5 percent 25 years ago) finally pushed most trustees into moving over to "balanced" portfolios for their employee benefit funds—that is, into common stocks balanced by still large commitments of funds in corporate or government bonds. The early improvement in total return (in the 1950s and 60s) caused many funds to swing from zero to 25 percent in common stocks, with the balance in governments and corporates, into as much as 100 percent of new money in common stocks. Indeed, in 1973, which proved to be the worst possible time, 103 percent of new money went into common stock, the extra percentage coming from sale of bonds.

The prime concern of pension investments in all those variations was the best rates of return for the pension fund commensurate with some risk position. The only "social" investing was perhaps the very best kind. Money was put where demands were best rewarded. Free enterprise's "invisible hand," in striving for better returns, satisfied society's need by best rewarding investments where the public's desires were best served. Social investment (some government or other body's conception of what ought to be supported by pension investments) was fortunately ignored in the past.

The 70s and 80s proved very difficult for common stock investments. Results varied immensely, not only from year to year but from one management technique to another. While it was quite clear that various stock selection approaches had widely varying results, it was equally clear that it was as hard to pick good managers (or investment techniques) as it was to pick the right kind of investments. Furthermore, last year's champion in terms of investment results often was this year's or next year's loser.

NEW SERVICES FOR TRUSTEES

Possibly because of these uncertainties a whole new profession came into being; Performance Measurement. Many companies offered their services to let trustees of plan assets know how they were doing compared to other similar plans, or to the various market indexes, or inflation rates, and so forth. Further, they would measure the "risk" taken by the fund manager. Risk usually was some measure of the variability in market value of the fund's portfolio. While such studies were informative and useful in the sense that trustees were made aware of how the total return of their funds varied (and most were astonished to know the variations), it still did not answer the problems of who should manage their money and how.

So still another service is offered to funds—for a fee, of course. We now have professional advisers who undertake to help trustees determine how to select plan assets managers. They'll advise what the "asset mix" should be—how much more risk should be or can be taken for greater rewards, what liquidity is needed, and so on. Services are available with as many new concepts as the imagination can generate. Most of these services are useful but costly. Most small funds managers need to rely on common sense rather than their pocket book.

To illustrate the difficulty in answering the questions we've just raised, let's look at what would appear to be an amazing phenomenon—the growth of Index Funds in employee benefit investment. An Index Fund is a portfolio of common stocks designed to do exactly what the market does as measured by some index like the Dow Jones Average or, most often, the Standard & Poor's 500. Several billion dollars are now invested in such funds, though they only became important as recently as the late 1970s. How can this be? All they promise is just an average performance of average total rate of return for a fund. The answer is that nearly three quarters of all pension funds do not obtain results as good as the S&P 500 Index, and some results are very much worse. The ability to obtain better results through superior market timing, switching the asset mix from stocks to bonds and back at opportune moments, and from better stock selection than the averages is very difficult to demonstrate consistently. The Standard & Poor's 500 Index performed better than the American Stock Exchange Index until 1977. But in 1978 and 1979 the total return from the AMEX Index was several hundred percent better than the S&P 500.

Past results are not a clear clue to the future results of investment improvement. But it is clear that there is a wide difference in results that will materially affect your employee benefit plan, the future of your workers and retirees, and the company or companies concerned. A 1 percent increase in return on investments will generally allow a fund to pay 33 percent more retirement benefits or require a 25 percent lower contribution to the fund. Investment performance is the key factor in the financial health of retirement plans, retirees, and the contributory companies.

ERISA SECTION 404—
FIDUCIARY RESPONSIBILITIES

Let us examine the Employees Retirement Income Security Act as it pertains to the investment of employee benefit plans funds. Key phrases and words are italicized for emphasis:

The Law: ERISA Section 404 (a)(1) states " . . . a fiduciary shall discharge his duties with respect to a plan *solely in the interest of the participants* and beneficiaries and—

A. *For the exclusive purpose of:*
   1. Providing benefits to participants and their beneficiaries; and
   2. Defraying reasonable expenses of Administering the Plan.
B. With the *care, skill, prudence* and *diligence* under the circumstances then prevailing that a *prudent man* acting in a like capacity and familiar with such matters would use in the conduct of an enterprise of a like character and with like aims;
C. *By diversifying the investments* of a plan so as to minimize the risk of large losses, unless under the circumstances it is clearly prudent not to do so, and
D. In accordance with the documents and instruments governing the plan . . ."

If funds are not so managed the Department of Labor will assist damaged beneficiaries in suitable legal action against trustees, investment advisers, banks, and other fiduciaries for appropriate redress with punitive penalties. In fact the bulk of such suits have been brought by the Department of Labor, although others may file suit directly.

ERISA suits being brought by the Department of Labor can be categorized generally as follows:

a. Failure to invest for the "exclusive purpose" of providing benefits to beneficiaries. Some suits involve unreasonable expenses, such as trustees of a Detroit fund meeting advisers at Caribbean vacation spots. Some involve loans made at rate unfavorable to the beneficiaries of the plan but perhaps favorable to company officers, present workers, or others with conflicting interests. Some involve lease backs with conflicts of interest, etc.
b. Failure to diversify. Some plans invested mostly in real estate loans—often to people otherwise involved in plans and at terms in conflict with the welfare of the beneficiary. Often social investment concepts limit or concentrate investments.
c. Failure to act prudently. In many suits trustees without investment experience have invested funds violating the prudent man rule " . . . familiar with such matters . . ." This is often called the "Prudent Professional" rule, meaning that if you are a trustee and not familiar with investing, you ought to hire a professional. Examples of cases involving suits in the above categories are:

1. *Donovan* v. *Harbor Administrators Inc.* Civil Action No. C81-3086 SW (N D Calif. 7-23-81)
2. *Morrisey* v. *Curran,* 2EBC 1365 (4-25-81)
3. *Marshall* v. *Leigh,* Civil Action No. 81-0089T (D.C. Massachusetts 1-15-81)
4. *Donovan* v. *Walton,* Civil Action No. 81-6281 Div—JAG (D.C. S.D. Florida 5-20-81)
5. *Marshall* v. *Mazzola,* Civil Action No. c-79-0134 (D.C. N.D. California 5-15-81)
6. Many others: *Donovan* v. *Guaranty Bank, Marshall* v. *Gloss Mutual Assoc., Newhoff* v. *Rankow, Donovan* v. *Nellis,* etc.

The Department of Labor and the courts are continuing to give considerable amplification of what is prudent investment through court decisions and through outlining *safe harbor* actions and prohibited transactions. In general one must follow the lodestar of what is for the best interest of beneficiaries and not for the interest of anyone else. If there is any appearance of conflicting interests in investments (e.g., loans back to the company), great care must be taken to substantiate that they were made at arms length, with no market concession, and with the beneficiaries interests held first. And finally, investment must be made prudently and professionally.

With these rules as our guide, let's examine how investments are currently made.

CUSTOMARY MANAGEMENT TECHNIQUES

Currently most employee benefit plans (funds) are invested in a mix of short-term or money market instruments, longer-term bonds, guaranteed insurance contracts (GICs), mortgages, and common stocks or equities. How that mix varies depends on a number of considerations. If the need for liquidity is high, a large portion of the funds will be in short-term items. But if current liquidity needs are low, investments can be made for long-term growth to obtain better total return and protection from inflation. The perceived need to cover many "soon to retire" profit-sharing plan participants or to provide funds for early retirements necessitates that an appropriate portion of the funds be invested in money market instruments or their equivalents. The market will affect the mix as well. Very high short-term yields make these instruments relatively attractive.

Low short-term yields cause many to seek other investments for their perceived liquidity needs.

The balance between longer-term debt instruments and common stocks also depends on the needs of the funds for liquidity. Guaranteed insurance contracts or bonds of appropriate maturity may be best for known needs of money—3, 5, or 10 years hence. But more important will be investment perceptions of interest rates, inflation rates, corporate earning rates, and the economy in general. If the investment manager believes interest rates will trend down while the economy is flat and corporate earnings are dropping, a switch to a larger proportion in bonds is wise. If they perceive inflation as rising, the economy as heating up, interest rates as rising, they should flee debt instruments (bonds) for equities (common stocks and real estate).

Remember, though, that no one knows the future for certain—the doomsayer tip sheet specialists notwithstanding. So prudent people will rarely be 100 percent in any one instrument. While "the human mind longs for certainty and repose, certainty is generally an illusion and repose is not the destiny of man" (Oliver Wendell Holmes). To be prudent, we must therefore keep diversified in our asset mix and keep alert in the way we change that mix. We may go from 1 percent in short-term items when interest rates are 5 percent, and then raise money market items to 25 percent or 50 percent when their return is 20 percent. We may go from 75 percent in debt instruments and 20 percent in equities to the reverse—20 percent in bonds and 75 percent in equities with 5 percent in money market instruments depending on the funds needs and our perception of the various markets.

Just what are short-term and money market instruments? Short term is generally defined as one year or less, while money market instruments are usually 60 days or less in maturity. They include cash in the bank (commercial or savings), one year or less certificates of deposit (CDs), Treasury bills, U.S. agency debt of one year or less maturity, bankers' acceptances (debts guaranteed by a bank that arise in foreign trade), commercial paper (short-term promissory notes of major corporations), "repos" (purchase of government securities at a discount to be repurchased by the seller at an agreed-upon rate), and money market funds.

Most major brokerage firms have a money market fund or funds they offer for sale. Similarly, banks and many major mutual fund organizations offer these instruments. Purchase is made at $1 a share, normally for some minimum amount, such as $1,000 to $20,000. The money in the fund is invested in T bills, CDs, commercial paper, and others mentioned above with an average life of 30 to 60 days. Each day the investor receives a proportionate share of the interest rates plus or minus market changes. (The market changes are generally quite small due to the short maturity schedule of the portfolio.) Each day the investment plus interest is reinvested unless the manager chooses to take this money out. There are, therefore, never any early cashing penalties such as savings and loan CDs and other instruments may have. Because money market fund managers have very large sums, they can invest in large amounts ($1 million plus) daily in any of the vehicles we discussed, thus getting the best rates available. Small-sized investments will receive fractionally lower rates. In addition, small pension fund investors get a share in a diversified portfolio which they would not be able to afford through direct investment.

Longer-term bonds, guaranteed insurance or bank contracts, and mortgages are all debt instruments whose stated rates of return and price depend on prevailing interest rates when offered. They include mortgage bonds and debentures of corporations (a large supply comes from public utilities) that have a fixed rate of interest paid semiannually with the principal to be paid in full at a specified data (maturity date). Relatively few corporate bonds are issued that carry a variable rate where the interest is tied to some other factor, such as the prime rate or CPI, and whose interest rate will go up and down as that factor varies. There are also convertible bonds which may, at the option of the holder, be converted at some stated ratio into the common stock of the corporation allowing the holder some degree of growth if the corporation's common stock does well.

Municipal bonds have sometimes been used as benefit plan investments. These are similar to corporate bonds but are issued by states, cities, school districts, and other municipal organizations. Their chief attractiveness lies in their tax-free interest payments. Since qualified plans are already tax-free, this advantage does not exist for the fund buyer. Taxable entities and individuals need this advantage and therefore bid up these bonds so that their yield or rate of return is relatively low and therefore not attractive to funds. And yet some funds do buy them—not as a wise investment but for other reasons, usually political. The public employee pension funds of the City of New York buying New York City's municipal bonds is a case in point. At present there are some court cases on the question of the prudence of such actions. Saving the city from economic disaster might be prudent for the participant of such funds, though it might not be the best investment from the standpoint of the safest and best return available to the pensioners.

Guaranteed insurance contracts were quite popular when the stock market was down in the middle 70s. They gave returns guaranteed by an insurance company or bank for a stated period of time (5 to 10 years, for example) with the first year being high for that time (8 to 9 percent) and for the remaining years at a rate that was more flexible but relatively high. The safety in such contracts becomes less attractive when interest rates rise. (For a short time rates of 20 percent plus were available.) Of course the insurance companies invested the funds entrusted to them in bonds and similar vehicles to cover their guaranteed return, the administration to selling costs, and to provide a profit for the insurance company.

Real estate mortgages have been popular with building trades pension funds. Some method of investigating the properties behind the mortgage must be set up. Usually an adviser that may be a real estate company, a bank, or a mortgage broker is hired. Additionally, mortgages pay off interest and some principal on a monthly basis. The cost of collection and bookkeeping can be high if done in-house. Again, such service is usually contracted for by employee benefit funds. Government guaranteed mortgage pools give added safety but typically come in fairly large size. The guarantees come from Ginnie Mae (Government National Mortgage Association) or Fannie Mae (Federal National Mortgage Association). Yields available after the costs of collection and bookkeeping are typically quite similar to long-term corporate bonds and vary for much the same reasons. Their "guarantee" by an agency of the federal government gives them added maturity safety but not market safety.

Equity investments for the most part are in common stock. Real estate, through mortgages that offer a small ownership position, sale and leasebacks, or direct investment, had considerable popularity toward the end of the run up in real estate in the 70s. Real estate, however, lacks the liquidity of common stocks and requires considerable management. Ownership of business and property through common stock or of property through real estate has given the best protection historically against inflation by providing a rising stream of earnings and therefore of dividends to pension funds. Again historically and on the average, equity ownership has provided a much superior return to that available from debt instruments. The problem is that results can vary widely from year to year and even more so from stock to stock. How does one protect oneself from such market variability or risk in a prudent manner?

Just as we first considered a varying ratio or asset mix among short-term instruments, long-term debt, and equities depending on the needs of the employee benefit funds and on the relative status of the market, so too does prudence indicate that a diversified common stock portfolio should be utilized to protect the investor from the unknowable future. Hindsight alone gives perfect results. The unknowable quality of the future is perhaps best illustrated by the 20-20 Hindsight Club. They alone made the following correct predictions for the decade of the 70s. They predicted that a vice president of the United States would be forced to resign for wrongdoing and that a new vice president would be appointed. Further they predicted that the president would then resign under a cloud affecting his whole administration and that the appointed vice president would become president, only to lose to a nearly unknown farmer from Georgia. Needless to say, only the "hindsighters," predicting in 1980 for the decade of the 70s, came up with this view of the future.

Therefore, to balance against the unknowns of the future, most investment managers, be they independent, bank, insurance, or in-house (direct employees of the fund itself) will follow an approach similar to this:

- *First,* determine the predictable needs and the timing of needs for money as well as the contribution flow of the fund. It is necessary to know the actuarial assumptions and any other guidelines or directions the trustees wish to issue.
- *Second,* set aside sufficient short-term funds to cover near-term needs plus a reserve for emergencies, again considering the flow of new funds from contributions.
- *Third,* complete studies of interest rate directions, the economy, and the market and make assumptions, subject to change, on which to base decisions about the proportions of investments between debt instruments and equities, bearing in mind the tolerance for risk or market value variation the fund has or should have.
- *Fourth,* for the equity portion of the portfolio, divide the funds among 5 to 15 different industries, selecting those which best fit the needs of the particular fund.
- *Fifth,* within the industries selected, analyze the varying companies available, picking those with the best potential for earnings, dividends, dividend growth, and market appreciation, again in line with the fund's objectives.
- *Sixth,* institute a program to buy the portfolio selected, buying rapidly if there is confidence about the near-term action of the market or waiting for dips if there is uncertainty about the market.
- *Seventh,* keep monitoring the fund's needs, individual stock selections, the market, the economy, and the mix between stocks and bonds.

SELECTING INVESTMENT ADVISERS AND DEALING WITH THEM

How do employee benefit trustees go about doing all this? Most often they hire a professional manager (investment adviser) to manage the funds. The selection of asset managers, or investment advisers, has become a profession in itself. For funds of size that can afford the service, an expert can be brought in who will assist the trustees in their selection of an investment manager. Smaller funds cannot afford such services and often turn to their actuary, plan consultant, administrator, broker, banker or other people thought to be knowledgeable. In the past this has been the typical approach for most funds—with some occasional conflicts of interest developing.

The professional seeking a money or asset manager most often uses the questionnaire form, sometimes coupled with performance measurement data and/or personal visits to investment management companies. The questionnaire asks about the number and experience of the people in the investment managers' organizations, about their investment philosophy and approach, about their past performance results, their registration with the SEC, the liability insurance they carry, and for references from present customers. They inquire as to the accounting and reporting procedures of the advisers, their computer capabilities, their back-up procedures, their investment decision-making methods, their information services, their failsafe devices for monitoring maturing or expiring items, their experience with equities, debt, and money market instruments, options, and real estate. Indeed questionnaires of 50 or more pages have been designed and used to obtain information for trustees of plans. Such lengthy forms best serve to inform the trustees of general areas that can be of real concern to them. Forms that are too lengthy are self-defeating in that trustees will not take the time to read all the information.

With long or short questionnaires, with professional help or without, the trustees need to notify investment managers of their interest in the possible use of their services. Names of such professionals can be obtained from brokerage houses with whom the trustees do business, from banks, other pension funds, actuaries, plan consultants, professional organizations such as the Western Pension Conference, the Yellow Pages of the telephone book, and even from other investment managers. *Pension and Investment Age* and many other trade magazines carry long lists of funds and their advisers from time to time—in brief, with just a little questioning, the problem becomes one of keeping the list of potential advisers short enough to handle.

After a preliminary screening, by use of questionnaires or the advisers' own brochures, by personal contacts, or the use of professional aid, a relatively small number of advisers should be selected for personal interview by the trustees. It is important to make sure that there will be good rapport between advisers and trustees, that the advisers understand clearly the objectives and approach desired by the trustees, including the cash flow needs that are anticipated. These points are best determined by personal discussion. Such interviews can be educational for the trustees as well, since each interviewee will be apt to point out items he can offer that he believes are his areas of strength and why those are important for the trustees' consideration.

Once a money manager has been selected from those interviewed, it is advisable to put agreed upon objectives in writing. Restrictions, special considerations such as what range of balance between bonds and equities should be followed (30 to 70 percent to 70 to 30 percent), and any other specific instructions should be clearly spelled out. This should include the fee structure, the number and frequency of reports, the accounting and custodial procedures to be followed, who should receive reports of trades, monthly and quarterly statements, and so forth.

Investment adviser fees are generally based on assets under management. Typically a small fund ($100,000 to $1 million) might have fees ranging from ½ percent for a simple bond portfolio; to 1 percent for a balanced common stock and bond fund; to 1½ percent for common stocks, money market instruments, and bonds; to 2 percent for common stocks, options, mortgages, bonds, and money market instruments.

Larger sums of money, $1 million plus, will have *lower* percentage charges. Indeed, most advisory firms will negotiate quite low fees on large sums to be managed ($10 million plus). Fees can run from ½ to 1 percent depending on the complexity of the investment program. Remember, although usually in goods and services you get what you pay for, there is no guarantee that a high fee will get you superior investment performance nor that a low fee saves you money after performance considerations. In fact, advisory fees become of little overall consequence if investment performance is at all satisfactory. We will discuss investment performance later. Note that fees are a percentage of assets managed and not a percentage of the gains. This is in accordance with the method approved by the Association of Investment Advisers and by the SEC. While payment as a percent of results may sound appealing, observe that it might push advisers toward taking large risks in the hope of large fees. If right, they gain; if wrong, you lose.

Once you have selected investment managers, how do you deal with them? The first step is to make sure that you have agreed on goals, investment objectives, rates of return, types of diversification, balance of equities, bonds, money market instruments, and so on.

The second step is to have the investment adviser make reports both written and in person on a continuing, periodic basis, such as monthly or quarterly. Trustees need to be sure that progress is being made toward the agreed-upon goals and that they do not stray from the guidelines, constraints, and objectives you have set (or, should you change objectives, that such changes are understood and agreed upon).

Finally, trustees should ask advisers to provide them with performance data, comparisons to leading indices such as the Dow Jones, S&P 500, Treasury Bills return, and others, in comparison with their results. Reluctance to comply should make trustees suspicious.

Should you be unhappy with results or feel that your directives are not being followed, bring your problems out for discussion with your adviser as soon as possible. All too often trustees are hesitant to speak up when troubled or confused. Don't be. If no reasonable solution can be reached or you feel no effort is being made to comply with your directions, consider changing your adviser. It is amazing, banks and advisers being human, how such open discussions and the possibility of a successor adviser will change neglect to attention.

OTHER INVESTMENT FUNCTIONS

Most banks that act as investment advisers lump their charges for that service along with their custodial and other services. These services can be split out, however. For example, you might hire an independent investment adviser, have a brokerage firm act as custodian of the plan's securities, and hire a contract administrator to handle your reporting to the Department of Labor, IRS, and others and to make payments and explanations to pensioners and beneficiaries. Some of these functions you might wish to perform "in house," meaning the corporation or fund would hire its own advisory staff to handle at least a portion of its pension investments. American Telephone & Telegraph has done this in addition to hiring outside counselors. Similarly, any one of the investment functions described above can be handled in a variety of ways. But remember, there is a cost for all these services whether they are billed separately or together.

Most often it is banks that act as the custodian of securities—whether or not they also act as the investment adviser. For the smaller plans ($2 million or less) this can be expensive. Today most large brokerage houses supply custodial service for "free" expecting the commissions from securities business as compensation. Even in this case they will discount commissions for most pension funds. Often brokerage firm statements are clearer and easier to read than bank statements. If the question of safety of your securities comes up, most large brokerage firms offer at least $500 million in Securities Investor Protection Corporation (SIPC) coverage for private loss of your securities, bankruptcy of the brokerage firm, etc., at very nominal fees relative to bank charges for custodial services. SIPC is similar to the FDIC that insures bank deposits.

Banks not only charge for custodial services on a periodic basis, but also have a fee schedule for all transactions that they are asked to settle. This can become quite onerous in accounts using stock options. In addition they generally provide savings accounts for cash flow at interest rates considerably below money market rates unless specifically required to do otherwise. Investigate alternatives to their custodianship.

Once you have selected an investment adviser and have agreed upon the desired returns, risk balance of investments, and any other special requirements, how do you monitor results? Again a whole new profession has grown to fill this need. There are several independent performance measurement companies throughout the country. In addition, many brokerage firms offer these services—either for cash or for commission business. (When services are provided in return for commission business, they are said to be paid for in "soft dollars.")

PERFORMANCE AND RISK MANAGEMENT

Performance measurement undertakes to give a quantitative rate of return on investments compared to some index of the market as a whole, such as the S&P 500, and adjusted for the risks taken. The rate of return includes dividends and interest received, option premiums and stock loan rates received, plus or minus realized gains or losses and plus or minus unrealized gains or losses. The total of these figures divided by the money invested and available for investment gives the real rate of return for the period covered (one quarter, one year since inception, etc.).

For example, $1 million invested for one year might show $10,000 in money market instrument interest, $50,000 in bond interest, $30,000 in dividends, $20,000 in option premiums received, $30,000 in realized and unrealized stock evaluation gains, minus $10,000 in bond market realized and unrealized losses. This would give a net dollar return of $130,000 for a real rate of return of $130,000 divided by $1 million, or 13 percent.

However, it is not enough to know the rate of return only; one must know how this compares to the market as a whole—say the S&P 500 Index. If the market was up only 10 percent including dividends, the 13 percent return would look good. But if the market was up 26 percent, it would appear quite bad.

This comparison still does not tell the whole story for some measure of the market risk taken must be introduced. Volatility of price (or market price movement) has been taken as a proxy for market risk. Where there is no movement in market price, there is no market risk. Once again, stock and portfolio volatility in market prices are compared to the volatility of market prices for the S&P 500. If the portfolio concerned has the same volatility as the S&P 500, it has a risk, or beta, of 1, that is it should be up or down 1 for 1 with the market. If its volatility, or beta, is 1.5, the portfolio should move up or down 1½ times what the market does. If the market was up 26 percent, the portfolio should be up 39 percent. If the market was down 10 percent, the portfolio should be down 15 percent.

Coming back to our first example, a real portfolio rate of return of 13 percent would be average, with a beta of 1 and a market rise of 13 percent. It would be a *superior* performance with a risk or beta of .90 and a market rise of 13 percent. And it would be an *inferior* rate of return with a beta or risk of 1.50 and a market rise of 13 percent, for indeed you should have had 1.5 times the 13 percent, or 19.5 percent to compensate for the risks taken. Common sense must be added, however, since past volatility or risk is not always indicative of future risk.

How your investment adviser performs is measured by the real rate of return received divided by the money under management (time weighted for cash flows in or out of his management) compared to the S&P 500 Index real rate of return adjusted by the risks taken as measured by relative volatility or beta. It was interesting to note that in 1980 the bond market had a higher beta or more risk than the stock market. While this is historically unusual, it was of little comfort to those who had planned on a large bond portfolio to reduce risk. In fact, bond market losses were substantial.

Obviously, care must be taken in the restrictions and guidance the trustees give their advisers. If the advisers were directed to invest solely (or in very large percentage) in corporate bonds, their relatively poor performance in 1980 should not be held against them. But if they were given latitude as to asset mix (i.e., they were able to change the percentages in stocks and in bonds), then any overinvestment in bonds should be charged against their performance.

Similarly, if there were specific "social investing" directions given (e.g., no investments in South Africa nor in cigarette or liquor companies, but investments to be made in municipal bonds or other perhaps socially desirable but economically questionable areas), then a resulting poor performance cannot be entirely levied against the adviser. The University of Chicago law school points out that a "trustee who sacrifices the beneficiary's financial interest for any other object breaches both his duty of loyalty to the beneficiary and his duty of prudence in investments." (Professors John Langbein and Richard Posner). Others claim you can invest successfully in socially desirable ways without sacrificing return. So long as investment return is satisfactory, you have nothing to worry about. Should returns drop below par "the price of yielding to social investing may be litigation costs and potential liabilities."

Performance measurement organizations not only provide trustees with relative rates of return and relative risk taken, but also undertake to answer why performance was superior or inferior. Generally, they try to determine whether the investment manager's selection of stocks was good or bad, whether his market timing as measured by changes in asset mix from more stock and less bonds to more money market items and less stock was advantageous or disadvantageous.

The difficulty is not only in assessing market selection and timing abilities, but also in the significance of measuring performance generally. This year's hero can often be next year's poor performer, or vice versa. On average most investment advisers perform just slightly worse than the market averages, so superior performance is apt to be followed by inferior performance, but not always. While past performance is not necessarily related to future results, it is nonetheless a fiduciary responsibility of fund trustees to monitor the results of the management of their funds to ascertain that their instructions and requirements are being met.

FUTURE INVESTMENT TRENDS

The future delights in hiding its intentions not only from those seeking the best investments, but from those wanting to know the newest developments in investment technique. What are some of the promising new trends in asset management?

We have observed that employee benefits investment has evolved from what was thought to be extremely conservative media, such as only government bonds, into better yielding instruments. Corporate bonds and common stocks have each had their period of greatest popularity. We have also seen actuarial assumptions of rates of return rise from less than 3 percent to 10 percent or higher. It would appear that in changing investment approaches we are making progress for the benefit of pensioners and other recipients, as supported by increasing actuarial assumptions.

We have also seen a developing trend in prohibited transactions. It was once thought excellent, for example, that Sears invested most of its profit-sharing funds in the company's own stock. Indeed it proved to be one of the most beneficial of all profit-sharing plans from the point of view of payments to past retired Sears employees. However, it ran counter to part of a developing body of law and regulations which held that the trustees of such employee benefit trusts should not themselves benefit from investments. Sears was considered to have a "conflict of interest" in the sense that such investment in Sears stock was thought to be beneficial to the company. A program was worked out so no new funds went into Sears stock from its own profit-sharing plan, thus effecting investment diversification. This was fortunate for the employee beneficiaries of the Sears plan as Sears stock in the late 70s did not do as well as formerly.

Similarly, trustees are enjoined from having plans under their control invested in real estate in which the trustees may have independent interests. Self-serving transactions—investments made to benefit anyone in a fiduciary capacity rather than to benefit pensioners or other recipients—are generally prohibited.

Because of this background of law and regulation, I do not believe that social investing will gain much headway despite the enormous pressures to do so. I believe that the beneficiary's interest must come first. An interesting suggestion was made to allow beneficiaries to have a choice in plans. One plan would continue to require investments to be made only for their best financial benefit; the other plan would state that investments would be made to help the impoverished cities, the building trades, or whatever socially desirable objective the trustees might have in mind and in whatever way they believed to be appropriate, with pension payments being therefore reduced! If such a choice resulted in only a small amount of funds thus becoming available for social purposes, let the proponents of social investing be happy in the knowledge that the invisible hand of free enterprise economics would nevertheless direct investments to those areas most in demand by the majority of people.

In sum, I do not predict social investing to be a large wave of the future—barring some political takeover from the left.

One very interesting and rapidly growing new investment tool that appears to be of significant importance to employee benefit plans is the use of options to decrease risk and to increase total returns to those funds. Options can be used speculatively as well, but selling fully covered calls against established positions is conservative. Selling calls brings in premiums of approximately 10 percent of market value and reduces the downside risk by that amount. Options (put and call) are the right to sell or buy 100 shares of stock at a specified price (the strike price) for a specified period of time not to exceed nine months. Most of the largest, financially strongest, and most actively traded companies' stock have options listed on one of the four different option exchanges. These options are bought and sold at prices established in open auction markets quite similar to the way shares of the underlying stock are bought and sold. They are versatile tools, and I expect that every knowledgeable money manager will use them as a method to add to total return while at the same time reducing risk. They are especially useful in employee benefit plans since the premiums received, being nontaxable to such entities, all accrue to the plan.

Another trend that is already quite well established is for benefit funds to add new and diverse money managers as they grow in size. Small funds usually begin with a single asset manager, usually a conservative one with a balanced stock-bond approach. As they grow in size they may note that different investment philosophies bring substantially different results. For example, an approach heavily weighted with bonds will not do well in rising interest periods but will do well with dropping interest rates. Similarly, a manager selling calls against a common stock portfolio will naturally outperform most other common stock managers in flat or falling markets. But he will likely not do better, though he will do well, in a very rapidly rising market. And finally, there are times when emerging lesser known companies' stocks will perform the best and times when they will perform the worst. So from time to time you might be interested in an asset manager who specializes in seeking out such situations.

If your fund is large enough to warrant the usually very modest added expense of more than one asset manager, it makes sense to investigate alternatives. (Large enough usually means around $10 million or so.) Be sure to get a good diversity of investment approach by your various money managers, however. All too often I have observed trustees adding new money managers to their funds whose approach and philosophy are nearly identical. Therefore, when they split their—say $50 million— fund into two $25 million parts for two managers, they find that the results are nearly identical no matter what the market or interest rate environment. But in those funds utilizing more than one manager with different management skills (e.g., options, emerging growth, or balanced), the results will vary, often extensively, thus balancing out for their total overall performance those times when any given approach will do badly or better than the averages.

The returns on real estate investment whet the appetite for direct equity investment—as contrasted to mortgage lending investment—for most funds. It seems likely that benefit plans may increase their investments in this media. If so they may likely repeat some of the problems encountered in common stock investment; that is, the funds may enter that market at or near the top of a long rise in real estate prices. Patience may be required at present price levels before an adequate total return may be realized, as it seems clear that, at least in many areas, the future potential of property has been fairly well discounted by price rises already seen. Care, too, must be taken to make sure that the lack of liquidity in real estate investments will not cause serious problems to your particular fund.

In summary, the management of employee benefit funds has become considerably more complex than it was in former years. But results have been greatly improved as measured by constantly increasing actuarial assumptions of rates of return. I expect both trends to continue.

Diverse management techniques, better performance measurements and management selection, more sophisticated use of options, risk measurement, and a broader selection of investment media are all waves of the future. But fundamental management procedures include solid research into investments, diversification and risk considerations, and accountability will continue to be of paramount importance.

For the decade of the 90s I believe the stock market will be the best answer for employee benefit investments. Not only does this market offer great liquidity advantages, it is probably the only undervalue market able to accommodate productively the very large present and future funds of employee benefit plans.

CHAPTER 10

EVALUATING BENEFIT PLAN EFFECTIVENESS

By Ernest Griffes
Contributing Author: David M. Gladstone

ARE EVALUATIONS OF BENEFIT EFFECTIVENESS
    WORTH THE TROUBLE AND EXPENSE?
WHAT IS THE OBJECTIVE OF EVALUATION
    TECHNIQUES?
EFFECTIVENESS OF EVALUATION TECHNIQUES
SELECTING THE TECHNIQUE TO BE USED
EMPLOYEE SENSING TECHNIQUES
COMPETITIVE BENEFIT STRUCTURE AND COST
    ANALYSIS
BENEFIT INDEXING AND VALUE COMPARISON
COST VERSUS IMPACT ANALYSIS
SPECIFIC PLAN COST VERSUS BENEFIT ANALYSIS
PRACTICAL APPLICATIONS OF EFFECTIVENESS
    EVALUATION
CORRELATION OF INDEXING STUDY AND
    EMPLOYEE SURVEY DATA

In Chapter 4, the concept of a Benefit Plan Life Cycle was examined and discussed. In summary, this concept presents the process of benefit plan development as follows:

- An idea for a benefit plan is conceived somewhere in the organization.
- The idea is evaluated in terms of company philosophy, employee needs, employee motivation, internal politics, competition for labor, and legal considerations.
- A plan is designed, and funding and financing are evaluated.
- Proposals are presented, revised, and approved.
- The plan is implemented and communicated.
- Administration is established and benefits provided.
- Over time employee reactions, internal politics, and external influences impact the operation of the plan.
- Eventually the question is asked: Is this plan doing what it was intended to do? Is it effective from the standpoint of cost, employee relations value, and organization objectives?
- The plan is then reevaluated.
- Fresh ideas are presented and reviewed, the plan is modified, and the cycle commences all over again.

Each aspect of this cycle has been examined and discussed throughout the chapters of this book, except for the process of evaluating the operation of the plan to determine if it is operating effectively in terms of cost, intended objectives, employee relations value, and consistency with organization objectives.

In this chapter we will examine the process of evaluating benefit plan effectiveness.

ARE EVALUATIONS OF BENEFIT EFFECTIVENESS WORTH THE TROUBLE AND EXPENSE?

Evaluating benefit plan effectiveness is, at best, an inexact art. At worst, it is a waste of time and money. Benefit plans have always been criticized for the simple fact that it is very difficult, some believe even impossible, to evaluate if they are effective in terms of positive employee morale, motivation, and productivity. The diversity of needs of the work force often means that no single benefit plan, or even combination of benefit plans, can meet all of the diverse needs. So, some employees will always be dissatisfied and therefore, to some extent, demoralized and demotivated by a set of benefit plans.

It is this aspect of benefits that makes them like a hygenic factor in

Maslow's hierarchy of needs: necessary, but of questionable value in positively motivating behavior, with the possibility of being a demotivational factor in the work environment.

Nevertheless, there is important value in undertaking efforts to evaluate the effectiveness of the plans. Employee attitude sensing and surveys, benefit indexing to make comparisons with competing employers, cost comparisons based on surveys, and benefit value comparisons based on employee perceptions versus benefit costs, are all useful as broad measurement of the effectiveness of the benefit plans and as one of several guides to benefit plan management.

But they are not 100 percent reliable measurements, in the sense that the results are absolute and totally dependable as the basis for action aimed at creating the ideal benefit plan. The results of attempts to evaluate the effectiveness of plans must be moderated and considered in the context of the total operating environment of the organization.

As a practical matter, the desire for more benefits is insatiable, and the limiting factor is always what the organization can afford and what trade-offs are to be made between competing demands for limited resources, regardless of what effectiveness evaluation studies reveal or imply about employee perceptions, needs, and desires.

WHAT IS THE OBJECTIVE OF
EVALUATION TECHNIQUES?

Thus, techniques directed at evaluating the effectiveness of benefit plans all seek to answer the basic questions:

- What are the intended objectives of providing benefits?
- Are the benefit plans accomplishing their intended objectives within the financial constraints imposed upon them?
- Are there changes that are required to move closer to accomplishing the intended objectives?

After defining the objectives (Chapter 3) and evaluating the effectiveness of the plans within the context of those objectives, possible answers by the benefits staff may be:

- Yes. Overall we think they are meeting objectives—nothing more needs to be done at the present time.
- Maybe. There are some indications that redesign may produce a

package of benefits that employees would value more highly at the same or lower costs. More study is needed.
- Maybe. Employees are generally satisfied with the benefits, but the cost is projected to exceed what we can afford. We may have to make some changes that employees will not like, but costs require this trade off. More study is needed.
- No. Employees are dissatisfied with the benefits and they already cost more than we can afford. Major change is required, and it will be difficult to effect. We can expect increased employee concern if we are to get costs under control.
- No. Employees like the benefits but the cost is projected to become greater than we expect to be able to afford. Changes are required.
- No. Employees are generally dissatisfied with the benefits, and the costs are low compared to other employers. We should make several changes to be more competetive in the labor market.

Subjective integrated organizational analysis of objective data derived from evaluation techniques that produces broad gauge answers such as these, is important and helpful in managing benefits.

EFFECTIVENESS OF EVALUATION TECHNIQUES

There are many techniques that have been developed by employers, academics, and consultants to evaluate the effectiveness of benefit plans.

Assuming that the objectives of providing benefits have been identified, the various techniques include:

- Employee sensing, attitude surveys, and perception surveys.
- Competitive benefit structure and cost analysis.
- Keeping up with the Joneses.
- Benefit indexing and value comparison.
- Cost versus impact analysis.
- Specific plan cost versus benefit analysis.

In this chapter we will examine each of these various techniques.

The history of evaluation is that employers have long conducted employee surveys to determine what employees perceive and think about benefits. Employers have also long been interested in how their benefits compare with those provided by other employers, both in terms of the benefits themselves and the associated costs.

Based on employee perceptions employers have traditionally made plan changes to meet employee interests and needs, based on the fundamental premise that if the employees are satisfied with their benefits they will be more productive employees.

Based on competitive benefit structure comparisons, that is comparing the benefits they provide with those provided by competing employers, employers have added benefits on the premise that to do so was necessary to compete for employees in the labor market.

Based on competitive cost comparisons, that is comparing the cost of benefits to the cost of benefits for competing employers, employers have also made changes, based on the premise that benefit costs contribute to the total cost of doing business and selling products and services, and if those costs become much higher than competitor's costs, then a disadvantage will occur in the ability to compete in the market place.

Traditionally, even beyond employee perceptions and structure/cost comparisons, there has been a tendency to "keep up with the Joneses" by modifying benefit plans simply based on what everyone else seems to be doing. This is not a genuine evaluation technique, but simply a human character trait, as it has translated into benefit management. A CEO returns from a conference convinced that everyone else is moving toward flexible spending accounts, for example, and insists that his company have the same plan as other companies.

During the 1970s, as the trends toward applications of computer technology and scientific methods to personnel management evolved, more precise techniques evolved for evaluating benefits. These more precise techniques have undertaken to evaluate, for example, how two benefit plans compare on a numerical basis, giving a value to each relative feature of the specific plan. This has been called, variously, benefit indexing or value comparison.

In the past, two pension plans may have been compared by simply listing the various provisions side by side, and assessing which plan was the better plan, a subjective evaluation that weighed each of the variables and made a simple judgment.

Benefit indexing and value comparison undertake to assign numerical values to each differing plan provision and then to draw a mathematical index of the relative value of the two plans, making the evaluation very objective and scientific.

Cost versus impact approaches undertake to compare the value employees place on a given benefit with the actual cost of that benefit and draw conclusions about the *employee impact value* the employer is getting for each dollar spent on the benefit.

Specific plan cost versus benefit analysis evaluates what it costs to deliver a dollar of benefits and whether that cost is reasonable or can be lowered by making some changes in plan design or administration.

SELECTING THE TECHNIQUE TO BE USED

Each technique produces useful information in plan design and management. But they do produce information based on the perspective of the technique, and thus they can produce conflicting results.

An employee sensing technique may indicate that employees are very interested in child care, a benefit not presently provided. A benefit structure comparison may indicate that only 20 percent of competing employers provide such a benefit. A benefit indexing study of overall benefits may indicate that overall the total benefits package is 10 percent better than competing employers. A comparative cost study may indicate that benefit costs are overall 5 percent lower than competing employers. Thus, four different techniques provide four conflicting perspectives. It is the challenge of the benefits executive to sort through such conflicting data and guide the organization to sound benefits management.

This indicates the need to be wary of relying on any given evaluation technique for benefits management. If there is a genuine intention to manage benefits scientifically, then at least two, and maybe more, of these techniques must be applied simultaneously in a given situation in order to have truly reliable information for decision making.

EMPLOYEE SENSING TECHNIQUES

Employee sensing is the popular term for obtaining information from employees about how they feel about benefits.

There are two primary methods of doing so—focus groups and perception surveys.

Focus Groups

Focus groups are a standard technique for information gathering. In this case they are focused on employee benefits. The important aspects of this application are (1) which employees or employee groups are convened, (2) what benefit issues they are focused on, and (3) who leads the discussion.

The focus group may be a diverse group, including employees from various levels in the organization, whose perspectives are different. The value of a diverse group is the interplay that occurs exposing the various perspectives and the conflicting interests. The disadvantage is that in such a diverse group the discussion can become unfocused, and may not produce the kind of concentrated information for which it was convened.

The group may focus on overall benefits, in which case a great deal of perceptual information may be gathered in a broad and general context. On the other hand, specific concentrated data on a given benefit will not be obtained. Or the group may focus only on specific areas of benefits, in which case the issues can be explored in depth, providing an opportunity to gather very detailed and specific information.

Who leads the discussion is important, as well as who is present for the discussion. If a benefits staff member leads the discussion, there may be a tendency to be defensive when criticism is leveled at the plans or administration. Or, the discussion can dissolve into a benefits communication session, in which it appears to participants that the purpose of the group was to sell them on some issue. This defeats the purpose of the group.

It is usually better to have the group led through the discussion by a noninterested third party, who can independently guide the discussion without any personal interest in the outcome.

The presence in the group of a particular person, such as a high level executive or manager, may have the effect of creating an atmosphere of caution in which there is a reticence to express conflict or criticism. Often there may be no official person in attendence, and the third party leader is asked to report the results of the group without attribution of comments to any attendee. This produces more reliable participation by the group in the discussion.

In evaluating the information produced by focus groups, consideration must be given to who was represented in the groups and how many employees were represented by participation in focus groups. In any search for information that is useful in benefits management, there may be a tendency to extrapolate the view of 1 percent of the work force that participated in a focus group to being the view of the majority of the workforce. The result can be misleading and if relied upon too much can produce a mistaken management effort.

Generally, focus groups should occur simultaneously with a general employee perception survey. Then the results of the focus group can enhance and add to the raw data gathered from the survey.

Employee Perception Surveys

Appendix 3 is an actual employee survey used to gather information from employees about benefits. This survey project was managed for Levi Strauss & Co. by David M. Gladstone who offers the following insights into the steps involved in management of a survey project:

1. The plan sponsor's benefits philosophy needs to be reviewed to determine the salient points that need to be compared with employees' perceptions.
2. The key programs about which the plan sponsor wants to obtain employee perceptions need to be identified.
3. The benefit elements in each plan that are to be the subject of the survey are then grouped by the events that trigger benefits, that is, illness, disability, death, retirement, and so on.
4. A list of questions is designed to elicit employee's perceptions about the benefits and how they would like to see the benefits designed and administered. These questions include queries about before and after-tax employee contributions and employee views on choices and flexibility.
5. The responses to the survey are compiled and evaluated. Generally, a 20 percent to 30 percent response rate to the survey is considered sufficient for a reasonably accurate portrayal of employee perceptions. Less than that response rate and the survey is probably not reliable.
6. A management summary of the results is prepared and presented.
7. As a communications process, a summary of the results is also provided to employees so they feel that their effort at responding was worthwhile.
8. The areas which warrant further analysis or more employee feedback are identified.

Mr. Gladstone also offers the following regarding focus groups as compared to the use of surveys:

1. Since the response rate to surveys is often well below 50 percent, an employer may consider that the time and expense do not justify a survey and choose instead to use focus groups.

2. The dialogue in a focus group may be of more value than a sterile single response to a pointed question.
3. In a focus group employees may be more open about their feelings, more willing to share their views, and feel that their contribution is of more value than in responding to a pointed question.

The survey in Appendix 3 is an actual survey and the results were actually combined with a benefit indexing survey conducted at the same time to produce actual management information for decision making. Some of the actual applications are outlined later in this chapter.

COMPETITIVE BENEFIT STRUCTURE AND COST ANALYSIS

Surveys of benefits are the most common method of evaluating competitiveness in benefit structure and cost.

For decades, employers have surveyed each other and asked questions like "What are you doing in benefits? What kind of pension plan do you have? What does it cost? What benefits changes are you thinking about?" and so on. Such surveys are now so numerous that, on occasion, a benefits manager succumbs to "survey overload" since there is a lot of work involved in responding to such a survey.

These surveys are important, however, so a benefits manager customarily determines which are most useful in their circumstances and chooses to participate on consistent basis in those selected, choosing not to participate in the numerous others that are offered.

The U.S. Chamber of Commerce survey has consistently been one of the most useful, being conducted on essentially the same basis for over 40 years. Many consulting firms sponsor such surveys for clients and prospects, both as a valuable service to clients and as a business development tool. Some such surveys are listed in the Reference Section of this book.

Such surveys gather data on the kinds of benefits being provided and the prevalence of benefits among employers of various sizes and geographical distributions. They also sometimes gather data on the cost of various plans. In evaluating the effectiveness of benefit plans, such surveys have served well for a long time, being used by plan sponsors to measure their position relative to their competitors and other employers in general. Modern data processing has made it possible for consulting firms to meet client needs for specialized data from such surveys. Clients may select a specific group of employers with whom they wish to compare data, and obtain very specific comparative data from the survey data base. This has made such surveys more useful.

However, for purposes of definitive evaluation of the effectiveness of benefit plans, such surveys are of limited usefulness, providing essentially only broad based data for establishing general reference points of competitive positions in benefit structure and costs. This information is important as one factor in the equation for benefits action, but seldom will such information be the dominant factor in a benefits decision.

BENEFIT INDEXING AND VALUE COMPARISON

The concept of benefit indexing and value comparison derived from the insufficiency of the generalized surveys in providing definitive comparative data on which to base benefit decisions and actions.

Whereas a competitive survey comparison may reveal the general relationship of plans with those of other companies, a benefit indexing study places a specific value on the relationship. Such a study reveals almost precisely the numerical value of the relationship, taking into account specific details such as narrow differences in plan provisions and benefits and the significance of employee contributions to the funding of the benefits.

Table 10–1, "Summary of Composite Indices By Company," illustrates such an indexing study, showing how the numerical values give a very definitive measure of the relative value of one company's benefits compared to selected other companies.

The benefits are numerically valued based on the total benefits being provided, and also valued based on the portion paid for by the employer with an adjustment for mandatory employee contributions. Thus, as seen in row 7 of Table 10–1, the Total Benefits may be valued at 126 (26 percent better than the average), but the Employer Paid Benefits are worth more to the employee (132 or 32 percent better) because other employers require to a greater extent mandatory employee contributions.

The numerical reference point is set at 100 for the average of all of the plans being examined, and then each benefit plan is measured against that reference point.

Generally, such a study functions off of the benefits provided and does not attempt to relate each employers costs to the benefit levels. A

TABLE 10–1
Summary of Composite Indices by Company

Co.	Overall Composite		Disability		Death		Retirement		Health Care	
	Total Benefits	Employer-Paid Benefits	Total Benefits	Employer-Paid Benefits	Total Benefits	Employer-Paid Benefits	Total Benefits	Employer-Paid Benefits	Total Benefits	Employer-Paid Benefits
1.	101	108	98	111	115	125	93	93	106	115
2.	99	105	110	127	143	156	78	79	89	93
3.	96	96	119	136	90	98	95	96	90	72
4.	110	87	80	14	181	129	91	85	101	101
5.	90	93	128	145	99	91	62	62	105	113
6.	127	125	104	116	113	112	161	162	97	83
7.	126	132	113	130	59	64	179	180	101	109
8.	78	81	89	100	98	93	43	43	111	120
9.	110	105	89	63	125	136	109	109	111	98
10.	121	128	95	109	137	149	141	142	91	99
11.	67	63	81	76	14	8	67	67	101	91
12.	93	95	94	90	74	80	94	94	107	112
13.	84	84	103	86	54	59	87	88	90	97

NOTES:
[1] An index of less than 100 in this table indicates that that plan is not as valuable (to employee group) as the average; an index in excess of 100 indicates that the plan concerned is more valuable than the average.
[2] All Employer-Paid Benefits indices were adjusted (compared to the Total Benefit indices) to reflect mandatory employee contributions, where applicable.

given employer then may have benefits that are 32 percent better than the average, but whether or not those benefits also cost 32 percent more than the average of the other employers remains unanswered. To truly evaluate the relative value of the benefit plans would also require a simultaneous indexing study of the costs of the plans.

An indexing cost study is much more difficult to conduct, only because information about the actual benefits is fairly easy to evaluate from written documents provided by survey participants, whereas the assembly of accurate and consistently valued cost data is much more time consuming and difficult, and often employers are unwilling to share such cost data with competitors.

Table 10–2, "Summary of Ranking for Various Benefits," illustrates the detail on the ranking of the indices of various provisions of specific benefit plans for the plan sponsor conducting the study. This detail informs the plan sponsor of strengths and weakness in specific aspects of each plan. An example can be seen in Item B (Death Benefits) of Table 10–2. While Group Life Insurance Death Benefits are slightly better than the average, Survivor Benefits in the pension plan are relatively weak, ranking 11th out of the 13 plans used for comparison. Thus, specific areas of concern are identified.

Table 10–3, "Summary of Index With High and Low Indices," provides a measure of the index for each measured provision of the various plans, thus highlighting the areas of relative strength and weakness in the benefits offered by the sponsoring employer.

Such definitive information provides the basis for specific benefit management planning and action, as is demonstrated in the description (later in this chapter) of how results from an employee survey and this benefit indexing study were combined in an actual case to produce a specific recommendation for benefits change.

COST VERSUS IMPACT ANALYSIS

As the principle for profitable retailing is, "buy low, sell high," so with benefits one of the principles of management is, "seek the highest possible value of benefits for employees at the lowest possible cost."

Of course this ideal balance is never actually achieved. Effectiveness evaluation is one of the processes by which plan sponsors seek to move always closer to getting the most value from every dollar spent on benefits.

TABLE 10–2
Summary of Ranking for Various Benefits

Benefit Area	Total Benefits		Employer-Paid Benefits	
	Rank	Index	Rank	Index
Current Protection Plans				
A. Disability:				
Short-term disability	6	104	6	104
Long-term disability	4	122	3	155
Composite	3	113	3	130
B. Death:				
Group life insurance	7	103	6	104
Pre-retirement survivor	11	57	9	70
Post-retirement survivor	11	14	11	15
Composite	11	59	11	64
C. Health care:				
Medical				
Major medical	4	103	2	112
Minor medical	11	84	7	94
Composite	9	97	6	106
Dental	2	119	2	120
Overall health care composite	6	101	5	109
Capital Accumulation Plans				
D. Retirement:				
Pension plans				
Benefit payable at age 65	7	102	7	103
Early retirement	9	101	9	101
Vested benefit available	10	85	10	85
Composite	9	100	9	101
Savings/Profit-sharing plans				
Short-term savings	1	339	1	339
Long-term savings	1	338	1	338
Composite	1	338	1	338
Overall retirement composite	1	179	1	180
All Benefits Combined	2	126	1	132

The technique of measuring cost versus impact attempts to relate the cost of a given benefit to the employer to the impact that benefit has on èmployees, as the employees express their evaluation of the benefit. The concept is fairly easy to grasp, the implementation is very complex and intricate to administer.

TABLE 10–3
Summary of Index with High and Low Indices for Various Benefits

Benefit Area	High	Company	Low
Current Protection Plans			
A. Disability			
Short-term disability	132	104	28
Long-term disability	132	122	53
Composite	128	113	80
B. Death			
Group life insurance	215	103	21
Pre-retirement survivor	214	57	19
Post-retirement survivor	219	14	0
Composite	181	59	14
C. Health Care			
Medical			
Major medical	107	103	92
Minor medical	131	84	58
Composite	114	97	85
Dental	127	119	53
Overall health care composite	111	101	89
Capital Accumulation Plans			
D. Retirement			
Pension plans			
Benefit payable at age 65	150	102	43
Early retirement	129	101	34
Vested benefit available	235	85	43
Composite	131	100	40
Savings/profit-sharing plans			
Short-term savings	339	339	0
Long-term savings	338	338	0
Composite	338	338	0
Overall retirement composite	179	179	43
All Benefits Combined	127	126	67

NOTES:
[1] Since the average index is 100 in each instance, an index of less than 100 in this table indicates that that plan is not as valuable (to employee group) as the average; an index in excess of 100 indicates that the plan concerned is more valuable than the average.
[2] An index of 0 means that the company concerned either has no plan or that the employee contributions more than offset the actuarially determined cost of the plan.
[3] The indices shown in this table were developed for *total* benefits provided in each area.

For a simple example, suppose employees are asked to estimate the cost of various benefits provided for them as a percentage of their salary. Since they have very little information on which to base such costs, their estimates will reveal something about how much value they personally place on that benefit. Further suppose, the average estimate employees make of the cost of group term life insurance is 2 percent of their salary.

If the actual cost of group term life insurance averages 1 percent of salary, then the cost/impact ratio is 1 : 2, indicating that this benefit obtains a very high employee perceptual impact relative to the actual cost of the benefit.

Based on the behavioral assumption that people act on their perceptions of reality, rather than on reality itself, the conclusion that might be drawn from this simple example is that providing employees large amounts of life insurance will be a very cost effective use of benefit dollars—they will place high value on large amounts of life insurance, but the cost will be very low relative to the value they place on this benefit.

Actually, the life insurance is of no dollar value to the employee themselves, since to collect the benefit they must die. But it is of great value to their peace of mind since they can be comfortable that should they die, their beneficiaries will be well provided for. Given the probabilities of death, the likelihood of actual payment of the benefit is very low. The perception of value derives from the large dollar numbers that are written on their group life insurance certificate—$100,000 sounds like a lot of money and gives a lot of comfort to a wife and family.

This is cost versus impact analysis. Actually implementing such an evaluation technique can be very complicated.

In 1981, professors Randall B. Dunham and Roger A. Formisano of the Graduate School of Business undertook such a study for an employer and drafted a lengthy paper on the study titled *Designing and Evaluating Employee Benefit Systems.*

The introduction to the paper sets forth the research process as follows:

> A systematic procedure for the evaluation and design of both fixed and flexible employee benefit programs was developed. The model created for this procedure compared the costs and benefits of alternative benefit plans so that management may "optimize" the investment in employee benefit systems.
>
> The research procedure operationalized the concept of "employee value" regarding particular benefits and benefit levels and tested the predictive validity of the information thus obtained. Several widely-held hy-

potheses about employee interest in benefits were tested. The research resulted in a computer-based, systematic employee benefit evaluation procedure which can provide management with a vehicle for analyzing and comparing the effectiveness of both existing and alternative benefit systems.

Employees were asked to construct their own ideal benefit plan by selecting from many options with related point values based on costs. A limit of 1,000 points placed the cost constraint on the benefits package.

Based on the actual plans selected by employees, and the points they allocated for various benefits, the benefits were valued as to what the employees would in effect be willing to pay for each benefit. These "employee values" were then compared to the actual cost of providing the benefits selected under a scenario of a fixed set of benefits for all employees and a scenario of a cafeteria approach to benefits that matched the individual selections.

From this compilation of data, value/cost ratios were developed for each benefit choice. The presumed utilization of this extensive data would be to design a benefits package for employees that maximized benefits with high value/cost ratios. This would optimize the investment in employee benefits, that is, obtain the highest employee value for the lowest cost.

The research produced some anamolies that illustrate why evaluations of effectiveness cannot be used alone as the basis for the benefit management actions. One of the lowest valued benefits by employees was the pension plan. The highest valued benefit by employees was an additional $30,000 of Accidental Death and Dismemberment Insurance. The lowest valued benefit by employees was a short-term disability income plan allowing the accumulation of one day per month toward short-term disability.

Reality is that the probability of short-term disability during a lifetime is very high, the probability of retirement is 100 percent, and the probability of accidental death is very low. Designing a benefit package around such employee choices would be irresponsible—like permitting a child to select their dinner from the choices between spinach, Twinkies, and Milky Way bars.

The authors of the study commented, "Another finding which has encouraged some organizations to reexamine their benefit packages is the level of widespread lack of knowledge by employees of the scope of their benefits package. Inaccurate and incomplete information is abundant."

The research is well done and well presented—the evaluation technique is very useful and sophisticated. The resulting information is very useful in managing benefit plans. The process is very intricate and complex. But in the search for more definitive and reliable data and the need to optimize the allocation of benefit dollars such sophisticated studies will become increasingly more frequent.

SPECIFIC PLAN COST VERSUS BENEFIT ANALYSIS

This evaluation technique is designed to answer the question "What does it cost to deliver a dollar of benefits in a given plan, is that cost reasonable, and if not, can it be lowered?"

The premise behind this technique is that dollars spent on benefits are most productive when they actually constitute a benefit in the hands of the employee. If $1,000,000 is spent on medical benefits premiums then ideally 95 percent of that should be delivered in actual benefits to employees, and the cost of delivery should be 5 percent. If 80 percent is delivered in actual benefits and the cost of delivery is 20 percent, then the delivery system is suspect.

This type of evaluation is simple to conduct. The total cost of a benefit plan is measured against the cost of delivering the benefits and the result is a ratio or percentage of the cost for delivery. This is essentially an internal measure, useful to the benefits manager in evaluating alternative delivery systems, such as an indemnity medical plan versus a self insured medical plan, or evaluating if the provider of the delivery system is competitive. There is no routine general survey data on such costs of delivery, although brokers can produce comparative studies if other companies are willing to share such data.

PRACTICAL APPLICATIONS OF
EFFECTIVENESS EVALUATION

The usefulness of evaluation techniques is the role the results of evaluations may play in benefits management and decisions.

The following is an actual case study of how an employee perception survey and a benefit indexing study were used in combination to develop recommendations for plan changes.

In 1983 a five-year plan for managing employee benefits in a Fortune 500 company was developed. The table of contents was:

I. Introduction
II. Executive Summary
III. Principles and Strategy for Benefits Management
IV. Evaluations of Competitiveness of Benefits Programs
V. Review of Employee Perceptions about Benefits
VI. Review of Benefit Trends and Costs
VII. Detail on Specific Recommendations for 1983
VIII. Planning for Medical, Disability, and Survivor Benefits
IX. Planning for Pension and Profit Sharing

Section III, Principles and Strategy for Benefits Management, established the necessary philosophy and principles base against which the plans were to be evaluated. Section III also contained an internal evaluation by the benefits staff of how they perceived each benefit as meeting that philosophy and principles base from the perspective of (1) primarily the employee, (2) primarily the employer, and (3) common goals. This evaluation also set forth issues related to each benefit.

Table 10–4 illustrates how this data was displayed. Eighty-one benefit programs and policies were so assessed as they applied to home office employees, field employees, retirees, executives, and all employees. In addition, six prospective benefit programs were evaluated in the same manner.

Section IV, Evaluation of Competitiveness of Benefits Programs, presented the results of the benefit indexing study. Tables 10–1, 10–2, and 10–3 are extracts from this section. This section also contained the correlation of information between the benefit indexing study and the employee perception study, as the background for recommendations for change. Some examples of how this information was correlated are set forth in the following subsection of this chapter.

Section V, Review of Employee Perceptions about Benefits, presented the results of the written employee survey. Appendix 3 is the survey that was used.

Section VI, Review of Trends and Costs, considered how trends might affect benefits decisions, and evaluated overall benefit costs as a percentage of payroll for a four-year period into the future, including some prospective benefit changes.

Section VII, Detail of Specific Recommendations for 1983, brought all of this research together in specific recommendations.

TABLE 10—4
Goals, Objectives, and Purposes

	Common Employee/Employer					Primarily Employee						Primarily Employer							Issues		
Benefits—Home Office	Economic Security	Reward Long Service	Savings/Capital Accumulation	Invest in Company	Tax Advantageous to Employee	Competitive in Labor Market	Flexible to Individual Needs	Add to Cash Income	Help in Short-Term Cash Needs	Save Money on Living Expense	Legally Required	Attract Employees	Retain Employees	Create Goodwill/Loyalty	Productivity Incentive	Golden Handcuffs	Cost Effective or Cost Sharing	Understood/Appreciated by Employee	Consistent with Philosophy	Provide Adequate Benefits	Need Changes?
Home office pension	Y	Y	Y			Y	Y		Y			Y	Y	Y		Y	Y	Y	Y	Y	Y
Home office profit sharing	Y	Y				Y	Y	Y				Y	Y	Y	Y	Y	Y	Y	Y	Y	Y

HO stock purchase plan	Y	Y	Y				Y	Y	Y	Y
Medical/HMO's	Y		Y				Y	Y	Y	Y
Life insurance	Y			N	N	Z	Z	Z	N	N
Short-term disability	Y				Y	Y	Z	Y	Y	Y
Long-term disability	Y				Y	Y	Z	Y	Y	Y
Accidental death	Y				Y	Y	Z	Y	Y	Y
Travel insurance	Y				Y	Y	Y	Y	Y	Y
Vacation		Y		Y	Y	Y	Y	Y	Y	Y
Holidays			Y	Y	Y	Y	Y	Y	Y	Y
Sick days	Y	N		Y	Y	Y	N	Y	N	Y
Employee assistance			Y	Y	Y	Y	Y	Y	N	Y
Relocation allowance			Y	Y	Y	Y	Y	Y	Y	Y

Legend: *Y = yes N = no Blank = not Applicable ? = Uncertain* The responses represent the opinion of the benefit staff. Y = yes, goals/objectives/purposes are met by this benefit plan. N = no, they are not met. Blank = the plan does not relate to the specific goal or purpose

7/82

CORRELATION OF INDEXING STUDY AND EMPLOYEE SURVEY DATA

The following are examples of how the data was correlated to form the background for benefit management actions.

Example 1—Benefits Overall

While only 67 percent of the respondents to the perception survey rated our benefit program better than that of other companies, the indexing survey emphatically points out that the benefit programs are among the very best (number one in employer-provided benefits and number two in total benefits available, among all 13 companies in the study). Further, the value of our benefit programs is about 32 percent better than the average company benefit in the study.

This misconception on the part of approximately 33 percent of the employees is significant relative to our actual ranking and indicates that a more positive and forceful communications program should be instituted.

Example 2—Medical Benefits

More than half (62 percent) of respondents would be willing to make contributions to the medical plan to maintain current benefit levels. The indexing study reveals that 6 of 13 medical plans (including ours) do not require employee contributions.

Nearly half (46 percent) of respondents would like to obtain supplemental health care coverage; a similar percentage (47 percent) feel that the present plan fully meets employee needs. Our indexing ranking was sixth, with an index about 6 percent better than the average plan.

In conjunction with the fact that there were a number of survey comments reflecting dissatisfaction with the current level of medical benefits, the results summarized above convey the suggestion that we should upgrade the medical plan and charge employees for some portion of the cost of improvements.

Example 3—Survivor Benefits

We rank 11th in total survivor benefits with an index that is 36 percent less than the average company. Of respondents to the employee survey, only 25 percent would like to obtain more survivor benefit coverage at their own expense, (75 percent don't feel the need) but only 34 percent perceive our plans to fully meet their survivor benefit needs (66 percent say present levels do not meet their needs). This is a mixed signal on the need for improved survivor benefits.

Employees perceive their survivor benefit plans should be strengthened, but they are not willing to obtain such coverage at their own expense. Our index ranking on the other hand, indicates that survivor benefits should be significantly improved.

If we make improvements, it will require a thoughtful and clever communications effort to maximize the employee appreciation of the improvements.

APPENDIXES

CONTENTS

1. SAMPLE BENEFITS DEPARTMENT ANNUAL REPORT
2. SAMPLE DISCUSSION PAPER
3. SAMPLE EMPLOYEE PERCEPTION SURVEY
4. LEXICON OF BENEFIT PLANS AND TERMS
5. "THE WINDS OF CHANGE"
6. "HOW TO USE YOUR CONSULTANTS MOST EFFECTIVELY"

APPENDIX 1: EMPLOYEE BENEFITS DEPARTMENT ANNUAL REPORT FOR 1979

The purpose of this brief annual report is to review for management the status of benefit programs at the close of fiscal 1979, to review the activities of the Benefits Department during the year, and to outline projected activities in 1980, including a major change in benefit management strategy.

Status of Benefit Programs

Indicators of the general status of benefit plan operations are:

- Comparative benefit levels
- Cost of benefits
- Administration
- Communications
- Legal compliance
- Employee perceptions

Comparative Benefit Levels

We participate annually in a noncash compensation survey. This is purely a quantitative survey of benefits that measures only the existence of various benefits and not the quality of those benefits and is thus limited in scope. We have appeared in the 70 percent to 85 percent range of this survey in each of the last four years.

Benefit Costs

A 1978 Chamber of Commerce survey indicated benefit costs at about 36 percent of payroll, including customary benefits as well as time off. By comparison our benefit costs in 1979 were:

Benefits	Percent of Payroll
Pensions	
Medical	
Life insurance	
Disability income	
Subtotal	
Stock purchase plan	
Profit sharing	
FICA, other payroll taxes	
Subtotal	
Total benefits	
Time off and other miscellaneous plans	
Total estimated as a percentage of payroll	

Administration

Benefits are being paid and inquiries being answered in a timely manner for all plans. Very few complaints have been received from employees, and those have been primarily with regard to medical claims. Last spring the insurance carrier moved claims facilities, and this has created delays. We have met with them several times and prevailed upon them to take a series of actions designed to improve claims service.

The Work Climate Analysis has not revealed any complaints about benefits administration.

Benefits administration is still largely manual and is hampered by delays in completing systems work necessary to greater efficiency.

The length of time of 60 to 90 days to make profit-sharing plan distributions is still a source of concern but because of the valuation process of assets by the trustee is the minimum time required. We have been making partial distributions of profit-sharing accounts to relieve this delay, when requested by employees.

Communications

All legal communications requirements have been met. Beyond that our communications program is among the best in the country.

Our benefit communications programs have won national awards in 1978 and 1979 for the benefits booklet and annual statement as well as for a film on health maintenance organizations.

Communications play an important role in employee acceptance, understanding, and appreciation of benefit plans. We have therefore pursued an aggressive program of communications, averaging one communication a month.

In 1979, we completed revisions of the benefits booklet to meet new legal requirements, instituted a semiannual profit-sharing statement, completed film strips on health maintenance organizations and retirement planning, and completed most of the work on a preretirement planning manual.

Legal Compliance

Through the Corporate Legal Department we have brought all benefit plans into compliance with all laws.

Employee Perceptions

An attitude survey regarding benefits has not been conducted since 1973. Responses in the Work Climate Analysis conducted during 1979 indicate a continuing very favorable attitude towards benefit programs among employees. This is significant because of extensive communications programs since 1976. This favorable attitude now should be based in a better understanding of the benefit plans, rather than existing as a carryover from a generalized good feeling about the company.

We are approaching the time when an attitude survey should be conducted to develop more specific knowledge for use in managing benefit plans.

Benefit Department Activities in 1979

During 1979 the Benefit Department activities included the following:

1. Installation of health maintenance organization.
2. Development of draft of benefit planning systems and philosophy.
3. Evaluation of all benefit plans.
4. Support services to international benefits functions.
5. Participation in evaluation of international profit-sharing concepts.
6. Development of a cash and deferred proposal for profit sharing.
7. Proposals on, and implementation of, executive benefit plans.
8. Evaluation of flexible benefit concepts.
9. A comparison of field benefits with competitors.
10. A study of the adequacy of pension benefits.
11. A projection of pension costs and liabilities.
12. Evaluation of a stock purchase plan concept for field employees.
13. Several meetings with insurance representatives to evaluate key man insurance concepts and voluntary life insurance programs for employees.
14. Evaluation of programs for dealing with stress in a work setting.
15. Implementation of benefit plan changes for 1979.
16. Rewriting of pension, profit-sharing, and stock investment plan documents.
17. Rewriting of basic benefits booklet.
18. Implementation of pregnancy as disability law requirements.
19. Production of annual benefit statement and introduction of semiannual profit sharing statement.
20. Participation in selection and installation of Master Trust arrangement for pension plans.
21. Evaluation of, and actions with regard to, security of records, privacy of records, and emergency preparedness.
22. Preparation of preretirement planning manual and presentation of several meetings around the country.
23. Distribution of stock service awards domestically and internationally.
24. Extensive work with MS on various systems under development.

25. Selection of new broker for medical/life insurance plans.
26. Development of retiree data base system.
27. Directed activities of eight retiree counselors.
28. Brought employees of various subsidiaries on to home office payroll.
29. Proposed record system for tracking time off due to illness.
30. Developed automated payroll link between profit-sharing systems.
31. Improved audit controls over medical plan.
32. Developed administrative manual for Data Center and Department Budget Control.
33. Prepared financial statements for various plans.
34. Conducted weekly orientations for new employees.
35. Conducted long-range planning meeting for staff.
36. Examined ways to integrate benefits planning with corporate planning.
37. Conducted study of work flow in Health and Welfare Plans group.
38. Developed retiree newsletter and preretirement training game.
39. Directed development of film strips on health maintenance organizations and retirement planning.
40. Implemented a word processing system for payment instructions to trustees.
41. Supported activities of pension and welfare plans administrative committees.
42. Established a local benefit managers group.
43. Staff members presented several speeches on retirement planning, aging issues, and benefits management around the country.
44. Made presentations on benefits to various employee groups around the country.
45. Staff members served on various company committees, including Credit Union Board of Directors & Loan Committee, and Foundation Advisory Board.
46. Maintained effective basic administration of all plans.

Benefit Department Projected Activities in 1980

The benefit management strategy adopted in the summer of 1976 with a three-year completion time frame was to:

1. Bring all benefit plans into full compliance with all legal requirements, in particular ERISA.
2. Develop reliable cost data on benefits and secure a measure of control over costs.
3. Develop and implement the best possible communications about benefits to gain maximum employee value from benefits.
4. Evaluate all plans for overlaps and basic gaps in coverage and/or basic deficiencies and correct same.
5. To organize the department and administration mechanism, staff and train the department employees to levels of competence, and secure control of department budget.

These objectives were essentially completed during 1979.

Accordingly, it is now appropriate to move on to a more sophisticated level of benefit management that includes development of an orderly benefit management and control system, orderly benefit planning integrated with corporate planning to support corporate goals, and presentation to management for consideration and discussion of a number of benefit concepts that are appropriate to a company of our nature with a mature benefits operation.

Benefit Department activities in 1980 will reflect the first significant movements into this new benefit management strategy. Many of the 1979 activities previously outlined have been directed toward building a foundation of information and knowledge on which to base 1980 activities within this strategy.

Benefit activities in 1980 will include:

1. Presentation to management for discussion of a benefit philosophy and planning system.
2. Presentation for discussion of a flexible benefits concept for the home office.
3. Presentation of results of a study of the adequacy of pension benefits.
4. Presentation of the results of a projection of pension costs and liabilities.
5. Presentation for discussion of profit-sharing concepts for field employees.
6. Presentation for discussion of key man life insurance concepts.
7. Presentations for discussion of whole life insurance concepts for employees.
8. Presentations for discussion of a program of voluntary stock options for employees.

9. Development of plans for integration of acquisitions into benefit plans.
10. Consideration of an Employee Attitude Survey.
11. Preparation to undertake an analysis of the quality of benefits as well as their quantity in comparison to major competitors in our salaried labor market.

APPENDIX 2: FLEXIBLE COMPENSATION (DISCUSSION PAPER, OCTOBER 1980)

Introduction

The purpose of this paper is to introduce the concept of flexible compensation into the company for discussion and consideration. The objective is to seek the establishment of a task force to investigate, evaluate, and make a recommendation by September 1981 as to whether or not we should implement flexible compensation and how this would be done.

The Concept

Flexible compensation (or *cafeteria compensation, flexible benefits, cafeteria benefits*) refers to the concept of providing employees an opportunity to make a trade-off between certain benefits and/or direct cash, selecting those benefits that are most useful and meaningful to them.

The idea is not particularly new in that employers have for decades offered employees "options" in benefit plans. Such options as selecting supplemental amounts of life insurance, selecting life insurance for family members, selecting the investment medium for profit-sharing funds, selecting the form of payment for retirement benefits, and so on are a form of flexibility in that they permit some degree of employee choice in their benefit coverages. Such options, however, usually require some form of employee contributions made in aftertax dollars.

What is new about flexible compensation is that tax laws since 1978 have opened the way for employees to make certain types of trade-offs between benefits with pretax, or nontaxable, income. For example, employees with no dependents may feel they do not need as much life insurance as the company is willing to provide, and may wish to exchange what they deem as "excess" life insurance for something that is more meaningful to them, perhaps one additional day of vacation during the year.

Also relatively new, and a major impetus for the movement toward flexible compensation, are the shifts in social attitudes of employees, particularly with regard to work.

The desire of employees for more participation and involvement in decisions affecting their lives, for more personal attention and consideration as individuals, coupled with changing lifestyles and social values, have combined to encourage employees to be more demanding in seeking rewards from employment that are more meaningful to them personally.

Thus, a great deal of interest has surfaced in the last three years regarding flexible compensation as a possible mechanism for both meeting individual employee's needs and simultaneously offering the potential for an employer to secure some real measure of control over the ever-expanding cost of benefit programs.

The State of the Art

As of mid-1980, less than 15 employers are known to have actually adopted some form of flexible compensation, most of them after 1976. So far, all such employers have reported very good results in terms of employee morale and acceptance and are pleased with their decision to implement such a plan.

All major consultants report that they are working with many clients on various stages of investigation of such plans and expect an increasing number of plans to be implemented every year.

The reason there are not more such plans currently is generally accepted as the usual reluctance to be first, and the desire of plan sponsors to have information on the experience of others in the process of deciding whether or not it is appropriate for themselves.

The Reasons in Favor

The reasons cited for favoring the adoption of some form of flexible compensation are as follows:

1. Greater control over corporate costs for employee benefits—at least to the extent of preventing uncontrolled increases. Future benefit cost increases, which would normally be assumed by the employer, may be passed to employees through the choices or may be assumed by the employer.
2. Employee appreciation and awareness of benefits, and their real value, are greatly increased. The process of communications

and considering choices requires genuine employee involvement and understanding of benefits.

3. Overall participation in plans by employees can be expected to increase. Employees will utilize the benefits more because they understand them better and choose benefits that are meaningful to them.

4. The employer becomes more attractive to potential employees; it is a good recruiting tool, at least until flexible compensation becomes commonplace, perhaps in 10 years.

5. The pressure from employees for new benefits can be minimized or at least accommodated without great extra cost since new benefits can be added as choices without expanding the total employer cost for benefits.

6. Individual employee needs can be more easily met by the individual choices since it is very costly to change a plan for all employees in order to accommodate the needs of only a few.

7. As inflation carries employees into higher tax brackets, the need for tax efficient benefits grows to preserve income. Flexible benefits can accommodate this need, giving employees opportunities to trade before-tax income for nontaxable benefits.

8. In an environment of wage controls, it is difficult to add new benefits because they reduce direct pay. With flexible benefits, new benefits can be added to accommodate employee needs without increasing the total cost structure or reducing amounts available for direct pay.

9. As social attitudes change and employee needs/desires/interests change, benefit plans can more easily be adjusted, (even discontinued) to accommodate these changes, thus refuting the psychology that once a benefit plan is installed it can never be cut back or eliminated.

10. Where a company has many diverse operations or is acquiring other companies, flexible benefits provide a vehicle for accommodating differences in benefit programs. They can also be helpful in accommodating the transfer of employees between organizations with different benefits.

11. Flexible benefits may provide a vehicle for easy and low cost compliance with laws on discrimination. For example, if under a flexible compensation program all employees are granted the same percentage of pay to use for benefit purchases then there

is no discrimination in benefits—all employees are treated equally.

12. Serious examination of flexible compensation forces the organization to carefully consider its philosophy toward benefits and direct compensation, a healthy exercise that will produce clarity and improvements, even if flexible benefits are not adopted.

The Reasons Against

1. The complexities of benefit administration and communication are greatly increased, as are the costs of administration. Extensive systems support is required, and some additional staff is required.
2. Some initial increase in employer cost for benefits will occur as adjustments are made in plans to accommodate employee choices.
3. Employee choices may involve converting part of future benefits into current benefits, such as would occur with a current cash option in the profit-sharing plan. In such cases, nonvested benefits that might have returned to the company or other employees upon early termination of an employee will be "lost."
4. Communications and the need for employees to make decisions can be quite complicated, and some employees may not be able to understand the plan and the implication of their choices. There is a risk of failure in adequately communicating the full implication of choices with the potential for additional employer liability and legal exposure.
5. The implementation and maintenance of a flexible program will be a drain on internal resources (staff and computer, etc.) for an extended period of time. It is complex and time-consuming.
6. If adverse selection occurs, and some is almost inevitable, the actual cost of a benefit plan will exceed to some extent the cost of a conventional plan.
7. Because the employees, through their choices, are the actual "purchasers" of a benefit, there will be constant pressure on the employer to select and maintain benefit coverages for the lowest possible cost.
8. Insurance carriers may be unable or unwilling to underwrite the optional benefits and reluctant or unable to provide meaningful assistance in the implementation and administration of the program.

9. The government may be unwilling to accept the tax losses that occur as employees exchange taxable income for nontaxable benefits and may impose tax laws that diminish the advantages of flexible compensation.

Types of Approaches

There are three basic approaches to implementing flexible benefits. Within these approaches the combinations of benefit options is almost infinite, limited only by the current IRS constraint that a three-way trade-off between cash, profit-sharing, and welfare plans is not currently permitted.*

These three approaches are defined as follows:

1. *Add-on Method.* In the add-on method, the employer maintains the existing nonflexible benefit program and provides an additional supplemental allowance. The allowance can be allocated among a number of options within the same benefits or new benefits. If the individual wants more than the supplement can buy, he or she can pay the difference through payroll deductions.
2. *Opt-Up/Opt-Down Method.* This approach starts with an existing program of benefits. Variations on the present coverages are developed as options—some of which have more value than the present coverages and others of which have less. An individual can choose to opt-up in value in some coverages and opt-down in others. If the person wants greater total value than the present program, he or she can buy the difference in value with payroll deductions. If the person wants less value in total than the present program, he or she receives the difference in cash (which is then taxable income).
3. *Carve-Out Method.* The carve-out method starts by cutting back present coverages to a core of nonflexible benefits. The core benefits are set at levels that provide adequate protection in the event of illness, disability, and death and that provide an adequate retirement income. The difference between the value of the old program and the value of the new core is calculated and made available to employees in the form of a flexible benefit allowance. The individual can spend that allowance among various optional

---

* This constraint was removed by tax law changes in 1981.

benefits provided in the program. And, if the individual wants more options than the allowance can buy, he or she can pay the difference through payroll deductions.

An employer could use any of these three methods effectively. The choice depends on the company's starting point and objectives. The add-on method might be appropriate when an organization is willing to spend more for its benefit program. The method allows the company to raise benefits in selected areas that give most employees something they want by letting each person choose how to spend the additional sum. This method also maintains future cost control by promising only a fixed allowance rather than underwriting all cost increases for new coverages.

Current Benefit Options

Existing benefits offer many options and choices to employees, in terms of both participating in benefits (additional life insurance, stock purchase plan) and in the form of benefit payments and investments.

However, what is not now available is the choice to exchange one benefit for another benefit, that is, to exchange some profit sharing for whole life insurance that would provide a paid-up life insurance policy at retirement age, for example.

A list of current benefit plan choices follows:

Elements of Choice in the Benefit Programs

The company has a standard benefit plan with several options already available. Employees have the opportunity to add to one or more benefit coverages through aftertax contributions or on a shared employee/ employer paid basis. Workers may select their own investment fund(s). There are also pension, holiday, and tuition options available. However, the company has a piecemeal approach to benefit options rather than a true cafeteria plan.

Survivor's Benefits

Option 1: The employee has a payment option in all survivor benefit coverages. He/she may select a lump sum payment or installments.

Option 2: Supplemental life insurance of two or three times an employee's annual salary is available in addition to basic life insurance, subject to a combined maximum of $300,000. A supplemental option of one times annual salary was offered in late summer, 1979. The company is underwriting a portion of this coverage.

Option 3: Employees can elect not to increase supplemental life insurance coverage in the event of a salary increase.

Option 4: Voluntary accidental death and dismemberment insurance is available in $25,000 increments up to $100,000 for the accidental death of the employee. After July 1, 1979, the maximum limit will be $250,000. The coverage is offered through payroll deduction, but the company subsidizes 10 percent of the premium to cover death due to an act of war.

Option 5: The employee may select voluntary AD&D to cover himself/herself up to $100,000. He/she may also opt for a family plan which covers the accidental death of dependents up to $50,000.

Disability Protection

Option 1: When an employee leaves the company due to disability he/she may request an early distribution of amounts held under his/her account in the profit-sharing plan and stock purchase and investment plan. These amounts are usually payable within 120 days after the individual reaches age 60.

Medical-Dental Benefits

Option 1: Beginning May 1979, the company will offer three HMO plans as alternatives to the medical plan. The three HMO packages will offer similar coverages in different localities. Premiums are fully paid by the company.

Profit-Sharing Plan

Option 1: There are two investment alternatives under the profit-sharing plan. Each year, the employee chooses to allocate his/her share of the company's contribution to account E, diversified investment, or account F, fixed income.

Option 2: Each year, the employee has the option to transfer 25 percent increments of the value of his/her portion of either account E or account F to the other account.

Option 3: Upon termination of employment, the individual selects to receive the vested portion of his/her accounts E and F in the form of either an annuity or a lump sum payment.

Stock Purchase and Investment Plan

Option 1: Employees may choose to contribute through payroll deductions to one of three investment funds. The options are account A, diversified investments fund; account B, fixed income fund; account C, employer common stock fund.

Option 2: The employee designates from 1-10 percent of his/her total wage to be contributed to the stock purchase and investment plan. A maximum of 5 percent of the total wage may be contributed to account C. An individual may change the percentage contribution at the beginning of each fiscal year. Contributions to fund C are matched by a company contribution of 50 percent of the employee contribution.

Option 3: The employee can withdraw the entire balance of any account to which he/she has contributed. At that time, contributions to the account will be discontinued.

Option 4: Each year, the employee has the option to transfer 25 percent increments of the value of his/her portion of either account A or account B to the other account. Participants who are at least age 63, or age 53 with at least 13 years of service, have transfer rights for funds in accounts C and G to enable them to transfer funds out of company stock into less volatile investments.

Option 5: Upon termination of employment, the individual selects to receive the distributions of accounts A and B in the form of either an annuity or a lump sum payment.

Pension Plan and Other Retirement Benefits

Option 1: The employee can choose early retirement if he/she is at least 55 and has at least 15 years of credited service. The individual may begin receiving his/her retirement pension at the time of termination or a later date. A pension started before age 65 is subject to actuarial reduction.

Option 2: The employee selects one of four forms of annuities through the pension plan. These include normal life annuity, half joint and survivor, full joint and survivor, and ten-year certain and continuous annuity.

Holidays

Option 1: In addition to eight fixed paid holidays, the employee can select two floating holidays from among 10-12 specified days.

Tuition Benefits

Option 1: The company reimburses tuition for any employee's work-related education. Reimbursement is nontaxable to the individual and is contributed on a sliding scale based on the final grade achieved in the course.

Deferred Compensation Plan for Executives

Option 1: Employees earning over $40,000 a year may elect to defer up to one third of pay and bonus to a future date, thereby deferring taxation of that income until it is actually paid.

Summary

Since 1976 the benefits function has been investigating and watching developments in flexible compensation. We now believe it is appropriate to consider the idea seriously for certain groups of employees.

I recommend that a task force be established to evaluate the issue and make recommendations in time to be incorporated into fiscal 1982 planning. Suggested members of the task force are:

Director of Compensation and Benefits, Chairperson
Vice President of Corporate Personnel
Director of Industrial Relations
Vice President of Personnel, International
A representative from each of the following departments:
Corporate Planning and Policy
Domestic Taxes
Legal Department
Management Services
Risk and Insurance Management
A representative from each Group/Division Personnel Unit

I request that this task force be granted a budget of $40,000 for fiscal 80-81 to secure advisory and other services to conduct its work, carried as a separately budgeted item in the employee benefits budget.

Flexible compensation may well represent the opportunity for a genuine breakthrough in modernizing compensation concepts and synchronizing them with the changing attitudes of the workforce.

Among the possibilities are such innovations as allocating pay increases into the flexible compensation system and letting employees decide how much they wish to take in direct pay and how much they wish to allocate to tax advantageous benefits; allowing employees to declare their own annual "bonus" by selecting the amount they wish and when to receive it and adjusting direct pay accordingly; including a percent of pay for benefits in the salary structure so that employees understand the value of benefits as part of pay; breaking the psychology of high cost benefits as "fringes"; breaking the psychology of comparison of pay between employees since individual benefit choices will affect the net pay.

Most important, flexible compensation may be the vehicle for "capping" the cost of benefits and for fixing the percent of payroll to be allocated to benefits.

APPENDIX 3: EMPLOYEE PERCEPTION SURVEY ON EMPLOYEE BENEFITS FOR HOME OFFICE PAYROLL EMPLOYEES, AUGUST 1980

TO: Home Office Payroll Employees

FROM: _____

DATE: August 29, 1980

RE: Survey on Employee's Perceptions Regarding Employee Benefits

As part of the long-range planning process for our employee benefits program, we have retained an independent consulting firm, Hazlehurst & Associates, Inc., to perform the enclosed employee perception survey. This survey is being conducted by an independent organization in order to maintain anonymity for the responding employees.

This survey will assist us in evaluating your perceptions and understanding of the current programs. We also expect to use the information for developing a long-range plan for employee benefits. In order to help us complete this effort, we urge you to take the time to fill out the enclosed survey and return it in the enclosed pre-addressed stamped envelope by September 19.

If you have any questions, you may call _____ , Manager of Employee Benefits, _____ . In making inquiries about this questionnaire, you do not need to identify yourself.

We look forward to your answers and comments on these important matters. Thank you.

SURVEY ON EMPLOYEE BENEFITS

Before we look at _____ employee benefits, we would like you to provide the following information so that the survey results can be analyzed by various characteristics (your name is *not* requested). Please check one answer for each of (1) through (9).

(1) Age:
Below 25 — 1. ( )
25 to 29 — 2. ( )
30 to 39 — 3. ( )
40 to 49 — 4. ( )
50 to 59 — 5. ( )
60 to 64 — 6. ( )
65 and over — 7. ( )

(2) Length of Service:
Less than 1 year — 1. ( )
At least 1 year but less than 2 years — 2. ( )
At least 2 years but less than 3 years — 3. ( )
At least 5 years but less than 10 years — 4. ( )
10 years and over — 5. ( )

(3) Annual Compensation:
Under $15,000 — 1. ( )
At least $15,000 but less than $25,000 — 2. ( )
At least $25,000 but less than $40,000 — 3. ( )
At least $40,000 but less than $60,000 — 4. ( )
$60,000 or more — 5. ( )

(4) Job Position (salespersons should check only the last box)
Grade 12 or below — 1. ( )
Grade 12 to 15 — 2. ( )
Grade 16 to 24 — 3. ( )
Grade 25 to 29 — 4. ( )
All other employees — 5. ( )
Salesperson — 6. ( )

(5) Number of Dependent Children:
None — 1. ( )
One — 2. ( )
Two or more — 3. ( )

(6) Work Location:
Home Office Area — 1. ( )
Field Location — 2. ( )
Sales Location — 3. ( )

(7)   Sex: Male   1.   ( )
                                                    Female   2.   ( )

(8)   Present Marital Status: Married   1.   ( )
                                                    Unmarried   2.   ( )

(9)   Are you covered by any other employee benefits not
      provided by _____ ? (For example, medical benefits of
      a spouse's employer, pension benefits with a former
      employer, insurance benefits you have purchased for   Yes   1.   ( )
      yourself and your family, etc.)   No   2.   ( )

Question 1: How would you rate _____ current employee benefit programs in
meeting each of the following needs? [Please check one answer for *each* of (A)
through (E).]
   (A)   Benefits to cover the medical, hospital, and surgical expenses of an illness
         or any injury
         ( )   1.   Very well
         ( )   2.   Adequately
         ( )   3.   Poorly
   (B)   Benefits to cover your dental expenses
         ( )   1.   Very well
         ( )   2.   Adequately
         ( )   3.   Poorly
   (C)   Benefits for your survivors in case you die
         ( )   1.   Very well
         ( )   2.   Adequately
         ( )   3.   Poorly
   (D)   Benefits to replace your earnings in case you become sick or disabled
         ( )   1.   Very well
         ( )   2.   Adequately
         ( )   3.   Poorly
   (E)   Benefits when you retire
         ( )   1.   Very well
         ( )   2.   Adequately
         ( )   3.   Poorly

Question 2: Please indicate below your belief in how efficiently you feel each of the
following benefit programs is run. [Check one answer for *each* of (A) through (F).]
   (A)   Health Care Plan
         ( )   1.   Have not used this plan
                    Have used this plan and my participation was handled:
         ( )   2.   Very smoothly
         ( )   3.   No major problems
         ( )   4.   Poorly
   (B)   Dental Benefits Plan
         ( )   1.   Have not submitted a claim under this plan
                    Have submitted a claim and it was handled:
         ( )   2.   Very smoothly
         ( )   3.   No major problems
         ( )   4.   Poorly
   (C)   Profit-Sharing Plan
         ( )   1.   Am not yet a participant *or* have not changed my investment
                    options under this plan

Have changed my investment options and the change was handled:
( ) 2. Very smoothly
( ) 3. No major problems
( ) 4. Poorly
(D) Stock Purchase and Investment Plan
( ) 1. Am not a participant in this plan
Am a participant and the ongoing administration has been handled:
( ) 2. Very smoothly
( ) 3. No major problems
( ) 4. Poorly
(E) Pension Plan
( ) 1. Have not requested personal information on this plan
Have requested information and my request was responded to:
( ) 2. Very smoothly
( ) 3. No major problems
( ) 4. Poorly
(F) Employee Purchase Plan
( ) 1. Have not used this plan
( ) Have made some purchases under this plan and the order was filled:
( ) 2. Very smoothly
( ) 3. No major problems
( ) 4. Poorly

Question 3: How well do you understand the following employee benefit programs and what they can do for you? [Please check one answer for *each* of (A) through (H).]
(A) Health Care and Dental Benefits Plan
( ) 1. Understand clearly
( ) 2. Understand pretty well but have a few questions
( ) 3. Do not understand
(B) Survivor Benefits, Including Life Insurance and Accidental Death and Dismemberment Insurance
( ) 1. Understand clearly
( ) 2. Understand pretty well but have a few questions
( ) 3. Do not understand
(C) Disability Benefits, Including Paid Sick Leave, Short-Term Disability Benefits and Long-Term Disability Benefits
( ) 1. Understand clearly
( ) 2. Understand pretty well but have a few questions
( ) 3. Do not understand
(D) Profit-Sharing Plan
( ) 1. Understand clearly
( ) 2. Understand pretty well but have a few questions
( ) 3. Do not understand
(E) Stock Purchase and Investment Plan
( ) 1. Understand clearly
( ) 2. Understand pretty well but have a few questions
( ) 3. Do not understand
(F) Pension Plan
( ) 1. Understand clearly
( ) 2. Understand pretty well but have a few questions
( ) 3. Do not understand

(G)   Employee Purchase Plan
    ( )   1.   Understand clearly
    ( )   2.   Understand pretty well but have a few questions
    ( )   3.   Do not understand
(H)   Holiday and Vacation Policies
    ( )   1.   Understand clearly
    ( )   2.   Understand pretty well but have a few questions
    ( )   3.   Do not understand

Question 4: Following up on the last set of questions, how well do you think _____ explains your employees benefits to you? [Please check one answer for *each* of (A) through (H).]

(A)   Health Care and Dental Benefits Plan
    ( )   1.   Very clearly
    ( )   2.   Okay
    ( )   3.   Not very well
(B)   Survivor Benefits, including Life Insurance and Accidental Death and Dismemberment Insurance
    ( )   1.   Very clearly
    ( )   2.   Okay
    ( )   3.   Not very well
(C)   Disability Benefits, Including Paid Sick Leave, Short-Term Disability Benefits and Long-Term Disability Benefits
    ( )   1.   Very clearly
    ( )   2.   Okay
    ( )   3.   Not very well
(D)   Profit-Sharing Plan
    ( )   1.   Very clearly
    ( )   2.   Okay
    ( )   3.   Not very well
(E)   Stock Purchase and Investment Plan
    ( )   1.   Very clearly
    ( )   2.   Okay
    ( )   3.   Not very well
(F)   Pension Plan
    ( )   1.   Very clearly
    ( )   2.   Okay
    ( )   3.   Not very well
(G)   Employee Purchase Plan
    ( )   1.   Very clearly
    ( )   2.   Okay
    ( )   3.   Not very well
(H)   Holidays and Vacations
    ( )   1.   Very clearly
    ( )   2.   Okay
    ( )   3.   Not very well

Question 5: Please rank the following benefit plans in order of relative importance to you. [In the parentheses next to the benefit program, put a number from 1 to 10. Number 1 should be assigned to the benefit program which you feel to be the most important to you; number 2 to the benefit program which you feel to be the next most important; . . . and number 10 to the benefit program which you feel to be the least important to you. Rank all 10 benefit plans, and use each number (from 1 to 10) only once.]

( ) 1. Health Care Benefits
( ) 2. Dental Benefits
( ) 3. Survivor Benefits, Including Life Insurance and Accidental Death and Dismemberment Benefits
( ) 4. Disability Benefits, Including Sick Leave Pay, Short-Term Disability Benefits and Long-Term Disability Benefits
( ) 5. Profit-Sharing Plan
( ) 6. Stock Purchase and Investment Plan
( ) 7. Pension Plan
( ) 8. Employee Purchase Plan
( ) 9. Holidays
( ) 10. Vacations

Question 6: Some of the benefits _____ require employee contributions (supplemental life insurance, voluntary accidental death and dismemberment insurance, Stock Purchase and Investment Plan, and, of course, Social Security and California State Disability benefits). All other benefits are paid completely by _____ . Along with the cost of everything else, the cost of your benefits increases each year. In fact, some benefits, such as health care benefits, have had larger increases than the cost-of-living for a number of years.

If you had to make contributions to maintain current benefit levels, which of the following benefits would you be willing to pay part of the cost for? [You may check more than one.]
( ) 1. Health care benefits
( ) 2. Dental benefits
( ) 3. Survivor benefits
( ) 4. Disability benefits
( ) 5. Retirement benefits (including cost-of-living protection after retirement)

Question 7: Which of the following benefits would you be willing to contribute toward in order to obtain *additional* benefits? [Please check one answer for *each* of (A) through (E).]
(A) Additional coverage of hospital, medical, and surgical bills
    ( ) 1. Yes
    ( ) 2. No
(B) Additional coverage of dental bills
    ( ) 1. Yes
    ( ) 2. No
(C) Additional survivor benefits, including life insurance
    ( ) 1. Yes
    ( ) 2. No
(D) Additional retirement benefits
    ( ) 1. Yes
    ( ) 2. No
(E) Additional income protection benefits in case you become sick or disabled
    ( ) 1. Yes
    ( ) 2. No

Question 8: One of the approaches that _____ is considering as a long-range possibility for your benefit programs would permit employees to make certain limited individual selections among various employee benefits. Under this "flexible" benefits system, _____ might provide certain minimum basic benefits (which would probably be less than the current level of benefits). Employees might then be allowed to choose additional benefits in specific areas (possibly with a requirement that employees pay part of the cost of the additional benefits). Employees might also be permitted to maintain (at no extra cost) the same levels of benefits they now have under the present plans; or to retain only the minimum basic benefits and get the remaining "credit" either in cash or through their Stock Purchase and Investment Plan accounts.

Please indicate below your relative interest in adding or reducing benefits in the following areas. [Please check one answer for *each* of (A) through (G).]

(A) Coverage of hospital, medical, and surgical bills
( ) 1. Would like to obtain more coverage
( ) 2. Present benefit levels are sufficient
( ) 3. I do not need as much as the present program provides

(B) Coverage of dental bills
( ) 1. Would like to obtain more coverage
( ) 2. Present benefit levels are sufficient
( ) 3. I do not need as much as the present program provides

(C) Life insurance and other survivor protection
( ) 1. Would like to obtain more coverage
( ) 2. Present benefit levels are sufficient
( ) 3. I do not need as much as the present program provides

(D) Income protection in case of illness or disability
( ) 1. Would like to obtain more coverage
( ) 2. Present benefit levels are sufficient
( ) 3. I do not need as much as the present program provides

(E) Opportunity to invest in a tax-sheltered savings plan (like the Stock Purchase and Investment Plan)
( ) 1. Would like to obtain more coverage
( ) 2. Present benefit levels are sufficient
( ) 3. I do not need as much as the present program provides

(F) Retirement benefits
( ) 1. Would like to obtain more coverage
( ) 2. Present benefit levels are sufficient
( ) 3. I do not need as much as the present program provides

(G) Time off with pay (for example, vacations and holidays)
( ) 1. Would like to obtain more coverage
( ) 2. Present benefit levels are sufficient
( ) 3. I do not need as much as the present program provides

Question 9: How well do you think _____ employee benefit program compares with the benefit programs of other companies? [Please check one.]
( ) 1. Much better
( ) 2. Slightly better
( ) 3. About the same
( ) 4. Slightly worse
( ) 5. Much worse

Question 10: Which of the following do you think best describes _____ total pay and benefits program? [Please check one.]
( ) 1. Both pay and benefits are above average compared to other companies
( ) 2. Pay is above average but benefits are below average compared to other companies
( ) 3. Pay is below average but benefits are above average compared to other companies

( ) 4. Both pay and benefits are about average compared to other companies
( ) 5. Both pay and benefits are below average compared to other companies

Question 11: Please rank the following employee benefit plans according to how expensive you think they are for the Company to provide for _____ employees as a group. [In the parentheses next to the benefit program, put a number from 1 to 10. Number 1 should be assigned to the benefit program you believe to be the most expensive; number 2 to the benefit program which you think is the next most expensive; . . . and number 10 to the benefit program you believe to be the least expensive. Rank all 10 benefit programs, and use each number (from 1 to 10) only once.]

( )   1. Health Care Benefits
( )   2. Dental Benefits
( )   3. Survivor Benefits, Including Life Insurance and Accidental Death and Dismemberment Benefits
( )   4. Disability Benefits, Including Sick Leave Pay, Short-Term Disability Benefits and Long-Term Disability Benefits
( )   5. Profit-Sharing Plan
( )   6. Stock Purchase and Investment Plan
( )   7. Pension Plan
( )   8. Employee Purchase Plan
( )   9. Holidays
( ) 10. Vacations

Question 12: Which of the following figures do you think most clearly represents _____ total cost of employee benefits (including governmental plans like Social Security and Workers' Compensation, vacations, holidays, sick leave pay, etc.) for Home Office employees, when measured as a percentage of their salaries? [Please check one.]

( ) 1. 20% of pay
( ) 2. 30% of pay
( ) 3. 40% of pay
( ) 4. 50% of pay
( ) 5. 60% of pay

Question 13: In order to design an effective _____ employee benefit program, it will be helpful to know a little about any of your own personal financial security programs. [Please *do not* include any benefits which are provided to your spouse by another employer.]

(A) Do you have any additional life insurance on yourself other than what _____ provides for you?
( ) 1. Yes   ( ) 2. No
If your answer is no, please go to part (B). If your answer is yes, approximately how much additional life insurance do you have? [Please check one.]
( ) 1. Less than 1 times your annual pay
( ) 2. Between 1 and 2 times your annual pay
( ) 3. More than twice your annual pay

(B) Do you have any additional disability income insurance other than that provided to you by _____ ?
( ) 1. Yes   ( ) 2. No

(C) Have you purchased any supplemental health insurance coverage for yourself?
( ) 1. Yes   ( ) 2. No

For other members of your family?
( ) 3. Yes   ( ) 4. No
(D) Do you have a regular savings program other than the Stock Purchase and Investment Plan?
( ) 1. Yes   ( ) 2. No
If your answer is no, please go on to Question 14. If your answer is yes, for what purpose(s) are you saving? [You may check more than one.]
( ) 1. To purchase a home
( ) 2. For home remodeling
( ) 3. To educate your children
( ) 4. For your retirement
( ) 5. Other (explain) _____

Question 14: Miscellaneous comments regarding your concerns, interests, or other feelings with regard to _____ employee benefit programs.

How long did it take to complete this questionnaire?
( )   15 minutes   ( )   30 minutes
( )   1 hour   ( )   1 hour+

THANK YOU FOR YOUR ASSISTANCE!

APPENDIX 4: LEXICON OF BENEFIT TERMS AND ACRONYMS

By Ernest Griffes

This lexicon is intended only to describe benefit related terms in a simple manner that enhances the reader's understanding of benefit concepts. It is not intended to be complete in describing the complexity of benefit plans or the full implications of laws or regulations.

AARP American Association of Retired Persons, the foremost membership organization representing the interests of over 20 million members age 50 and over, although membership is not actually age restricted.

actuarial valuation or actuarial report The mathematical valuation of the liabilities and funding requirements of a pension plan as conducted by an actuary and presented to the client in an actuarial report.

actuary A mathematically trained person who uses mathematical and statistical concepts in the calculation of funding and costs for pension, health plans, life insurance, and other benefits.

actuarial assumptions Any of several assumptions that actuaries may make about the work force covered by a pension plan that are used in the calculation of the funding requirements for the plan.

ADEA Age Discrimination in Employment Act, which raised the permissible age for mandatory retirement.

ADP test   Antidiscrimination provisions test, a test of 401(k) plans that is conducted annually to determine if contributions favor the highly paid employees. If they do, such contributions of the highly paid must be returned to the employees, thereby reducing their tax advantage in the plan.

adverse selection   A process of selection that works against the cost of the plan. This occurs primarily in health plans when employees have an opportunity to choose coverages and those who are healthy choose minimal coverages while those who are not healthy and likely to have large claims choose for high coverages. The result is a higher cost for the plan because the spread of risk and premiums are distorted by the adverse selection.

age discrimination   Any practice or provision in a benefit plan that has the effect of creating a disadvantage to older employees over young employees. Of particular significance are Early Retirement Incentive Plans or "Window Plans" providing special benefits for older long service employees who may elect to retire during a specific narrow window of time. The significance in such plans is that whatever incentive is offered it must be offered to all employees in the eligible group and there may not be any influence or duress exerted on individuals to either encourage or discourage them from retiring.

age protected group   Related to age discrimination, basically anyone over age 40 is in the age protected group per ADEA.

alienation or assignment of benefits   Refers to procedures under which benefit entitlements of an employee may be assigned or alienated to some other person or agency, such as in a garnishment of wages or in a divorce suit.

amendment   Refers to changes made in a benefit plan that are incorporated into the plan by amendment of the plan document.

annual additions   Refers to the annual additions to an employees accounts in a defined benefit or defined contribution plan or a combination of such plans that arise from added employer or employee contributions or forfeitures during the year. The significance is that such total annual additions are subject to limitations which are generally the lesser of the total of 25 percent of the salary of an employee or $30,000 (as adjusted for inflation from time to time). For this purpose employee contributions of deferred salary in a 401(k) plan are treated as an employer contribution and nondeductible employee contributions to such a plan are includable in this total as well after 1987. The result is to discourage the provision of savings plans with employee-only after-tax contributions and cash or deferred type plans.

annuity   A form of payment of pension benefits in which the benefit payments are spread out over a given period of time, such as the life of the participant, or, if a joint and survivor annuity, over the life of the participant and a spouse or qualified person.

APPWP   Association of Private Pension and Welfare Plans, a plan sponsor membership organization involved in interacting with legislators on behalf of plan sponsors on issues of benefits legislation and keeping members informed of legislative activities.

ASO Administrative Services Only, refers to an arrangement with an insurer to provide only services of administration and claims payment for a medical benefit plan, or when the plan sponsor is self-insuring the actual benefits payable under the plan. In such cases the insurer bears no risk and does not underwrite the benefit coverages. Such arrangements are designed to provide insurers a competitive opportunity to provide services similar to those provided by a TPA.

ASPA The American Society for Personnel Administration, an organization of professionals in the human resources field.

ASPA The American Society of Pension Actuaries, an organization of actuaries engaged in pension activities, as compared to actuaries engaged in life insurance and other fields of actuarial science.

beneficiary A person designated by an employee to receive the employees benefit entitlements should the employee become deceased.

benefit Any of an endless variety of plans, programs, and policies that an employer may provide for employees which are beneficial to the employees.

benefit plans audit Generally refers to a process of conducting a general audit of the entire process of managing a benefit plan or set of benefit plans for the purpose of establishing if the plan is in order, is meeting legal requirements, is being effectively communicated to employees, is cost effective, and is generally accomplishing the employers objectives in providing the benefit. May also refer to the process of auditing claims payments in a medical or other benefit plan to ascertain that they are being properly paid in accordance with plan provisions.

benefit statement A written communication provided to employees that sets forth or states the benefits to which they are entitled as a result of their employment with an employer.

broker A person or agent who intercedes between a plan sponsor and various insurance companies to negotiate contracts for the benefit plan on behalf of the plan sponsor and to otherwise advise the plan sponsor on matters related to the plan.

cafeteria plan A plan in which employees have a choice between a "menu" of a variety of benefits, usually on the basis of a trade-off of one benefit for another. Interchangeable with flexible benefits. Under Section 89 not to be confused with an eating facility provided for employees which is subject to certain provisions of Section 89.

cash or deferred plans   A generic term referring to plans such as a 401(k) or profit sharing plan in which participants have some choice as to whether to take salary or company contributions in cash or defer a portion of the salary or the company contribution on their behalf.

CEB   Council on Employee Benefits, a private membership organization of large private plan sponsors formed for the purpose of providing a means of regular interaction among members on benefits issues of common interest.

CEBS   Certified Employee Benefit Specialist course offered by the International Foundation of Employee Benefits to provide formal training and professional designations for nonactuarial employee benefits professionals.

child care plan   Any of a variety of plans and programs that provide employees assistance with the costs of child care while working.

claim   An employee's request for payment of benefit entitlements under the provisions of a benefit plan.

CODA   Cash or Deferred Arrangement, see **cash or deferred plans.**

comprehensive plan   A medical plan that provides for payment of medical expenses on a comprehensive basis. An example would be a plan that provides that the employee pays the first $200 of expenses as a deductible, then for medical expenses of any kind for the next $1,800 of medical expenses the employee pays 20 percent, and the plan pays 80 percent, and thereafter over $2,000 of total expenses the plan pays 100 percent of medical expenses, all during a fixed period of time such as one plan year. The advantage of such a plan is that it is easier to administer since each claim does not need to be checked against a schedule of services and related amounts payable. It is also easier to communicate to employees and for them to understand what benefits the plan pays.

controlled group   A term referring to many forms of organizational ownership affiliations that have the effect of several discreet employers being actually one employer for certain benefit purposes. The significance is that if a controlled group circumstance exists, then all of the related groups must be tested together for purposes of anti-discrimination testing of benefit plans.

co-payments   A method of cost sharing with employees in which the employee and the employer share the cost of a medical service according to the provisions of the benefit plan.

COBRA   Consolidated Omnibus Budget Reconciliation Act of 1985 which established the legal requirements for extending medical benefit coverage to former employees and dependents of former employees.

defined benefit plan   A pension plan that provides predetermined benefits according to a prescribed formula. The funding and contributions are determined by actuarial calculations.

defined contribution plan A plan in which the amount of contributions are determined by some formula and each participant has an account that accumulates contributions made for them. The ultimate benefit is the balance in their account. Profit sharing and similar plans are in this category.

DEFRA Deficit Reduction Act of 1984.

deductible The amount of a claims for medical care that is to be paid by the employee before the plan begins paying benefits in accordance with the provisions of a health plan. For example, if the deductible is $200, then the employee must accrue and pay $200 of medical expenses before the plan begins paying benefits. A cost control technique.

dependent Refers to spouse or children (sometimes parents or others) of an employee who are legal dependents of the employee for purposes of benefit coverages.

determination letter See **filing.**

document or plan document Refers to the legal document that establishes a benefit plan and sets forth all of the provisions for qualifying for and receiving benefits as well as administering the plan and investment of fund assets.

early retirement or early retirement plan Provisions within a pension or similar plan permitting retirement prior to a normal retirement, or a special plan providing incentives to retire earlier than would normally be the case.

EBRI Employee Benefits Research Institute, the foremost research organization on employee benefits issues, often requested to provide reliable data to legislative bodies regarding benefits, and the premier source of research data for plan sponsors.

ECFC Employers Council on Flexible Compensation, a membership organization that focuses on issues related to providing flexible benefits.

election Refers to an employees opportunity to elect certain aspects of coverage under a benefit plan, such as electing to participate in a savings plan by making employee contributions.

employee contributions The employee's contribution to the cost of benefits. May be mandatory to participate in a medical plan or may be voluntary as in a savings plan.

enrolled actuary An actuary enrolled with the federal government under provisions of ERISA and thereby authorized to conduct pension evaluations, sign actuarial reports, and practice on behalf of clients before federal agencies.

ERIC Erisa Regulations Industry Committee, a membership organization formed following the passage of ERISA in 1974 to provide a regular forum for discussion of benefit issues related primarily to very large employers.

ERISA   The Employee Retirement Income Security Act enacted in 1974, the major pension legislation that established many of the legal principles governing the management of pension and welfare plans.

ESOP   Employee Stock Ownership Plan, a plan by which employees become shareholders of the employer by the employer making contributions that purchase company stock on behalf of the employees.

evaluating a benefit plan   The concept of conducting employee surveys, benefit comparisons, cost comparisons, and so on, all for the purpose of evaluating if the provision of a benefit plan for employees is really effective in achieving plan sponsor objectives.

exclusion   A medical service for which no payment is made under the provisons of a health plan. An example might be an experimental form of medical treatment, such as acupuncture, that the medical profession has not accepted and which an insurer therefore will not insure.

experience rating   A process by which an insurer adjusts the premiums charged up or down to reflect the actual claims experience of a plan for a particular employer. Primarily applicable to large employers where the statistical experience for claims across a large homogeneous work force approximates the experience of the population as a whole so that better experience than would normally be expected creates lower costs for that employer, and higher claims than normal create higher costs for that employer.

FASB   The Financial Accounting Standards Board, a professional accounting organization that establishes standards for accounting. In reference to benefits, it sets standards for accounting for the cost of pensions, pension liabilities, retiree medical benefit liabilities, and so on.

fee for service   Refers to the manner in which a medical service is provided, in this case on the basis of a fee for services rendered. This is to distinguish this payment method from a fixed fee method as used by an HMO in which a fixed fee is paid in advance and whatever services are necessary are rendered for that fixed fee and no additional charges are made for service.

FICA   Federal Insurance Contributions Act, the formal title of Social Security.

fiduciary   In benefit plans refers to persons who administer and/or provide services to a benefit plan. The concept of a fiduciary in benefit plans derives from ERISA, which places burdens of personal responsibility on such persons to fulfill their duties solely in the interests of plan participants. Failure to do so may create personal liabilities upon such persons.

filing   Commonly refers to the filing of the required plan documents and information with the IRS to secure approval of the plan, to assure that it meets legal requirements, and assure the contributions to the plan will be tax deductible to the employer and such contributions or benefits will not be currently taxable to the employees. The IRS will provide a "determination letter'' so indicating. May also refer to filing any number of other forms with various federal and state agencies.

financial planning programs Any of a variety of plans and programs provided for the purpose of assisting employees with personal financial planning and education in personal financial issues.

Findpro© The Financial Independence Planning Program, a financial education and planning software program used by plan sponsors to enable employees to project their financial needs for retirement, to communicate the role of the plan sponsors benefits in attaining those retirement goals, and to build participation in 401(k) plans, created by and available by contacting the author of this book.

first dollar coverage Refers to a plan that pays medical expenses from the first dollar of expense incurred, as compared to a deductible plan in which the employee must pay first dollars of expense before the plan will pay any benefits. Many plans have eliminated first dollar coverage as a cost containment measure on the premise that if the employee has no personal investment in obtaining a medical service they will tend to use more medical services than they really need, thereby increasing the cost of the plan.

flexible benefits The term describing a variety of plans in which employees have choices of benefits and opportunities to trade some benefits for others, used interchangably with cafeteria benefits.

forfeitures Portions of an employer's contribution on behalf of an employee in a defined contribution plan that are given up or forfeited by an employee as a result of termination of employment prior to becoming vested in those contributions.

FSA (1) A Fellow of The Society of Actuaries, a professional designation signifying the highest level of actuarial competence; (2) Flexible Spending Account, as used to describe a Section 125 plan; or (3) in pension funding the Funding Standards Account.

FUTA Federal Unemployment Tax Act, see **unemployment compensation.**

guaranteed issued Refers to an insurers agreement with a plan sponsor to guarantee the issuance of a minimum amount of life insurance on all employees covered by a group life insurance plan, even if some members of the group have medical problems that would otherwise indicate that the issuance of such insurance coverage was not an actuarially sound risk.

hard dollars Refers to cash payment made to a consultant, broker, actuary, or other service provider for services provided to a plan sponsor in management and administration of benefit plans. See **soft dollars.**

HCE Highly compensated employee as used for determination of discrimination in 401(k) plans and under Section 89.

health and accident plans   A general term referring to benefit plans that provide medical care or other benefits in the event of illness or accident.

HMO   Health Maintenance Organization. This is a medical service organization of various forms that provides health care services for a fixed and flat fee.

IFEB   International Foundation for Employee Benefits, a member organization providing information, education, and certification for professionals in the employee benefits field.

indemnify   Refers to a protective process by which a plan sponsor may take legal actions such as approving a resolution by a board of directors that provides that employee fiduciaries administering a benefit plan for the employer will be indemnified or protected against personal liabilities that arise from their performance of those fiduciary duties, so long as they have performed them in good faith and there has been no fraudulent or criminal act involved in their performance of the duties.

indemnity plan   Refers to the traditional type of insured medical benefits plan in which an insurer agrees to pay certain benefits according to a schedule of payments, in effect to indemnify the insured employee against certain medical expense losses.

integration or integrated plan   Refers to a pension or other plan that provides benefits that will be paid related to or integrated with benefits that are payable from some governmental plan, such as social security or workers compensation.

investment elections   Refers to an employee's right to elect how to have an account, in a profit sharing or savings plan, invested, usually from three to five different forms of investments that are offered.

investment manager   A professional investing service that manages the investment of assets in a pension, profit sharing, or other similar plan.

IRA   Individual Retirement Account. A tax advantaged means of saving for retirement that is primarily beneficial to people not covered by an employer pension plan of some form.

IRC   Internal Revenue Code, various sections of which establish the tax principles for operation of benefit plans.

ISPP   International Association of Pre-Retirement Planners, a member organization of professionals in the field of retirement planning programs.

key employee   Similar in intent to a highly compensated employee but refers to an employee (sometimes even a former or deceased employee) who is an officer or stockholder but not necessarily also highly compensated. The significance is that key employees must be included as a highly compensated employee for various antidiscrimination tests, even if they are not highly compensated.

leased employee   Refers to a person who works in the employ of an employer but for whom the employer pays a third party a fixed rate, and the third party provides for payment of wages to the person, payment of required taxes on employment, and provides the persons benefits. A leased employee is differentiated from a temporary employee by the fact that the arrangement with the third party provides for long-term utilization of the person, generally defined as one year or more.

limitation year   A twelve month period selected by the employer that constitutes the plan year for purposes of antidiscrimination testing.

LTD plan   Long-term disability plan, a plan providing income benefits to employees in the event of long-term disability.

mandatory retirement   Means that retirement may be required and enforced at a specific age. Generally mandatory retirement may not be required or enforced except for certain very limited jobs, such as airline pilots, where it is deemed that the public interest is served.

major medical   Refers to the provisions of a medical plan that provide for major claims. Such major medical provisions may provide for an overall limit on how much a plan will pay in total for a given claim.

matching contributions   Refers to an employer contribution that is made as a matching contribution to an employee contribution in savings plans, such as the employer will match each $1 of an employee contribution with an employer contribution of $.50.

MDIB   Minimum Distribution Incidental Benefits rules, refers to various rules designed to assure that the primary purpose of benefits is for the employee and that payments to beneficiaries is incidental and not primary.

MDR   Minimum distribution requirements, as set forth in various laws and regulations that provide for procedures for distributing accounts to employees under various circumstances.

Medicaid   A common title for state programs providing medical care.

Medicare   That portion of Social Security that provides for medical benefits. Part A of medicare provides for Hospital Insurance Benefits, and Part B provides for Medical Insurance Benefits.

MIB   Medical Information Bureau, a private organization that maintains files on individuals similar to a credit reporting agency but containing data on the medical history of each individual as reported by hospitals and physicians. Such files are usually checked by insurers or underwriters when considering an individuals applications for various forms of insurance.

minimum premium plan   An arrangement with an insurer of a medical plan that provides that the plan sponsor pays a minimum premium for benefit coverages, and at the end of specified period pays an additional amount if claims have exceeded prearranged limits. The purpose of such a plan is to allow flexibility in the cash flow of the employer since the employer pays only a minimum premium that is expected to cover the bulk of claims expense based on prior plan experience.

money manager   A professional investing service that manages the investment of assets in a pension or similar plan.

morbidity rates   The statistical and mathematical data based on rates of disability or illness for various ages and populations used by actuaries to compute the probabilities of same for establishing premiums for disability and health care plans.

mortality rates   The statistical and mathematical data based on death rates for various ages and populations used by actuaries to compute the probabilities of death for establishing life insurance premiums or for funding in pension plans.

multiemployer plan   Refers to benefit plans sponsored by unions for members who may be employees of many different employers, hence *multiemployer*.

normal retirement   The age provided within a pension or similar plan at which customary retirement may occur. Retirement prior to this age is referred to as *early retirement* and after this age is *late retirement*. The normal retirement age may no longer be made mandatory for most categories of employees.

OBRA   Omnibus Budget Reconciliation Act of 1987, notable in benefits for funding limitations on defined benefit plans, actuarial calculation constraints, plan terminations, PBGC premium increases, estate tax exclusions for stock sales to an ESOP, and constraints on reversion of excess plan assets in a pension plan.

out of pocket expenses   Generally refers to the employee's expenses paid for medical services in excess of the deductible in a comprehensive plan.

PBGC   Pension Benefit Guarantee Corporation, a federal agency formed by ERISA for the purpose of insuring pension benefits provided by employers in defined benefit pension plans.

plan sponsor   An employer or union sponsoring a plan that provides benefits for employees or union members.

pooling   A technique for spreading the risk of large unexpected claims by pooling the claims experience of several plan sponsors so that each individually does not bear the risk alone.

PPO   Preferred Provider Organization, a medical service organization that provides medical services at lower cost under an arrangement to serve the majority of employees of a given employer.

private pension plan or plan   Refers to a benefit plan sponsored by an employer, as compared to a multiemployer plan sponsored by a union.

premium or premium rate   The amount or rate charged by an insurer for providing benefit payments under an insurance contract.

premium delay   A contractual arrangement under which the plan sponsor may delay payment of premiums for a period of time, usually 60 or 90 days, with the insurer's concurrence. The purpose is to assist the cash flow of the employer.

premium tax   A tax charged by many states on premiums paid by an employer to an insurer for providing benefits for employees. Avoiding premium taxes as a cost control measure was one reason for the shift by large employers towards self-insuring benefits for employees. Many states have responded by levying a tax on self-insured plans as well.

preretirement planning   See **retirement planning.**

provision or plan provision   Refers to the written statements contained in a plan document that provide for how all aspects of a benefit plan are to be managed.

PSCA   Profit Sharing Council of America, a member organization dealing with issues in profit sharing plans.

QDRO   Qualified Domestic Relations Order, a legal order directing the distribution of benefit assets in divorce or other marital circumstances.

QJSA   Qualified Joint and Survivor Annuity.

QPSA   Qualified Preretirement Survivor Annuity.

qualification   Of a benefit plan, the process of qualifying a plan with the IRS by meeting all requirements of various laws and regulations so that the plan sponsor is assured of the deductibility of contributions made to the plan.

rate   Refers to the premium rate.

REA   Retirement Equity Act of 1984, further liberalized the permissible mandatory retirement ages as earlier increased by ADEA, in effect eliminating mandatory retirement.

retention   An added charge in the premium charged by an insurer for insuring a benefit plan. The purpose of the charge is to provide the insurer with a fee for various services provided, such as plan administration, payment of claims, booklets, and a profit margin.

retirement   In the social context generally means separation from the work force at a later age and living in a state of receiving pension payments and no longer making a contribution to societies productive economic processes. In the context of benefit plans means termination of employment at an age of entitlement to benefits from a pension or similar plan, whether or not pension payments actually are commenced or separation from the work force has occurred.

retiree or pensioner Former employees now retired from the employer and collecting pension payments.

retirement plan A common term for a pension, profit sharing or similar plan providing for the accumulation of benefits towards retirement.

retirement planning Any of a variety of programs designed to enable employees to understand and manage the personal and financial issues of preparing for retirement.

risk charge An added charge in the premium charged by an insurer for insuring a benefit plan. The purpose of this charge is to spread among many plan sponsors the risk of unexpected large claims, so that each plan sponsor or the insurer do not individually bear the risk for such a claim.

salary reduction or salary deferral Generally refers to the process of 401(k) and Section 125 plans in which employees choose to reduce salary or defer salary and have the salary applied toward some benefit purpose.

SAR Summary Annual Report, a legally required annual report to participants of a benefit plan setting forth information about the funding and financing of the plan.

savings plan Generally refers to any of a variety of plans that allow employees to save by making contributions into a plan, most commonly a 401(k) plan.

section *xx* Refers to sections of the Internal Revenue Code.

section 79 The section of the IRC that establishes the premium costs for life insurance that are includable in taxable income.

section 89 Section 89 of the Tax Reform Act of 1986 that established qualification and antidiscrimination requirements for health insurance, life insurance, and other nonpension benefit plans.

section 125 plan Also called a Flexible Spending Account or Salary Reduction Plan in which employees choose to have salary reduced on a pre-tax basis and have the reduced portion of the salary applied for the purpose of paying for a variety of nonpension benefits.

section 401(k) plan Also called a Salary Deferral Plan, a plan in which employees choose to defer some portion of salary and have that portion invested for future purposes of retirement income.

section 457 plan Refers to deferred compensation plans for governmental, academic, and other nonprofit organizations. Such plans permit employees of such organizations to defer compensation on a tax advantaged basis similar to 401(k) plans of for profit organizations.

section 501 (c) (9) The IRC section that provides for the formation of a VEBA (see **VEBA**).

self-administration Administration of a self-insured plan by the plan sponsor themselves, as compared to having the administration of the plan performed by an insurer or TPA.

self-insurance Benefit plan funding approaches in which the employer absorbs the risk for benefit payments rather than insure the plans with an insurer who would bear the risk. The significance of self-insuring is that an employer expects to experience lower costs for the benefit.

SEP Simplified Employee Pension, a simplified and easily installed pension plan used primarily by small employers.

service of process Refers to the manner by which legal suits are filed against a benefit plan.

social security The generic term for the Federal Insurance Contributions Act (FICA) that provides for the federal government to collect contributions from employers and employees and pay a variety of pension, disability, and medical benefits to those employees and their dependents.

Society of Actuaries The professional organization that trains and certifies actuaries.

soft dollars Insurance or brokerage commissions paid to consultants, actuaries, brokers, investment managers, or other providers of services by a plan sponsor in the management of a benefit plan; often accepted as payment for the services in lieu of hard dollar cash payment for the services.

SPD Summary Plan Description, a legally required communication document about a benefit plan containing information about the rights of participants in the plan.

split funded Refers to funding of a pension plan by using life insurance and other investments to fund the benefits of a pension plan, as compared to using only non-life insurance investments.

stop loss limit A limit established in self-insured plans on the amount of claims. Beyond the limit, an insuror will absorb some or all of the claims, for which the employer pays a premium to the insuror.

TDA Tax Deferred Annuity, most commonly applied to pension annuities purchased by employees of nonprofit organizations under Section 457 plans, but may also refer to other forms of annuities that may be purchased by individuals and that contain provisions for deferral of taxation on the annuity.

TSA Tax Sheltered Annuity, essentially the same as a TDA.

TAMRA 1988 Technical and Miscellaneous Revenue Act of 1988, notable in benefits for technical corrections to several TRAs affecting coverage and nondiscrimination tests, distribution rules, increase in excise taxes on reversion of assets in pension plans, IRA deduction limits, rules for SEPs, ESOP distribution rules, Section 89 clarifications as well as changes to group life plans, educational assistance plans, group legal service plans, cafeteria plans, and dependent care assistance plans.

target benefit plan A pension plan in which contributions are based on a targeted benefit computed by a formula but the actual benefit paid is based on the assets in a participants account that have accumulated from those contributions.

TEFRA Tax Equity and Fiscal Responsibility Act of 1982, notable in benefits for provisions that establish limits on benefits and contributions on behalf of employees.

top heavy or top heavy plan Refers to a pension or similar plan in which the preponderence of benefits (generally 60 percent or more) accrue to highly paid employees. The consequences of a plan being top heavy are generally that benefits for other employees must vest more quickly than would otherwise be required by law.

TPA Third-Party Administrator, an administration service provided for the purpose of administering claims in self-insured plans, or in plans such as Section 125 plans.

TRA *"xx year"* Tax Reform Acts for various years—especially TRA 1986, notable in benefits for the provisions of Section 89, minimum vesting standards, more strict integration requirements, and numerous other changes to pension and defined contribution plans.

TRASOP Tax Reform Act Stock Ownership Plan, an ESOP that is entitled to special tax credits pursuant to provisions of various Tax Reform Acts.

travel accident plan A plan providing benefits for loss of various body functions or life in the event of an accident that occurs during travel.

underwriting or underwriter Refers to the process of insuring or an insurer who for a premium payment agrees to bear the risk (underwrite) of claims against a benefit plan.

unemployment compensation A state and federal program for providing minimal compensation to unemployed workers during periods of no work, funded by required contributions by employers.

usual, customary, and reasonable (UCR) Refers to the basis by which an insurer determines what amount should be paid for a particular health, hospital, or medical service under a medical plan, based on statistical data gathered about the usual and customary fees charged by many different providers of such services. Often the basis of contention between an employee and the insurer over how much of a claim is covered, since individual physicians providing a service may well charge more than the usual and customary fee, so the employee must pay the portion of the fee that is not covered under plan provisions for payment only of the usual and customary fee.

VEBA   Voluntary Employees Beneficiary Association, a trust formed under IRC Section 501 (c) (9) to provide various medical benefits for participants in the trust. A self-insured plan may be managed through use of a VEBA, or several small employers may form and join in a VEBA as an alternative to each using a traditional insured plan.

vesting   The process of earning an entitlement to benefits in a pension or other plan based on meeting service requirements with the employer.

welfare plan   A misnomer that derives from references to WPPDA and ERISA and refers to essentially any employee benefit plan that contributes beneficially to the welfare of employees. In the employee benefit context this term is not to be confused with the common usage of the term *welfare* as it refers to government plans for providing benefits to the disadvantaged persons in society.

window plan   A plan providing special incentives to retire early during a narrow window of time, after which the special incentives are no longer available.

workers compensation   State and federal programs for providing compensation and medical expense payments to employees injured while on the job, funded by required employer paid premiums.

WPPDA   Welfare Pension Plans Disclosure Act, enacted in the 1940s for the purpose of requiring disclosure of information about pension and welfare plans.

APPENDIX 5: THE WINDS OF CHANGE*

By Vic Zink

Five years ago this spring, I had to turn over the presidency of this fine organization to Russ Schuck just before the spring meetings. The reason: my boss wanted me to do some different things and to start out by spending May 1976 in Europe. The winds of change have been very much a part of my life since that time. I have ridden them around through the Industrial Relations organization worldwide back to exactly what I was doing five years ago. Therefore, it is obvious, at least for me, that "change" is not necessarily synonymous with progress.

Many of us here today have grown up together in the benefits

---

* Keynote address to the spring conference of the Council on Employee Benefits, May 1981— reprinted with permission of Mr. Zink.

business, and it's nice to be able to say both hello and goodby again to so many of you. The largest change of all for me is only months away. If things go the way I hope, Ken Olthoff will take my job as of July 1, and I will retire officially a couple of months later. I plan to cast at least my immediate future on the winds and see what they blow in.

Let me assure you right at the beginning that I am not going to tell you how things are or will be at General Motors and then simply urge you to spread the gospel. I recognize full well that what is good for General Motors is not necessarily good for you. In fact, many of the things we thought would be good for General Motors turned out not to be. All of these we now blame on the unions. That's fair, isn't it? Through the years they've taken credit for all the good things.

Moreover, I'm not going to talk very long. I've sat out there through many of these wishing the speaker would get on with it.

I started out with General Motors 35 years ago as an English professor at our engineering college in Flint. In 1953, after I had spent a year selling Oldsmobiles in Montana, Jim Gillen, one of the deans of the benefits business, needed an English teacher to bring a little class to employee benefits; so he brought me to Central Office. I was to stay for two years and then go on to greater things. But I was a slow learner. In the intervening years, I was on the ground floor in a lot of concepts we take for granted today: HMOs, major medical, dental plans, retirement planning, 30 and out, survivor income benefits, increases for pensioners, joint union-management administration, pension investment policy, substance abuse programs, health care cost containment, and even ERISA. I have gone the full route overseas from imposition of U.S. benefits to local option, and there is no magic wand there either. My most important duty through the years was dealing with the unions. I got my baptism early. The issue of employee involvement in paying for health insurance was a strike issue as long ago as 1955—and there I was up in Canada as the strike lasted for 155 days. It was the first and last issue I ever totally won with the UAW—and then only until the next set of negotiations. I have been a key member of the General Motors bargaining team for many years and its spokesperson at times. I have sat almost directly across the table from Walter Reuther, Leonard Woodcock, Irv Bluestone, and Doug Fraser of the UAW. The only reason for citing this history and dropping these names is to point out that I cannot blame our current benefit design and cost problems on anyone else. I was there. I was, in fact, largely responsible.

You should also know, as you listen and take account, that I am a born-again middle-of-the-roader. Even when I was asked early this year whether I supported President Reagan, I said without thinking, "That depends." I would like to think that this kind of statement rather than lack of ability kept me from getting a job with the new administration. But it is our responsibility as benefits people to be in the middle. It is our job to represent the needs of employees and the demands of the union (if there is one) to top management and to do that to the best of our ability. It is our job to represent the points-of-view of the corporation's managers to the unions and to the employees—and to do that job as effectively as possible. It is our job to reconcile those points of view and reach agreement or consensus and design plans which will protect employees and their families against the vicissitudes of life, induce them to be appreciative and productive, and still enable management to operate at a profit. It is easy to say, "Here it is; it's good for you; take it or leave it." It also builds the ego to present management's monumental no's. But our job is not the easy route; it is to stand squarely in the middle of the second guessers and let come what will. If that means being the conscience of management, so be it. If that means crying reason with the union, so be it. If that means compromise, as it almost inevitably does, then we must be able to balance the pendulum there, too.

One of the problems with the middle of the road is that you don't get invited to parties at either end. Publishers don't pay you for writing books about it. You don't get on talk shows. Sometimes "you don't get no respect." After a recent talk at a hospital conference, one of the southern administrators, in a most affable tone, said, "I congratulate you, Mr. Zink. At least you have the courage to come down here and reveal your ignorance in person." And here I am, doing it again. It reminds me of an old ditty

> "I've let it all hang out
> As is the current trend.
> I've said it as it is
> And lost every single friend."

I guess what I'm saying is, among all the things I believe in as a result of years of sometimes bitter experience, the most important is that we must stand up and be counted. Our epitaphs should read, "You may not have agreed with him, but you always knew where he stood."

Moreover, the things we stand for are important. We are no longer dealing with the fringe; we are an integral part of the surrey. Our business is no longer the cottage industry, the adjunct to the insurance industry, it was when I started out. In 1953, we spent 9 cents an hour on pensions and insurance for hourly employees—about 4 percent of payroll. In 1980, we spent $4.15 an hour on pensions, insurance, and supplemental unemployment benefits—about 23 percent of a huge payroll. And that only tells part of the story. Government required benefits have soared from 4 cents an hour to 95 cents; the cost of paid time off work from 10 cents an hour to $2.14 an hour. Moreover, we are not only big business, we are many businesses—the health insurance business, the life insurance business, the pension business, the savings and loan business. Actually there isn't much left for an employee to take care of entirely by himself. As a former boss once said, "We don't hire employees; we adopt them."

Some of the changes the winds have cast upon us are dramatic, such as the increase in health care costs since the late 60s, the burgeoning costs of early retirement, and ERISA. Others simply represent shifts in direction. But whether the changes are great or small, overt or subliminal, they have materially changed the characteristics of the benefits job. But have we changed our thinking, our operations, our outlook, our approach, our organization in kind? Have we done all we can to assure that our bosses have real appreciation for what our people do? Or is their attitude primarily related to the fact that costs, dammit, are out of hand? Are we really in the main stream of our operations? Are we a part of the small meetings where things are really decided? Or are we still the good old technicians over in the corner—the repository for those who can't cut it somewhere else?

Let me return for just a moment to costs. In 1975 at GM, for example, we spent about $2 billion on benefits for our U.S. employees. Last year the figure was well over $4 billion—an increase of more than 100 percent in five years. The cost for every vehicle we built in 1975 was $450—in 1980 over $900. Our health insurance costs alone in 1980 were almost $3,000 for every working employee. What hurts the most is that these costs increase even more per employee and per car in bad times when we can least afford it than in good times. Something has to change.

For a wide variety of reasons, I have always favored negotiation of benefits rather than costs. Jim Gillen was an ardent advocate of this approach, and I learned at the master's slide rule. But in industries like ours we may have to change to stay competitive. If we do, with a union like the UAW across the table, a lot of other issues will become compelling: investment policy, carrier selection, joint administration, porkchopper politics, you name it. Are we ready for them? I recently read a statement attributed to Earl Wilson, the columnist, which went like this: "It's a fast age. The impossibility of yesterday has become the luxury of today and the necessity of tomorrow." The unions are showing some signs of enlightened self-interest, but the zebra is not going to start wearing spots. Stan Brams, former publisher of *Labor Trends,* wrote the following in his 30th anniversary issue:

> If there is one moral we can draw from our 30 years of labor relations watching, it's that labor will continue, for better or for worse, to hatch new ideas, create new targets, call for the unprecedented—and almost always succeed.

In spite of existing "cradle to grave" coverages, in spite of unemployment, in spite of noncompetitive labor costs, our employees and their representatives will continue to seek ways to pad the cradle and decorate the grave as soon as the present economic wake is over. Will we be ready for them?

Much of the complexity and expense in our business has also come from Washington. But with Reagan in the saddle all that is downwind now. Right? Don't be too sure. One good thing about being a middle-of-the-roader is that you don't have to flipflop with each change in the administration. How about the scenario about regulating employers so that employees will choose lower cost health insurance and save the country from health care regulation? Don't misunderstand me. I love baseball, hotdogs, apple pie, Chevrolet, and all of the new administration's cost cutting proposals. But no one is perfect. Can we afford not to remain vigilant? Some of our worst regulatory hours in the past have come from well-meaning "friends" on the far side of the Potomac. Is there anyone ready yet to place implicit trust in the new crews at HHS or the Labor Department? In a recent *New Yorker* cartoon, an executive behind a huge desk is answering the phone: "Harrison here—sailing along on the new winds from Washington." Well, the new winds from Washington can still carry a lot of regulatory dust for somebody. I, too, am concerned about the time and expense and duplication of effort involved with the NAM, the Chamber of Commerce, the Business Roundtable, the Washington Business Group on Health, and ERIC, not to forget the CEB. But what is the alternative? The pension and health insurance areas, in particular, deserve our best thinking both at home and in Washington because they take the bulk of the benefit dollars and mean the most to our people.

Starting this September, for example, I want my retirement income secure, and I would like it to keep pace with the cost of living. I want my health and life insurance continued—and maybe a company picnic or two. As you can see, my point of view is changing already. It reminds me of another ditty:

"Driving, I hate pedestrians.
I curse at every dumb one—
Deplore their whole jaywalking tribe.
Till the moment I become one."

We need resolution of the problems with social security financing; the issue of mandatory, universal pensions; the question of automatic adjustments for cost of living; the growing political influence of retirees. Moreover, in spite of a banquet table of predictions to the contrary, there will be continuing strong emphasis in our industry on early retirement, at least through the mid-80s. The stage is set for hard work.

In health insurance, we in the auto industry have been among the pacesetters—whether for good or for ill depends upon your point of view. It is not a coincidence that all of our latest health insurance plans have been designed so that the patient shares the costs through co-payments at the point of service. But these are only frosting on the cake. We need rearrangement of hospital, surgical, and medical expense coverages, both to broaden coverages in nonhospital settings where care can be provided most appropriately from a cost as well as quality standpoint, and to provide for cost sharing in the highest cost areas. Twenty-six years ago this spring I spent my days, nights, and weekends working with Charlie Siegfried, former vice chairman of the Metropolitan Life Insurance Company, and some of his people on just such a plan. In negotiations that year, the union wouldn't even hear us out. We advanced much the same plan in 1979, eight sets of negotiations later, with the same result.

Now, thank God, a solution is in sight. Competition will be introduced into the system—through legislation and regulation, of course—and the marketplace will solve all our health cost problems. And I keep shutting out that small, cynical voice in my ear that keeps saying, I thought that was what Nixon's HMO law was going to do for us.

In the meantime back at the paperwork factory, if any person out there really has a workable solution to the health care cost problem, you can quit your job, consult part time, and buy this part of Virginia for your kids when you retire next year.

Well, I've talked too long already. At last fall's meeting, I understand Pete Pestillo of Ford told you how important you're all going to be in the 1980s. I hope he's right. You should be. You should have a strong role in policy as well as administration. You should be a strong voice for employees, a key member of management, and an integral part of your bargaining structure. In order to do your job most effectively, you have to be a lawyer, a psychologist, a diplomat, an accountant, and a writer. You are also expected to be an innovator, a leader, and a rock of integrity. And if you are all those things, you surely ought to be paid more.

In short, I'm proud to have been associated with you through all these years. I recognize as you do that worthwhile changes usually result not from one dramatic incident but by good people chipping away year after year. As you keep chipping on the benefits while I'm chipping on the golf course, I wish you continuing challenges and at least an occasional success. Change is inevitable and constant. I know that you will continue to do your best to see that it results in a better environment both for our companies and for our employees.

Thank you for inviting me.

APPENDIX 6: HOW TO USE YOUR CONSULTANTS MOST EFFECTIVELY*

By Ernest J. E. Griffes

We have all chuckled occasionally about the pundit's view of expert consultants: "People who live more than 50 miles away" or "They are consultants because they don't actually know how to do anything—so they can only tell others how to do it."

As a client user of many consulting services and firms in my role as director of benefits at Levi's, my experience is that there are certainly times when we want or need consultants and there are many useful contributions they can make toward getting the job done.

On the other hand, we frequently don't use them as well as we could

---

* Reprinted with permission from the the March 1983 issue of "EMPLOYEE BENEFITS JOURNAL", published by the International Foundation of Employee Benefit Plans. Statements or opinions expressed in articles published in the JOURNAL are those of the authors and do not necessarily represent the view or positions of the International Foundation, its officers, directors or staff.

and so we end up paying more for their help than we need to. Not using consultants properly results in diminishing their motivation and ability to help us effectively.

The proper use of consultants is the focus of this paper—determining when we need or want a consultant's assistance, selecting the proper consultant for our need, using him efficiently and effectively, evaluating his performance for us and establishing an equitable price for this assistance.

How Do We Determine That We Need a Consultant's Assistance?

There are times when we really need a consultant's expertise and support because we need to solve a perplexing problem and we need knowledgeable advice. Usually we can recognize these events very quickly and we have no doubt about our need. In the jargon of the consulting profession, this kind of assignment is referred to as one that calls for the "expert" factor of the consulting role. We want an expert to tell us what to do. In these kinds of situations we sometimes have what consultants term "heroic expectations"—that is, we expect that the consultant will be a hero and solve our problem quickly and easily.

There are other times when we want a consultant to perform some task for us that we probably know how to do and could do, if we had the time, the staff, the resources, etc. Consultants call this sort of assignment being used as a "pair of hands," because their role is primarily mechanical in nature, rather than primarily creative or innovative. It is interesting that during difficult economic times consultants more often are called on to perform these mechanical duties because certain work must be done, the staff is short and overloaded and it is less costly to use the consultant than to recruit and hire a staff member or try to justify another headcount in the budget.

Then there are times when we just want to talk things over with a knowledgeable resource, explore one or several ideas, discuss some different viewpoints, gain some fresh insights into our problems and some fresh information. Perhaps we want some encouragement or support, or training for our staff people.

There are times when we need a consultant who is a recognized expert to come forth in support of an action we propose because our management wants some independent reassurance that our proposal is sound. Personally, I always resented this application of a consultant but have sometimes found it essential to enacting a new idea or program successfully.

Lastly, there are times when we have a foreboding sense that something is wrong but we don't know what it is, or we have the feeling that we should be planning ahead for something but we aren't sure what it is. Perhaps some new law is enacted and we know it affects us but aren't sure how. All of these are instances where we feel the need to have a consultant talk the problem over with us and assist us.

In summary, then, there are times we clearly need a consultant and know it, there are times we need mechanical assistance and there are times we just want some time with a consultant to talk things over.

This last use of consultants—just to talk—I find most interesting. It is similar to having an annual physical examination, or feeling a pain and calling the doctor to discuss what the problem might be. As director of benefits at Levi's, I allocated money in the budget each year for personal consulting use. I used it to pay for brainstorming sessions, for getting new knowledge, for checking out ideas and so on. Usually once or twice a year I would take a full day in or out of the office with the consultant to refresh my information and knowledge. Some of the budget was used to have the consultant spend a day or two with key support staff in general training sessions. This procedure was also an effective use of our consultant.

Having determined that we need or want some consulting advice, how do we go about selecting a consultant? For many of us, we have already established these arrangements and we know who we want to talk to. Other times, we are intrigued by some tantalizing idea that a consultant or marketing agent dropped on our doorstep during a new business call, so we might want to talk to the new person rather than to our usual consultant. Sometimes, our established consulting arrangements are letting us down and we seriously want to consider a fresh consulting arrangement.

Let's discuss briefly how to proceed with selecting a consultant.

Selecting a Consultant

Consultants are individuals. Each has a different work style, a different experience and background and a style of interaction. Consultants often have a special field of expertise because they have dedicated themselves to knowing all there is to know about a particular area.

A client needs to take the time to assure himself that the consultant has the specific knowledge and expertise to address the issue at hand. Beyond having specific knowledge, the consultant should operate in a style that the client feels comfortable with.

It is ineffective to hire a cash compensation consultant to perform a study of controlling health care costs. Neither is it effective to hire the best health care consultant if his personal style makes you feel uncomfortable. In either case, the consulting effort will take longer and cost more than it should. The cash compensation consultant will become educated at your expense; feeling uncomfortable with a consultant will interfere with the project.

An important point to remember, then, is to make sure that your consultant is appropriate to the task and that you can relate well to each other.

How Can You Determine If the Consultant Is Appropriate to the Task?

First, you as the client must take responsibility for identifying the areas in which you need assistance. Sometimes this task is easily done; at other times, identifying the problem *is* the consultant's task.

If you determine that your pension plan is out of date, you also have established that the consulting assistance you need is in the benefit plan design area. You then seek a consultant whose experience or reputation is in the area of benefit plan design. When employees are grumbling about the profit-sharing plan but you don't know why, then you may need to discuss the problem with several consultants to get varying viewpoints. If the problem finally is isolated as a communication issue, then you have established that a communications consultant is what you need. Sometimes, maybe all you want to do is talk through your benefit plans, do some brainstorming about new ideas or do some strategic planning. Then you would seek a consultant with a broad practical background in benefits management.

The interesting point is that you as a client are in charge of selecting the consultant. Traditionally, companies have locked into one consulting firm for all their needs. Many times, this arrangement works out very well. However, it can lead to a relationship in which the client loses control through deepening dependence on one firm. A client should always be in control of the consultant, define the consultant's work and hold the consultant to the highest standards of performance.

After you have identified the area in which you need aid, you select your consultant. Unfortunately, this task can be time consuming, but careful selection is important. The right consultant for your needs will get the job done better, faster and at less total cost.

Let's discuss the realities of selecting a consultant.

Remember that the cardinal rule of consultants is that it is essential that the consultant have some billable time every week. When you interview consultants, it is only fair to be direct. Indicate in advance what you want to know about them and some information about your problem. This way, they can be prepared and time is not wasted.

It is unfair to consultants to expect them to provide you free advice by using the interview as a vehicle for getting information to solve your problem. I must admit to being guilty of this tactic once or twice myself as director of benefits at Levi's. This idea is very tempting, especially when your consulting budget is very limited. However, remember that you are really after a relationship of trust and integrity, where both of you can collaborate to solve your problem. This relationship begins the first time you meet, so it really isn't useful to play games.

Since there are many potential consultants and you usually only use one for a given problem, be courteous to those consultants you do not select. Tell them why you chose someone else, or why you didn't feel comfortable with them. This procedure helps establish an honest relationship with a consultant that you may wish to use in the future. It also helps the consultant learn from the experience.

During the interview process, be conscious of how you feel about the consultant—what your intuition is telling you. Your sense of how comfortable you feel tells you a great deal about what it may be like working with him. Once you have embarked on a project, you will need control to use him effectively.* You get messages from your very first discussions and it pays to listen to those messages.

There is one curious way of establishing the integrity of the consultant. If he sometimes admits that the job may be done better by someone else with more direct experience, then you have a good indication that he is aware of his limitations and is honest enough to admit it. Such an admission is by no means an indication that he is inadequate. This consultant may be a good choice because he will work exceptionally hard to prove he is capable of the task.

---

* Use of the word *him* is for convenience only, since there are many highly qualified women consultants in the benefits field.

Consultants, like most of us, have a fairly substantial ego to satisfy. You might be wary of the consultant who casually declares the ability to do any task. Expressing confidence and self-assurance may sound great, but it is not a guarantee that the job you need done will be done well. It is possible that the ego being expressed will get in the way of accomplishing the task; important details may be treated lightly.

Now that you have identified your problem and selected a consultant, how do you use the consultant most effectively so that the job gets done on time, in a quality manner and at an equitable cost?

The Consulting Contract

The customary process of retaining a consultant involves the proposal letter from the consultant specifying what he will do, how long it will take and approximately what it will cost. The client then modifies the proposal or accepts it and the job begins. In consulting jargon, this process is called "contracting." Contracting is so important to the successful completion of a job that we will consider it here in some detail.

Recall that we sometimes hire consultants as the "expert" and sometimes as a "pair of hands"; however, the most effective utilization of a consultant occurs when we enter into a collaborative partnership to get the job accomplished. This process of collaboration, taking a 50/50 responsibility for accomplishing the task, is very important.

Consider what effective utilization of the consultant encompasses:

1. A clear understanding of what is wanted from the consultant and what he requires to complete the job
2. A clear understanding of who will do what, when and why
3. A clear understanding of the expected outcome of the work
4. A reasonable timetable for accomplishing the task. Too short a timetable leaves little room for adjustments that may be necessary and can force the consultant into a lower quality job. Too long a timetable permits the project to languish or can lead to loading it with unnecessary activity. Either way, the consultant is not used effectively.
5. A result from the consultant's contribution that is useful and meaningful
6. Maintaining control over the project, knowing what the consultant is doing at each step and controlling the final report of his work

7. Assurance that the cost of the consultant's work is equitable and bears a reasonable relationship to the magnitude of the problem, the effort required and the amount of new ground to be broken in accomplishing the assignment.

If all of these factors work smoothly and satisfactorily, we have literally a 100% effective utilization of the consultant and a perfect completion of a project—the objective in every consulting assignment.

The first six factors must be outlined and established before any work is begun. They are the contracting process and that is why the contracting phase is so important to effective use of the consultant.

I like to think of this process as being similar to preflight planning, since I am a private pilot. I want to have clearly in mind and in notes just how every leg of the flight will be flown, where alternative airports are in case of trouble and what the destination airport is like so I can increase the chances of a successful landing and completion of the trip. The contracting phase of the assignment, when properly done, goes a long way to assure a cost-effective and useful end product.

As the client, to obtain full effectiveness from the consultant, we must share in the collaborative effort of establishing this contract, as time consuming as it may be. To do so pays big dividends in cost savings and quality results. A failure of the client or the consultant to lay out this contract carefully can produce disaster instead of success.

There is another important reason for laying out a careful contract—it gives us a measuring stick by which to evaluate the consultant's performance. This subject is the next one we will consider.

Evaluating Consultant Performance

As corporate managers, we are all subjected to setting objectives and having our performance measured against the accomplishment of those objectives. The same process can and should be applied to the utilization of our consultants.

The section on the contracting phase discussed how objectives are set. At least annually, we should sit down with our consultants, review every project and give them a performance evaluation on those objectives.

The performance evaluation should include review of at least the following factors about the consultant:

1. Contribution to a clear understanding of what was to be done,

by whom and when. This factor measures avoidance of mis-understandings, wasted effort and money and unusable results.

2. Willingness to play a collaborative role in accomplishment of the projects. This measures the consultant's acceptance of responsibility. From the perspective of company management, the benefits manager, *not* the consultant, is responsible for the results. So, the benefits manager (or client) must expect an honest assumption of mutual responsibility for a successful result. If the consultant does not share responsibility and the result is unsuccessful, the outcome can be bitter accusations, faultfinding, mutual recrimination—or worse, loss of a job or a consultant.

3. Attention to details, follow-through and full completion of each phase of a project. These items measure the consultant's attention to the project and to the client, as well as his reliability and dependability. Credibility and trust are the standards here.

4. Timely completion of the work

5. The overall quality of the project—its usefulness, completeness, appearance, etc.

6. Honesty in making appropriate demands on the client when necessary to successful completion. Sometimes as clients we need to be pressed by the consultant when information is needed or feedback is necessary for completion of a project. Although we may be intimidated by this tactic, it is a measure of a good consultant that he will get our attention when necessary. After all, it is in our best interest that he does so.

7. Attentiveness to client needs—returning phone calls, visiting the client's office, understanding political and organizational factors affecting the work, etc. These factors measure the consultant's sensitivity and genuine interest.

8. Cost effectiveness—not necessarily the lowest cost, but a cost that makes reasonable sense relative to the effort and results achieved.

Some of my colleagues in both consulting and client roles tell me that this effort is all a waste. The only thing that really counts is the results—if they are all right, then everything is all right.

However, I believe that attention to these details goes a long way toward assuring a successful result. Then, no one has to lose sleep over the outcome of the project. Equally important, discussions about performance establish understanding and trust that in turn create a basis for increasingly effective working relationships. Such a relationship is in the best interest of both parties.

Evaluating the Cost of Consultant Services

Now we come to the final subject, which is the most difficult to discuss—judging if we are paying the right price for the consulting services. Consultants, like doctors and attorneys, provide needed services and yet they often are working with subjects that have an aura of mystery about them. One idea from our consultant, developed in a one hour discussion, may save us thousands of dollars. What was that one hour with the consultant worth? What should we pay him for that one hour? If the doctor saves our life, what dollar amount would reward him properly? It is this kind of enigma that confronts us when trying to judge if we are paying a fair price for our consultant's services.

To try to get some perspective on this problem, it helps to classify consultants' services into two categories:

• Those services that can be billed directly for actual time spent and services rendered
• Those contributions that the consultant makes which cannot be valued in terms of an hourly billing rate.

How Consultants Bill for Their Services

Usually, there is an hourly rate, e.g., $100 an hour, which consists of the consultant's salary plus his contributions to the maintenance of his company. If he is successful within his firm, he must bill a certain minimum number of hours regularly to pay his way. This hourly rate reflects his reputation, experience and ability. A consultant who charges $200 an hour may be able to solve the client's problem in one hour, whereas a less experienced consultant may take three hours at $100 an hour, thus costing the client more totally.

Hourly rates are a measure to watch because that is what we will pay. But hourly rates shouldn't alarm us, as the issue really is how many hours we will use. How many hours depends on (1) how good the consultant is, i.e., how quickly he can help us and (2) how often we choose to use our consultant.

Beyond the hourly rate that really pays for the consultant's knowledge, ability and brainpower, consultants customarily bill separately for "out-of-pocket expenses" or "administrative expenses." These expenses are sometimes difficult to evaluate. They can include everything from copies, phone expenses and travel to a dollar contribution for utilities and rent.

This practice is most common—that is, an hourly rate for brainpower plus an aggregation of administrative expense. It serves to keep the hourly rate lower and present the appearance of lower cost to potential clients. But, I repeat, it is the number of hours used that determines our cost, more than the hourly rate.

Some consultants have chosen to charge very high hourly rates that include factors for administrative overhead; thus, their out-of-pocket expenses are lower. But the resulting cost is the same, and they bear the burden of comparing to other consultants unfavorably because of the higher hourly rate.

When consultants quote a price for a single project they compute their expected time and expense and add in a factor for breathing room in case more time is needed. As clients we need to have such a number for budgeting to determine if we can afford the work.

The consultant tends to quote high and as clients we often need lower numbers to justify the project. This differential is unfortunate because it is a point of contention that detracts from the collaborative effort to get the job done. The resolution sometimes is that the consultant lowers his numbers in order that we as clients can buy. Often both parties know full well that the end result will be something different—maybe higher, maybe lower.

Since consultants must also meet rent and payroll, some retainer relationships are developing that serve both parties very well. The retainer may be set at some modest level reflecting an expectation of a certain volume of service over a month or year. The consultant can actually reduce fees because of the stability of cash flow and the client can feel freer to call without getting into the issue of what the call will cost. If substantial added work or projects come along, they are dealt with in the usual proposal fashions.

Is the Price Right?

With this background we now come to the final issue in the effective use of consultants: evaluating if we are paying an equitable price for services—a price that is fair and reasonable for both parties.

We start answering this final issue by excluding the ridiculous at both ends of the scale—the price that is obviously too high or too low. If fees are clearly too high or too low, then it is obvious that the nature and scope of the project is not understood and we return to the contracting phase.

Assuming that the cost quoted is in the commonsense ball park, the client is always entitled to ask for an explanation of what is included. The consultant should be able to defend the cost openly. If the quoted cost seems reasonable, it is better to proceed without rancorous negotiation; insist on detailed invoices to justify the cost as the project progresses.

There is after all a point of presumed trust and integrity in this relationship that permits the client to trust that he is not being deceived and permits the consultant to feel that he will be able to receive a reasonable fee without time-wasting arguments. If such trust and integrity are not operative, then we return to square one—selecting a consultant—and start over.

Eventually, there comes a point where the client feels he has or has not received his money's worth. That point may occur several months or several years into the relationship. The resolution to this issue rests with both parties:

• *Consultant role.* Be diligent in developing proposed costs; compute them carefully and once you have presented them, stay within that budget unless a major change occurs. Bill honestly for actual work; don't puff up the billings with extra hours, but seek fair compensation for work done. Above all, provide the client with very detailed statements of time and expense so that the client has a basis for defending the fee if challenged by auditors or others.

• *Client role.* Be sure that the assignment is clear so that the consultant can develop accurate costs, allow for changes (since many projects can branch out), assess if the cost proposed seems reasonable and factor in "unanticipated" items that occur. Then, go with it. If the gut feeling seems wrong, confront the consultant, clear up any misunderstandings and proceed from there. Insist on very detailed billings, so that you can defend the expense, and pay the bill quickly as a gesture of confidence and trust. This procedure will enable the consultant to survive in his own world—be it the large consulting organization or the one-man shop.

Summary

A great deal of material has been presented in this paper, but effectively using your consultant settles down to those things that characterize all good and mutually rewarding business transactions:

- Openness and clarity of meaning, desires and intentions
- A clear plan of expectations
- An assumption of mutual responsibility for success
- Attention to detail and followthrough, full completion of each phase of the transaction
- Attentiveness and sensitivity to the needs of all parties
- Every party contributing fully and to the best of his abilities
- A logical, defensible and fair price for service, rendered in detail, and accepted and paid in an atmosphere of trust and integrity.

Reasonable attention to these principles will assure effective use of the consultant, successful completion of the project and a contribution to the success of the client in his organization.

REFERENCES

1 SUBSCRIPTION NEWSLETTERS, BOOKLETS, PERIODICALS
2 PRIMARY ORGANIZATIONS INTERESTED IN BENEFIT ISSUES
3 MAJOR BENEFIT CONSULTING FIRMS IN THE UNITED STATES
4 PRIMARY REGULAR BENEFIT PUBLICATIONS AND SERVICES
5 PRIMARY BENEFIT SURVEYS

REFERENCE 1: SUBSCRIPTION NEWSLETTERS, BOOKLETS, PERIODICALS

1. *The Mercer Bulletin*. William M. Mercer, Incorporated—Monthly, 1211 Avenue of the Americas, New York, NY 10036. In Particular, "Employer Attitudes toward Compensation & Productivity," vol. VI, no. 2, December 1980; "A Proposal for a New Consumer Index," vol. VI, no. 11, November 1980.
2. *Labor and Investments*. The Publication of Labor, Pension and Benefit Funds, and Investments—Monthly, Industrial Union Department, AFL-CIO, 815—16th Street, N.W., Washington, DC 20006.
3. *TPF&C Letter*. Towers, Perrin, Forster & Crosby, Consultants to Management, Located in all major U.S. cities. In Particular, "Inflation Protection Purchased Through Indexed Pension Program," Issue 181; "President's Commission Recommends Raising Social Security Benefit Age," Issue 183.
4. *Cafeteria Compensation: Present Status and Future Potential*. A TPF&C Research Study, 1973, Towers, Perrin, Forster & Crosby, Philadelphia, PA.
5. *Wyatt International News Letter, Wyatt Washington Commentary*. The Wyatt Co., 1990 K Street, N.W., Washington, DC 20006.
6. *CEBS Newsletter*. Certified Employee Benefit Specialist Program, P.O. Box 69, Brookfield, WI 53005.

7. *Health Sciences Report.* Harvard School of Public Health, 677 Huntington Avenue, Boston, MA 02115. In Particular—Spring 1980 issue.

8. *Profile of Employee Benefits*—Survey of Benefit Practices—Annual, The Conference Board, New York, NY.

9. *Employee Benefits*—Surveys of Benefit Practices—Annual U.S. Chamber of Commerce, Washington, DC.

10. *High Employment and Income Maintenance Policy.* U.S. Chamber of Commerce, Washington, DC, 1976.

11. *Private Pensions and the Public Interest.* New York State School of Industrial on Labor Relations Report, Fall 1974, Cornell University, Ithaca, NY.

12. *Stress on the Job.* New York State School of Industrial on Labor Relations Report, Winter 1975, Cornell University, Ithaca, NY.

13. *Private and Public Pension Plans in the United States.* Institute of Life Insurance, New York, NY, 1967.

14. *Financial Management of Company Pension Plans,* Patrick J. Davey, The Conference Board, New York, NY, 1973.

15. *Retirement: Reward or Rejection.* J. Roger O'Meara, The Conference Board, New York, NY, 1977.

16. *Hay Huggins Bulletin.* Hay Huggins Co., Philadelphia, PA 19103. In Particular, "Total Benefits Planning," December 1980; "Protecting Private & Public Sector Employees against Losses in the Purchasing Power of Their Pensions," October 1980.

17. *International Foundation Digest.* International Foundation of Employee Benefit Plans, Brookfield, WI.

18. *Hansen News/Views.* Published by A. S. Hansen, Inc., 1080 Green Bay Road, Lake Bluff, IL 60044. In Particular, "Are Your Benefits Staying Ahead of Competition?" vol. III, no. 3, 1980.

19. *Health Care Cost Containment News.* Published by Health Research Institute, 44 Montgomery Street, 5th Floor, San Francisco, CA 94104. In Particular, "Solving the Productivity/Health Care Cost Challenge," Fall/winter 1980/81.

20. *Johnson-Higgins Benefit Newsbeat.* Published by Johnson-Higgins, 95 Wall Street, New York, NY 10005.

21. *1980 Social Report of the Life and Health Insurance Business.* Clearinghouse on Corporate Social Responsibility, Washington, DC.

22. *Beating the High Cost of Health Care.* Research Institute of America, Inc., New York, NY 10017.

23. *Aetna Backgrounder.* Aetna Life & Casualty Insurance Co. In Particular, "Health Care Costs," June 1980. Offices in all major cities.

24. *Observations on Changes in Retirement Practices.* Richard A. Van Deuren, Esq., Reinhart, Boerner, Van Deuren, Norris & Rieselbach, Milwaukee, WI.

25. *Kwasha Lipton Newsletter.* Kwasha Lipton Co., Engelwood Cliffs, NJ. In Particular, "Pensions and Inflation," June 1980.

26. *What's Ahead in Personnel?* Industrial Relations News, Enterprise Publications, Chicago, IL.
27. *Managerial Values for Working.* AMACOM, New York, 1975.
28. *Arthur Young Co. Executive Compensation Letter.* Arthur Young Co., New York, NY.
29. *Hewitt Associates Compensation Exchange.* Hewitt Associates, Lincolnshire, IL. In Particular, "Hot Topics in Employee Benefits," January 1980.
30. *Buck Consultants for Your Benefit and for Your Information.* George B. Buck Consulting Actuaries, Inc., New York, NY. In Particular "Universal Social Security Coverage—Has Its Time Come?" no. 54, April 1980.
31. *Executive Compensation and Benefits Report.* Warren, Gorham, Lamont, Inc., 210 South Street, Boston, MA 02111.
32. *Quarterly Newsletter.* Edward H. Friend & Company, 1800 K Street., N.W., Suite 1500, Washington, DC 20006. In Particular, Transition Issue: 70s to 80s. "The Case of Full Indexing of Social Security Benefits" by Robert Meyers, December 1980.
33. *Thinking about the Future* (A periodical publication). Alexander & Alexander, 1211 Avenue of the Americas, New York, NY 10036. In Particular, "Twelve Faces of Inflation," August 1978.
34. *Emphasis* (Quarterly). Tillinghast, Nelson & Warren, Inc., Tower Place, 3340 Peachtree Road, Atlanta, GA 30026. In Particular, "Inflation: Is There No Hope?" September 1980.
35. *Hall Ways to Better Benefits.* Frank B. Hall Consulting Company, 1415 Kelleem Place, Garden City, NY 11530. In Particular, "Salary Deduction Life Insurance," August 1980.
36. *American Medical News.* 535 North Dearborn Street, Chicago, IL 60610.
37. *Benefits Forum.* Dan McGinn & Associates, Inc., 1150 South Olive Street, Los Angeles, CA 90015.
38. *Nutshell*—A monthly digest of Employee Benefits Publications. The Country Press, Inc., P.O. Box 5880, Snowmass Village, CO 81615, (303) 932-3416.
39. *EBRI: Notes.* Employee Benefits Research Institute, 1920 N. Street, N.W., Washington, DC 20046.
40. *Benefits Briefs.* Tillinghast, Nelson & Warren, Tower Place, 3340 Peachtree Street, Atlanta, GA 30026.

REFERENCE 2: PRIMARY ORGANIZATIONS INVOLVED IN BENEFITS

1. American Society for Personnel Administration, Compensation and Benefits Committee, 606 N. Washington St., Alexandria, VA 22314 (703-548-3440).

2. American Society of Pension Actuaries, 1700 K Street, N.W., Suite 404, Washington, DC 20006.
3. Association of Private Pension & Welfare Plans, 1725 K Street, Suite 801, Washington, DC 20006.
4. The Conference Board, 845 Third Avenue, New York, NY 10022.
5. Council on Employee Benefits, C. S. Lazaroff, Secretary/Treasurer, The Goodyear Relief Assoc., 1144 E. Market Street, Akron, OH 44316.
6. Employee Benefits Research Institute, 1920 N Street N.W., Suite 520, Washington, DC 20036 (202-659-0670).
7. International Foundation of Employee Benefit Plans, P.O. Box 69, Brookfield, WI 53008-0069 (414-786-6700).
8. Society of Professional Benefit Administrators, 2033 M Street N.W., Suite 605, Washington, DC 20036 (202-223-6413).
9. National Health Policy Forum, 1919 Pennsylvania Ave. N.W., Suite 505, Washington, DC 20006.
10. Health Insurance Association of America, (202-223-7780).
11. Profit Sharing Council of America, 20 N. Wacker Drive, Chicago, IL 60606.
12. Profit Sharing Research Foundation, 1718 Sherman Avenue, Evanston, IL 60201.
13. Society of Actuaries, P.O. Box 91901, Chicago, IL 60693.
14. U.S. Chamber of Commerce, National Employee Benefits Committee, 1615 H Street, N.W., Washington, DC 20002 (202-393-1728).
15. Employers Council on Flexible Compensation, 927 15th St. N.W., S 1000, Washington, DC 20005 (202-659-4300).
16. Practising Law Institute, 810 Seventh Ave, New York, NY 10019.
17. Western Pension Conference, P.O. Box 7440, San Francisco, CA 94120.
18. International Society of Pre-Retirement Planners, 11312 Old Club Road, Rockville, MD 20852 (1-800-327-ISPP).
19. Washington Business Group on Health, Washington, DC.
20. ERISA Regulations Industry Committee, 1750 Pennsylvania Ave N.W., Suite 1201, Washington, DC 20006.
21. ESOP Association, 1100 17th St. N.W., 5310, Washington, DC 20036 (202-293-2971).
22. Midwest Pension Conference, Detroit, MI, Barbara Hall (313-471-4300).

REFERENCE 3: MAJOR BENEFIT CONSULTING FIRMS

1. Alexander & Alexander, 1211 Avenue of the Americas, New York, NY 10036 (212-840-8500).
2. George B. Buck Consulting Actuaries, Inc., 2 Pennsylvania Plaza, New York, NY 10001 (212-279-4400).
3. Edward H. Friend & Company, 1800 K Street N.W., Suite 1500, Washington, DC 20006 (207-785-9080).

4. Frank B. Hall Consulting Company, 1415 Kellum Place, Garden City, NY 11530 (516-741-3600).
5. A. S. Hansen, Inc., 1080 Green Bay Road, Lake Bluff, IL 60044 (312-234-3400).
6. Hay/Huggins Co., 229 S. 18th Street, Rittenhouse Square, Philadelphia, PA 19103 (215-875-2300).
7. Hazlehurst & Associates, Inc., 400 108th Ave., Bellevue, WA 98004 (206-455-9272).
8. Hewitt Associates, Inc., 100 Half Day Road, Lincolnshire, IL 60015.
9. Foster & Higgins, Inc., 125 Broad Street, New York, NY 10004 (212-574-9000).
10. Kwasha Lipton Co., 429 Sylvan Avenue, Englewood Cliffs, NJ 07632 (201-567-0001).
11. Dan McGinn & Associates, Inc., 1150 South Olive Street, Los Angeles, CA 90015 (213-747-6501).
12. Mercer-Meidinger, Inc., 2440 Grinstead Drive, Louisville, KY 40204 (502-499-1240).
13. Milliman & Robertson, Inc., 1301 Fifth Avenue, Suite 3600, Seattle, WA 98101 (206-624-7940).
14. Segal Associates, Inc., 57 Post Street, San Francisco, CA 94014 (415-392-0930).
15. Tillinghast, Nelson & Warren, Inc., Tower Place, 3440 Peachtree Road, Atlanta, GA 30026.
16. Towers, Perrin, Forster & Crosby, Three Penn Center, Philadelphia, PA 19102.
17. Watkins Ross & Co., 505 Waters Bldg., Grand Rapids, MI 49503 (616-456-9696).
18. The Wyatt Company, 1400 Ohio Savings Company, Cleveland, OH 44114 (219-696-6250).
19. Coopers & Lybrand, 400 Rennaissance Ctr., Detroit, MI 48243 (313-446-7100).

REFERENCE 4: PRIMARY REGULAR BENEFITS PUBLICATIONS AND SERVICES

1. *Benefits International Magazine,* 30/32 Queen Annes Gate, London SW1H9AB, England.
2. *Benefits News Analysis Magazine,* 388 East Main Street, P.O. Box 3081, Branford, CT 06405 (203-481-9240).
3. *Business Insurance,* Crain Communications, 740 Rush Street, Chicago, IL 60611.
4. *Commerce Clearing House Pension Services,* 4025 West Peterson, Chicago, IL 60646.

5. *Compensation Review,* American Management Association, 135 West 50th Street, New York, NY 10020.
6. *Employee Benefit Plan Review,* Charles Spencer & Associates, Inc., 222 W. Adams Street, Chicago, IL 60606 (312-236-2615).
7. *International Benefit Information Service,* Charles Spencer & Associates, Inc., 222 W. Adams Street, Chicago, IL 60606 (312-236-2615).
8. *Pension Reporter,* Bureau of National Affairs, Inc., 1231 25th Street N.W., Washington, DC 20037.
9. *Pension World Magazine,* Communication Channels, Inc., 6285 Barfield Road, Atlanta, GA 30328.
10. *Pensions & Investment Age,* Crain Communications, 740 Rush Street, Chicago, IL 60611.
11. *The Personnel Administrator,* Magazine of the American Society for Personnel Administration.
12. *The Personnel Journal,* A. C. Croft, Inc., 866 West 18th Street, Costa Mesa, CA 92627.
13. *Prentice Hall Pension Service,* Sylvan Avenue, Englewood Cliffs, NJ 07632.
14. *Research Institute of America, Inc.,* 589 Fifth Avenue, New York, NY 10017.
15. *Employee Benefits Journal,* IFEBP, Brookfield, WI 53008-0069.

REFERENCE 5: PRIMARY BENEFIT SURVEYS

1. Hay Non-Cash Compensation Survey, Hay Group, 229 S. 18th St., Philadelphia, PA 19103.
2. Profile of Employee Benefits, The Conference Board, 845 Third Avenue, New York, NY 10022.
3. Employee Benefits, U.S. Chamber of Commerce, 1615 H Street, N.W., Washington, DC 20062.
4. Hewitt Survey, Hewitt Associates, 100 Half Day Road, Lincolnshire, IL 60015.
5. Bankers Trust Company—various surveys, Bankers Trust Company, New York, NY.
6. Segal Surveys, Martin Segal Co., 730 Fifth Ave., New York, NY 10019.
7. Foster Higgins, 125 Broad St., New York, NY 10004.
8. Hansen Surveys, 1080 Green Bay Road, Lake Bluff, IL 60044.

INDEX

Absenteeism, 21
Accounting Principles Board, 15
Accrued benefit method, 265–66
Actuaries, 259–60
Actuarial assumptions, 260–62
Actuarial funding methods, 265–70
Add-on method of flexible compensation, 337
ADEA; *see* Age Discrimination in Employment Act
Adjudication of benefits, 214
  capabilities, 226
Administration, 138–56; *see also* Benefits
  management
Administrative expenses, 114, 208–9
Administrative services only contract, 227, 258
Age Discrimination in Employment Act (ADEA)
  amendments, 47–48, 73, 74, 135
Aggregate cost method, 266–67
Aging, 13, 22–24
AIDS epidemic, 210
Alcoholism coverage, 279–80
Ambulatory surgical coverage, 279
American Society of Pension Actuaries, 11
American Stock Exchange Index, 287
American Telephone & Telegraph Company, 296
Andrus Gerontology Center (Los Angeles), 128
Annual benefits report, 94, 327–33
Asset accumulation, 18; *see also* Plan assets
Asset management, 282–303
Asset valuation, 264
Audit program, 272–73
Authorization-for-change form, 97–98

Bank of America, 172–73
Banks, securities custodians, 297
Barber, Randy, 19, 32 n
Batch processing, 226
Benefit catalog, 93
Benefit department, 38–43
Benefit indexing, 91, 313–15
Benefit Information Center, 170–72
Benefit planning system, 50–53, 62–80
  controlling change, 96–97
  developing trends, 89–92
  long-range planning, 86–89, 92–94
  short-term action, 95–96

Benefit plans, 28–29, 65–69; *see also* Defined benefit
    pension plans; Group life insurance;
    Health-medical plans; *and* Long-term disability
  administration, 114, 138–56
  annual report, 327–33
  assets, 18–20
  business cycles and, 20–22
  claims administration, 207–30
  company costs, 14
  competitive benefit structure/cost analysis, 312–13
  controlling changes, 96–97
  consultants, 370–81, 385–86
  coordination, 223–24
  cost and return on investment, 111–17
  cost control, 231–81
  costs of changing programs, 45–46
  cost versus impact analysis, 315–20
  effectiveness, 304–25
  employee attitudes, 101–9
  employee communication, 157–206
  employee contributions, 114–17
  employee-designed, 319–20
  employee sensing techniques, 309–12
  employer-paid, 115–16
  evaluation applications, 320–25
  expenditures for, 17–18
  flexible compensation programs and, 333–42
  flexible plans, 134–35
  funding, 208–10
  government interest in, 10–14
  impact on productivity and behavior, 117–20
  indexing and value comparison, 313–15
  information sources, 382–84
  integration, 132–33
  Internal Revenue Code Section 89, 11
  investment earnings, 114
  life cycle, 121–23
  listing of plans, 237
  need versus reward, 118–20
  new assumptions, 6–7
  new paradigm, 24–31
  objectives of evaluation, 306–7
  older-age workers, 128–29
  organizations, 385
  pension fund liabilities, 14–16
  planning and design guide, 53–58

Benefit plans—*Cont.*
  primary function, 25
  publications and services, 386–87
  reasons for cost escalation, 25–26
  reasons for providing, 101
  and retirement age, 22–24
  social role, 123–35
  specific assumptions, 29–31
  specific plan cost versus benefit analysis, 320
  stockholder interest, 14–17
  survey organizations, 387
  taxation of, 135
  top-level executives, 16
  and turnover reduction, 110
  types of evaluation techniques, 307–9
  unusual family arrangements, 134
  value of evaluation, 305–6
  wages tradeoff, 3–4
  weaknesses of systems, 131–32
  work/life attitudes, 7–10
Benefits adjudication, 214
Benefits bulletin, 162
Benefits executive, 71–94
Benefits ideology, 2–7, 101–35
  restructuring of assumptions, 45–46
Benefits management, 35–38, 44–58, 81–89
  administrative procedures and needs, 138–50
  claims administration, 207–30
  cost control procedures, 231–81
  employee communication requirements, 157–92
  employee financial education, 193–201
  plan asset management, 282–303
Benefits payments, 209–10
Benefits race, 111
Benefits short-range planning, 70–80
Benefits statements, 172–92
Benefit system model, 26
Bere, J. F., 35, 59 n
Bernstein, Merton C., 19–20
Blue Cross/Blue Shield, 209, 211–17, 218–19
Bluestone, Irv, 365
Brams, Stan, 368
Briggs, B. Bruce, 33 n
Brokerage firms, 297
Business cycles, 20–22
Butler, Robert S., 33 n

Cafeteria plans, 134–35, 333–42; *see also* Flexible
  compensation programs
Califano, Joseph A., Jr., 13, 32 n
Carve-out method of flexible compensation, 337–38
Catastrophic risk, 249–50
Certified Employee Benefit Specialist program, 37
Civil Service Retirement System, 116
Claims administration, 208–16, 227–30, 271–73
Claims administrators, 216–30
Claims checks, 215
Claims payment systems, 225–27, 271–73
Commissions, health plan, 248
Common stock investments, 292–93
Company loyalty, 109–10
Comparable worth, 106, 133–34
Competition, in benefit plans, 110–11, 312–13

Consultants, 370–81, 375–86
Contract administration, 247
Coordination of benefits (COB), 214, 226, 227, 272
Corporate finance, 282–84
Cost(s), 111–17, 232–39
  communication budget, 163–64
  of consultants, 378–80
  of plan changes, 45–46
  self-administration, 220–21
Cost analysis, 312–13
Cost containment, 273–81
Cost control, 26, 239–54
  versus benefit cost reduction, 232
  claims administration, 271–73
  defined benefit pension plans, 259–70
  long-term disability plans, 257–59
Cost price index, 275–76
Cost shifting, 233
Cost versus benefit analysis, 320
Cost versus impact analysis, 315–20
Cottage industry resurgence, 120
Council on Employee Benefits, 116
Custom reports, 226

Data base, 171–72
Davey, Patrick J., 383
Death benefits, 133, 254
Decision making, 44–47
Defined benefit pension plans, 259–75
Demographics, 22–24
Dental plans, 271–73
Department of Labor, 288
Depressions, 21–22
Designing and Evaluating Employee Benefit Systems
  (Dunham and Formisano), 318
Disability assumption, 262
Disability income plans, 56, 65–80, 339; *see also*
  Long-term disability
Donovan v. Harbor Administrators Inc., 289
Donovan v. Walton, 289
Dow Jones Average, 287
Drucker, Peter F., 19, 32 n
Dunham, Randall B., 318

EAP; *see* Employee assistance programs
Economic security needs, 25
Ehrbar, A. F., 14–15, 32 n
Eligibility determination, 212–14
Employee assistance programs (EAPs), 208, 223
Employee benefits; *see* Benefit planning system
Employee Benefits Research Institute, 18, 289
Employee communication, 157–206
Employee contributions, 114–17
Employee disclosure rules, 143
Employee perception survey, 311, 342–50
Employee Retirement Income Security Act (ERISA),
  5, 11, 47–48, 73, 103, 111, 116, 125, 133, 135,
  138, 158, 257, 259–60, 261, 263–64, 265, 270,
  273, 284
  employee disclosure rules, 143
  record-keeping rules, 151–53
  Section 404(a)(1), 287–89

Employees, 101–11
  handicapped, 134
  ideal plan design, 319–20
Employee sensing techniques, 309–12
Employee stock ownership plans, 108
"Employer Attitudes toward Compensation and
  Productivity," 108
Employer certification, 213
Employers, 3, 109–13
  benefit administration, 138–56
  benefit department, 38–40
  benefit statements, 172–85
  cost control procedures, 231–81
  direct access to administrators, 229–30
  employee communications, 157–206
  introduction of long-range plans, 92–94
  pension fund liabilities, 14–16
  plan asset management, 282–303
  product discount plans, 236
  role of benefit planning system, 62–63
Entry age normal cost method, 267
Equal Pay Act, 73
Equity investment, 292
Evaluation of plans, 305–25
Expenditures, 17–18; see also Cost(s)
Explanation of benefits (EOB) form, 212, 215
Externally managed investments, 285

Families, nontraditional, 134
Fannie Mae investments, 292
Federal National Mortgage Association, 292
Fiduciary requirements, 287–89
Financial Accounting Standards Board, 15–16
Financial accuracy standards, 228
Financial data capture and reporting, 214–15
Financial education, 193–201
FINDPRO program, 194–201
Flamholtz, Eric, 60 n, 136 n
Flanigan, James, 9, 32 n
Flexible benefit plans, 134–35, 338–42
Flexible compensation programs, 92–94, 108, 333–42
Flexible work arrangements, 131
Focus groups, 309–12
Formisano, Roger A., 318
Fortune, 14, 38, 99
401(k) plans; see Section 401(k)
Fraser, Douglas, 365
Fringe benefits, 1–3
Frozen initial liability method, 267
Funding, 208–10; see also Self-funding
Futurists, 8

General Motors, 21, 365, 367
Gillen, James, 367
Ginnie Mae investments, 292
Gladstone, David M., 60 n, 173, 185, 311
Glossary of terms, 201–6, 350–64
Government
  agency disclosure rules, 143
  benefits legislation, 103–4
  and disability plans, 67–68
  and employer paternalism, 109–10
  integration with benefits, 65

Government—*Cont.*
  interest in benefit plans, 10–14
  social role of benefits, 125–35
Government National Mortgage Association, 292
Great Depression, 102
Griffes, Ernest E. J., 231 n, 370
Group Annuity Mortality Table, 261–62
Group Annuity Table, 261–62
Group life insurance, 124, 253–54
Guaranteed insurance contracts, 291–92

Handicapped employees, 134
Hanna, William E., Jr., 192
Harbrecht, Paul P., 32 n
Hardy, Dorcas R., 186
Hazlehurst and Associates, 342
Health maintenance organizations (HMOs), 229
Health-medical plans, 133, 242–53, 275–81, 339
  cost control, 242–53, 271–73
  goals, 56
  managed care concept, 223–24, 229
  post–65 workers, 128–29
  tests for, 11
Hierarchy of needs theory, 102–3
Higgins, Foster, 208, 217, 220, 227
Holmes, Oliver Wendell, 290
Hunt, Frederick D., Jr., 11, 32 n

Income replacement, 66–67
Income shifting, 19–20
Incurred claims, 245–46, 258
Index Funds, 287
Individualism, 7–8
Individual level premium method, 267–69
Inflation, 21
  future, 29
  health care and, 276
  indexing disability plans, 76
Information on developing trends, 89–92
In-house investment decisions, 285
Insurance; see also Group life insurance
  carriers, 75, 217–18
Integrated processing, 229
Integration of benefits, 132–33
Internal Revenue Code, 65; see also Section 401(k)
  and Section 125
  disability plans, 74–75
  Section 89, 11, 135,
  Section 501(c)(9), 251–52, 255–57, 258
Internal Revenue Service, 5, 11, 253, 265, 284
International Foundation of Employee Benefit
  Plans, 37
Interplan Data Reporting system, 219
Investment(s), 284–87, 289–93
  earnings, 114
  in options, 301
  social, 299, 300–301
  risk management, 297–99
  trends, 300–303
Investment advisers, 294–97
Investment yield assumption, 263–64

Job security, 9
Job sharing, 131
Kahn, Herman, 33 n
Kann, Ray, 21, 33 n
Killian, Ray A., 60 n
Koenenn, Connie, 31 n

Langbein, John, 299
Leshin, Geraldine, 3–4, 31 n
Levi Strauss and Company, 311
Liability costs, 232
Life cycle, 121–23
Life expectancy, 13
Life insurance; *see* Group life insurance
Lifestyles, 9, 134
Limited liability, 258–59
Long-range planning, 86–89
   annual benefits report, 94
   benefits catalog, 93
   developing trends, 89–92
   introduction into organization, 92–94
   for short-term action, 95–96
Long-term bonds, 291
Long-term disability (LTD) plan, 254, 255, 257–59
Long-term employment, 9
Love, Douglas A., 282, 303 n
Loyalty to employers, 109–10
LTD; *see* Long-term disability
Lump-sum payment, 265

Major diagnostic categories, 215
Managed care concept, 223–24, 229
Management, systems approach, 95; *see also*
   Benefits management
Mandatory retirement, 47–48, 74
Market price movement, 298
Marshall v. *Leigh,* 289
Marshall v. *Mazzola,* 289
Maslow, Abraham, 102–3, 306
McClung, Nelson, 13, 32 n
Medical costs, 126
Mercer, Michael, 136 n
Mercer and Company, 1–8
Military Retirement System, 116
Minimum premium arrangement, 227
Minimum premium contracts, 252–53
Money market instruments, 289–91
Money purchase plans, 274
Moody's Investor Service, 283
Morale and benefits, 104–5
Morrisey v. *Curran,* 289
Mortality assumption, 261–62
Motivation, 108–9, 117–20
Municipal bonds, 291

National Employee Benefits Institute, 36, 40
National health insurance, 126
"National Policy on Retirement Income," 11
Need benefits versus reward benefits, 18–20
Needs, 102–3, 118
New York City, 17, 291

Nielsen, Niels H., 86 n
North Will Rise Again, The (Rifkin and Barber), 19

Ogden, Frank, 8
Olthoff, Ken, 365
O'Meara, J. Roger, 383
Open population method, 270
Options market, 301
Opt-up/opt-down flexible compensation plan, 337
Ordinary risk, 249–50
Outpatient surgery, 279

Paine, Thomas, 23, 33 n
Paradigm, 24
Part-time employment, 131
Paternalism, 3, 109–10
Past service liability, 266–67
Peer review organizations, 277–78
Pension and Investment Age, 294
Pension funds, 14–20; *see also* Plan assets
   investment history, 285–86
Pension plans, 340; *see also* Defined benefit pension
      plans
   administrative procedures, 140–42
   private, 127
   size of assets, 294–95
   and Social Security, 132–33
Performance agreements, 227–28
Performance measurement, 286–87, 297–99
Personal Earnings and Benefit Estimate Statement,
      185–92
Person-to-person contact, 162–63
Pestillo, Peter, 369
Plan assets, 130–31, 282–303
Planning for employee communication, 159–64
Plan utilization, 211
Pooled premiums, 253
Population, 13, 22–24
Positive benefits management, 47–50, 63–64
Posner, Richard, 299
Preadmission testing, 279
Preferred provider organization (PPO), 208, 211, 223
Premium stabilization fund, 248
Premium taxes, 248
Premium waiver, 254
Preretirement income, 275
Private pensions, 127
Product discount plans, 236
Productivity
   benefit impact on, 117–20, 133
   compensation motivated, 17, 108–9
   declining, 21
Profit sharing plans, 108, 274, 339–40
   Sears Roebuck, 302
Projected benefit method, 266
Prudent professional rule, 28

Rand Corporation, 8
Real estate mortgages, 292
Recession, 21–22, 76
Replacement ratio, 262
Request for proposal, 221–22, 224

Reserve requirements, 246, 251–52
Retention charges, 246–48, 253
Retirement, 127–29
    extending age limit, 74
    goals of benefits, 55
    terminology of, 201–6
Retirement age, 22–24
    assumption, 262
    government legislation, 47–48
Retirement Income Projection Report, 195–201
Return on investment, 111–13
Reuther, Walter, 365
Reward benefits versus need benefits, 118–20
Rifkin, Jeremy, 19, 32 n
Risk, 249–52, 286–87
Risk charges, retention, 247–48
Risk management, 297–99
Ritter, Robert, 19
Roosevelt, Franklin D., 3
Rothschild, L. F., 19

Safe harbor actions, 289
Salary scale assumption, 263–64
Same-sex marriages, 134
Schuck, Russ, 364
Schulz, Richard, 32 n
Sears Roebuck, 300
Second-opinion surgery programs, 278
Section 501(c)(9) trust, 251–52, 255–58
Section 401(k) Salary Deferral Plans, 114–16, 233
Section 125 Salary Reduction Plans, 114–16, 233
Securities and Exchange Commission, 16
Securities Investor Protection Corporation, 297
Self-administration, 220–21
Self-funding, 249–54, 258
Sex discrimination, 129
Shapiro, Max, 14, 32 n
Shock claims, 210
Short-range planning, 70–80
Short-term actions, 95–96
Short-term investments, 289–91
Sick days, 118
Silicon Valley, 111
Social investing, 299–301
Social justice, 106
Social role of benefits, 123–25
Social Security Act, 138
Social Security Administration, 185
Social Security benefits, 11–12
    benefit statements, 185–92
    costs to employer, 103
    and defined benefit pension plans, 262
    fillers, 23
    funding, 127–28
    and private pensions, 132–33
    replacement ratio, 262
    tax rate increases, 240
    unfunded liabilities, 17
Software improvements, 229
Special-purpose communication, 162
Standard and Poor's 500, 287, 298

Stockholders, 14–17
Stock purchase plans, 340
Stocks, 16, 292–93
Stop-loss insurance, 250–51
Summary plan description, 158
Supplemental unemployment benefits, 129
Survivor's benefits, 56, 338–39
Systems approach to management, 95

Tax deferral plans, 114–15
Tax Equity and Fiscal Responsibility Act, 127, 128
Tax identification numbers, 225
Tax policy, 3–4, 254–57
    benefits for wealthy, 135
    municipal bonds, 289
    results, 24–25
Tax Reform Act of 1986, 11, 116, 135
Termination assumption, 261
Third-party administrators (TPAs), 209, 219–20
Third Wave (Toffler), 120
Thirty-and-out retirement, 22–23
Thrift and savings plans, 276
Toffler, Alvin, 120, 136 n
Total compensation concept, 36
20-20 Hindsight Club, 293

Underwriting gains or losses, 248–49
Unemployment compensation, 17, 129–30
Unit credit cost method, 266
United Auto Workers, 367
United States Chamber of Commerce, 16–17, 235, 312
University of Chicago Law School, 299
Utilization data capture and reporting, 214–15
Utilization review (UR), 208, 211, 216, 218, 223, 278

Vacations, 118
Value comparison, 313–15
Van Deuren, Richard A., 384
Volatility of price, 298
Voluntary Employee Deductible Contributions, 116

Wages; *see also* Flexible compensation programs
    and productivity, 19
    tradeoff for benefits, 3–4
Weeks, David, 5, 24, 31 n
Welfare and Pension Plan Disclosure Act, 5
Western Pension Conference, 294
Wharton School of Economics, 37
Wilson, Earl, 367
Window periods, 23
Woodcock, Leonard, 365
Work behavior, 117–20
Workers' compensation, 17, 131
Work ethic, 7
Work/life attitudes, 7–10
Workshops, 195
Zink, Vic, 364